PIMLICO

505

LOVE LETTERS

Judith Adamson is the author of several books, including *The Dangerous Edge*, a political biography of Graham Greene, and *Charlotte Haldane: Woman Writer in a Man's World*, a biography of J.B.S. Haldane's first wife. She selected and introduced the essays in Graham Greene's much acclaimed last book, *Reflections*, and is Professor of English at Dawson College, Montreal, Canada.

# LOVE LETTERS

Leonard Woolf & Trekkie Ritchie Parsons
1941 – 1968

———

# EDITED BY JUDITH ADAMSON

PIMLICO

Published by Pimlico 2002

2 4 6 8 10 9 7 5 3 1

First published in Great Britain by Chatto & Windus 2001
Pimlico edition 2002

Pimlico
Random House, 20 Vauxhall Bridge Road,
London SW1V 2SA

Random House Australia (Pty) Limited
20 Alfred Street, Milsons Point, Sydney
New South Wales 2061, Australia

Random House New Zealand Limited
18 Poland Road, Glenfield,
Auckland 10, New Zealand

Random House South Africa (Pty) Limited
Endulini, 5A Jubilee Road, Parktown 2193, South Africa

The Random House Group Limited Reg. No. 954009
www.randomhouse.co.uk

A CIP catalogue record fo this book
is available from the British Library

ISBN 0-7126-6473-4

Papers used by Random House UK Limited are natural,
recyclable products made from wood grown in sustainable forests;
the manufacturing processes conform to the environmental
regulations of the country of origin

Printed and bound in Great Britain by
Biddles Ltd, Guildford

This book is affectionately dedicated to
Elizabeth Inglis and Anneliese West,
without whom it would have been impossible

Trekkie Parsons, 1950s
Leonard Woolf, oil by Trekkie Parsons, 1945
Leonard and Trekkie at Charleston, June 1969

# Contents

# Acknowledgements

For permission to publish this correspondence I am greatly indebted to the University of Sussex, copyright holder, and to Sheila Dickinson and David Dunbar Dickinson, executors of Trekkie Parsons's estate. For Trekkie's diaries I am very grateful to John Pugh. Without the additional trust and help of Elizabeth Inglis and Adrian Peasgood at the University of Sussex Library, Baroness David, and Anneliese West, I could not have completed this book.

Many other people have helped me with information. I would like to thank especially: Peter Alexander, Olivier Bell, Peter Blunt, Douglas Brewer, Betty Dagg, Alessandra Duncan, Nancy Fortescue, Angela and John Graham, Bryan Healing, George Hildebrand, Vera Kaden, Carol Kidwell, James King, Yvonne Klein, Norman MacKenzie, Ursula McCracken, Kerry McSweeney, Mary Meigs, Ursula Mommins, Richard Monaghan, Ian Norrie, S.P. Rosenbaum, the late George (Dadie) Rylands, Lukie Scott, Tim F.S. Scott, Francizka Shlosser, Ray Smith, Frances Spalding, Hope Spater, Frederic Spotts, Barbara Trigger, Jane Turner, Jenny Uglow, Serge Vaisman, Enid Whitham, and Jennie Yates.

Michael Bott, at the University of Reading Archives, deserves special mention for his generous assistance. I am also grateful to the staff of the following libraries and institutions: Agnew's Gallery (Richard Kingzett); The Bloomsbury Workshop (Tony Bradshaw); Clare College, Cambridge (Roger Schofield); the Centre for South Asian Studies, Cambridge University (Lionel Carter); Devon County Council (Josephine Halloran); the Department of Education, Edinburgh (Kate Moulin); Flora Stevenson School, Edinburgh (Ian Marchant); Leeds University Library, Brotherton Collection (Christopher Sheppard); the Royal London Society for the Blind (Natalie Feast); Tynecastle High School, Edinburgh (John Campbell).

Finally, I want to thank Alan Adamson, always my first reader, for his unfailing encouragement and essential critical comments.

This work was supported in part by a grant from the Social Sciences and Humanities Research Council of Canada.

# *Editorial Notes*

Because Trekkie preferred the name Ritchie to Parsons, I call her Trekkie Ritchie throughout. For brevity, she appears in my annotations as TR, Leonard Woolf as LW, and Ian Parsons as IMP, as he always signed himself; others are denoted by their initials where identity is obvious.

No letter has been abridged, and the correspondence has been edited as little as possible to maintain its casual intimacy. Both Trekkie Ritchie and Leonard Woolf used ampersands and many abbreviations; I have left these except where clarity indicated that the full word would be appreciated in square brackets. Editorial additions and explanatory notes also occur within square brackets, as do suggested readings of illegible words, which are accompanied therein by a question mark. Neither correspondent used apostrophes consistently, rarely including one in 'don't', and both used '%' for degrees of temperature; these I have left unchanged.

Despite the tremor of his hand, which sometimes made the most simple tasks difficult, Leonard's handwriting is easy to read. I have transcribed his letters as closely as possible. Trekkie's calligraphy is less legible, particularly when she was hurried or writing, as she sometimes did, with a lithographer's crayon. Her punctuation is conversational; she often omitted it entirely. Especially during the war (which may mean she was saving paper), she frequently left a long space between sentences to indicate a new paragraph. I have indented paragraphs in place of these spaces, and have corrected her punctuation, but very loosely and only when necessary for understanding. I have been more heavy-handed with her spelling. Trekkie was a dreadful, imaginative and self-protective speller. At first Leonard teased her about it; her misspelling of 'desert' as 'desart' became his in letters to her. She persisted in spelling across as 'accross'; around, 'arround'; extraordinary, 'extrordinary'; nonsense, 'nonesense'; Italian, 'Italien' (these I have corrected throughout). Some of her misspellings seem phonetically induced, others have a hint of the Scottish accent of her Aunt Fuzzells. So careless a speller was she that, in letter 124 for example, Fuzzells appears as Fuzzles, Fuzzells and Fuzzels within a few lines. Unless in the context it seemed appropriate to leave them, I have corrected the misspellings to make reading easier.

At some point Trekkie numbered her own (but not Leonard's) letters. She numbered them in two batches: the first contained 176 letters, the second (beginning July 1958) contained 62. Sometimes she numbered two letters as one; in one place, I matched ink and paper folds to find she had numbered a page which was part of one letter as though it were separate from it. The letters she numbered 131 to 139 (late October 1949–January 1950) are missing from the collection, and others referred to in the correspondence are not there. I have edited into my annotations parts of the diary she kept intermittently, placing inclusive dates in brackets at the end of quotes; a few pages are missing from these books; about twenty-five have been cut out following an Easter trip in 1958.

Leonard almost always dated his letters accurately; Trekkie rarely gave more than the day she was writing, at best the day and month. In some places this caused a considerable problem, especially where the contents of a letter showed her numbering to be wrong. In renumbering, I have kept as closely as possible to Trekkie's ordering of the letters, but some had to be moved to maintain continuity.

The correspondence is housed in the University of Sussex Library at Falmer.

# *Introduction*

'A young woman has appeared on the scenes, called
by the rather absurd name of Trekkie Ritchie. Have
you heard of her?'

Vanessa Bell to Jane Bussy
(9 January 1945)

'She's an artist, a serious one. Her enormous blue eyes
are blind with intensity of observing. Chic is an
extraordinary quality – she pierced that party like a
knife, every time she came in sight one was aware of
a complete purpose in apparel, and other women who
were just as expensively, as intentionally dressed, either
looked fumbling or fashion-plates. I liked her a great
deal.'

Sylvia Townsend Warner to Valentine Ackland
(7 July 1955)

At Easter 1949 Trekkie Ritchie Parsons opened an ordinary unlined black
book, the kind she might have used for sketching, and wrote: 'Now
without more ado I must try to write a diary. It is ridiculous to enjoy
reading other people's as much as I do and not try to write one myself.'
Because she remained in two minds about making the private public, even
in what ought to be the most private of places, she started and stopped the
diary many times before Leonard Woolf died in 1969. On this she and
Leonard agreed: disclosing the personal was not on. Why then did
Trekkie not destroy her diary and the correspondence of her long,
intimate friendship with Leonard? Had not a clerical error been made
when he altered his will, an error which landed their letters in probate
court, she probably would have, for she was an entirely unpretentious
woman.

    In April 1969 Leonard was suddenly incapacitated, probably by a stroke, and although he soon recovered enough to answer mail and with help to correct the page proofs of the last volume of his autobiography, he understandably decided to revise his will. It was little different from the one he had made in 1959. Trekkie Parsons remained his executrix and residuary legatee (something she was astonished to learn she had been for the past ten years), and a few legacies were increased. Those to the son and two daughters of his brother Philip Woolf were unchanged, although a typing error in the new draft credited them with £5,000 each instead of the £500 Leonard wanted them to have. The error went unnoticed when the will was prepared because the secretary checked her engrossment against her incorrect draft rather than against the 1959 document on which Leonard's solicitor had pencilled the alterations. It was overlooked again when Leonard signed the new will and, feeling unwell, asked his solicitor to read aloud only what had been revised.

When Leonard died on 14 August proof of error was readily provided and the legal situation considered straightforward. Nevertheless, Philip's children contested the will and his son, Cecil Woolf, accused Trekkie of 'undue influence', claiming that 'further particulars would be given after discovery'. This allegation complicated and delayed the probate hearing until July 1971, when the charge was dropped and Woolf's counsel was forced to admit it should never have been made. The will was accepted as Leonard had intended it and, as executrix, Trekkie was finally free to turn Leonard's papers and Monk's House over to the University of Sussex, where today the papers (including this correspondence) form an important archive; the house is now owned by the National Trust. But 'after discovery' had meant that Trekkie's private letters to Leonard and his to her had been exposed to legal eyes in order to show, as she was obliged to say on the stand, that there had been no 'improper relationship' between herself and Leonard. The newspapers wasted no time in reporting details of the hearing.

Trekkie was then sixty-nine. Nothing could have been a greater violation of the liaison she, her husband Ian Parsons, and Leonard had kept private for decades. It was not that they had concealed anything – Trekkie had lived half the week at Monk's House for the better part of twenty-six years and she and Leonard had travelled together many times to France and Scotland, to Greece and Israel in 1957, to Ceylon in 1960, to Greece again in 1961, to the United States and Canada in 1966. They simply had never spoken to even their closest friends about what was no one's business but their own.

To a large degree silence had brought them the privilege of living outside the customary constraints of marriage. Trekkie and Leonard loathed sexual gossip, and quashing rumour would have been foremost in her mind when she entered the probate court. Carrying out her duties as Leonard's executrix depended on her doing so – and how she would be remembered. That day she was spared further embarrassment when the inventive marital arrangement the letters revealed was dismissed as 'one of those literary and social friendships which are quite remarkable in the history of literature'. But the 'undue influence' charge had turned her correspondence with Leonard – the private calligraphy of love – into the opposite of what it was and Trekkie never forgot the indignity. In preserving these letters as final proof against the absurd allegation, she courageously decided that privacy was less important than restoring the integrity of her life with Leonard and Ian. How lucky for us that she did.

Trekkie was born Marjorie Tulip (her mother's maiden name) Ritchie on 15 June 1902 in Durban, where her architect father, Alan MacGregor Ritchie, had followed his sister from Scotland. Her childhood moniker stuck and Trekkie Ritchie became her professional and preferred name. In *The Drama of the Year in South Africa*, the popular nature study book for Natal children by her aunt Mary Ritchie, she is remembered as a precociously observant child who treks about collecting botanical specimens to paint – scarlet pea-flowers off the kaffir-boom at the edge of the family paddock, jacaranda blossoms from the swarm of blue above their whitewashed cottage. But in Afrikaans 'trek' is also a strong desire, as in 'trek hê in' – to 'have a strong inclination for' something. So while the child trekked about, she did everything with a charming determination well known to those who knew her as an adult.

Alan Ritchie had joined the British Army to fight the Boers; when World War I began he returned to Britain and enlisted as a major in the Royal Artillery. In 1917 Trekkie followed with her mother and siblings; her twenty-year-old sister, Alice, went to Newnham College, Cambridge; her eighteen-year-old brother, Pat, joined the RFC. Trekkie was just fifteen and was sent to school in Tunbridge Wells; in summer she lived in Scotland with a second Ritchie aunt called Fuzzells, who was a teacher like Mary, but rather formidable.

In 1920, the same year that Alice moved to Geneva to work in the League of Nations Secretariat, Trekkie went to the Slade to study with Philip Steer and Henry Tonks. It was an exciting time for British painters and lithographers; technical developments in the printing of colour had affected especially children's books, and the hiring of artists for posters and other graphic work, most notably by London Transport and Shell, quickly created a group of what we would call today commercial artists. That Tonks encouraged Trekkie is evidence enough of her talent, for he was a scathing critic who intimidated many bright young painters. When she married fellow student Peter A. Brooker in 1926 she looked forward to a promising career, making her living in the expanding commercial arts and painting alongside.

Alice had returned to London by then and was selling books for the Hogarth Press. She was also writing fiction. In 1928 Leonard Woolf published her first novel, *The Peacemakers*, based on her experience in the League of Nations, and in 1930 (with a dust-jacket designed by Trekkie) *Occupied Territory*, about post-war Germany where their father, then a colonel, was commanding his regiment. Soon after Alice began a third novel, which she never finished. Virginia Woolf said she alternately wrote and burned it. Leonard felt that like many good writers she was intimidated by her own high standards.

In the late twenties Trekkie and Peter lived a lean bohemian life in London. She and Leonard first met when she delivered the jacket for *Occupied Territory* to the Hogarth Press in Tavistock Square. She was 'extremely beautiful', he recalled in *The Journey Not the Arrival Matters*; she remembered that she was terribly nervous and that Leonard had put her immediately at ease. In the next two years the Press commissioned four more covers, including those for John Hampson's popular *Saturday Night at the Greyhound* (1931) and Vita Sackville-West's *All Passion Spent* (1931). Trekkie was skilled at reducing complex literary themes to flat simple shapes; for R. M. Fox's *Drifting Men* (1930) she heightened the spareness of a circle of desolate figures with a sinister edge of shadow; on Hampson's cover she dramatised the lure of a moonlit house with a hard contrast of hatched sky.

These commissions led her to other publishers. One was Chatto & Windus, where she met Ian Macnaghten Parsons, a handsome and talented young man who in 1928 on graduation from Cambridge had become the firm's typographer. By 1930 he had been made a partner; by 1934 Trekkie had divorced Peter, married Ian and committed herself to making their house at 25 Victoria Square a welcoming spot for friends and colleagues. She was an excellent cook and hostess, and for a couple of years seemed expertly to balance her domestic, lithographic and painting commitments. Chatto & Windus had perhaps the most distinguished list in London at the time and a reputation for excellence in design. Trekkie did her first book for them in 1935: *English Drawings*, an anthology of pictures she liked from Matthew Paris to Duncan Grant, which she edited and introduced.

Yet by 1936 Alice was so worried about her she told Leonard that Trekkie's paintings were unlikely ever to be exhibited. When he suggested Vanessa Bell and Duncan Grant might give an opinion of them, Alice wrote back that in Trekkie's 'gloomy view' there was no point. The problem, she said, was that Trekkie was not 'the least smart' with dealers accustomed to artistic 'stunts'. Trekkie was certainly bruised when her paintings were rejected, and being shy and still youngish lacked the artistic confidence to persevere with gallery owners. Like Alice, she had high standards; whereas she was quick to part with illustrations for dust-jackets, magazines, Christmas cards and whatever other commercial work came her way, she hoarded and destroyed paintings all her life. She did exhibit in those years, regularly in the 'Artists of Fame and Promise Exhibitions' at the Leicester Galleries, at the Goupil Gallery, with the New English Art Club, and the London Group; her portraits were especially good. But probably by 1936 Trekkie had begun to see herself more as the lithographer and illustrator she was becoming than the great painter her sister wanted her to be. Ian's admiration for printed work of every kind buttressed her lithographic talent; the Midget books she would soon write and illustrate for Chatto & Windus were a natural extension of her early interest in botany, and showed her to be an inventive and instructive author for children.

When war broke out in September 1939 she and Ian joined the Auxiliary Fire Service. Ian wanted to fly, but being thirty-three was offered instead a commission in the RAFVR and sent in January 1940 to France on staff duties. He returned after Dunkirk to spend long hours at the Air Ministry interpreting photos of airfields in occupied Europe, and when the US entered the war at the end of 1941, he was sent to America for several months to instruct US intelligence officers to do the same. From then until August 1944, when he returned to France, he was often away on long assignments. Trekkie became a land girl, then answered incoming calls for the War Office at Petersham to which she rode every day on a motorbike.

On 28 March 1941 Virginia Woolf drowned herself in the River Ouse. She and Leonard had moved to Monk's House seven months earlier when their flat at 37 Mecklenburgh Square was rendered almost uninhabitable during the Blitz. Rodmell was on the path of German bombers heading for London and from August to November 1940 there had been dogfights over the downs behind the cottage. One day the planes were so close that Virginia and Leonard had lain face down under a tree in the garden with their hands over their heads. Another day a Messerschmitt had been shot down on nearby Mt. Caburn. At night, when the bombs were dropped on London the windows of Monk's House shook. For someone like Virginia whose health depended on nourishing food which was becoming difficult to find, and on periods of rest and lack of excitement, it would seem that circumstances could not have been worse.

When Leonard died in 1969 Trekkie found this anguished note (now in the Archive) among his papers: 'They say: "Come to tea and let us comfort you." But it's no good. One must be crucified on one's own private cross. It is a strange fact that a terrible pain in the heart can be interrupted by a little pain in the fourth toe of the right foot. I know that V. will not come across the garden from the lodge, & yet I look in that direction for her. I know that she is drowned & yet I listen for her to come in at the door. I know that it is the last page & yet I turn it over. There is no limit to one's stupidity & selfishness.' However much Virginia insisted in the letters she left that she owed all her happiness to Leonard, that he had been 'entirely patient' with her and 'incredibly good', his remorse for being the man whose life she had decided she could no longer 'go on spoiling' must have been overwhelming.

Leonard's diary shows that two months after Virginia's death, in May 1941, he began to visit Alice Ritchie whenever he was in London. She was dying of cancer at Trekkie's house in Victoria Square and Trekkie was grateful to him for sitting with Alice while she was at the War Office. In his autobiography he wrote at length about sharing with them that terrible watch when time has stopped and 'the universe is hesitating, waiting, in fear, regret, pity, for the annihilation or snuffing out of a life, a living being'. On 24 October Trekkie wrote to tell him that Alice had been moved to the Westminster Hospital. Leonard had already sent £100 to help with expenses. Alice died three days later and Trekkie returned the cheque, thanking him for the comfort it had given her sister to know she would not be a financial burden. She invited him 'for lunch or any evening for dinner'. Of the first time he went alone for tea he remembered that her 'beauty & the beauty of your room & pictures, & your mind & moods appealed enormously to me'.

So their friendship began, in mutual loss and the dangers of war, and their correspondence with Trekkie's invitations to Victoria Square and her thank-yous for the freesias and strawberries Leonard left on her doorstep in appreciation. In May 1942 she had to give up her job at

Petersham because she was plagued by repeated bouts of quinsy and flu, which eventually left her close to pernicious anaemia. She shared her lithographic miseries with Leonard, and her enthusiasm for the Midget children's books she was doing. Then in November she wrote that Ian was again being sent on an assignment and asked if she might come to Rodmell when he left. She stayed at Monk's House the night of 12 December and within a month returned with her paintbox and meat ration.

Soon afterwards she began her 'first proper painting since the war started'. Leonard bought an ink drawing from her and the Hogarth Press commissioned twelve illustrations and the jacket for Barbara Baker's *The Three Rings*. She thanked him for his encouragement and took him with her to Whipsnade and Kew, where she drew from life for her book commissions. He began to call her his 'Dearest tiger' and to feed her eggs and toast in the dilapidations of his bombed Mecklenburgh Square flat as she made her way home through the blackout after her lithography classes. By March, Leonard's letters were playfully amorous. By May, he confessed he had thought, 'I don't know for how long now, it would be impossible to feel for anyone as I do for you.'

Trekkie was caught off guard by his attentions and flattered by his interest in her work. She admitted she had come to rely on him 'in a major way' and, perhaps without realising her coquetry, sent him a poem about the physical passion of her cat for his. At the same time, although she later said she had never wanted to re-marry, she had committed herself to a second husband and was wary of Leonard's emotional dependence on her. 'I want you to love me,' she wrote him in May, 'but not as an epidemic disease'.

He continued to send presents to 'Dearest tiger, my dear dove, or dear owl, pussy –, or grocer's cat', without heeding her warning that 'the tiger is too true and has always stalked about in me too ready to show its teeth and claws'. When he pressed ahead, she snapped back; when he became frightened that his persistence would drive her away, she added her old white coat to the things she left at Monk's House and became his 'dearest & most perverse of tigers'.

Especially in war Cupid's arrows fly in unlikely directions; twenty-two years apart in age, Leonard and Trekkie were deeply in love by the end of 1943. His flat in Mecklenburgh Square had become impossibly uncomfortable and the lease of 24 Victoria Square was available. At first he thought himself 'sensible enough to see that I love you too much to make it wise to come and live next door to you'. But while Trekkie cautioned that he might discover she 'hadn't got such a very nice character' after all and then have to pretend she had because 'it would be awful to live next door to someone you didn't like', she encouraged the move. Ian, who probably did not yet realise how permanently attached they were, thought it a good idea and helped sort out the lease.

In mid-September Leonard offered Trekkie half of Monk's garden and more of the house. When she turned him down, he made plans to extend Virginia Woolf's writing lodge into a proper studio for her, and began to search harder for a cottage close to Monk's where she and Ian might live. In October she reported from London that 'the electric man came to join you in holy matrimony to the service', and Leonard moved next door in Victoria Square. Just before Ian was returned to France the following August, Trekkie moved into Monk's House for nearly a year, and during this time signed a lease for Iford Grange two miles away, which she and Ian called home until 1954, when they moved permanently to Juggs Corner above nearby Kingston. In London, they gave up their Victoria Square house to share the first and second floors of Leonard's. The stage was set for a most unusual domestic compact.

From the first Leonard knew 'that there was nothing I couldn't say to you, that I could go on talking to you forever.' In 1944 he told Trekkie, 'it is the extraordinary harmony & harmonies in you dearest, that make you so different from everyone else'. Five years later she wrote in her diary, 'I would like to have known L when he was young and when I was too. Would we have been as perfectly sympathetic as we are now, I wonder', and without sentimentality decided yes. For years Leonard had borne a great responsibility with Virginia; his relationship with Trekkie was so easy and agreeable that he talked about it in musical terms: 'I get a thrill or vibration of complete harmony, the kind of answering thrill which one gets from some divine phrase of Mozart'.

Yet from the first Trekkie refused to be the idealised woman his early letters show he anticipated. However tired and sick she was during the war she was unexpectedly resilient. She responded to his offer of Monk's House and garden with a resounding no. And when life then became particularly pressing because they had fallen in love and Ian would soon return from the war, she had the stamina to imagine a different narrative for them all, and to sustain it. Leonard's old friend Dadie Rylands told me, 'Trekkie gave him the happiest years of his life. Leonard was very lucky to meet her.' She was equally lucky to meet Leonard, and to be married to Ian Parsons, without whose integrity and gift for friendship they could not have reorganised their lives as they did. Maximum personal freedom had always been a central desire of the Bloomsbury group, but Trekkie and Ian were not of Bloomsbury, and post-war publishing circles did not lend themselves to openly unconventional arrangements.

Theirs fell into a practical pattern. Trekkie went to London on Monday to attend publishing events with Ian and to entertain for him. When Chatto & Windus absorbed the Hogarth Press in 1946, leaving Leonard editorial control without the financial and administrative responsibilities of publishing, the combined list was unrivalled: Hogarth writers included Freud, T. S. Eliot, Chekhov, John Maynard Keynes, Gorki and, of course, both Woolfs; Chatto's names included Aldous Huxley, William Faulkner, Norman Douglas and several successful journals. The firm grew rapidly and many publishing deals were clinched over dinners provided by Trekkie. Leonard came to London on Monday afternoons or Tuesday mornings, depending on his Hogarth and *New Statesman* meetings. He and Trekkie returned to Rodmell together late Tuesday afternoon. She went to her own house at the weekend when Ian arrived, bringing his dirty laundry. Leonard picked her up early Saturday to shop with him in Lewes. There was more entertaining, and friends often stayed the night.

That this arrangement needed the support of trusted housekeepers and gardeners is obvious. But without Trekkie's energy things would never have run so elegantly. She was a visual person who created beauty equally on her dining table and in her studio and she held this arrangement together with delicate deftness. As the complexity of their lives increased, she rose to the intricacies of the schedule. She took holidays with them separately, sometimes with Leonard arriving as Ian left. She attended publishers' conferences, which were especially important between 1955 and 1961, when Ian was president and then an officer of the Publishers Association. Ian's mother, Mabel, who died in 1951, was demanding and unsympathetic and Trekkie, who had lost both her own parents by 1932, was bound by fierce familial loyalty to her Ritchie aunts, Fuzzells in Scotland, and Mary (Faanie) who came to live with the Parsons when she retired from Natal.

Stories of the hospitality at Juggs Corner abound – Trekkie and Ian cooked superb meals together; they danced together so beautifully that everyone else preferred to sit and watch; they argued plenty, and never more passionately than about poetry, which they recited competitively from memory; Ian was said to remember more, but Trekkie increased her repertoire almost to the day of her death. If this all sounds a bit too perfect – someone I spoke to did call the scene 'a well-oiled act' – friends recognised the Parsons' commitment as a married couple. They also remembered how very easy and affectionate Trekkie and Leonard were with each other. When Trekkie was at Juggs and something went wrong at Monk's, she went immediately to Leonard. She cooked for parties there too. Leonard taught her about music, which they listened to every evening; she painted there almost daily in the studio he renovated for her, and printed in her lithography room. Ian enjoyed gardening, but Trekkie and Leonard were the serious botanists; their plants and animals became an increasingly important bond. Although she loved both men, Trekkie was closer to Leonard, and for all her sophistication, the simple things she shared with him delighted her most. Among the list of pleasures in her diary are: 'picking primroses along a sheltered bank on a sudden warm spring day; falling asleep in a drowsy thymy hollow of the downs; finding a new wild flower; climbing a high springy tree on a blowy blue and white day; the first meal in France if all is auspicious; coming back to find that something you didn't expect has burst into bloom; seeing a letter you have been ardently waiting for lying on the table'.

Whatever rows took place as tensions and jealousies rose – about Ian's long affair with his business partner Norah Smallwood for example – they rarely found their way into Trekkie's letters. I have added to the record the conflicted feelings she disclosed in her diary about Norah, and about the eternal female struggle to find a fair balance between nurturing other people and her own work, the bitterness that spilled over when her family or social obligations occupied too much of her time, the doubts she had about her artistic capabilities. If her double responsibilities sometimes made her miserable, they also gave her pleasure. In any case, she faced them with admirable irony. One morning when things were getting her down she wrote in her diary a 'conversation between TR and IV (Inner Voice):

IV   You are becoming defeatist – you are a coward.
TR   I don't think being abusive is any help.
IV   I am not abusive. I think it is a good thing to look it in the face – call a spade a spade.
TR   How tired a spade must be of having people always looking in it's face & calling it a spade. Has a spade a face anyway?
IV   That is a Red Herring.'

Every marriage is an invention with its own limitations. This ménage à trois – or more accurately, ménage à trois à trois ménages – was based on devotion, stability and equality. It grew, adjusted to its contradictions, changed, lived in Trekkie's memory when Leonard and then Ian died, and has an afterlife in these letters.

One can hardly imagine such a correspondence being carried on today. It obviously depended on frequent and rapid postal services. It hung also on Trekkie's and Leonard's ability to sustain an epistolary romance and to appreciate how feeling, indeed life itself, is validated by the very act of recording it. This correspondence is not the same as the closed record of a journal; it is a shared process in which the small acts of life are celebrated in the telling. Our e-mail may be faster and have the same sense of privacy, but it leaves no trace of corrected misspellings, the different curls of hastily written and carefully considered words, the smudges caused by a restless cat in the lap, a spilled cup of tea or a sneeze. Even the simple choice of paper and ink reveals character.

That these letters were written for each other's eyes alone does not make them artless. Leonard's sentences are beautifully clear and Trekkie's phrases well turned, her descriptions painterly vivid and filled with pungent observations. The correspondence is spontaneous and fresh. Trekkie's humility and humour in the face of illness and the daily chores of war, along with Leonard's tender solicitude in turning a boiled egg into a feast for his tiger, give us an enduring sense of the oasis they established for each other against darkness and danger. Leonard was as dogged in love as he was in politics, and as creative. To read the Athanasian creed rewritten for his amorous purposes is to enjoy a playful, inventive intelligence. To read Trekkie's early admonition of his advances is to know the *angst* of a deeply moral feminist who never wanted a second husband and in essence now had two. Her discussions with Leonard about what a woman ought to be, about the struggle of balancing a painter's life with personal loyalties, love with duty, have a very contemporary flavour. Although her correspondence with Leonard falls off once the daily routine had been established, it is remarkable that its epistolary continuity is never lost. In a way the dates on the letters make no difference to the story; two years can pass without a written word and the subsequent letters read as though there had been no interruption in the dialogue.

Even in the last letters when Trekkie is travelling with Ian and one would expect nothing more than repeated I-miss-yous and accounts of hotels slept in, food eaten, her sharp observations ring through: 'The moment when one sees Greece from the air is something which we in this age have invented.' In the soft blue light of a first evening in America 'all New York looked like a Monet', but next day comes the biting discovery that Americans 'have *no* idea of conversation. You all sit round a long way away from each other & shout across' – this from the house of Alfred and Blanche Knopf! Leonard's last letters are filled with lively home news about shared animals and the garden, and clear-headed, often humorous revelations about ageing. 'A very old man with a bald head' whom he met at a London dinner in 1968 and thought 'must be ten years older than I am,' turned out to be 'Michael MacCarthy whom, when I was 35 and he a small boy . . . we used to take out for treats at Richmond.' When Harold Nicolson died shortly after that Leonard wrote to Trekkie, 'I am beginning to feel that I am an only survivor.'

In 1977 Sylvia Townsend Warner cautioned Trekkie to give this correspondence 'to Sussex if you feel you should . . . But let Sussex wait.' Publishing it while Ian was alive was out of the question, but when he died in October 1980 Trekkie raised the possibility with Chatto & Windus, and in 1984 made provision for her friend, the writer Jeanne MacKenzie, to publish it after her death. As it turned out Jeanne died first, in October 1986. Trekkie helped Frederic Spotts with his 1989 volume of Leonard's letters, allowing him to publish eleven addressed to her. When Peter Alexander was working on the Woolfs in 1991 she gave him access to the cache for a couple of hours; she then resealed it, 'not' she told him 'because it is secret, but because it's private', and returned it to the University of Sussex Library vault, where it remained unopened until her death in 1995. With it, and sealed with the same red wax, was a bundle containing the legal papers from the probate hearing.

It is easy to clip a correspondence for effect, more risky to allow it to be its own narrative. I took the decision to publish all the letters Trekkie left us because I think the life they represent worth preserving, and because it is her story, not mine. The coincidences that brought Trekkie and Leonard together are several. Their love was passionate and especially during the war years erotically charged. But just short of her ninetieth birthday Trekkie told Peter Alexander that it was not sexual, and nearer the end of her life she made a point, unsolicited, of saying the same to two other people. The question seems to me irrelevant, but the circumstances of these disclosures make me think it possible that in this instance Trekkie's usual truthfulness may have succumbed to a deeper need for privacy – one might say to her habit of privacy. If she had not wondered before, the sting of the probate fiasco would certainly have brought to mind how her relationship with Leonard might be recorded. While wanting to help Peter Alexander, she may well have felt the need to protect herself when he dared to ask her what no one else had, even to control how she would be written into the story of Leonard's life. It would rightly have been very important to her not to be dismissed as Leonard's mistress.

Trekkie gave Leonard his happiest years, but Virginia's long shadow was always over her shoulder and if there is any sadness in the story this is it. Surely the reason Leonard wrote only one book between Virginia's death and the first volume of his autobiography, *Sowing*, which he started twice before finally publishing in 1960, is that he was occupied editing seven volumes of Virginia's essays and unpublished fiction in those years. When he was sorting Virginia's diaries, Trekkie wrote about them in hers. When Trekkie inherited Monk's, where she felt more at home than in her own house and cared for as lovingly, she knew it would be remembered as Virginia's home, and Leonard as Virginia's husband. As Leonard's executrix it became in part her responsibility to make sure of this. Which is why, in a way, this is Trekkie's story more than Leonard's, for although this correspondence will change our view of him, his life is remembered elsewhere.

Judith Adamson

# THE LETTERS

# Letters 1-72 (October 1941-July 1943)

In June 1940 Ian returned from France to spend long hours at the Air Ministry interpreting photos of airfields in occupied Europe. The Blitz began on 7 September and is generally said to have ended on 16 May 1941 with a great night raid on Birmingham. In those months Britain was under continual bombardment and, although other cities were hit, London was the major target. Not until after three years of war were as many soldiers killed in battle as women and children were at home. At night Londoners sought protection in Tube stations, and in family-sized shelters which could carry the debris of two floors. Those who moved about the city did so by moonlight, while powerful searchlight beams crisscrossed the sky looking for enemy planes. When the bombs eased, the blackout remained. In October 1941 Trekkie was answering incoming calls at the War Office in Petersham. Her sister Alice, whose novels had been published by the Hogarth Press, had been ill with cancer since May at the Parsons' house in Victoria Square, where Leonard had frequently visited her. In August she had been moved to a nursing home and now, very close to death, taken to hospital.

1: Friday 24 October 1941 *25 Victoria Square*

Dear Leonard,

I have been meaning to write to you for some little time. It is hard to write news you do not want to send or the other person to hear. You knew that Alice[1] had been moved into the Westminster Hospital for treatment,

1. The Ritchie children, Alice MacGregor (1897–1941), Alan Patrick (1899–1961) and Marjorie Tulip (Trekkie) (1902–1995), were born in Durban, Natal, and moved to England during World War I. Alice studied at Newnham College, Cambridge (1917–20), then worked in the League of Nations Secretariat, Geneva. From 1928 she edited *International Women's News* and travelled for the Hogarth Press, who published her novels *The Peacemaker* (1928), *Occupied Territory* (1930) and, posthumously, her children's book *The Treasure of Li-Po* (1948) in a jacket and with illustrations by TR.

she wrote to you from there I think. She had this treatment for a fortnight & last Monday they decided to give it up. She apparently does not respond to it. She has been growing very markedly weaker since the middle of last week. And I felt it was no use hoping any more. And on Monday the Dr confirmed this. They give her a great deal of dope now & are steadily increasing it. She is herself when she wakes though she is confused from time to time & this maddens her. And I have besought them to let her wake as little as possible now. I see her each evening for about an hour, sometimes she is quite tranquil & though weak, is herself, at others she is confused & I wonder if my going does more harm than good because she forces herself to think when I am there as she would not with the nurses.

I am writing all this to you because I know how much you valued each other. I know that your visits were a very great comfort & happiness to her.

I will write again. Please don't bother to answer this.

> Yours
> Trekkie Ritchie

2:    [Saturday] 1 November 1941                    *25 Victoria Square*

Dear Leonard,

I would have written to you before but I have been ill & am still in bed with Quinsy. It is getting better now. Thank you for your letter. I cannot take in a world without Alice at all.

I must explain about your cheque. It gave Alice the very greatest comfort & satisfaction that you lent this money to her so spontaneously, and I was able always to say, now don't worry about money you know we have heaps, and she really did feel comfortable and happy about it. I had actually enough to meet the expenses of her illness & at first said so but she always said, I hate you spending all this on me etc. so that when you so generously sent her this cheque I said no more, and let her think we were using it, and as I did not in fact have to, I send it back to you with the greatest gratitude. I shall never forget either that you lent it her, or the sweet and friendly way you did it, and it certainly bought her a £100 of comfort.[1]

---

1. After *Occupied Territory* Alice began but could never finish a third novel, which she wrote and destroyed several times. In August 1941, when she had to be moved to a nursing home, she had asked LW to lend her £100 'on the poor security of an unfinished book'. She died on 27 October 1941.

I hope we may meet sometime soon. Are you never in town on a Tuesday for lunch or any evening for dinner?

Yours with much gratitude

Trekkie Ritchie

---

3:   [Monday] 10 November 1941                    *25 Victoria Square*

My dear Leonard

Thank you for your very kind letter. I think I am quite all right financially but I haven't had everything in yet. If I find it does not work out I will ask for your help, and do thank you very much for your kind friendliness.

I look forward to seeing you – will you let me know when is convenient for you.

Tuesday is the only day I am here during the day, Being my leave day.[1] Any evening would do of course as I am back by 6.30 & would be very pleased if you would dine. Whatever suits you best.

Yours

Trekkie

---

4:   [Monday] 2 February 1942                    *25 Victoria Square*

My dear Leonard,

Will you be in town on Tuesday week, it will be the 10th. If you are I wonder if you would be free to come to tea at Vic Square. I would so much like to see you. I haven't written before as I have been having a distracting time with no domestic help, which when one is out all day is most disheartening.

I enclose a small anthology which Alice & Ian[2] & I selected during this summer while she was ill.

---

1. At the outbreak of war TR joined the Fire Service. She then became a land girl, and now worked in the War Office at Petersham, where she answered incoming calls.

2. Ian Macnaghten Parsons CBE (1906–1980) and TR married on 30 August 1934. The son of Edward Perceval Parsons and Mabel Margaret Macnaghten, he was educated at Winchester College and Trinity College, Cambridge, where he obtained a first in the English Tripos, and edited *Granta*. He joined Chatto & Windus, publishers, in 1928 as typographer, became a partner in 1930, chairman in 1956, joint chairman of Chatto & Jonathan Cape in 1969 when the firms united, and joint chairman (with Max Reinhardt and Graham C. Greene) of the larger firm when The Bodley Head joined them in 1973. Among other responsibilities, he was managing director of

If you can't manage the 10th the following Tuesday the 17th would suit me equally well.

I have now had all the bills in, & find I can meet them without involving myself. So that I shall not need to accept your kind offer of help, but do most gratefully accept the friendship that prompted it.

 Yours
 Trekkie

5: [Saturday] 7 February 1942      *at the office*

My dear Leonard,

How frightfully sweet of you to bring me such an enchanting box of flowers. I came home last night nearly crying with cold & very low & found the box on the doorstep, and literally screamed with joy when I opened it. I have arranged the freesias in a shallow white Wedgewood compotier out of which they frill in the most entrancing way.

I've never seen that pure red cyclamen before. It is a lovely colour. You must have a very successful green house. It is a thing I have always coveted. It must be so nice to have somewhere to garden out of the wind.

When the rain came the other day I felt very homesick for a place to garden in; but now it has hardened up again & I find it hard to believe in your freesias.

I have lost your London address & so send this to Rodmell.

Would much like to see you soon when you can manage it.

Thank you again for my lovely surprise.

 Yours
 Trekkie

*The Geographical Magazine* (1935–56), typographical consultant for Hazell, Watson & Viney, printers (1949–52), director of Duralin Bookbinding Products (1960), the Scottish Academic Press (1969), Sussex University Press (1970), and the Hogarth Press. He was president of the Publishers Association (1957–9) and the Society of Bookmen (1969–80), and was one of the defenders of the Net Book Agreement before the Restrictive Practices Court in 1962. His many publications include *Shades of Albany* (1930), *The Progress of Poetry* (1936), *Poetry for Pleasure* (1952–6), *Men Who March Away: Poems of the First World War* (1965). With TR, he joined the Fire Service in September 1939. He served with HQ British Air Forces in France (1940), with Chief of the Air Staff until 1944 (being made Flight Lieutenant in October 1942), and Air Staff SHAEF as Wing Commander (1944–5). He was awarded an Hon. D. Litt. (St Andrews) in 1975.

6:    [Friday] 15 May 1942                              *25 Victoria Square*

My dear Leonard

I have tried to ring you up once or twice at Rodmell but there was no reply & I have lost your London telephone number. I have had to give up my job as the constant sitting seems to have had a bad effect on my inside. But what is nice is that I am doing the little books[1] I think I spoke to you about. I am having to work hard & very fast as they want to publish 18 this autumn, and there are 12 drawings to each book. I can't tell you what it is like to be out of that office & in my own room again, and drawing.

Will you ring me up and come & see me. I am almost always here now unless I am in the museum.

Rose[2] had a miscarriage & has now gone back to Penge to try again.
Yours ever
Trekkie

7:    [Monday] 6 July 1942                              *Chiswick Press*

My dear Leonard

How awful. I should have thought the front door would have burst open of its own accord if it saw strawberries wanting to come in. I expect I was at the Press,[3] where I am at the moment, that's why this is in pencil as the only alternative is litho ink & posting you a stone. It was kind of you & I am desolated to miss you & the strawberries.

I have been up here at Arnos Grove every day for the last month putting my drawings on the stone. I expect & fear a colour proof this week. I have warned them that I shall redraw all if I don't like it.

Will you come to dinner next time you are in town. We are hardly ever fixed up except Wednesdays. Which night will it be, this week or next? I cook the meal when I get home so you will not mind if it is not grand —

1. The Midget Books were published by Chatto & Windus, beginning 1942. There were 30, grouped into 7 series: Nature Pictures, In Other Days, In Other Lands, Bible Stories, How and Why Stories, First Pictures, Nature Studies. Owing to wartime paper shortages, these brightly coloured little books were cut from leftovers after standard size books were printed. Measuring 2½ by 3½ inches, and 12 pages in length, including cover, the first 18 (1942) were printed in editions of 35,000, the second and third 8 (1944 and 1946) of 20,000. They sold for 2d each.
2. Rose was TR's Persian cat; Penge, another, with whom she was being bred.
3. The Chiswick Press was on Brunswick Road close to the Arnos Grove Tube station. It printed many of TR's children's books; in 1942 she did all her lithography there, drawing directly on to the stone. Eyre & Spottiswoode, publishers, bought the Press in 1943 (see letter 105).

Rose is very nearly a mother.
Please send a card & say which night. I do want to see you.
> Yours ever
> Trekkie

8:   [Monday] 9 November 1942                    *25 Victoria Square*

My dear Leonard,
   Thank you so much for the delicious pears. I came back from Scotland
on Sunday morning to find them waiting for me. It was kind of you. Ian
is being sent away on a special job in a week or two. I will write & ask if
I may come for the night. It is easier to get away when I'm on my own as
I haven't any help just now. I often hate having anyone to stay so I hope
you'll say no if you feel the same. It was lovely in Scotland & I walked
miles.
> Yours ever
> Trekkie

9:   [Saturday] 5 December 1942                   *25 Victoria Square*

My dear Leonard
   May I come & see you on Saturday next and stay the night? It will be
the 12th[1]. If this is not convenient I could come another time. Don't worry
about comfort. I am now nearly a Yak.
> Yours ever
> Trekkie

10:   Monday 14 December 1942                    *25 Victoria Square*

My dear Leonard
   I am posting back your box with this. I carried both home after all. No
cabs, & as I'd carried it so far down a long platform it seemed craven to
leave it. I feel rather mortified about the apples. You should have let me
pay because I *asked* for them. I have packed them for the aunt who will be
very pleased. I have just heard Ian has arrived. It's a relief.

1. This was their first weekend alone at Monk's House, Rodmell. LW's diary reads 'work, Trekkie
came, walk. [13th] Work, did apples, Trekkie left'.

I keep on thinking about the light in your house & will come back & paint. Perhaps in January if I may.

Thank you very much for Saturday.

You should not get tired of pictures. Something is wrong if you do, I mean with them. I think you should be able to look at them indefinitely. Rose is cool & distant. I am afraid ours is a Marriage à la Mode.

> Yours ever
> T.


11:    Saturday 19 December 1942

My dear Leonard

This is the last lithograph I have done – it was for the Geographical Magazine, and I had some printed without the lettering. The design is somewhat spoiled as there should be about an inch & a bit on the bottom which had to be cut off. I am fired about the Albion press[1] & am finding out what I can, and am liable to turn the basement into a litho works. Would Saturday 2nd Jan be at all a suitable date for me to come with a paint box? And is an easel one of the things your house has, if not I'll bring a small one. It does seem rather soon to suggest coming but it is so much easier when I am alone. I hope you got your box back safely.

It was kind of you to write.

> Yours
> T.


12:    Saturday 26 December 1942                    *25 Victoria Square*

My dear Leonard

Thank you for your letter. The friend I was expecting can't now come & so I could come to Rodmell on Thursday instead of Saturday, & shall by the same bus & train if that is really all right for you.

I am very gloomy, dining last night at my ma-ma in laws[2] with seven others all on eighty. I came home feeling like something you have picked

---

1. An Albion press was easier to work than the older ones TR had been using because different blocks for the same print could be placed on it simultaneously and more correctly adjusted. However, she soon discovered it inadequate.

2. Mabel Margaret Macnaghten Parsons and TR were not fond of each other and, according to relatives, TR thought her father-in-law, Edward (Ted) Perceval Parsons, weak.

& forgotten to put in water. The old girls talked about their habits — a piece of brown bread & honey, I *never* take anything else for breakfast; the old boys about their crashing abilities — I can do anything I like with people of that class, never have any trouble, everyone says its perfectly marvellous how I manage them — and so on & on.

The Recording Britain Trust[1] will not have me. I sometimes think I must be a very good artist to have been so persistently discouraged.

Don't you admire this passionate pink paper,[2] it should be richly scented.

I shall come unless I hear from you not to

Yours ever

T.

And I shall bring my meat ration which you cannot very well refuse. Do you smoke cigars?

13:   Wednesday [6 January 1943]

My dear Leonard

There should have been a flag flying from Vic Sq to day. I have started on the canvas of the painting from your window. The first proper painting since the war started. I am so grateful to you that I felt I must write & thank you all over again. I do hope it will go on all right. I am taking classes from 6–8 on Mondays & Weds at the Central[3] to learn about taking your own pulls & offsets & so on. The man there is trying to find me a press.

I have carried this letter from my aunt[4] about in my handbag for about five days. I'm sorry.

1. In 1939 the Ministry of Labour and National Services Committee on the Employment of Artists in Wartime decided to initiate a visual record of places and buildings of national interest, particularly those thought to be exposed to possible war damage. The project was sponsored by the Pilgrim Trust and published by Oxford University Press in four volumes entitled *Recording Britain* (1946–9). The work of 97 artists was included; the collection of 1,549 works was eventually transferred to the Victoria & Albert Museum.

2. TR's first letters to LW are on blue 25 Victoria Square letterhead. From here on they are almost all on pink paper and written in pencil or black ink. Most of LW's letters are in green ink on white or blue paper. Some, especially the final ones, are typed and signed in blue ink.

3. Central School of Arts and Crafts, Southampton Row at Theobald's Road.

4. Fuzzells (Elizabeth Ida Ritchie), sometimes spelt by TR with a double 's', sometimes with a single 'l', sometimes ending 'les'. Fuzzells taught in school first at Flora Stevenson in Edinburgh, and from 1912 was First Assistant to the headmaster (in those days always a man) at Tynecastle School. TR spent her first summers in Britain with her. Fuzzells was a genuinely good, Christian woman, but humourless; on New Year's Eve 1951, TR said mischievously to her: 'If you always believe it is more holy to give than to receive, you force everyone else to be receivers & reserve the holy part to yourself,' but Fuzzells was impervious to the fun (Diary, 1.2.51).

Yours ever
            T.
I recognized the paper & guessed where you'd got it from – it had a faint
smell of cigars about it.


14:   Thursday [14 January 1943]                    *25 Victoria Square*

My dear Leonard
    Thank you for your letter. It is kind of you to think of me, and I should
like to do the drawings very much if the author is satisfied with your offer
& Mr Lehmann[1] with me. What shall I do, take the Midget [book]s or wait
until you hear from the author?
    This house has been a bed & breakfast establishment since I got back
and I think longingly of the marsh & gold hay.
    I am going to see the man at the Central about litho presses now. It is a
hopeless black dark London day.
        Yours ever
            T.


15:   [Tuesday] 19 January 1943                     *Monk's House*

My dear Trekkie,
    John Lehmann was here over the week end and he agrees with me
about the children's boo[k] so that we shall be very glad if you will do the
illustrations and jacket.[2] He asked me to say – I hope you wont think this
impertinent – that he thinks the animals should be very much alive in the
illustrations. [H]e will send you the proofs as soon as ready; it may take a
little time as the author is making some alterations in the text.
    I hope you are painting and that it is going well.
        Yours ever
            L.

1. John Lehmann (1907–1987), writer and publisher, became apprentice manager of the Hogarth
Press in 1931. After 18 months he left for Vienna and Berlin. In 1936 he began to publish *New
Writing*, which he took with him when he returned to the Hogarth Press in 1938, after buying
Virginia Woolf's share for £3,000. In September 1940 when the Woolfs' flat in Mecklenburgh
Square was bomb-damaged and the Press, whose premises were in its basement, was moved to
Letchworth, Lehmann became entirely responsible for its day-to-day running.
2. Barbara Baker's *The Three Rings* was published in March 1944 with 12 of TR's lithographic
illustrations, in a white jacket printed in grey and orange.

16:    [Wednesday] 20 January 1943                                    *25 Vic Sq*

My dear Leonard

Thank you for your letter. I am so glad the Hogarth Press will have me. I look forward to doing the book very much. It seems to me most reasonable to want the animals lively, and so they shall be. I am painting all the time. My pianist friend came from Oxford[1] & sat five days for me, & I have got the painting from your house as far as I can until I have another look. If you have not been dewed with people could I come in a fortnight's time? I have got a slight cold & this in spite of Little Victor. It is kind of you to offer to ask your printers about a press. I asked the man at the Central on Monday & he said an Albion would not do. It must be a lithographic press. The ones there are made by Winston. The thing is that the bed of the press moves across as you turn the handle. I understand the Albion kind screw down and are pressed in one movement on the work? Perhaps this isn't right but certainly the litho kind move across as you turn the handle. I did my first proof on Monday; I am glad I thought of taking the course; it is much quicker than trying to learn alone. I had a box of snow drops sent me from Devon so the worst is over.

    Yours ever
     T.


17:    [Tuesday] 2 February 1943                                    *25 Vic Sq*

My dear Leonard

When I get home from Rodmell I am always hoarse & this is due to incessant talking so that I feel there's nothing to choose between me & those mothers & sisters in law we were talking of. I hope you are a little hoarse too?

I had to give the ticket collector at Victoria my ticket in my teeth as I had so many bits & pieces, but found an outside man to carry them here for me. Rose's honeymoon had perhaps been rather too exciting for her as I found that she was a little sick, was shedding her hair & had written a poem. She seems to have found out that you are a publisher & insists on my sending it to you for 'your opinion'. She doesn't really want this as she is inordinately conceited. She only wants your praise.

---

1. Probably Gypsy Lucas, a schoolfriend whom TR continued to paint well into their old age. She visited TR every January.

I'm no longer cool aloof & well bred
Now I'm calling for Wave & his marriage bed
With ears laid back & front close to the floor
I want once again what I've had once before.
I shake with desire
I burn like a fire
I'm passion's slave
As I fell for Blue Wave.[1]

It is rather mean of it to be such a distinctly better day as soon as I get back to town. I felt rather ashamed that I hadn't wanted to come back as everyone was very nice to me and not at all aggrieved at me being late. The man who is finding us a press came this morning, & all is very hopeful. He will come & be Old Stone Man & as he is also a printer he knows everything. He says he can find us stones & everything else so that I think we will very soon be fixed up.

The house has been so full of people all day I haven't had a chance to look at my painting yet, but to-morrow will be normal again.

I enclose this snapshot[2] to amuse you. It was taken just before we came to England.

I think you know how happy I am at Rodmell & being that am grateful so I won't say it all over again.

Yours ever
T.


18:    Wednesday [10 February 1943]            *25 Victoria Square*

My dear Leonard
    The painting is done & is rather stodgy I am afraid but perhaps you'd like to see it even so, as it has a somewhat historic interest. If you are to be at Mecklenburgh Sq next Monday night I could bring it round after lithography and leave it for you to see in day light & without me breathing down your neck. I would have eaten before going out & would be with you at about 8.15 if I didn't lose my way [through the blackout]. This has been a horrid week, wind & wet & I am in bed with flu & the prospect of my sister in law[3] for all Sunday. I have been drawing a Stylosa Iris [*unguicularis*] mostly. Rose & I are at a loss to

1. A cat of LW's with whom Rose was to be mated.
2. Not in the Archive.
3. Doreen Parsons (married Jasper Blunt).

know what qualities we have in common & she's a bit miffed. Alice is helping me do my doll's washing in the photograph. The dolls were a never ending story which we played for years & which had almost nothing to do with the actual dolls though they were the beginning of it all. This has been such a swamping week it already seems months since I was at Rodmell.

Yours ever<br>T.

19:   Saturday [13 February 1943]                                   *Vic Sq*

My dear Leonard

I could have come another night when you were going to be in town. I feel rather appalled that you should come on purpose, I know the painting is dull. I shall, I hope, paint a lot of pictures at Rodmell & perhaps something will come of them. If it hadn't been for the sad story of the elm[1] I would not have shown you this one. As for me, you are wrong I fear. Gentleness is a quality I dote on but do not possess. The tiger is too true & it has always stalked about in me all too ready to show its teeth & claws. Rose is now all dove. She has settled down to making her kittens & is soft & purring & affectionate & only thinking lovely thoughts so that they shall have every chance. On Monday I shall be rolling my stones from 6–8 & then it is so late to eat, so I shall have had something before, & be coming away from the Central School two blocks above Holborn Station at eight. But I shall find my way and there is a moon. How awful your day sounded & not really enough consolation to know at last all about women tracers.

Yours ever<br>T.

1. There were two great elms with interlaced boughs on the bank edging the lawn at Monk's House, which were called Leonard and Virginia. They were in the picture TR had sketched on her second visit and by 6 January had begun to paint. The one under which VW's ashes were buried had blown down in a gale that first week of January. When LW died in 1969, TR buried his ashes under the other; it later succumbed to Dutch elm disease.

20:    Tuesday [16 February 1943]                                    *25 Vic Sq*

My dear Leonard

You so surprised me last night with that Sowerby[1] talk that I think I more scolded than thanked you. And I still feel so hurt & don't quite know how to begin. I've wanted one since I first saw it, when I was a child trying to identify flowers. I had no notion how good the engravings were. And now I can hardly wait for it to arrive. So I can only say thank you Leonard dear for being so kind to me. And that is what I meant last night when you said 'for what?'

I hope you didn't feel a navel gazing stupor stealing over you last night – I was rather tired from stone rolling & felt I was pretty stupid. My iris is sweet & crisp & I am keeping it at the cold end of my room. It is astonishingly beautiful. It is so sunny this afternoon perhaps your elm looked a little bit like the painting. You must look at it (the painting) in a good light or you don't see the colour as it's so pale. The coloured study is the one I did from the path.

These seeds are some I had from Buryard. They make very delicious little marrows like (to look at not taste) cricket balls. I wish I had more.

Next week when you are in town will you come & see my Press. I will scarcely have it by then.

Yours ever
T.

21:    Thursday [18 February 1943]                                  *25 Vic Sq*

Oh my dear Leonard the Sowerby has come, & this afternoon the Press. And everything smells of spring & I think its a good thing I have had two bad nights else I'd go straight through the roof like the great aloe at Kew. And you do realize don't you that this is all your doing except for the spring smell. I know good will come of the Press. I have so many lithographic ideas. As for Sowerby, it is all over my floor & I can't believe it's mine. I feel as I did when I was eighteen & given my small string of pearls.

1. James Sowerby (1757–1822), engraver, whose books and illustrations of English natural history are well known. These were probably a set of hand-coloured flower plates, from first and early editions, which TR later had bound into seven volumes, and which she kept all her life. Her sharpness with LW would have come from embarrassment about the extravagance of his gift.

Will you please say when you can come – to, or not to a meal as you prefer. Whenever suits you.

Reticulata[1] has been sitting for me all morning. Can you gather from all this how thankful I am?

Yours ever<br>T.

22:  Sunday [21 February 1943]                                    *25 Vic Sq*

My dear Leonard,

Your letter took ages to come – not till Friday afternoon. I think it had been censored to see if you were telling me all about convoys.[2] Anyway I am glad you like the painting. I have a great feeling against selling pictures hot from the brush. In case one doesn't like them & afterwards wants them back, so I will lend it you for the present. The study I will give you because I like it & if I liked the picture better I'd give you that, though I really am greatly against giving away pictures but this is quite a special thing. The ink drawing I will sell you for £2, so now that is all straight and as you are so very good at working me out you will understand my quirks. I am sorry to write in pencil but Rose & I are having tea on the mat. She has drunk all my milk very messily & has spattered her forehead with it. She is very secretive about whether or not she is making me kittens. I hope you are coming to see the Press this week. I could come to Rodmell for Sunday night if you'd like me to? I might be going away for a fortnight after that.

Yours ever<br>T.

1. Iris reticulata comes from the Caucasus, grows about 6 inches tall, and has a delicate scent of violets.
2. From the Battle of Britain when squadrons of German bombers trimmed the trees as they flew over Rodmell, military convoys crisscrossed the Ouse Valley and searchlights swept its night skies. After 1942 the Downs were extensively taken over for troop training. There were constant air-raid warnings at the south coast towns and anti-aircraft fire from the large guns at Offham and Southease, on Firle Beacon and Caburn, was audible in the village. Further danger and noise came from aerial dogfights and aircraft droning in both directions. The Home Guard watched for German invaders from six-sided brick pillboxes built up the valley, one in the field next to Monk's House. There was often a ban on non-residents coming into the area, and the movement of locals was sometimes controlled.

23:   [Tuesday] 23 February 1943                    *Monk's House*

Dearest tiger, I find I can get up Monday so I'll expect you 8.15 at Meck. Square & I shall try to tame your ferocity with a diet of tea, toast, butter, & one boiled 'shell-egg'. Can you imagine any diet less appropriate, more ridiculous for Blake's tiger?[1] Only, if you really find it too tiring after the two hours & the rolling of lithography, to come on to Mecklenburgh & then your journey home, you mustn't do it, & just ring me up & tell me to go to the devil, which willingly & yet unwillingly I will do.

I wasn't really sure that I could manage Monday when you suggested it, because I thought they might have fixed a Labour Party meeting here that night for Robson[2] to speak on the Beveridge report (I hope & expect you don't know what that is)! Luckily, when I got back here tonight, I found they have fixed it for Tuesday.

I enclose a cheque. Thank you again for the sketch & loan of the picture. There is a palimpsest below the black & white of the cyclamen & below that of a room, the colour in which is lovely. I must say I like the cyclamen.

> Ever your
> L

24:   Wednesday [24 February 1943]                    *25 Vic Sq*

My dear Leonard

Alas it *is* a toast & tea tiger. In bed all yesterday with a new cold & a roaring inside; got up at once to day as I couldn't bear it in bed any more & I spent the day painting my [iris] reticulata & cyclamen. But had the Dr this hour who says yes it is a poor kind of out of condition beast and has

1. In 'The Tyger', *Songs of Experience* (1794). LW continued to call TR 'Tiger' and, until August 1943 when he contradicted his earlier interpretation of it, to refer to Blake's poem (see letter 82 and note).
2. William Alexander Robson (1895–1980), an expert in administrative law and local government who became Professor of Public Administration at LSE. He and Kingsley Martin launched the *Political Quarterly* in 1930, which he edited jointly with LW from 1931 to 1940, and 1946 to 1959 (LW did the job himself from 1940 to 1946 and remained literary editor until 1962). His wife Juliette Alvin (d. 1982) was a violincellist and a pioneer in music therapy. Their children called the Woolfs uncle and aunt; VW signed her letters to them Aunt Virginia. The Beveridge Report was published on 2 December 1942 by an interdepartmental committee on Social Insurance and Allied Services headed by Sir William Beveridge. This major restatement of social policy, which had wide repercussions two years later as the basis of the Government's proposals on national insurance, sold over a million copies.

given it a bottle of medicine which will quickly cure it. And it must be more in the air. So I think I'll offer to come as garden boy to you & Percy.[1] Everyone lately has said I look tired or thin or both & I know they mean I look like this drawing [sketched through the letter]. It is very depressing so I hope I shall come back from Lyme sleek & glossy.

Your reticulata are the best ones. Irene[2] brought one from Hertfordshire not nearly so good a colour nor half as sweet. What a delicious smell it is. A very violet coloured smell. I haven't gone to the Central tonight but I shall on Monday & will come to Meck Sq. I have *heard* of the Beveridge Report but don't know about it. Is it a good idea? So that's where the cyclamen painting went, I couldn't find it. I often do that & people get two pictures instead of one & never know, because I don't remember until too late to ask for it back, & they never look behind. The room is this one & I did a painting of it just before the war which turned out quite well. Thank you for the cheque. I do hope you are seeing a committee or something on Monday?
    Love from
        T.
Rose lay on my chest in bed yesterday & looked all through the [Rosace?] vol of Sowerby – she wasn't interested in any other order.


25:    Thursday [4 March 1943]    *Bay Hotel, Promenade, Lyme Regis*

My dear Leonard
    It *is* magic casements opening on the foam. I was so afraid the hotel would after all not be near enough the sea, but it almost has its feet in it. We shared our taxi from the station with people who went to yours. This one is ugly but comfortable & good food & the usual collection of old tabs with one or two old tibs. Tearing along, doing last minute things, and not to keep the taxi waiting I fell headlong down Victoria Street & tore a great hole in my knee & stocking so came away in a dishevelled state with Ian's hanky tying me up.[3]

1. Percy Bartholomew had been Leonard's gardener since 1928.
2. Irene Beatrice Hawkins (b. 1906), painter, illustrator and close friend of TR, had been in Ware, Much Hadham and Westmill, Hertfordshire, painting for the Pilgrim Trust's 'Recording the Changing Face of Britain' project. Trained at the York School of Art and the RCA under Rothenstein, she illustrated books for Faber & Faber (1940–53) and designed jackets directly on to the stone at the Curwen Press. Her work was exhibited at NEAC, in Brighton, Ditchling and at the Southover Gallery in Lewes.
3. TR was accident-prone and, when older, boasted about her scars. She usually disinfected cuts carefully because of a tendency to infection.

I am eating so much that I will be much more like the grocer's cat than a tiger when I get back. Ian is being very good & walking very willingly. We were out all day to-day & saw heaps of birds including among the less usual ones a Dipper – Nuthatch, Bullfinch & Grey Wagtail as well as all the Tits. The marsh tit was particularly charming. He was on a branch of Pussy willow in the evening sunshine, & his own grey & silver colours were repeated in the willow all but the little jetty head. We saw too, simply heaps of spangly bright yellowhammers. I always think they look as if they had been too eager to sniff flowers & had charged at them with their heads down & got covered in pollen. I agree about the country side, it isn't especially what I like to paint. And the building is really worse than most places. Horrid scattered chicken farming shacks all over the hillsides.

Now look what I've done. Taken two sheets instead of one so I shall have to go on some more or it will be a waste.

We have decided to stay here until we come home on Sunday week, it seems such a bore moving & difficult when it must be done by bus or train. I have brought painting things & hope to get something done but am a bit nervous for fear they fuss about me being a spy, the way they did to poor Irene in Yorkshire.[1]

I hope you have been calm & had no more colds? I still snuffle but it is going I think. From the look of the gardens here Monk's House will be over before I see it again, I fear. I take back what I said about that Pyrus [pear tree] –? There is one full out here over a stream & it looks simply lovely.

love<br>T.

26:    [Monday] 8 March 1943                                    *Monk's House*

Dearest Tiger, I enclose Vol 2 (or part of it) of a letter I began writing to you last Wednesday night after the Robsons [William and Juliette] had gone to bed. I put Vol 1 in my pocket meaning to post it in London on Thursday & didn't, partly because I hadn't an envelope & partly for the reason given in this piece of Vol 2. & now I think I had better destroy Vol 1 & send you Vol 2, which was written on Friday.

I got your letter this morning. It is possible that if you eat & sleep

1. In Yorkshire Irene Hawkins painted a house in Castlegate and the Lodge in Thirkby Park for *Recording Britain*.

enough you may become a zoo tiger, but I can't imagine anything changing you into a grocer's cat. I'm afraid Lyme country is not really very good, but I do hope you've found something to paint. When you come here, as I hope you may, in 2 weeks time it will be daffodils, Crown Imperials, & hyacinths, but the first flush of spring will alas be over.

I could not at the time tell you how honoured & touched I was to have the printing machine hanselled by your drawing of me & to be given the first pull.

Ever your

L

And then – to be honest – I'm not sure that subconsciously I wasn't afraid that it might not bore & annoy you. And still am. So I may never send it but go on to the end of my life carrying it in my pocket & adding a paragraph to it from time [to time] for the mere pleasure of writing to you.

In that case I must add this, again for the sake of honesty. There is something to be said more than the above for the Robsons of this world – & for my poor unrewarded Robsons in particular. (They have left me today). I like bore Willie despite the monumental boredom of his brain & thought. I like Juliette; she is a 'nice woman' with sense in her head & character. And she played Bach suites which made up – almost – for everything – one which I had never heard & is practically never played, because it is practically unplayable – it was extraordinarily beautiful & also gentle & mysterious. I do wish you could have heard it. I see now after 6 days observation how Juliette treats Willie. She wouldn't of course admit it even to herself & he would be outraged, if you even hinted it, but in fact she treats him exactly as if he were a child. Why are practically all women so much more civilized than men? They almost all treat us almost always as children, except when for a moment they treat us as tomcats or stallions. They are quite right – I see it clearly after the last six days – to do so. Unless they treated us with our intolerable conceit, violence, & tediousness as if we were children who know not what they do, they simply could not live with us at all. Several times when poor Willie was being more absurd & peevish & dictatorial than usual, I noticed that unmistakable mother's smile flit across Juliette's face, the smile of affectionate apology for the wilfulness & violence of 'only a child'. Being myself – I suppose & admit – also a man, I felt humiliated, knowing him to be right & not a pin's difference between me & Willie, & when I willingly enraged Willie by repeating several twists of a statistical statement made by him in a 'serious' political discussion: 'I don't believe a word of it', I saw that the smile was now including me.

At any rate the barometer has gone up & I've had the pleasure of thinking of you having a divinely still, sunny day. That's what it has been here.

27:   Wednesday [10 March 1943: postcard]                    *Axminster*

We are going to walk along the Axe today. I tried to get a picture of the house you told me of 'The George' to send you but there aren't any. It is nice & so is the bench in the street in front of it. I don't expect you'll be able to read this as I am writing with a minute blunt pencil chained to the Post Office – the pencil is not me. How very bad of you to send me only vol II, of course I want vol I. I agree with what you say about the treating as a child. It is just what I am useless at. I cannot switch about like that. I haven't painted at all. But like the country much better than at first. I seem to be very slow to settle in a new landscape unlike the Colonel or the amateur lady sketcher who paints 'a pretty bit' almost instantly. But I am walking miles & am becoming fatter & pinker every day. I fear you may find that it isn't Tiger & Dove but Owl & Pussy Cat.
        Love T.

28:   [Thursday] 11 March 1943                    *Monk's House*

Dearest tiger, my dear dove, or dear owl, pussy -, or grocer's-cat, it is most confusing the way you seem to be changing into a Protean menagerie. The psychological contradictions & permutations of the gentle tiger & fierce dove were, as I explained to you, complicated enough. Now that you have added an owl & two cats, the result must be bewildering. I have indicated above, I hope with the greatest delicacy, the degrees of my affection for the various manifestations. I stand by the tiger, even when red in tooth & claw. And what shoulder & what art could twist the sinews of thy heart?[1] I have always thought it must be magnificent to have a heart like that. No wonder you cant treat us like children.
        I am sorry I destroyed vol I, if you would have liked to see it. The following is a Snopsis (as film people say) of it so far as I can remember it:

1. From Blake's 'The Tyger' (see letters 23, 82, and notes).

Ch. 1  An oasis in the Robson desert
  " 2  Close-up of a tiger disappearing into sulphurous fumes of Holborn tube
  " 3  Strange effect on black-out, Orion, & Pleiades
  " 4  Close-up of tiger on Tavistock Square area surrounded by dustbins
  " 5  Ditto on St George's Square with George V dying in background
  " 6  Ditto on Victoria Square with world falling about ears
  " 7  Curses & shrieks of host overwhelmed by guests & doddering & tottering onto old age & grave
  " 8  Scenes of second childhood connected with a barometer

I'm glad the country improves but it must be rather sad not to paint. Everything here is rushing out & if you don't come soon, you'll find it has reached the 'autumn tint' stage in March. But of course when you get back to the Home Counties you'll find them much behind the West.

Good night, Your
      L.


29:   Monday 15 March 1943 [postcard]

I'm home. In view of the snopsis it would be egotistical to go on about vol 1 but I do regret it. May I come for Saturday & Sunday please, the usual train on Saturday, and I would have to come home on Monday afternoon. I do hope it will be all right & that you are not going to be invaded by 'guests'. I did two studies of the Cobb [a black-backed sea gull TR was sketching for her Midget Books] so it wasn't quite barren.

     love
      T.


30:   [Tuesday] 16 March 1943 [postcard]       *Monk's House*

Yes, I shall look forward to Saturday. There will be no guests, no curses, no smirks, only daffodils, hyacinths, & crown imperials.

      Yr L.

31:   [undated; probably Monday 22 March 1943, left at Monk's House]

My dear Leonard

I have now added my old white coat to the things that stay behind.
W[ave] is more beautiful than ever this afternoon & I really am nearly
demented. It seems useless to try to paint. I'm not sure I wasn't wiser
[written over] when I chloroformed myself into an office worker. The
word I can't read myself is wiser.

I rolled my flowers in a paper poke & tied them outside my case so
I haven't taken the box. Thank you for them & for letting me come
& quiver in your 'grounds'. Really dear Leonard thank you very
much.

Love
T.

32:   [Tuesday] 23 March 1943

Dearest tiger, What do you think of this letter to Peter?[1] I have again
forgotten his surname, a Freudian suppression, I expect – our powers of
forgetting are, as Fanny Price said, peculiarly past finding out. I should
like to read his answer.

Yr
L

How I wish that one could relieve you of some of the weight of the world,
& events, & life, but one of the horrors of life is that one can practically
never relieve any one, however fond, or the more fond, one is of them.
The most one can do is to offer an exquisite pair of shoes, as Peter did, or
an extra large boiled egg, as I did.

23/3/43 [enclosure]                                   *37 Mecklenburgh Square, WC1*

Dear Peter

I am not sure whether you will remember that we once met, on Jan 20,

1. Peter A. Brooker, TR's first husband. They met at the Slade while students of Henry Tonks and
Philip Steer and married in early 1926 to live a bohemian life for a few years in a garret on Gower
Street and country cottages in England and France. TR said the marriage was a mistake from the
beginning. He had sent her a pair of shoes from West Africa.

1936.[1] Even if you do, I am afraid that you may consider this letter an impertinence & will not believe me when I assure you that it is meant to be the opposite.

One of the worst things of which one can be guilty is, I think, injustice, & I hate to know that I have been unjust & made no attempt to repair it. The only possible reparation is too often confusion & apology.

I was unjust to you on Jan 20, 1936 & have continued to be so acutely at intervals for 7 years until last Saturday. The nature of the injustice can best be explained by the cause of my realizing it. I realized it when I saw the shoes you sent to Trekkie. I realized that the person who had the taste to choose those shoes, send them in the middle of the second world war from West Africa to England, & send them to Trekkie in particular could not be the person whom, as I wrongly thought, I met on Jan 20 1936. Hence this letter, confession, apology.

> Yours,
> Leonard Woolf

## 33:    Thursday [25 March 1943]

My dear Leonard

I enclose as you see a very quick reply from West Africa. I liked your letter so much that I would have liked to send it & see what the authentic one would have been. But it would not have done. Poor unhappy Peter, alone in Africa living all his life with his head turned over his shoulder (which I should think began when he was about five) would only have had all his complexes fed by it. So I have done what I can myself.

I believe the fearful Rodmell grieving is due entirely to me not being fixed to a continuing painting for which I have collected a large amount of material. This would make a sense of continuity & stop that awful 'days & moments purely flying' feeling. And perhaps, as Ian sensibly pointed out, I shall find I can get fixed to a picture even with a railway journey between me and the 'motif' when the landscape has settled into summer & stopped this wild spring conjuring trick. The study of your house with its debated lilac roof has come off after all, I think I may be able to finish the green house from memory. During the moment, you are right, no one can do anything. But great eggs and what goes with them make grateful dove cats return after the flight, and I could never under estimate them. The

1. In letter 37 LW corrects this date to 1 March 1932. VW's diary for 21 January 1936 reads: 'The King died last night. We were with Alice Ritchie'.

awful feeling of time passing I think I never had until Alice's death. I had always felt it was still quite early morning, now it seems to be tea time.

I think one of these days when you are in town you should force yourself away from your meetings & come to Kew. The magnolias are just bursting their little plush sheaths. And the stork has got his little hill wildly sprinkled with daffodils and I don't wonder he's put up notices with Private on them to keep it as much to himself as possible.

Rose is back looking a little pale & interesting and lying more limply like a tippet than ever.

What an immense letter.

     Love

      T.


[Enclosure, in TR's hand)

Dear Mr Woolf

Yes I do remember meeting you at St George's Sq.[1] some years ago.

I suppose I ought to feel delighted that you have taken the trouble to compliment me on my taste. But that is not how I feel. I have never been able to see why a small group of intellectuals should imagine that they have a monopoly of 'taste', when in my experience most literary people have rather poor taste at any rate in any visual way.

The shoes you admire are the work of the local Africans who have never had the advantage of having their taste 'trained' and who are in my opinion greatly superior in almost every way to the English who come here to 'civilize' them, and are quickly ruined when they are subjugated to this process.

     Yours

     Peter Brooker


34:   [Monday] 29 March 1943               *Monk's House*

Dearest tiger, Your Peter letter was admirable. I suppose he would probably have taken it in that way, though he was mistaken in thinking that it was that kind of taste – the 'artistic' sort – that I was thinking of.

The time passing is a terrible feeling. It comes, I think, some time or

1. SW1, Alice Ritchie's flat.

other to every one. But you are too young for it; you still have what I think is probably the best part of the day before you. It is when evening really comes and one realises that there are only a few hours before bedtime that the moment comes when one must stand up and defy fate. And that, I believe, is really the only way to meet it and to deal with God, death, and life. If only one can recognize fate as fate, the inevitable as inevitable, even one's own fate becomes impersonal. Then you can stand up and defy the universe, which is the only right attitude for a human being; 'I dont like you,' you can say, 'I dont like what you do and are going to do to me; I despise you and your ways; but the responsibility is yours, not mine; so go ahead, go your way, and, while there is still time, I propose to go mine.'

This is more a sermon than a letter, I'm afraid. It is written to the accompaniment of a continual wailing of syrens, alerts and all clears following one another at intervals of five minutes all the morning – which seems to be appropriate.

Would you come to Kew with me if I could snatch an afternoon next week? I had thought to come up tomorrow, but all my engagements have got into a tangle and I think I shall make that an excuse for cutting them all, staying here, and doing some work in quiet. But I shall be up Tuesday, Wednesday next week. Do you hate dining in restaurants. If you don't, would you dine with me at the Akropolis Restaurant in Percy Street on Wednesday, the 7th; it is a Greek restaurant which means that the food is Turkish and, I think, rather good.

Ever Your<br>L.

35:    Thursday [1 April 1943]                                  *25 Victoria Square*

My dear Leonard

You were such a trial to me yesterday. All morning I was rolling away at you and not to mince words you sullenly & obstinately filled in & scummed up.[1] Thus in a rage I snaked off your ear, this did me no good as I had to resensitise you & try to put it back – now I have gummed &

1. TR was printing a lithograph of LW's head. The printed and nonprinted areas lie in the same plane in lithography. The process begins with a drawing in crayon or ink on limestone. The fats in the crayon adsorb the stone, forming a greasy image. When treated with a solution of gum arabic, the undrawn areas are sealed from further contact with the grease. This can be removed with acidic resensitising solutions if the nonprinting areas scum up with unwanted deposits. In this way the image can be added to or, as here, corrected.

left you. After all that you'll be surprised to hear that I would come to Kew on Wednesday afternoon if you can get away. I hope these wild winds aren't destroying the magnolias. Except for that I like this big buffeting but non vicious wind.

The attitude you suggest is exactly the one I employed against the Blitz & it worked perfectly. The trouble about all defiance is that [it] is to some extent exhausting.

I don't at all object to dining in Restaurants, but I shall be stone rolling until eightish on Wed. That makes it late in a restaurant & they have mostly eaten everything. And anyhow I prefer tea & toast at Mecklenburgh Sq even if there isn't a tiger's egg, but perhaps this doesn't sustain you enough? More slippers have come from Peter. Sambo's Sunday shoes this time [drawing of shoe], red & yellow & green with buck hide soles with the hairs left on on the outside. They expect to have bare brown legs not stockings in side them.

　　Love
　　T.

36:　　[Saturday] 3 April 1943　　　　　　　　　　*Monk's House*

Dearest tiger, How terrifying are the words you don't, as you say, mince! Terrifying, because they not only apply to lithography but life. I am sure that I am sullenly scummed up and snaked off. And then you have resensitized me, but dont, please, gum me up and leave me finally snaked off and scummed up. Your use of words unminced shows that you ought to be a writer as well as a painter.

Defiance is exhausting. But the attitude should not be pure defiance, but a mixture of defiance and resignation. It was the Greek attitude to fate. The defiance which leads to acceptance of and contempt for one's own fate. That is what makes their heroes like Prometheus and poor old Oedipus so admirable; they shriek with agony or rage, and yet deep down they quite calmly defy and accept the inevitable.

Alas, Wednesday is impossible. I am secretary of a Labour Party committee[1] which meets at 2 to deal with a memorandum on Abyssinia

---

1. LW worked indefatigably for the Labour Party although his politics were often left of its ideology. He was appointed honorary secretary of the Labour Party's advisory committees on International and Imperial Affairs in 1919 and helped write hundreds of policy analyses and recommendations before he resigned in 1945 with Labour's electoral victory. In 1922 he stood unsuccessfully for the Combined Universities Labour seat. His book *International Government*

which I have written and therefore must attend. (I know your interest in my political occupations). Could you possibly come to Kew on Thursday afternoon; I would pick you up at Victoria Square about 2. You can tell me on Wednesday, as I shall expect you in Mecklenburgh Square for tea and toast about 8; you will see the Square for the first time in double summer time daylight.

How I wish you were here today. The garden has suddenly changed from yellow to blue and violet, hyacinth, scillas, grape hyacinth, and aubretia; there is a pear tree in full flower, and one or two fritillaries in the grass. I do hope your painting has been going well.

Ever your
L.

37:  [Friday] 9 April 1943                                    *Monk's House*

Dearest tiger, I just want to say that I do hope you will manage to come here on the 28 or 29. Because the niece[1] who has just married writes and asks whether she and he (who has 10 days leave) can come here for two or three days in the following week and I have said any time after May 4. So that if you failed me the week before I should not be able to see you here until the summer was almost over.

When I got to the place last night on the road where I always think that I shall see Sally[2] again in four minutes, I became intimidated by a vision of your disapproving face (and Hippy and Henderson) and said to myself 'Now, I must not allow any show of emotion on either side.' Sally must have had a flash of telepathy, for she was on me almost before I was inside the garden gate. I tried to be as cold as a cat-lover or a tiger in order to win your approval, but dont pretend that it was a complete success. However when I got inside the door and Peat[3] immediately came screaming down the staircase to greet me, I felt on much safer ground.

(1916) helped form Britain's proposals for a league of nations; *Empire and Commerce in Africa* (1920) analysed imperialist greed. His other political publications include *Imperialism & Civilization* (1928), *Quack, Quack!* (1935), *Barbarians at the Gate* (1939) and *The War for Peace* (1940).
1. Judith Stephen (1918–72), anthropologist, daughter of Adrian and Karin Stephen, had recently married photographer Nigel Henderson.
2. A black-and-white Cocker spaniel the Woolfs had bought for £18 in June 1935 after Pinker (Pinka) died. Pinka had been given to VW by Vita Sackville-West in July 1926; she was the model for Flush.
3. A cat

The evening we dined with Alice, you, and Peter was that of Tuesday, March 1, 1932, so that it must have been very near the time when you left him. The whole day came back to me in a flash, an absurd tea beforehand at Ottoline's, and the menace behind us of Lytton's death and our having before us the appalling task of going down to try to prevent Carrington from committing suicide. (The other time we dined with Alice when George was dying, I now remember, to meet a man who was, I think, a civil servant). I reburst into a rage when I found it was March 1, 1932. I never saw you again until February, 1942.[1] I put it all down to Peter and shall write him another letter retracting all I said. It infuriates me to think that I never saw or spoke to you for 10 years. However I must not begin that or I shall rewrite the first vol. of the letter I didn't send for that was its subject.

There were goldfinches at the pond today after breakfast.

I do hope you enjoyed Winchester and solved the problem of Murray[2] and the widow.

I should like to become your tiger with the sponge one day next week, but it looks hopeless as the only time I shall have free at all is on Tuesday morning. I have to be up on Monday, but must go back here Tuesday evening, and then come up for the day on Thursday.

> Ever your
> L.

38:    Sunday [11 April 1943]                                    *Vic Sq.*

My dear Leonard. God forbid that I should come between you & Sally. I think you wilfully misunderstand me. Having a much more tender heart & lively conscience than you the thought of Sally's brooding devotion would weigh on me when I was in London; but having allowed her to get into that state about you the least you can do is to leap on her as ardently as she does on you.

Winchester was not bad but I was glad to come home. We had one long good walk, all day on Friday. Murr[a]y never mentioned the widow. I

1. George Duckworth, Virginia Woolf's half-brother, died on 27 April 1934. TR remembered meeting LW before the 1932 dinner when she delivered her jacket design for Alice Ritchie's *Occupied Territory* to the Hogarth Press. The book was published in March 1930.
2. Frederick Murray Hicks (1883–1967), barrister and teacher, was housemaster of DuBoulay's, Ian Parsons's house at Winchester. He was Flight Commander in the RFC (1914–18), and awarded the Croix de Guerre (1917). He remained a close friend of Ian's, and sometimes travelled with the Parsons. The widow is unknown.

told him he was the most like a Puritan of anyone I knew but gave him no advice. He was piqued about the Puritan and said I was talking vaguely & it was unusual in me & I must define what I meant & got out dictionaries. But I didn't think I could define what I meant more clearly without perhaps giving mortal offence so I went to bed. The water meadows looked lovely – soft melting green & grey.

I left Peter the following January. So you can hardly blame him for the next ten years. What I can't understand is that I remember doing 6 wrappers in all for the Hogarth Press[1] – and I only remember seeing you the first time with Alice's. I suppose I must have sent the others by post. It is all very strange, but perhaps we wouldn't have liked each other ten years ago.

Tuesday is hopeless. I must air Ian on Tuesdays. I will come to Monk's House that week D.V. meantime you must walk round the apple trees looking pretty frostily at them. If I don't see you this week will you be able to come any time the following one & meet my aunt [Fuzzells] again. She would be so delighted as she took what she would describe as 'a thought' for you.

Rose was extremely pleased to see me & blew in my face & even which is very rare sat on me. I do remember now that the man you met at Alice's was Dennis Kincaid,[2] he was a judge in India went out again & was drowned bathing almost at once. I liked him.

Love from
T.

39:    Tuesday 13 April 1943 [postcard]                    *Monk's House*

If your brother has not, & you can still get, Bird Flight by Aymar published by Lane, he might like it.[3] It is mainly photographs. I have a

---

1. TR designed dust-jackets for 11 Hogarth books: Alice Ritchie's *Occupied Territory* (1930), R. M. Fox's *Drifting Men* (1930), John Hampson's *Saturday Night at The Greyhound* (1931), Vita Sackville-West's *All Passion Spent* (1931), Bonamy Dobrée's *St Martin's Summer* (1932), Barbara Baker's *The Three Rings* (1944, with drawings), Tom Hopkinson's *Mist in the Tagus* (1946), Norah & William Montgomerie's *Scottish Nursery Rhymes* (1946, with drawings), N. Brysson Morrison's *The Winnowing Years* (1949), *The Following Wind* (1954), *The Other Traveller* (1957).

2. Dennis Kincaid (1905–1937) wrote *British Social Life in India: 1608–1937* and books about Shivaji, the founder of the Maratha Empire.

3. Air-Vice-Marshal Alan Patrick Ritchie, CBE, AFC, then Air Officer in charge of a bomber command group. Through Alice Ritchie, LW had known TR's brother since the early twenties when Pat tried, but failed because of a problem with the plane, to take the Woolfs up from Hendon. Gordon Aymar's book was an apt choice for a flier; it included 200 action photos of birds.

sneaking hope that even your 'tender' heart will be allergic to the photo overleaf [of an English Springer spaniel]. I did enjoy the printing. I see that Hooker gives the tulip as indigenatis in some southern counties.

 L.

40: Wednesday 14 April 1943        *Vic Sq*

My dear Leonard, Sowerby says 'doubtful native'. Mrs Loudon & the Kew Johns accept it. I think perhaps we had better devote the rest of our lives, me to going about planting the bulbs in old chalk pits, you to getting an act of Parliament passed to make it a capital offence to dig up wild flowers. And I think also you must pass an act that only I can plant things about the country or some unprincipled people might put delphiniums in woods & have riots of colour. I have succumbed & am painting the yellow tulips at this moment.

 Yesterday we tried to print & everything went wrong again. Rollers were the trouble I think.

 The great jar of hyacinths is in the window. They are the best I ever saw.

 I think you are madly generous about hyacinths.

  Love T.

41: Monday 19 April 1943 [postcard]

You must know that I have proofed the Pink & what is more printed an edition of 20 through the yellow *and the blue*. I don't mean I've done all this to-day. But I have done it. To-day would have been a washout anyway. Fuzzels had to rush to Derby as Tim[1] has burnt herself rather badly. Would it be possible to bring the study of the room with the yellow cloth, which is behind one of your drawings on Thursday? I might be going to sell it. I think of lending you the painting of that. Face is down but tooth is still sore. My yellow tulips still smell sweet & look lovely. They smell half way between apples & roses. T.

---

1. Elinor (Tim) Agnes Ritchie and Pat were married on 5 January 1943. They lived in Egginton, near Derby, and in London. When Pat retired from the Air Force at the end of 1945 they lived at Buxhall in Suffolk, where he successfully farmed peaches.

42:    Friday [23 April 1943]                                      *Vic Sq*

My dear Leonard. I have printed the blue. What a relief. It went on in just
the same way, no result at all time after time, & the old man never came.
Today he did & *he* got no better results than me; we had an awful morning
with me alternately glowering & screaming at him & everything he said.
Then at the end we tried a glazed roller he had brought & it worked,
proving that the whole trouble had been the newly covered roller. It has
all aged me very much.

Thank you so much for taking that trouble about the house.[1] We both
agree with you it is too near Hailsham & too far from Lewes. I am very
relieved you say it is too far from Lewes too, as I am glad to know that
you don't feel Robinish about the whole plan which after all you well
might.

Fuzzells & I walked all round all the Parks this afternoon and really I
can't accept the Laburnum – lilac this year. *Every*thing is out even a rose
bush. I have never seen the leaves lovelier. No rough winds & no frosts
have made trees full of flawless leaves. There are two huge white
chestnuts trailing their skirts in the Serpentine & billowing about in a
most voluptuous way near the Kensington end.

Will it be all right for me to stay until Monday? I am writing for a
haggis which may not come (you can eat it it has no pig) Shall bring my
meat & cheese & absolutely insist on having bread & cheese for lunch
unflanked by lobsters or prawns or any delicatessen from Lewes. How
thankful I am about the blue.

        Love T.
I hope you won't go to London on purpose. I think I'd feel very strange
there without you & perhaps I'd get influenced by Sally & just sit
paralysed until you came back.


43:    [Monday] 3 May 1943                                  *Monk's House*

Dearest tiger, I simply cannot help writing to you to tell you what you
must know – the extraordinary pleasure it is to me when you are here. I
had thought, I don't know for how long now, it would be impossible to
feel for anyone as I do for you. You may not have a sweet nature or be
gentle or possess any of the qualities a woman ought to have – I believe,

---

1. LW was looking for a house close to Monk's for the Parsons to rent.

as always, everything you say – and then I say the answer must be a woman ought not to have the qualities which a woman ought to have, otherwise why should I get such pleasure from everything about you – exist to watch you, talk to you, listen to music with you? To you, being you, this may sound foolish, but I don't think it is because it's the only way of thanking you for the last five days.

Your L.


44:   [Monday] 3 May [1943]                     *Vic Sq.*

Dearest Leonard. I slept all the way to Victoria but not so deeply as to miss the smell of my lilac which successfully drowned that of the Southern. Rose gave me a tremendous welcome so that I hadn't the heart to mention the bath to her. From a slight indication in her figure I think I may confidently expect kittens.

One of the very nice things about Monk's House is how firmly it stays in my head when I have come away. I keep on seeing the garden through the flowers on the sill & the cyclamen with the marsh behind it. Each time I have been I come away filled up with flowers. Only I feel a little guilty that I take too much of your time. Each time I resolve that I shall efface myself & then I don't do it.

I must go to bed. We have had dinner out & poor Ian has had to go back to the office. I tell you (in order to forestall you) that all the Laburnum between Rodmell & Lewes is full out.

I wish I could have had another three sittings on the head of you, because I like it, and later on it will be too late & have set the pan.

Love T.


there's another love now.
See where he comes, like to a greedy sparrow
Who from the poor Martin his frail love nest snatches.[1]

Hope it will be all right for Judith's young man to eat the garlic. I remember in the Arabian Nights the bride cut the bridegroom's toes off because he had eaten it at dinner.


1. LW was probably right in suspecting these to be TR's lines.

45:   Tuesday [4 May 1943]

Now I must write another letter because I have come in from my liver puncture & found yours. It doesn't sound foolish but from the first I have been really surprised that you should enjoy my company and I have thought that it must be 'the novelty'. This has given me as Fairlie would have said a precarious feeling. I wish Proust had written me in ten volumes. I would insist on your reading every word and that would be the end of any novelty, and if it wasn't the end of me my foundations would be fixed on a rock. I am as you said a pessimist and so I would like you to know the worst as I have come to rely on you in a major way.

　　We aren't going to Derby. Ian can't get away. Poor Pat [Ritchie] will be bitterly disappointed. I couldn't get him the bird Flight book at Hatchards this morning & my chilblain is so sore I couldn't bare to go else where so I have for him a Hooker like yours & a book on gardening. The Dr says I was heading straight for pernicious anemia, but am better & my skin has begun to loose the 'lemon yellow' tint. Had you noticed this or its departure?

　　　　Love T.

46:   [Wednesday] 5 May 1943                                    *Monk's House*

Dearest, I'm quite sure it isn't novelty, though what it is exactly I don't know, unless – unless – unless – could it be possibly simply you? No sensible man will pretend to *explain* the antics of the heart – or brain for that matter, least of all his own, for which, in my case, he acquires, about the age of 25, an unfathomed contempt. But I shouldn't be afraid of 10 vols of Proust or 10 years of time on you. In fact I could, I believe, give at least ten reasons – good ones – for enjoying your company & will when I'm not, as at the moment, menaced every minute by the coming of guests & the Labour Party.

　　First Judith [Stephen] telegraphed to say she'd come Thursday. Then she telephoned to say she'd come today. Then she telephoned to say she could not be quite certain whether they would be able to get off in time to come today. Then Vanessa [Bell] telephoned to say Quentin [Bell][1] was in bed & would not be able to come today!

---

1. Vanessa Bell (1879–1961), painter, sister of Virginia Woolf, lived with Duncan Grant at Charleston farmhouse, near Firle. She and her husband Clive Bell (1881–1964) had lived there during World War I, then used the house for holidays until 1939, when she moved there permanently. Her younger son (with Clive Bell), Quentin Claudian Stephen Bell (1910–1996), had had TB and was exempted from military service. He was working at Tilton, Maynard

Does that mean Derby is a complete acquittal for you or only a reprieve?

I did notice the lemon-yellow tint, as you call it, when I thought you certainly did not look well & I noticed you losing (not loosing, Dearest tiger) it – in fact this week you had loost it altogether. It rather reminded me of the lemon yellow Tamil or Sinhalese women & children. I do hope you'll be all right now.

Did you compose the love-nest lines? I think you must because of the attitude towards the sparrow. They are very good, but I should think libellous of the sparrow.

It really is cruel that the weather should have changed the moment you left. At any rate, I shall see you again on Monday.

I met Mary Ann[1] talking volubly to two nuns outside your door yesterday.

> Your
> L.

47:   Wednesday [12 May 1943]                                    *Vic Sq.*

Dearest Leonard

I was going to write to you any way because though I ought in deserving to write to huts in the Persian desert & prison camps in Germany I like to write to Rodmell.

I got caught in a wild tearing tempest of wind & rain on Monday coming down from Hyde Pk Corner & was blown in & out all the way down. Rose whose inside is it seems upset had arranged a surprise for me in the upstairs lav (being baulked of the bath as the door was shut.) The upstairs lav has no black out so I had to do what was necessary by the aid of a torch. You can judge if our goodnights were tender. The tooth was pulled out yesterday, the dentist & I both behaved well. He was neat & determined (it was very firmly fixed to me) and I maintained an unbroken phlegm; from that I got home at six o'clock with my face just beginning to come to & the gum to bleed a fairish amount, to find the man who is washing the paint had left Rose shut in the sitting room with disastrous

---

Keynes's farm half a mile away, and potting. After the war he became Lecturer in Art Education at Newcastle (1952–62), Professor of Fine Arts at Leeds (1962–7), Slade Professor at Oxford (1964–5), Professor of the History and Theory of Art at Sussex (1967–75). He wrote many books including *The Impossible English* (1952, with Helmut and Alison Gernsheim), *The True Story of Cinderella* (1957), *Ruskin* (1963), *The Schools of Design* (1963) and *Virginia Woolf* (1972).
1. The Parsons' housekeeper.

results. So that when she joined me later in the kitchen & asked to be fed we had the following dialogue.

Rose.  Can you meet your Pussy's Eye
      Hear her wild & anguished cry
      And not feed her 'ere she die?
T.    Yes I can. And this is why.
      They're too loose that Pussy's bowels
      That is why I hear her howls
      Coldly, and her frenzied yowls
      Bring her neither Fish nor Fowls
        She must on arrowroot sustain
      Beating heart & eager brain
      Until she's learnt the way again
      To be a Pleasure not a Pain.

This morning my face is swollen & I have a very strange look. I think if I ran round & showed it to Mabel she might stop telling me I should be a 'little fatter in the face'. It gives me an aggrieved look in the eye & makes my mouth small & petulant. I also feel a little sick.

I would feel quite different about my Rodmell box if you'd come and choose it with me.

Fuzzels will be with me on Monday next if you could come & have tea with us. She'd be delighted & so would I.

I've written you a ¼ of the pink sheet – nearly.

Love
  T.

48:  [Thursday] 13 May 1943               *Monk's House*

Dearest of tigers, I was glad to get your pink letter this morning & hear how you were. I am sitting in the garden trying to work in a sweltering sun.

I wish I could come Monday, but I feel I must be firm with myself & return here. I really have an engagement at 4.30 in London, but decided to cut it & stay here to do some work which I ought to get through next week. I know I wont if I come up.

I have to come up Thursday to make a speech in the evening. Is there any chance of your printing that day? Perhaps I might look in at 11 & see whether you are? And take you to get a paint box?

Your adventures with Rose & your lyrical & sanitary conversation with her made me laugh until I cried. Are cats the only things which move you to write poetry or will you one day break into an Ode to Sally?

I should like to give you my 10 reasons, but mustn't, if only because I *must* get back to a dreary piece of work which I broke off at the thought of you. Hence the paper & pencil. I wish you were painting on the other side of the yew hedge.

I rather feared you would be caught by the deluge Monday night. It was quite fine when I left you at the Tube, but it was pouring before I got home.

I think there must be a battle going on over the Channel, the noise is so terrific.

I do hope your face has returned to normal, dearest tiger.

> Your
> L.


49:   [Thursday] 20 May 1943                    *37 M[ecklenburgh] S[quare]*

Dearest, I think this [handkerchief] must be yours. I have to be up in town on Wed. next & probably not on any other day. If there were a chance of your coming here to tea-egg supper I would stay up for Wed. night. But the fact that I enjoy your company makes me unwilling to be importunate. So that if it would tire you or bring the moment when you are bored by me nearer, just say so. When we were talking of Ascot, it came over me that one of the reasons why I like being with you is your extraordinary integrity.

I have made my speech, the all clear has sounded, & so I must go to bed. I hope your hare was good.

> Goodnight, dearest tiger,
> L.


50:   [Saturday] 22 May [1943]                              *25 Vic Sq*

Dearest Leonard. It won't be boredom that makes me not want to see you, but it may be because you remind me of lithography. After a wretched night last night in which I kept sitting up in bed and bawling as loudly as I could I went into the basement to print the grey stone. I went with my best morning strength because I'd started the afternoon before & the stone didn't seem friendly and so I wanted to give it every chance – and it is no use. I have now redrawn it rather widely; it can't help being a bit wild because it has all gone on so long now I have really lost the thread of the picture. So I shall try again to-morrow with the new stone & if it doesn't work right I shall adjust the press & put myself through it. The stone went wrong not because of bad printing but something I must have done to it when I made some corrections after the proof. I don't want to do lithography at all – I want to be a beautiful woman & cherish my finger nails while other people cherish me. If I haven't gone through the Press I would like to come on Wednesday night. Thank you for this £1, & thank you for the handkerchief.

      Love T.

How beautifully my cheque matches this paper.


51:   [Monday] 24 May 1943             *Monk's House*

How like my dearest & most perverse of tigers. I pay a tribute to your integrity & you reply by return that your ideal is to be cherished as a beautiful woman with pink nails – knowing well that pink nails are the one thing which would shake my faith in your integrity. Knowing too quite well that you are a beautiful woman & cherished as such. But I wish you didn't have bad nights & such lithographic miseries – I'm beginning to feel guilty of the latter. I still hope & look forward to seeing you Wed. with or without pink nails – which at any rate should prove to you my love & loyalty.

   Thanks for the pink cheque

       Your

        L.


52:   [Thursday] 27 May 1943         *Monk's House*

Dearest, I hung the picture over the mantlepiece this morning. It is good of you to lend it to me. I like it immensely. It is not dull or tedious. But it is austere, which seems to me right & you in your art, for the austerity of beauty is in your painting what I mean by the integrity in your living.

I had my talk with John [Lehmann].[1] He began about everything but the matter which we both were thinking of – which is the eastern method of manoeuvre & bad tactics, in my opinion. Tension until I suggested that we should settle our difference. Considerable tension but I did *not* lose my temper. We parted amicably but with toes still dug in.

When I got back here tonight, I did wish you were with me to see the pond covered with the blood red & the cream waterlilies & bright blue sky reflected in it.

The devil is I so often want to be with you. I shant see you now really for 3 weeks, I suppose, which seems a terrible long time. I told you it was a week of bad things raining on me. You know, its really rather awful to be as fond of anyone as I have become of you the last six months, dearest tiger. I suppose it's all right if you're 3 or 6 or 36 (though I doubt it), but it's disgraceful at 63. The happiest people must be those whose affections are nil or tepid (I wish at the moment Peat's were – he wont leave me in peace), they dont get the supreme pleasure of the oasis but then they also miss the pain and emptiness of the desert & the desert is unfortunately so much larger as a rule than the oasis. You would never guess, I believe, that every time you say, as you do, 'Well, good-bye, Leonard' & look at me with the sternness & at the same time kindness which I like so much, before disappearing into the Russell Square tube, as I turn away I think of Thucydides, the greatest and most astringent of all historians. The reason is that no one for the last 2,500 years has succeeded in giving a more perfect description of that desert feeling which comes over me in Bernard Street than Thucydides. (He himself says it was Pericles who said it & he may be right. I daresay Pericles heard it from Aspasia.) 'It is as though the spring had died out of the year.'[2]

I hope you'll forgive me for writing another volume like this. It's

1. In 1943 there were two major causes of bad feeling between John Lehmann and LW at the Hogarth Press. The first was over LW's having to pay a much larger sum than Lehmann (a full partner only from 1938) when the Inland Revenue claimed back taxes for end-of-year stock-in-hand which LW had not made provision for in his meticulous but unconventional accounting. The second was a misunderstanding about Virginia Woolf's foreign rights. TR would soon disagree with Lehmann about the printing of her lithographs for Barbara Baker's *The Three Rings* (1944). Along with the Parsons' increasingly close friendship with LW, this disagreement may well have contributed to LW's decision, when in January 1946 he was given the chance, to dissolve his partnership with Lehmann and arrange with IMP to have Chatto & Windus absorb the Hogarth Press (see letters 99 and 101).
2. Brilliant Aspasia so charmed Pericles that he became her pupil, then lover and husband. Her influence subjected him to ridicule and censure, but Socrates was proud to be among her scholars and Plato said that her instructions helped form the greatest orators of the age. Thucydides began to write his famous history after his banishment from Athens in the eighth year of the Peloponnesian War. A classical scholar, LW had long been interested in Aspasia; there is a short manuscript about her among his papers in the University of Sussex Library.

really your fault. I begin to write you a short letter to thank you for the picture & you make me think aloud on paper. At any rate I'm glad to think you'll see the border. My recollection is that Edinburgh is a nice place. But if you can snatch even one day for the Cheviots you should. You'll see a new thing in light & sky. And I know the hills are made for you. They are cousins to our downs, but quite different & yet you cant mistake the relationship. Have you ever been to Abbotsford? If you haven't you ought not to miss that, just to see what the human mind is capable of in the way of houses if it really sets its mind to it.

Goodnight my dearest tiger, & forgive me my trespasses.

Your

L.

53:   [Friday] 28 May [1943]                                              *25 Vic Sq.*

Leonard dear would you like me to come this next week end – Friday 4th. It seems we are to go to Derby on the night of the 14th so that I wouldn't be back in London until about the 26th or so. So many dates makes me feel trapped, but they are all accurate as I have my diary open in front of me. Your roses are so sweet they make all the sitting room scented.

I have no other sensational news for you. Ian read me a few of Barker's[1] poems last night. I liked two & not any others at all.

love from T.

54:   [Saturday] 29 May 1943                                              *Monk's House*

O my dearest tiger, what an angel you are. This morning's letter from you is like an answer to the whinings which I posted to you yesterday. Dont be so annoyed by the whinings as to say that after all you wont come next week. I shall be up Monday & Tuesday, return here Tuesday night, and come up for the day Thursday. So that I *would* like you to come Friday, and if you found that you could and would come Thursday afternoon, I should like even that.

There seems after all to be something in the legend of Isis and Osiris.[2]

Love from your

L.

1. George Barker (1913–1991). *Sacred and Secular Elegies* had just been published.
2. Isis and Osiris, the moon and the sun (symbolised by the cow and the ox) in Egyptian

55:    Sunday 30 May [1943]                               *Vic Square*

Dearest Leonard. You do distress me. I like to be an oasis, but not to create desarts [sic] and if there is more desart than oasis your only reasonable act is to eliminate me. And you are so reasonable & I don't want to be eliminated so what are we to do? Couldn't you arrange not to have a desart, you who are so very much 'captain of your soul'? I have you for an oasis too & now that I begin to be sure you are not a mirage I am very comfortable and hoped you were the same.

   As for 36 & 63 what has that to do with feeling? You cannot really believe what you say about it being best to be tepid. You *know* that it must be hateful to be so.

   I want you to love me you see – but not as an epidemic disease all covered in spots & then quite cured – and certainly not if it gives you this desart feeling. What it really comes to Leonard dear is that I want your affection, it does make me happy but only if it makes you so too. Or my conscience & your reason must say *don't* love.
                     T.


56:    [Monday] 31 May 1943                    *37 Mecklenburgh Square*

Dearest, I was terrified to read your letter, but am relieved, because you are, as always, absolutely (or 90%) right. I ought not to have written that letter; it was due to the despicable desire of the human soul – male – when alone at midnight with pen & paper in its hands to posture in self pity & whine. At any rate I think you know that the last thing I would want to do is to worry or distress you. And when you tell me to use my reason, I know quite well – at 3 p.m. – that 3 hours with you on Monday evening outweigh enormously 3 weeks without you. You know how I treat Sally & the tone of voice in which I say: 'Shut up & go to your basket,' if she starts whining & whimpering with love – well, if you ever hear me begin whining again or see the spaniel look in my eyes, say 'Shut up & go to your basket' or write it on a postcard & I promise to obey.

   Remember however that though one may be captain of one's soul, no

---

mythology, taught the cultivation of the land. They governed with reason and benevolence and when Osiris was murdered by his brother, Typhon, Isis put the mangled pieces of his body into separate wax statues, which she gave to the priests, who continued to honour Osiris. LW's implication is that he will be restored by TR's return to the land.

one, as the poets have been saying for 3,000 years, is captain of his heart.
So I shall continue to love T.
Your

L.

57:    [Wednesday] 2 June [1943]                                      *Vic Sq*

Dearest Leonard. Thank you for your letter. Well then that's all right.
But you do know that it isn't your telling me about the desart but your
being in it that I mind. As for Sally you know I have always regarded that
relationship with some misprision (today I can't even spell up to usual
standard. We have had no sleep in this house for three nights and last
night was the worst, it was like the Castle of Otranto, knocks at the door
sudden ringing of bells & so on. It all began with a car left again waking
us at 1.30. I nearly cried thinking how it would spoil work to-day. Then
we rang up the police again & Ian waited up for him & I went back to bed
but not to sleep. Half an hour later there was an ominous knock at the
door. I thought it was the police & that Ian had gone to sleep on the sofa
so dashed down stairs in a very thin nightgown, opened the door to find
Ian & a policeman on the steps the door having shut behind them when
they were looking at the car. The bell which then rang violently all
through the house was the alarm clock which had I think got nervous, so
I fled upstairs again & buried it in bed because of Irene who I thought
might still be sleeping, and strange enough she was. Can a sentence stay
so long in a bracket & shall I come out of it now?) So you can see you can
hardly expect me to treat you like her & luckily you don't remind me of
her at all. Mabel [Parsons] doesn't approve of you. She goes silent when I
say I'm going to Rodmell for the week end.
                love
            T.
I wish you'd seen your flowers after I arranged them. The pinks are
frothing in a big white tureen & the roses extremely elegant in the small
urn.

58:    [Monday] 7 June 1943                                    *Monk's House*

Dearest, I feel I may have been importunate in asking you to come on
Wednesday. So if you don't feel like it or you're tired I trust you to ring

me up & say so. You have given me three completely happy days & I shall, I promise you, not enter the Desart by thinking of them & you. (That is not a very good sentence; what I mean is that the thought of them & you will keep me out of the Desart). For I continue to love T. & literally every time I see her, more.

      Your
      L.

59:   [Thursday] 10 June 1943          *37 Mecklenburgh Square*

Dearest tiger, I had just signed this cheque when the telephone rang & it was you. It was angelic of you to ring up, because I went to bed last night & woke this morning miserable at the thought of having depressed you & the last thing I wanted to do last night. And now your voice has made the whole day – everything – quite different for me.

Dont rush about too much in this oppressive hot house atmosphere. You looked so beautiful in your earrings[1] yesterday, but too tired.

Goodbye, dearest, & tell me, when you have a moment, of all the queer things which will certainly happen to you in Derby, Scotland, trains, inter & etc.

      Love from your L.

I meant to say last night that I should like to buy the picture here if you will sell it. I know now that I like it immensely. If you will sell it, let me know the price.

60:   [Friday] 11 June [1943]          *25 Victoria Square*

Dearest Leonard. Thank you for the cheque. It is nice to think of my box waiting snugly at Monk's House. I have just fallen up stairs & raised a great weal on my arm. I suppose it is because my slippers are always too big & I always run that I fall about so. I have also bruised both my hip bones with my stones yesterday. I knock them with the stones when I carry them from the bench to the press. I have hips rather like those cows you see sitting in meadows with theirs jutting out like clothes horses. This letter is now reminding me of my ex German Marie[2] who used to regale

1. LW had bought her ear-rings for her 41st birthday, 15 June.
2. An earlier housekeeper who returned to Germany just before the war.

my friends of either sex with detailed descriptions of just how her figure differed from mine. '*I* have de hingy bosom, de madam has *not* de hingy bosom but *I* have not the sticky out behind.'

It is terrible to have to leave two lithographs nearly mixed & ready to be cooked. My headache has at last gone. For two days it felt as if the works in my head had come out of their tone box & were lying unprotected on top.

If you have to tell me something of vital importance I shall be at The Cottage Egginton near Derby until Thursday morning & the Glen Balerno Midlothian is the best address after. I think of the water lilies & the roses & our descent on Church Farm a great deal.[1]

    love T.

I haven't had time to use a dictionary on this letter so I used pink paper to make up.


61:   [Wednesday] 16 June [1943]        *The Cottage, Egginton*

Dearest Leonard. I forgot my dressing gown & my hot water bottle & cut my thumb just before leaving to keep the whole thing traditional.

The country here is really very paintable. Pat was right though I didn't believe him when he said so. Fat slices of English meadows with the green river Dove full to its banks twisting through them. Heaps of white elder flowers & fields leading away to fields with occasional elms & a slightly bumped irregular horizon line. And though the weather is beastly, in one way these huge dramatic skies with great purple grey clouds reflecting the sun light down on to the meadows so that they are bright gold, much lighter than the sky, suits this landscape very well. This is a pretty garden with some good things in it. There are a whole lot of Penstemon not out yet which Pat says are reported to be plain red. I have told him to get seed or cuttings for you if they are. I find I am thinking of that fig tree garden at Monk's House in a slightly different way from the rest.[2]

I read your Fire Brigade book[3] before leaving. It is an accurate

1. Tim Ritchie was in Egginton, Aunt Fuzzells in Balerno. TR had taken LW to see Church Farm, which the Parsons rented at Herstmonceux.
2. Penstemon is a native North American rockery plant. TR and LW were both first-rate botanists; they gardened energetically at Monk's House, restructuring the beds and searching for new plants and seeds. The fig-tree garden was to be TR's; in mid-September LW offered to give her half of the entire garden (see letter 98).
3. Probably Henry Green's stories about his fellow firemen who were bored and getting on one another's nerves published in *New Writing and Daylight* (Summer 1943) by John Lehmann.

representation of the sordid atmosphere – The people don't come alive to me. And I doubt if I hadn't had my nine months in the same sort of place if I'd have found it very interesting. As it was he recalled it very strongly to me – he left out the incessant thieving but perhaps that was for libel. The sordid self seekingness of it all was very true. And when I tell you that one of our couples spent the initial stages of their courtship with her sitting on the edge of the bath while he squeezed her spots you will believe that not much time was wasted in fine perypheral [sic] emotions.

I have been cold ever since I left London and I still have a headache. I can't think why because I don't usually. I like my niece[1] but except that I think she may be going to have enormous hands like me, I see no likeness to any of us. I shall be glad to go tomorrow morning. I am becoming very sunk.

Love from T.


62:   [Friday] 18 June 1943                                *Monk's House*

Dearest, I have nothing of vital importance to tell you, but even so, I'm going to write to you. It was pleasant to see your handwriting this morning. But I wish you hadn't this headache. You ought to take life easier – you seem always to be on the run & one can't do that if like you one lives intensely inside oneself. No one can live intensely inside & outside perpetually & I thought you looked terribly tired the last week or two. You ought to sit still for two weeks meditating with a paint box.

I have one thing to tell you. I went today to Brighton to see Miss Higginbotham of Ward's. On the whole encouraging. She was very interested. She confirmed prices, i.e. she thought 3 guineas for a hand printed & 10/6 for machine printed copy about right – she volunteered these prices when I asked her what she thought one could ask. She thought she could sell 10/6 copies, but said that one could never be certain, it all depends on whether a thing 'goes'. In the ordinary way she doubted whether she could sell a 3 guinea copy, but she might on a special occasion, e.g. if she had an exhibition of say Printing in War Time & you let her have some hand printed copies to show.

I am glad you think of the fig garden as different from the rest. The geranium from Church Farm has settled down there & opened a flower. Isn't it right that the first plant to go into your garden should come from Church Farm?

1. Pat and Tim Ritchie's first child, Athene.

Here is a fact which gave me peculiar pleasure – & I think it will you too. The other night I was reading the life of a 17th Century naturalist, John Ray. He published a Catalogus Plantarum Angliae. He gives the names of the various plants & the places where they were found. I noticed that he included Helianthemum polifolium [rock rose] as found on 'Brean Downs in Somersetshire near the Severn Sea'. I looked it up, rather idly, in Hooker who says that 'in Britain only on Brean Downs in Somersetshire & Babbacombe near Torquay in Devonshire'. Dont you like to think of Helianthemum polifolium growing for 300 years on Brean Downs & obstinately refusing to grow anywhere else?

I had a strenuous time this week at the Labour Party Conference & the New Statesman – incessant talk, lunch, dinner, dinner, lunch talk. I was glad to get back. Last week when I got back, I found a first class domestic row going on. I had told Louie[1] she could have any gooseberries if she wanted to make jam for herself & she could pick them herself. She told me that Percy had been infuriated & had abused her violently. Then Percy came & 'gave notice'. I told him that I never meddle in other people's quarrels &, as he knew, always accept notice when it is given to me by anyone, as my experience is that there are better herrings in the sea than have ever come out of it my way. This seemed to depress him, so I said I hoped he would come & see the place sometimes after he has left – which seemed to depress him still more. This week he seems entirely to have forgotten it & talks about what he is going to do in the garden in the autumn.

This is an inordinately long, dull letter. I must go & write about Mrs Sidney Webb. Maynard Keynes[2] asked me some time ago to write something about her for the Economic Journal & I understood he would

1. Louie West Everest (1912–1977) was cook/housekeeper at Monk's House from 1934 to LW's death in 1969. She lived in one of the two Park Cottages nearby, purchased by the Woolfs in 1929 to make it possible for them to live alone at Monk's. Her sister-in-law Anneliese (the German-born wife of brother Harry) became TR's housekeeper after the war. When Bert Everest died in the early sixties, Louie married Conrad Mayer. Both Louie and especially Anneliese often sat to TR for portraits. Percy Bartholomew lived in the other Park cottage.

2. Beatrice (1858–1943) and Sidney (1859–1947) Webb founded the Fabian Research Bureau and the *New Statesman*. She died on 30 April and LW had written to Sidney Webb of his affection and admiration for her. In his obituary (the *Economic Journal*, June–September issue) he wrote that they 'seemed for the purposes of thinking and writing, and perhaps living, to have become a composite personality'. John Maynard Keynes (1883–1946), economist, one of the most extraordinary and influential Englishmen of his time. He was one of LW's oldest friends and, as Chairman of *The Nation and Athanaeum*, his boss. He went to Cambridge the year after LW who, with Lytton Strachey, recruited him for the Apostles. After marrying ballerina Lydia Lopokova (1891–1981), he purchased Tilton, neighbouring Vanessa Bell. He was Fellow and Bursar of King's College, Cambridge, founder and Chairman of the Cambridge Arts Theatre, a Director of the Bank of England and Trustee of The National Gallery.

not want it until the middle of July. When I got back here, I found a letter from him saying he wants it by next week. What a curse Editors are! I spent last night from 6 to nearly 1 reading again her autobiography. Have you read it? It is a very remarkable, fascinating book. But I dont know what I am to say about her.

I'm afraid you must be having horrible weather, if it's anything like what we have – I have been soaked to the skin three times in the last week bicycling to or from Lewes.

I cant leave off you see – so good bye, my dearest tiger – how glad I shall be to see you again

      Your

       L.

Dont you think the enclosed [picture] gives one a pleasant feeling of a winter evening before railways, telegrammes, cars, wireless?


63:    Thursday [24 June 1943]          *The Glen [Balerno]*

Dearest Leonard. I believe there is a letter from you pursuing me around Scotland. It should arrive here again tomorrow. I am in bed with a violent inside & fairly high temperature. It is going down (well both are) I don't know how much because Ritchies don't have thermometers. The Dr took it this morning & it was nearly 103 & then I'm sure it went up some more. It sounds quite important doesn't it. But now I am much better, have combed my hair & can write this. He says if I lie still for 36 hours & eat nothing I can most likely come South on Saturday night. I do hope that will be so. If I do come I will be going to lithography on Monday & Wednesday. If you were in town either day [I] would come to a Mecklenburgh Sq dinner (being a regular listener you will have heard the special B.B.C. announcement that their meals must no longer be called by the misleading name of egg teas.) If you read Irene's letter on the back you will hear all about Rose.[1] I hope you will be able to read this. I hardly can myself. It was lovely at Clovenford. I will tell you about [it] next week.

          love from T.


1. The cat had disappeared the previous Saturday; Irene Hawkins had phoned the police and rung every bell in Victoria Square, then found her in the garden. The concern was to keep her home until her kittens were born – five on Sunday.

64:    Friday [25 June 1943]                                    *Balerno*

Dearest Leonard

I don't know if my other letter will reach you before this. I am not to be allowed to travel to-morrow night, though my temperature is down this morning. So I will have to come by day I hope on Monday. How tiresome it is. I feel much better but pretty limp. I think it must be a bug as the Dr says a lot of people have had the same. Mine seems to have been worse because of walking about with a temperature. Now I lie like a log so perhaps it will do me good in the end.

I had your letter this morning. Yes I like the Helianthemum growing only in its own place. The wild flowers were beautiful at Clovenford masses of meadow cranesbill you know the big soft blue one it was in the valleys and yellow cistus[1] on the hillsides, and on one high top we had a delightful surprise, all the grass was thickly sprinkled with blue purple & yellow pansies on slender stems so that they were nodding & blowing in the wind. In the valleys the wild roses were at their height, & such variety of colour. The brightest peppermint pink down to pure white. In the cottage gardens round about there were lovely old roses. The nearly black flat one with curled back petals called either 'Belle des Jardins' or 'Belle de Province' and lots of heavy sweet pink ones.

I like the winter evening. No days & moments quickly flying there.

I will ring up when I do get home. This is a waste of time. But I am lucky to be doing it here in a nice sunny room & a black bird singing outside and darling Fuzzels running in & out.

The Dr who is quite bearable & has no soothing manner is quite appalled that I call myself Miss Ritchie – 'It's against the law' he shouted at me as he left this morning.

　　　　love from
　　　　　T


65:    [Sunday] 27 June 1943                          *Monk's House, Rodmell*

My dearest tiger, Ian has just rung up to tell me of your misfortunes. I am so sorry for you, dearest; you seem to be plagued by one thing after another. You really must be sensible and vegetate until you are

1. Clovenford is near Galashiels, in Walter Scott country. The cranesbill was probably Geranium *pratense grandiflorum alpinum*, which has purple-blue flowers. The rock (or sun) rose Cistus is a Mediterranean native and not as hardy as Helianthemum, a native of Britain.

completely well. I am sure you ought to do absolutely nothing but eat, sleep, and paint for at least a fortnight.

I had not had a letter from you which I gathered from Ian you had written, but I expect it takes days for it to reach here from Scotland. My week has passed in writing about Mrs Webb, at the grindstone of the New Statesman, writing letters to the Collector of Taxes, and weeding that abominable rose bed. Tomorrow I go to London and have to be there until Thursday, so perhaps I may get a momentary glimpse of you if you are back by then. I suspect, however, that really you ought to go on doing your vegetating in Balerno – which shows you how unselfish I am, for I long to see you again. At any rate, I do hope that I shall hear that you are better.

Love from your<br>L.

66:   Tuesday [29 June 1943]                    *The Glen, Balerno*

Dearest Leonard

It was nice to have your letter this morning. I didn't expect it as the posts here are fearful owing to a new system. There is now no chance of getting south before Saturday. I had hoped for Wednesday but have still hardly started to eat, I bang against my own bones in bed. I am really better this morning & though not dressed am lying on a rug on Fuzzels lawn half in the shade of a Wych elm with the burn rushing below & a wren shouting in my ear. The weather is superb & has been for four days, as if Scotland had suddenly decided to prove beyond doubt that of all climes Scotland's was the best. Not a cloud in the sky no wind just little breezes that dusk & quiver. I ought not to repine, but I long to be back.

When I was iller I had a curious demonstration of visual imagination which I will tell you about when I see you.

I would like to see what you have written about Mrs Webb.

There is to be a children's party here this afternoon, about 50, another to-morrow described as 'the big lot'. I haven't asked how many that means. There was one on Saturday of 40; last night Fuzzels had a jumble sale (in Edinburgh) & made £18 and when I arrived she had one blind & one lame woman staying, each had been here about a month. She enjoys it all so much & is so efficient it is a marvel to see her. The parties are the best kind, you can apparently do just as you like. Take all your clothes off & bathe in the [Bavelaw] burn, make daisy chains, or as one small sober boy did turn the passage into a tram car & spend an hour & a half opening & shutting the garden door. It took all Fuzzels benign influence not to let this last drive me (who was in a room opening off the tram car) into a state of lunacy. But you would marvel – I am almost entirely dove when with Fuzzels.

I feel so much better to-day I begin to be confident for Saturday. I would like you sometime to come here – it really is remarkable.[1]

Love from T.

67:    Wednesday [14 July 1943]

Did we say I was calmer Leonard? You could light a bonfire from the me on the other side of the road. As soon as I got home everything went hopeless. I had arranged for Mary Ann to wait until I got back to receive Mabel [Parsons] who was to call on her way from a Bazaar with a sack of potatoes & some smoked salmon. When I got in M. A. was there & Mabel hadn't been. Then the Dr came to puncture my behind, then Mabel rang up to say she had knocked & knocked & not got in. It seems Mary Ann had nipped out to get buns for the dressmaker who was sewing upstairs & must have buns like a bear, and Mabel came at that moment. Then Ian came expecting to have lunch at home (which he never does) but he thought there'd be smoked salmon & he'd have a sandwich. Then Irene came with her sandwich in her pocket to eat it with me on the mat in a quiet girls way as we used to. The Dr couldn't break into the glass tube of stuff to put it in me. I gave him knives scissors & my lithography file. After all of them had gone I had to go out to get something & couldn't get home because all the roads were lined by sailors with bayonets because of General Sikorski.[2] When I got in I had to throw the buns to the dressmaker & make more tea for Eddy who is in bed & then Mabel came

1. Built in Balerno in 1805 as a flax mill, The Glen later housed a grain mill, then burned inside in 1910. Fuzzells bought it in 1921, rebuilt the interior, and lived in its lower section until 1956, making use of a primitive electrical system run from a wheel in the mill-stream, supplemented by candles and oil lamps. The upper floor was used by her pupils and former girls from Tynecastle School, Edinburgh, as a dormitory. They came for weekends and holidays to walk in the hills, garden, keep bees and discuss Club projects. These included planting trees, raising money for the Tynecastle Child Garden and the nursery school founded by Fuzzells in 1929, and holding children's parties. Their Fellowship Group met once a month in the 'Quiet Room', where the window was permanently open so birds could fly in. TR said that if Fuzzells had not taken so 'close a personal view, living with a little company of disciples, instead of working in a larger way' she would had been 'a notable reformer in education' (Diary, 2.1.51).
2. Head of the Polish government in exile in London during the war.

with the smoked salmon & I pressed her most warmly to have tea & she did & I was perfectly sweet & mad as a hatter & now I have won through & go to the Central half an hour late. I didn't make myself late writing this because I had to wait for the vegetables to cook because it has come round to another meal. This paper is the right colour [pink].

Love T.

68:     [Thursday] 15 July 1943                                    *Monk's House*

Yes, dearest, we spoke before our time in St James's Square. I felt the heat through the envelope & was almost afraid to open it as I thought some appalling catastrophe had befallen you. When you describe two or three hours of your life, I always think of one of those spiral nebulae in which fiery particles whirl spirally upwards. I wish you were calmer & yet of course I don't really wish you anything but what you are, for your fiery spirals are what make you the most lovable person I know & a walk with you from Victoria to St James's Square an enchanting adventure.

What a different life we had. I spent yesterday afternoon from 2 to 6 in Committee Rooms in the House of Commons, first soberly discussing nutrition in Africa & then attending a meeting to discuss a memorial to Beatrice Webb. As I had ¾ of an hour before my train I thought I would walk past Victoria Square on the chance of seeing you dashing off to lithography. Then in Birdcage Walk I decided that it was much too late & that you would have started ages ago. So I wandered off conducting an imaginary conversation with you. But I daresay you really hadn't started.

The subject index which I looked at on the desk was the wrong one. There are quite a number of books on rats. I also forgot to show you the card catalogue. We shall have to go again.[1]

I have not heard from Judith [Stephen] yet.

Love from Your L.

69:     Sunday 18 July 1943                                       *Monk's House*

Dearest tiger, I failed to get hold of Judith last night or any one connected

---

1. TR had searched the London Library for photographs of the rats and other animals and plants she was drawing for *Bells Across the Sands* (1944), a 26-page book of rhymes (mostly by TR) and pictures printed for Chatto & Windus at the Chiswick Press. LW often helped her in the Library, at Kew Gardens and the zoo.

with her and I'm afraid I shall hear nothing from her now until Tuesday.

I enjoyed my dinner last night. I had not seen some of the younger members before, but the pleasant thing is that owing to the nature of the society one is on terms of complete intimacy at once. They were of course all in the army or air force, very nice and extremely intelligent. I went back with some of them to a flat in Bentinck St[1] and sat there until nearly 2 talking. I thought of you several times and what you said about the women in your office and I'll tell you why when I see you. But I also thought of you as we came into the flat because with immense dignity two blue Persian cats advanced to meet us. I dont want to hurt Rose's feelings, but they were even more dazzlingly beautiful than she.

How pleasant it was to sit and talk to you for that hour and to watch you shell peas

   Ever Your
    L.

70: Monday 19 July 1943        *Monk's House*

Dearest, I have received this from the Lewes agent this morning & send it on because you may think of looking at it tomorrow being Tuesday. It is just the right distance from Lewes – I imagine it is on the green at Ringmer. I don't very much like Ringmer itself but there is good country just south of it behind Caburn.

Here is Mrs Nolan's terrifying last. Who is Tom Doyle?[2]

   Love from your
    L.

1. LW's diary shows that he went to the flat of Richard Llewelyn Davies (1912–1981) after dinner on 17 July 1943. Davies and Virginia Woolf's niece Ann Stephen (b. 1916) were getting a divorce. They had married in 1938.
2. Nancy Nolan was a Dublin (Drumcondra) woman who first wrote to LW on 9 February 1943 after reading a novel of Virginia Woolf's. Her letters, which she persisted in sending until LW's death, were exceedingly long and about her life and friends, including Tom Doyle. As a publisher who felt it polite to reply, LW was susceptible to such correspondences, which sometimes got out of hand. There are about 600 letters from Nolan in the Archive, and only slightly fewer from an American woman, Evangeline Levine. According to Frederic Spotts in *Letters of Leonard Woolf*, Levine once flew from California to London carrying on her lap a plant which she insisted LW must have. She took a taxi to Monk's House, put the plant on the doorstep without realising LW was in the garden, and returned to America.

71:   Saturday 24 July 1943                                    *Monk's House*

Dearest, I actually rang you up last night because I thought you would be amused to hear further developments with regard to 22 V.S. I had practically given up thoughts of it when I saw you disappear up Tottenham Court Road. From there I went to the New Statesman Board of Directors Meeting. After the meeting Kingsley Martin[1] took me off for a cup of tea and to persuade me to write an article for next week in part dealing with a pamphlet which I had been reading in the train. We were looking at the pamphlet on one page of which I had made calculations as to what the rent of 22 V.S. worked out at. He asked me what they were and I told him. He got very excited as he wants a flat and cannot find one. I gave him the particulars. Late last night he rang me up again still more excited. Dorothy Woodman, with whom he lives, had dashed off at once to see the house and fell in love with it. Would not I take the house and let the bottom flat to them? Meanwhile I had been sent the particulars by the agent and of course they were far less favourable than what they said over the telephone. The rent works out at about £400 a year. That rather dashed Kingsley, but he is going to see the house on Monday morning. So there you are.

I feel that he may urge me vehemently to take it and as my mind is rather torn asunder I dont know what will happen. The truth of course is that one of the very strong pulls is the thought of being so near you, dearest tiger. But I am sensible enough to see that I love you too much to make it wise to come and live next door to you. I might so easily make myself just a nuisance to you, which I am more likely to be saved from doing with half of London between you and me. So that the question of whether the rooms are good enough and the rent too high is complicated by the fact that love has its reasons of which the Reason knows nothing. And one of those reasons is your character which is the nicest I have ever come across.

I am lunching on Monday with Kingsley to hear developments and I anticipate a furious argument, because it is of course a fascinating house. I shall have to display my Reason but not my reasons.

1. Basil Kingsley Martin (1897–1969), editor of the *New Statesman* from the time it amalgamated with the *Nation* in 1931 until 1960, when he became editorial consultant. He was an outstanding journalist and spokesman for the left and although he and LW had furious disagreements they remained close colleagues and friends. Dorothy Woodman, his companion for more than 30 years, was a political analyst and the author of many books and pamphlets on politics and social history. LW looked at several houses in Victoria Square before he bought number 24, next to the Parsons'.

In an hour or two Leslie, Judith and Nigel[1] descend upon me. It is nasty weather which consoles me for the fact that you are not here.

        Ever your
        L.


72:    Monday morning [26 July 1943]

My dearest Leonard. This is a practicle [sic] letter; apart from that aspect of it I will only say that I would like you for a neighbour if you would like it. I know I would. Ian says that rent is much too high. He says when we were all given a chance of a new lease about two years before the war the Estate asked him for a premium of £800 & a rent of £125 for an 18 year lease. He got them instead to take a rent of £150 P.A. & he agreed to spend £300 on the house. He says he is sure that the woman who owns the lease would not have paid a higher premium than £1,200 and that as you know the ground rent is £150 She is asking far too much. All these figures are correct as I wrote them on a piece of paper when Ian told me. I am going to get some lithographic inks in your neighbourhood also a piece of glass, so I shall leave this at Mecklenburgh. The other thing is would you like sharing with people you know? Perhaps living next door you would find out I hadn't got such a very nice character, but you would have to go on liking me in spite of it because it would be awful to live next door to someone you didn't like. I shall bring my cheese & meat with me, also I mean to bake a cake but this may be a failure. It is a thing I have hardly ever done.

        love T.

1. Judith Stephen had been engaged to Leslie Humphrey for a short period before marrying Nigel Henderson.

# *Letters 73-194 (August 1943-15 July 1944)*

By August 1943 Leonard's letters were openly amorous. While Trekkie warned him to work 'back to a safe . . . [intellectual] position', she helped him find a house in Victoria Square. When illness and professional rejection reduced her artistic confidence, Leonard encouraged her to exhibit her work and played her 'tough' with the galleries; when the drudgery of war depressed her, he cheered her up with flowers from the country and brought fruit and vegetables to supplement her food rations. Against the dangers of London he offered her three-quarters of Monk's House and half his garden. When she refused he scoured East Sussex to find a suitable cottage for her and Ian. In May 1944 at the end of a mini-Blitz he wrote: 'To know you has been the best thing in life.'

73:   [Tuesday] 3 August 1943                           *37 Mecklenburgh Square*

Dearest, I rang you up before I left this morning but got no answer. I wanted to ask you:
- A)   Whether you got back all right & without too abominable a journey;
- B)   Whether a black flag was flying from 25 Victoria Sq. and to tell you
  - 1)   How much I love you;
  - 2)   How much I miss you;
  - 3)   No flag flies or ever will from Monk's House.

You make even the little things of life – eating a mutton pie under a fig tree – as beautiful, exciting, & amusing as you are yourself. I think I've said that before but I shall say it again. I wish you could have come up with me this morning – no crowd at all.

 I love you, dearest tiger

       L.

**74:**   Tuesday Morning, 3 August [1943]                    *25 Vic Sq*

My dearest Leonard. As you always know just what is in every letter before you open it I might have sent you the envelope only & left you to fill in the letter for yourself, but as I am not quite sure you would have got it word perfect I have decided to write it after all. The train was full so I went first & had only one other in the carriage so that my Zinnias & I travelled in great comfort – they are burning fiercely this morning. There seems to have been no Rose crisis & the kittens look well but this morning Rose looks at me with a sultry look & says, Where's Wave? Ian is to have to-day & to-morrow off and so I shall be in my familiar train again at 12.45 hastening back to Lewis [sic]. If we can get in we mean to spend the night there & come back on Wed night or early on Thursday morning, it seems very strange.

Of all the times we have had at Monk's House this last was the best of all. Leonard dear it is always you who say kind things to me but you must know how greatly I value you & how certainly I would come to Polegate, or even Bexhill? Though I felt Friday morning when I was painting in the corn field that I seemed to bring you disasters I was glad each time that if you were to have them I should be there.

I shall see you soon shan't I?

love T.

I shall not tear up my poem as I like it.

Do you think that its kind
Or likely to bind
Me closer to you my dear

When you say that the smile
Which I hoped would beguile
Is really a sinister lear [sic]?

**75:**   [Wednesday] 4 August 1943                    *Monk's House*

Dearest, I found your letter here this morning. I did not know what was inside it before I opened it. You know very well that you are excepted from all general statements made by me or which in future will be made by me. I love to get a letter from you & particularly this one.

Elspeth Huxley was a short, large bosomed female & we sat one on each side of a table with a microphone hanging between us. She said I was all wrong & out of date. I had to spend an hour with her & Miss Benzie. Miss Benzie's bracelet fell off twice.[1]

I am editing the New Statesman next week. I shall if I can come several times to V.S. & look to see what flags are flying. Wouldn't you dine on Wednesday then at Meck. Sq. or the Acropolis or somewhere? I don't know yet whether I shall come up Tuesday or Monday. Kingsley insists upon coming here for the night on Friday, & I doubt whether he will really go on Saturday.

It is strange to think of you so near at Lewes. I might have met you in the High Street this morning when I went to buy a bit of fish.

> love from your
> L.

Even if I did know what was inside your letters, I could not know the spelling. So you must go on writing me more & more.


76:   [Thursday] 5 August [1943]                                  *25 Vic Sq*

I think I spell correctly but you can't read my writing.

Dearest Leonard. It is interesting about the po[w]der. I didn't know that was a cure. Rose was so bad with diarrhoea as a kitten she was nearly reared on arrowroot. Would it cure humans?

I wasn't so near you and your fish on Wednesday after all. Lewes had only one single bed to let so we went on to Eastbourne & I'm glad we did, it was so strange there. It is a deserted town, streets & streets of empty houses and groups of soldiers walking about with clanging feet. Winds & wild things grow all over the place – there is no one at all on the front & only one hotel that faces the sea is functioning as a hotel. A few old couples who won't be frightened off walk slowly about, any girl with the right number of features (or probably without) can have her pick of soldiers from almost any country. But the lovely thing was the sky on Thursday evening. I never saw anything more beautiful. Over Beachy Head it was cold pale blue ribbed with little lines of violet grey cloud – the

---

1. Elspeth Josceline Grant Huxley (b. 1907), author, went to Africa in 1913 and returned in 1925 to study at Reading University. She married Gervas Huxley in 1931 and travelled widely with him in the thirties in Africa, Australia and America. She wrote about her Kenyan childhood in *The Flame Trees of Thika* (1959) and its sequel, *Mottled Lizard* (1962). Miss Benzie worked for the BBC.

headland jutting against it dark warm kharki [sic] & the tide was out so the shore below was also ribbed with pale water trickled between rich dark bottle green rocks. It is stupid to describe it & I couldn't paint. Next day we spent on the Coghlan's farm[1] stooking oats. It was delightful. I've never stooked before. But the elegance of my legs is ruined for weeks to come with your bramble & their stubble.

I can come to dinner on Wednesday. Have you written to the dog people? Rose is awful, bawling for Wave day after day.

     Love T.

77:   [Thursday] 12 August [1943]          *25 Vic Sq*

My dearest Leonard.

I hope you will open this first or you may think the other parcel is something delicious & it is only your own boxes full of reserve paints. I am always bitterly disappointed if a parcel isn't something very nice.

This drawing hardly seems worth sending. I wish I had done more, but she didn't like being drawn, it made her uneasy. I am glad you have decided not to have a Spaniel again it is much better not.[2] I think a sheep dog with brown eye brows would be very nice. I wish I could find one for you.

I was in the Park painting all morning and have been drawing tigers since tea.

It is always the same, you see I don't think I've enough pictures for a show. I may have given you the wrong idea about that toe nail. I used to try very often to show pictures but always fruitlessly & always it made a bad upset & interruption & so that is why I have turned even more sullen.

I could come to dinner on Monday. Why don't you come to dinner here on Wednesday?

     Love T.

1. North of Cooden, near Seafield School at Little Common. Owned and run by Granville and Patrick Coghlan, Seafield had been evacuated to Two Bridges in Devon; the Parsons would visit there at the end of August. IMP attended Seafield before going to Winchester.
2. After Pinka and Sally, who had just died and whom TR had tried to draw, LW got a sheepdog, Merle.

78:   [Thursday] 12 August 1943                                *Monk's House*

I enclose Nancy [Nolan]'s latest

My Dearest, You didn't leave a pink & black nightdress, but you did leave a minute pocket handkerchief which I posted through your letter box on my way to the train.

   I shall not know until Monday morning whether I have to come up on that day or Tuesday so if it is just the same to you it would be safer to say Wednesday for you to come to supper at Meck. Sq. But if you would prefer Monday let me know as in that case I should come up on Monday afternoon.

   You will think over the many things I tried to say last night? Editing destroys the mind & after 48 hours of Kingsley & Gt Turnstile & writing articles I was too dull & jaded to be able to put into words what I wanted to say about the things which really matter, you & your work. Most people if you stripped off them, like skins off an onion, their various qualities – beauty, ugliness, charm, intelligence, talents, gifts, masks, virtues, vices – you would find inside them just nothing; but you are one of the rare people who if you were pealed like that, would at the end present to the peeler a perfectly hard, solid object, Trekkie, an adorable Trekkie, but something far more important, an artist Trekkie. I am sure of that, & I am absolutely certain that I'm an infallible judge of the absence or presence of solid cores in people. Of course, my judgement of whether you can get or have got the painter core on to your pictures is not infallible & is probably worthless, but for what it is worth, I'm absolutely certain that in one or two of the pictures I've seen the hard, solid (& still adorable), master painter Trekkie. But I feel that life has made you depressed to some extent & uncertain about yourself, just at the moment when it is most important that you should be ruthless with yourself & still more with this accursed outside world of public & dealers so that you may, as I'm certain you can, triumphantly get this solid Trekkie out of you onto the pictures. And for some curious reason this getting out process is nearly always only possible if the artist faces the outside world & flings his works of art in their face, again & again & again, if they refuse to read, or look at, or listen to what he writes, paints, or composes. I doubt whether any artist can withdraw into himself & make his art into a private or secret thing without damaging his art. So my heart gave a bound of joy when you said you were thinking of a show, for I'm sure it's right & I had been thinking of these things but feeling that I had no right to say them to you & possibly I might only worry & pain you if I did. You've got to be tough to the outside world, but, dearest, do consider whether you wont let me be your tough when it comes to the Agnews & the Macdonalds. You must know what pleasure I would get from being allowed to do it.

One other thing. You said you thought my judgement might be prejudiced by my feelings for you. Of course, I expect, to some extent it is. I think that when one loves anyone physically & mentally, their works produce in one something of the same excitement & exhilaration that they do personally & that therefore one's judgement is prejudiced. But only up to a point, or momentarily. If one is by nature critical, as I am, & consider it an absolute duty to be honest in that kind of judgement, after the first moment of pleasure & excitement, one does become impersonal & one sees not Trekkie's picture, but just a picture, & then one can judge impersonally – for what it's worth – whether that picture has that strange, solid object Trekkie – an impersonal (though still adorable) Trekkie – translated into & informing it & what value it & the impersonal Trekkie have.

I am still dull, jaded, & tainted with journalism & I daresay all this may read silly & pompous. But just as you have that rare solid core, so there is a solid core in all these words – the truth about your painting & my passionate belief in it & you. So if the words are silly, you must forgive your devoted

L.

PS 1.    I meant to take the name & address of the agent of No. 15[2] & like an idiot forgot. Would it be a great nuisance for you to ring them up & tell them to send particulars & key to you? And then we might look at it on Wednesday? But don't do it, if it's a nuisance.

PS 2.    You once wrote a letter to me while cooking dinner. That's what I've been doing with disastrous results to the dinner. I burnt one milk pudding, one saucepan & some macaroni, & reduced a potato to a kind of watery gruel.

1. Thomas Agnew & Sons Ltd, 43 Old Bond Street. Duncan Macdonald was a dealer at the Lefevre Gallery.
2. LW had visited 24 Victoria Square with Kingsley Martin two days earlier. He returned on 25 August with a builder (White), and had the lease in hand on 3 September.

79:   Friday 13 August 1943 [postcard]

I can't unpack the parcel to add this to the letter inside, so you have an immense post from me two packets & a p.c. Ian must work late on Wednesday so I can dine with you that night, will you dine here on Monday? I think I shall go along to Fennemore at the Nat Gal when I come out of the Park at lunch time. T.

P.S.   I bought the Listener this morning because it had such a lovely head on it & I saw it had you & E.H. inside. It seemed to me she just said everything was fine & dandy. I would have to read great long reports to know the truth.[1]

80:   Saturday evening 14 August 1943                              *25 Vic Sq*

Dearest Leonard. This will be even worse written than usual because I have caught a cold & I have gone to bed in hopes it will quickly cure it. It came on without any warning at lunch time to-day, perhaps it will be gone tomorrow. Everything that you say in your letter which I got this morning is true (you wrote it while you cooked the dinner & I read it while I got the breakfast & yet it is not at all a kitchen letter) I mean everything about it being bad to be secret. I know it and have really tried not to be. It is the thing that, apart from individual paintings at given moments, has most depressed me; because it is impossible not to say to yourself at low moments that doors are not shut in your face for nothing. And yet I do believe unshakably, underneath everything, in the hard core; if I hadn't I would not have been painting without ceasing for twenty years. Your extraordinary sympathy and belief in the core coming at this moment stimulate & revive me more than you may believe and than I can tell you, except I hope pictorially. You are like very unusual medicine which does one an immense amount of good and is at the same time extremely nice to take. I want to say also though I think I hardly need, that I do not accept all this love & faith as a matter of

1. On 12 August 1943 the *Listener* cover showed a young Masai warrior from Kenya. In 'A Challenge to Us All: The Views on the Responsibility of Colonial Empire' (recorded on 4 August 1943, see letter 75), LW made three divisions of colonies: 1. those like Ceylon with some experience of self-government who should be given it immediately after the war; 2. those like Malaya where people were not as politically advanced and the situation was complicated by strategic considerations; 3. those of primitive people. Elspeth Huxley thought self-governance a long way off and colonial problems more to do with poverty than politics.

course even if I may look as if I did. And I would not accept it at all if I didn't believe that it is on the whole nicer for you too. And I will let you be my tough. But I haven't many pictures. I have always weeded them out & there have been about three people who have bought the good ones from time to time, and pictures have to be for sale in shows don't they?

Rose is sitting on my stomach. She is far fondest of me when I'm in bed. I tried to get the key of number 7 for you but the Estate say though it is empty it is on lease & they may not tell me who has it. I will get the key of 15 on Monday.

I shall have to go to Whipsnade to see an elephant; how do you get there; will you come too?[1]

　　　love T.

PS.　I think your Irish Flame [Nancy Nolan] is fearful.


81:　Thursday 26 August 1943　　　　　　　　　　*25 Vic Sq*

My dearest Leonard. Here is the oven thing so that you will not burn your hands. I am sorry about it's nasty colour. I have spots this colour (the [pink] paper not the cloth) all over me; my harvesters [sic] are raging. If I was run over & taken to hospital they'd put me in an isolation ward. At sunset last night they suddenly got worse; do you think it was colour sympathy? I feel very low, & it is raining & I have got the American to dinner to-night & the Lewes Policeman says I may not come into the area. What shall I do to be saved? I feel as if they had left the plug out of me & it's all run out in the night.

One thing at any rate; Ian now entirely agrees with me about his Wing Co & is going to make moves for a transfer as soon as he comes back from Devon. I am glad about this whatever it may mean.[2]

I must go & work. Don't be too sympathetic. I should not bleat like this. I am a sponge. Do sponges bleat?

　　　Love

　　　T.

1. The elephant appears in Barbara Baker's *The Three Rings*.
2. IMP had been in France with the RAF from January to June 1940, when he was posted to the Air Ministry in London. He returned to France in August 1944. Thereafter TR largely gave up living at 25 Victoria Square to stay with LW at Monk's House. LW continued to search for a permanent home for the Parsons in Sussex; in October 1944, with IMP's encouragement, TR signed a 10-year lease on a house at Iford, about 2 miles from Rodmell. After IMP was demobilised in the autumn of 1945, 25 Victoria Square was sold and the Parsons shared LW's house at 24. The unidentified American was probably military.

Dearest Tiger, I do hope the mental goose flesh didn't last long. I hate to see you worried in that way. I wish I could analyse it out of you. It is, I'm sure, a very complicated & subtle thing & my mind at the moment is not up to the task though I've been thinking of it & you off & on ever since I saw you yesterday.

I've been thinking of you in other connections too. You've become so intertwined in my thoughts & feelings particularly here & in the garden that when you aren't here I have continually a strange sense of your presence & absence at the same moment. There has just been a violent storm of rain with a clear sky in the west [in the margin is: 'I'm afraid this is a sneeze'; the green ink of the text is smudged and overwritten in black ink, used for the rest of the letter] & a great rainbow over the church, & we were looking at it together as we did only a few weeks ago & yet you weren't here. And last night when I got back in the evening it was incredibly beautiful with a sky like the sky we had at Whipsnade, but quite different here, & the sun & long shadows chasing one another very slowly & softly across the water meadows & up Caburn. I walked on the terrace, & it was just as though you were by my side telling me all about the clouds & yet hopelessly different because you weren't. The garden too at the moment is, I think, rather wonderful, having burst into a new florescence with clouds of Japanese anemonies, & they also were strangely coloured by this feeling of presence & absence, because you haven't seen this particular moment & yet seemed so near.

I sent you 4 figs in a tin. I chose them not quite ripe as I thought they might travel better & be ripe when they arrive. But this may be a mistake. If so, let me know & I'll send really ripe ones another time.

I forgot to tell you that I examined the Tiger, tiger poem with great care again the other evening, & came to the conclusion that we were wrong & that 'What dread hand? And what dread feet?' must refer to God. All the other whats refer to God or the materials or instruments which he uses to make you. Secondly you are always refered to in the second person – thine eyes, thy heart. Thirdly I don't believe that you have hands in the poem.[1]

I began this letter after tea but am finishing it long after dinner & in the

1. 'The Tyger' is one of William Blake's most disputed lyrics. In later copies, 'and what dread feet?' was changed to 'formed thy dread feet' and 'forged thy dread feet'. The poem's questions are clearly meant to be unanswerable; today the 'immortal hand or eye' is generally thought to belong to man, who makes the tyger (mental darkness) and its opposite, the lamb.

interval have developed a violent cold in the head which perhaps accounts for why I felt so muzzy in the brain.

Still more Belladonna lilies [amaryllis] have begun to poke out their pink snakelike heads.

Good night, dearest. Write to me from Dartmoor if it's not a nuisance to you & write a short story.

> Ever your L.

I liked the picture you did by the orchard.

The caption of the lithograph should be '*We* don't believe a word of it.'[1]

Did you ring up St Pancras Enquiries about the voice?

I found Hackett's letter correctly filed in the year 1929, isn't that a triumph of useless organization?[2]

83:   Friday 12.45 PM 27 August 1943 [postcard]            *London*

I think 10 miles is too far don't you it makes it nearly as bad as C. Farm.

The American had gone as far as I am concerned & will have as far as Ian is tomorrow. He says the English can't understand how the Americans just *must* have a cup of coffee & a sandwich before they go to bed.

> Love T.

84:   Friday night 27 August 1943 [postcard]

Don't you think you ought to have the chimney swept before your room is painted. I go to Philip & Lewes Vic 1909, 89 Lillington St S.W.1. I thought of it & then forgot to tell you. Will you need to have black curtains sewn & have you someone to do it. My Mrs B will if you haven't. I have had to redraw the annunciation[3] on a new stone – infuriating. It really comes out that you mustn't resensitize for all they say, because if you do it destroys the quality. I spent the whole afternoon at it & only

1. TR had done a lithograph of LW saying to the Archangel Gabriel: 'I don't believe a word of it.' The phrase, which reflected their joint scepticism, became their mutual adage.
2. Francis Hackett (1883–1962) had been co-editor of the *New Republic* (1914–22). Irish-born, he lived in America, and eventually Denmark. LW sometimes consulted him on Irish questions. LW kept fastidious records of everything from finances to the number of apples he harvested each autumn and the pieces of music he listened to each evening. As evidenced here, he also had a fine sense of irony, especially about himself.
3. For a Midget Book in the Bible Stories Series, *The Birth of Jesus*.

hope it will now turn out well. I hate p. cards but you must forgive it, am just going to bed, have packed swept my room & made 3 lbs of plum jam.
  love T.
most succulent figs arrived


85:  [Sunday] 29 August 1943            *Monk's House, Rodmell*

My Dearest Trekkie, I hardly ever call you this now except when I announce that the bathroom is empty. But I don't see why I should always call you by the same name, & I like Trekkie.

  I bicycled to Halland this afternoon to see the house, as it seemed absurd not to find out what it was like if you thought it really sounded possible. It took me exactly an hour with a strong south west wind behind me to get there & 1½ hours to get back with an equally strong wind in my face. The place is not bad, but I doubt it's being quite good enough. I was shown over it by the owner, Mrs Ronky, with the bloodiest of bloodred hands & face to match. It is in a part of the country which I dont much care for, not the Laughton-Ripe bit, but about 3 miles further north on the Blackboys-Hawkhurst road or just off it. It stands bang on a minor road. I wish you had been with me to see it; it would have amused you. It is two typical Sussex cottages thrown into one, with a nice front & back, but nothing to make a song about. Inside everything has been done for comfort, warmth, & convenience. Radiators everywhere & hot cupboards & even in the coldest weather you wouldn't want more than two hot water bottles. They have rather disembowled it & filled it with rather ugly wood which goes badly with a few cherished ancient oak beams & ye olde fireplaces. A good deal of the horror could quite easily be removed, but the real objection is that most of the rooms are too small. There are two sitting rooms on the ground floor & 3 bedrooms above, but only two are fairsized. I don't see where you would get a proper room to paint in. You would make a beautiful garden. It slopes down from the house facing, I think, south or southwest, more or less in terraces, with a large wood on the left & apple & plum trees below. The wood, with a deep glade in it which you look into almost from the house, could be made lovely. But, as I said, I don't think it's quite good enough. I wish I could find you something next door to Monk's House; if I come & live next door to you in London, I think you ought to come & live next door to me in the country.

  I do hope your depression has lifted, dearest. If anyone has the right to face this damned outside world with confidence & to be happy, it's you. And you must & shall. You have in yourself everything which matters — & after all, what else really matters?

Only perhaps the weather. Which here yesterday was fiendish & today is thoroughly unpleasant — which has made me think more than once of you on that grey, grim Dartmoor & to pray that by a miracle, while the wind is howling here & a sea fret blotting out the downs when it isn't raining, the sun is shining on you — as it always would, if this were a sensible world.

And the Lewes policeman, curse him. This is utterly wretched. Did he say anything at all or just a formal refusal? I think we were wrong to ask for a general permit & that there would have been a better chance if we had waited until you were coming & asked for definite days. My only hope is that the whole thing is temporary; there are no troops here now. I dont think I can stand Rodmell without sometimes seeing you here.

On Friday Kingsley rang me up — the weathercock going round twice over. First, he had asked me to edit the N[ew] S[tatesman] in the week beginning Sept 6 — now he had changed his mind & could I do it the following week? Secondly, he & Dorothy were seriously considering Mecklenburgh Square — could I arrange for them to go over the flat that afternoon?

This letter rivals Nancy Nolan's in length. Am I becoming a male Nolan? Do you see any symptoms?

Love, dearest tiger, from your

        L.

I bicycled back from Halland across country & at the bottom of a hill near Glynde I had to show my identity card to a soldier who was talking to a countryman with a bicycle. I did not look at the man, but as soon as I started to walk up the hill he came too. 'You don't remember me, Sir,' he said. I looked at him — a wizened, elderly, wryfaced little man who vaguely stirred memories. 'Will Dudman,' he said. Then I remembered Will Dudman who was a youth working on Asheham farm 30 years ago, fell in love with our cook, & used to throw boxes of chocolates in at her bedroom window. A Shakespearian character of the half-wit clown type even to his name. Now a wizened, elderly man on a bicycle. He rode by my side for two or three miles talking the whole time & when I could understand what he said it was still the Shakespearean clown. As a boy, he said, he wore suits three sizes too big, which was pleasant in the winter, because you could keep warm in school by jumping about in your own clothes. He left me suddenly at a turning saying inconsequently that he was going to 'the bungalow, as I've done every Sunday these 20 years'.[1]


86:   Sunday 29 August 1943          *c/o Patrick Coghlan, Seafield, Two Bridges, Princetown, Devon*

Dearest Leonard. I think it was the lunatic who wrote in red ink wasn't it? This is all I can lay hands on & I think it is better than expecting you to read my writing in pencil. You will see that I didn't give you the address very accurately. We had a fearful journey down sitting on the floor of the guard's van. Ian who had worked straight through the night before, slept with my stomach for a nice pneumatic pillow. We were greeted by swirling mist but so many kisses & hugs & warm fires & hot bottles & cream for tea that I was ashamed for not having much wanted to come. It is still wet in a rather remorseless way but I have seen a buzzard & had a nice wet walk along the Dart.

  I don't wonder very much that I am entwined round Monk's House for it is so entwined round me. Every detail is fixed in a series of the clearest pictures in my head, from big general things like the look of the sky & land down to tiny details of sprays of leaves or bunches of fruit or spiders in hedges. Do you remember how wonderful the lily near the gentry's pool looked in the morning light? How much I want to see the Japanese anemones. I can't bear to think that I may not even if I could come. May I have dinner with you on Tuesday instead of Monday? Pat [Coghlan] is coming back with us on Sunday & I shall have him until Tuesday morning. If I come straight from the Chiswick I would be with you about sixish. I am sorry you got that cold. That is how mine came, like a thunder storm but it went quickly too. This is a poor dull letter but I must write it & walk quickly to Princetown with it or miss the Post. The figs were in perfect condition when they arrived.

  Love from  T.


87:   [Tuesday] 31 August 1943                          *Monk's House*

My Dearest, I have just had your letter. I wrote you one of Nancy Nolan

1. Should be Dedman, the local verger and the Woolfs' original gardener.

length & addressed it to The Two Bridges Hotel where you may find it waiting you. I thought it was wrong as you will see by the envelope. I can just catch the post now. I love you, dearest, & look forward only to Tuesday.

L.

88:  [Wednesday] 1 September 1943 *Two Bridges*

My dear Mr Woolf. Your Trekkie so surprised me. I thought you were working back to a safe S. Butler–Savage position.[1] So I hasten to forestall you & shall conclude yours truly if I remember. It is odd how formal it looked, & had I been in bed I would have got up at once. It was all nonsense about the address. Pat was just pulling my leg. Your letter came without delay, though Tavistock isn't really right. It was very kind to bicycle to the house, I think perhaps it was as well after your account that Ian prevented me from buying it at the breakfast table. I don't like that part at all & had not realized it was there.

The weather has been bad, & to-day is the worst. Yesterday I weeded celery all the morning the latter half with a very fine example of Dartmoor yokel; he made a date with me to do more to-day but it has rained absolutely steadily the only change being that until tea the rain was falling from left to right of the window pane & since tea from right to left. I have been working on the elephants & tigers & they are almost done.[2] We have had one good walk, not a long one but a pleasant one yesterday afternoon along the Dart & we bravely flung off our clothes & jumped in, it was cold but not petrifyingly though it made my behind ache, this always seems to be the bit of me that aches first for cold. It did it so violently once when I bathed off the north most point of Skye I thought I had fixed it like that & that it would always ache.

Murr[a]y [Hicks] is coming here to-morrow for the night. He has fitted us in, I am not clear where he is coming from or going to.

We *did* ask for a specific permit. We asked for leave to come about the middle of Sept & again about six weeks later. Yes he just said regretted

---

1. I.e., to an intellectual friendship such as painter and writer Samuel Butler (1835–1902) had with Miss Savage, the only woman of importance in his life and the person who urged him to write about his severe childhood in *The Way of All Flesh* (posthumously, 1903). TR seems to have asked LW to send formal-looking letters to her at the Coghlans', but there may also be a letter (of 30 August) missing which would better explain this sentence and the following paragraph (see letter 90 and note).
2. For *The Three Rings*.

unable to allow. I wish we had waited because I think that was the most feverish moment by all accounts. The matron here comes from Brighton & was telling me about it there. Perhaps it will not be for long.

If doing nothing is good for me then this week should restore 'the bloom' for I am doing nothing except eat huge meals with glasses of buttermilk between. Sleep is not good & not because I have weakened but because we are joined every night by a footballing mouse. Whatever I do he manages to find something small & hard to dribble across the boards with the maximum clatter. Last night he took a lump of sugar out of the knapsack I had in the train; it is astonishing the noise one mouse can make with a lump of sugar. I have tried, so far unsuccessfully, to find you my dog. I go into the bar in the evenings & ask the company. It is rather nice to stay in a house that has its own bar especially one like this which is only used by real locals, if there are no soldiers about. The conversation is carried on with so many asides & obscure references to things the outsider knows nothing about that it is very hard to get the drift sometimes for half an hour at a time. I liked your Will Dudman very much. This is an (ora? [sic]). N. Nolan too. She has infected us both for length at any rate. I shall not be able to bear Thursday Friday & Saturday all as wet as to-day.

With love dear Mr Woolf
    Yours truly
    T. Ritchie

89:    [Friday] 3 September 1943                        *Monk's House*

My Dearest, I meant to write to you yesterday, but couldn't because I had the Labour Party[1] meeting here & Quentin [Bell] stayed the night & came early in order to play bowls. I have been thinking and thinking about you & your work this last slowly passing week, with not a sight of you, & I have so much I want to say. I want to say it, but not that I should seem over insistent & nagging, worrying & disturbing to what is inmost in you. I think you do know that it is because you & your work – which means too your happiness – are to me now infinitely the most important things in life. And not, I really believe, merely that you & everything connected

1. LW took an active part in Rodmell life, and was a member of the local Labour Party from the thirties on. Meetings were held at Monk's House or the Church of England primary school, of which he was school manager for many years. He was also treasurer of the Cricket Club, clerk of the Parish Council and president of the Rodmell Horticultural Society. TR too attended Labour Party meetings and, when they were there, so did her aunt Faanie and sometimes IMP.

with you are so personally dear to me. I can judge you objectively, as the philosophers love to say, & I know that 'objectively' too you are really important because of what you have it in you to produce. From that point of view far the most important of anyone I know, & after all, as you always say, I do know quite a lot.

I think you have got to a vital stage in your painting life & that you can & must burst out into a new & superb florescence like the Japanese anemones in the garden. And it depends almost entirely – & that's why I feel I must write so insistently – upon your having, your regaining self confidence which in a subtle way you have lost. I think that you've got to face the fact that you've lost it, & deliberately conquer it & that as soon as you do, it will have an astonishingly releasing effect upon you & your work. If you were not you, there are very good reasons why you should no longer be confident – & that too one must face & not belittle. I am sure it began with Peter & the frosting attitude at the very moment when sympathy & encouragement were essential. And then, as you said in your letter once, it is impossible not to be affected by the continual shutting of doors in one's face. This is one of the main things one must face. I set no store of any sort or kind by failure & success. I mean that there is no relation between success & real value or importance. You might be a complete failure to the end with public, agents, shows etc. & it wouldn't make a shiver or quiver for one second in my belief in your value & importance as a painter. But it would be silly to pretend that success or failure does not have important effects upon even the greatest artists, even those who deep down set no real store upon them. I think success has a releasing effect upon them even when they really know that it means essentially nothing. It is pleasant in itself & it relieves them of the worry of having to consider what their impact upon the outside world will be.

Failure has just the opposite effect. It forces one in upon oneself. This may produce the privacy & secrecy which we talked about. If one is by nature a tough, one damns the outside world, sets one's teeth, & produces masterpieces which no one pays any attention to until one is senile or dead – even so I think the effect is not good. But if one is not a tough – & I dont think you are – even if deep down you remain certain of your solid core, superficially your self-confidence will be affected. The devil of it is that it may affect you as an artist & then two things happen. First, the outside world is always enormously impressed by self confidence & vice versa, & as it has an uncanny instinct for spotting them, a vicious circle is set up. Secondly, the artist who has superficially lost confidence often unconsciously continuously underestimates his powers & therefore does

70

not fully use them – he becomes too unambitious, in a sense, in his works – he is always, as it were, writing sketches & short stories when he should be writing full scale novels – & as he is always producing below his real power, he is perpetually conscious of something lacking in what he produces.

I believe that something like this has happened to you, & the problem is to reverse the process. You have something in you – I feel it, see it so often, dearest, that I cant be mistaken – so strong & so beautiful, something of immense importance, that you must break through this spider's web which prevents you often from giving full expression to it. How to break through? Of course, the main thing is simply to be confident, to see things exactly as they are – it sounds a lame conclusion, & would be with anyone but you, for one of the things which I adore in you is the way you do see things exactly as they are with your great eyes wide open (& that is why those 'blue pools' are the most beautiful eyes I've ever seen). But I believe there's another thing to do, though here my ignorance of the art of painting makes it difficult for me to know how it would apply there. But if you were a writer, I should say: 'In your next book, instead of choosing a theme & form which you think within your powers, choose ones which you think a good deal above your powers. And having done so, force yourself all through not to think of it again until the whole book is complete. Except that you may occasionally say to yourself: "There's nothing I cant do."'

I must catch the post. What a letter! I wont apologize because you know what causes it.

It was the most perfect morning here – I do hope you had it too.

The lease of 24 V.S. has arrived – White has sent his estimate – the electricity people may not put in power points. So I feel I am nearer Vic. Sq.

I long to see you again, dearest tiger.

     Your devoted
     L.


90:   [Saturday] 4 September 1943       [On *Political Quarterly* paper]

Mrs I. M. Parsons (legal name),
25 Victoria Square, S.W.1.

Dear Mrs Parsons,

I was very glad to get your letter of the 1st inst. in answer to mine of the 30th ult.[1] and to see that you were well. I hope however that the weather improved, that you slept better in the latter part of your visit, and that the ache in your behind proved to be temporary.

I am writing this in order to make it clear that, in our future relations however much you may wish to get into the position of the late Miss Savage, I shall be totally unable to play the part of the late Mr Samuel Butler. I think it is only fair to you to make this quite plain before any further misunderstanding occurs. My general attitude towards you is, I think, sufficiently clearly indicated in my subsequent letter (for the length of which I now apologize) which you should find awaiting you on your return to your London house, as I posted it yesterday, the 3rd inst. I can, of course, understand that you may think it desirable to work back to what you call a safe position and theoretically a strong case might be made out for it. It would be hypocrisy upon my part to pretend that I am not extremely glad that, so far as I am concerned, this is now impossible. As the reason is in yourself or, to go still further back, in the Almighty who is, I presume, ultimately responsible for making Mrs I. M. Parsons what she is and therefore for her effect upon the undersigned, I suggest that you accept the position prior to your letter of the 1st inst.

I am looking forward to meeting you again on Tuesday, September 7th, at about 6 p.m. at 37 Mecklenburgh Square, W.C.1.

Will you allow me to express my love and devotion to you and
Believe me, dear Mrs Parsons,
    Yours very truly

    Leonard Woolf
    (Leonard Woolf)


91:   [Thursday] 9 September 1943                    *Monk's House*

Dear Miss Ritchie

I am glad to be able to begin like this instead of with the more formal Mrs Parsons, as I gathered that you really prefer on principle not to use your husband's name, & after our talk in Brunswick Park (which I enjoyed very much) I feel I know you as I did not before &, if I may say

1. There is no letter of the 30th ult. in the Archive. Either LW means of the 29th ult., which this letter seems to refer to, or the letter is missing (see letter 88 and note). This kind of playful, semi-legal discussion continued sporadically until LW's and TR's lives settled into a pattern with his move to 24 Victoria Square and her rental of Iford Grange.

so, much more intimately (& I do not easily get on terms of intimacy with people).[1] As a man, I probably dont take exactly your view about the married & maiden names of women. I find personally that if I don't like a married woman, I definitely get some pleasure in calling her by her husband's name, Mrs X, & I should not call her by her maiden name, Miss A. I think that this is really because subconsciously when I say 'Mrs X' I am also saying to myself with some malicious pleasure: 'Thank God, *he* (X) has got it'. But it works the other way when I like Mrs Y, & the more I am attracted to her, the more willingly would I forget Mr Y. I realize that your view is very different, being impersonal & as it were sociological & I respect it & you enormously. But when you like a person & are a man, as I am, it is difficult to regard her objectively simply as a sociological case.

May I say again how much I enjoyed our rather curious lunch & talk in Brunswick Park? After I left you, I signed a lease for a new house which, strangely enough, will make me quite a near neighbour of yours, & I venture to hope that this may make it more likely that we may become better acquainted. I write this from my country house or cottage; it is unfortunately in a defence area; otherwise I should have asked you some day to honour it & me with a visit.

I am at any rate very much looking forward to meeting you again next Monday.

> Yours very sincerely
> Leonard Woolf

There was just one point in our talk which I trust you'll forgive me for referring to. I think you were quite right about my clothes & hair, & I have long known that unfortunately I can never become respectable in the Athenaeum sense. But you described my condition so vividly that at the moment it gave me an almost physical shock. It may have been merely the usual amusing & imaginative way of your speaking (which I so much admire) & I may be making a mountain out of a molehill. But I must confess that on thinking it over, I have become more & more uneasy. I agree, as I said, about the clothes & hair, but I really am, I believe, in perhaps more essential respects a perfectly normal man, & it would distress me that you should think otherwise. Perhaps I gave you a false impression by my awkward & too reserved behaviour, for just as I do not fit into the atmosphere of leather chairs in the Athenaeum, I am

---

1. On 8 September LW lunched with TR in Brunswick Park, Bloomsbury, then accompanied her to the Chiswick Press before he signed the lease for 24 Victoria Square and returned to Lewes by the 5.35 train.

unaccustomed to more agreeable atmospheres, e.g. to sitting in public parks with attractive young women. In fact the following quotation from de Gourmont's letters Intimes à l'Amazone[1] exactly describes my state of mind:

Sans doute, je n'ai pas l'habitude de me promener avec les jeunes femmes [le soir] au Bois de Boulogne (or rather au Parc de Brunswick): c'est pourquoi je n'ai commencé à me plaire à la situation que lorsqu'elle a pris fin. Non parce qu'elle n'était pas agréable, mais plutôt [parce] qu'elle l'était trop et qu'elle supposait un état d'esprit dont rien ne me prouvait qu'il était le vôtre. [Et puis la lune du Bois ressemble trop à un globe électrique.] Vous m'avez terriblement intimidé: pourtant votre voix était douce et naturelle. C'est peut-être cela qui me déroutait, votre naturel, et cependant je n'attendais pas de vous une autre attitude, – mais comme le naturel est très rare chez une femme, il faut y être préparé.

Telle qu'elle fut, elle restera dans mon souvenir, cette promenade, longue et brève, où je n'eus d'autre inspiration que d'écouter votre voix comme une musique ironique (l'ironie était en moi contre moi-même).[2]


92:     [Friday] 10 September [1943]                      *Chiswick Press*

Dear Leonard.

May I call you that? It is unusual to find a man over thirty who will eat buns with one in a Park. And this is because if 'le naturel est très rare chez une femme' it is almost unheard of to find a man who is not a stick insect.

---

1. Because Rémy de Gourmont (1858–1915), writer and founder in 1890 of Editions Mercure de France, suffered from lupus, he led a secluded life. *Lettres à l'Amazone* (1926) are essays and 'lettres' addressed to one of his few intimates, Natalie Clifford Barney, the American expatriate writer and Parisienne saloniste in the years preceding World War I.

2. LW has adapted the quote (from the *lettre intime* dated 20 August 1910) to his purposes. His deletions are within the square brackets in his letter and are not included in this translation: 'Of course, I am not in the habit of walking with young ladies in the Bois de Boulogne (or rather in Brunswick Park): that's why I didn't begin to enjoy the situation until it was over. Not because it wasn't pleasant but rather because it was too pleasant and because it presumed a state of mind which nothing suggested was yours. You intimidated me frightfully: although your voice was soft and natural. This is perhaps what baffled me, how natural you were, and yet I was not expecting of you a different attitude – but as the natural is very rare in a woman, one has to be prepared for it.

'Such as it was, this walk remained in my memory, long and short, where I had no other inspiration than hearing your voice like an ironic music (the irony being with me against myself).'

He covers himself with the large desks & country clubs the leather chairs or the more subtle University sticks of his particular respectability. It was this which I did not find in you & tried rather awkwardly to express. I am sorry that you should have interpreted my remark in any other way, as it was really meant, I hope you will believe, as a great compliment.

I am glad to hear that you are to become a neighbour in London. Oddly enough I have written to the Police at Lewes to ask for a permit to allow me into your district next week end – but am not too hopeful that they will let me come. If they do, I should very much like to come & see you if I may.

      Yours
       Trekkie Ritchie

I am sorry to write in pencil, the only ink here is lithographic ink & if I used that I should have to send you a stone.


93:   [Tuesday] 14 September 1943       *37 Mecklenburgh Square*

Mr Woolf presents his compliments to Mrs Parsons and begs to assure her of his complete and eternal adoration. If at any time she finds it possible to spare him a fragment of her affection, however temporary, he will be extremely grateful. Meanwhile he ventures to thank her for the delicious biscuits, which she was good enough to leave for him and which he has just eaten for lunch. (This letter may be inserted at either beginning or end of series.)


94:   [TR to LW] 15 October 1942   *Messers Pounce & Havem Solicitors,*
     [true date probably                  *Old Screw Lane, E.C.2*
     Wednesday 15 September 1943]

L. S. Woolf Esq.

Sir,

We are instructed by our client Mrs I. M. Parsons of 25 Victoria Square S.W.1. to inform you that she has received your letter of the 14th inst. While she does not wish to threaten or intimidate you she wishes you to know that she is keeping this & all former letters & that she will not hesitate to use them in evidence against you should there be the slightest falling off in your affection as she sees it.

      Yours truly
       F. Havem

95:   [Thursday] 16 September 1943          *Monk's House, Rodmell*

Dear Trekkie,

I was so glad you abandoned 'Mr Woolf' in your last letter & I hope I'm not presuming in abandoning Miss Ritchie for Trekkie.

I enclose a pink worm pill for Rose. It is one which the vet. gave me for Peat. It is as well to give it in the morning after at least 12 hours fast.

Is it possible that you write political books under the pseudonym of Sir Edward Grigg, K.C.M.G., K.C.V.Q., M.C., M.P.? I ask because in what seems to me a former life (in which I wrote letters to you beginning Dearest), we had only one disagreement – about the meaning of the word misprision. Coming back in the train to Lewes after leaving you at Leicester Square I was reading a book of his which I said I would review for the B.B.C. & came on this sentence:

'We should hesitate to throw misprision on the word "Empire".'
Did you write that?

When I got back – But I must begin this letter again

———————————————

Dearest of tigers, My feelings have got the better of me & I cant keep up the Dear Trekkie strain any longer, for you are dearest & not dear to me. Especially because I can't help really hoping that I may really have you here again. They have put back the buses & there are other signs of slackening & there is a rumour from soldiers that the ban will be lifted next week or even this. I don't think you know what it means to me when you come here & I have you all to myself for 3 or 4 days. 3 or 4 days of pure, unmitigated happiness are the rarest things in life – but that's what it is. I suppose its foolish to be so over optimistic, but if – if the rumour is true, would there be any chance of your coming next week?

I gather that you have sent me a solicitor's letter, because I told you in the 3rd person that I adore you. I repeat it in the first person & I've never adored you more than in Leicester Square at 2.30 p.m. on September 16, 1943, for the extraordinary truth is that it is more every time I see you. Ever your

          L.

I do hope they send me on your letter, I long to see why a solicitor's letter. There seem to be only two possible reasons to me for receiving a solicitor's letter either to be cited as corespondent or sued for libel. You can't cite me as corespondent so it must be libel. But is it libellous to say 'I adore you' even if the adoration is complete & eternal?

96:    [Friday] 17 September 1943                    *Monk's House, Rodmell*

Messrs Pounce & Havem
Old Street Lane, E.C.2.

Dear Sirs,
    I have this morning received your letter of next October 15. I note its
contents and am glad to observe from its date that you agree with me that
any thing connected with Mrs I M Parsons is not temporal but eternal. If
a letter written by her solicitors a month hence is the same as a letter
written about her a month previously, it is improbable that affection for
her will be, is, or was affected by time or tides. You have my full
permission to use this letter in any way you or she may consider desirable.
        Yours faithfully

        Leonard Woolf


97:    Doesn't the paper look lovely with this envelope? You are only
getting such a grand one because I have none other here.

[Friday] 17 September 1943                        *Chiswick P[ress]*
        This is a straight letter.


Dearest Leonard. If you would come to Durban for two hours to see me
you would probably rather have a pencil letter than none. I slept all night
long last night & bounced out of bed so lively that I had washed the rug
the girls have their lunch on before I knew it myself. Then I dashed up
here & am redrawing seven of the illustrations.[1] I came to this decision
last evening & am so glad I did. I wasn't happy about them before I had
the proof & when I saw it I was sure – I had got them too heavy. I shall
have all done by Monday night & the proof on Tuesday so I shan't delay
Lehmann & now Green can go into the way they are to be bound with
him as the redrawing means they will be transferred up, & so can be laid
down in any order.
    Last night Irene & I got involved in going out to dinner[2] to meet two

1. For *The Three Rings*.
2. LW would have appreciated TR's reference in the following story to his own 'I don't believe a
word of it' (see letter 82 and note), and to Fanny Burney's *Evelina* (1778), subtitled *The History of
a Young Lady's Entry Into the World*.

Germans, one of them does lithography. I think he wants to draw on our stones – but we neither of us liked him so we don't think will let him. They were both very oppressive & domineering so I remembered what you have so often said about me being too modest & I spent all the evening saying 'I don't believe a word of it' or 'I entirely disagree'. I daresay I am emotionally starved as your Pole asserted but really I begin to think that only English people have really pleasant manners. (This doesn't mean that I think *mine* were pleasant last evening but that theirs were not). Remind me to read you a bit in Evelina which is pure Alice in Wonderland. Doesn't that surprise you? The garden must have looked heavenly in the morning's light, I think of it so much I most likely will create a wraith of myself which you will see lurking about the place. What a terrifying thing for someone who is frightened of ghosts to create one out of their living self.

Love T.

98:    [Saturday] 18 September 1943                    *Monk's House*

This is a very straight letter.

Dearest, It's curious that we should have to announce to each other now whether our letters are straight or crooked. I've just returned from the Manor House, Denton [now a Newhaven suburb]. I don't quite know what to say. The house itself is very good indeed. An old, grey, flint squarish Sussex farm house (1724 in a stone on the front) – beautiful, I thought. The rooms too are very good. Two on the ground floor, one large, one not so large. Then an admirable staircase & upstairs a rambling old house with ups & downs all over the place & room after room, some small, but all, as far as I could see, good & some admirable, especially one large bedroom which you might use as a studio. Then upstairs again two attics – one very large which fascinated me & again I thought of you painting in it. A good kitchen. The house was full of soldiers, colonels & officers – quarters, rather grander than any I've struck in this war. It made it difficult to ponder things properly, as I was shown over it by a somewhat Eton & Sandhurst subaltern & I had to try (unsuccessfully, of course) to appear respectable. The garden is very odd. It is almost impossible to see what it could really be like as there are enormous tin huts all over it put up by the military. It is in two parts. The house stands bang on the road through the village & most of the garden – the vegetable garden & a large orchard, very badly neglected – is on the other side of the road from the house. Behind the house is the flower garden or what remains of it, mostly paved, with a small water lily pond. In it is a gigantic tithe barn which must have been beautiful but is rather spoilt. It & all the outside buildings are in bad repair, while the house itself is good.

So far, there is very much to be said in its favour. In fact, if one could take the house & put it somewhere else, I should be inclined to say 'Buy it'. The objection to it is its situation. It is right on the village road. It looks from the front on to a nice down across the village. But the down, particularly to the south, is covered with eyesores. A row of villas & a row of very ugly cottages. Also a good deal of the village which one sees is composed of those extraordinary rashes of tumbledown black wooden buildings which spread over allotments & fill me with depression. Another objection according to Eton & Sandhurst is the drainage – the house & whole village drains on to an open swamp not far from the house.

The kitchen garden & orchard are at present let to a villager. I routed him out & had a long talk with him. He was a very 'superior', but not a very nice man. He said that most of the people living in Denton were a bad lot & terrible thieves. The bone factory no longer exists – it actually was in the tithe barn. The previous owner committed suicide, but he thoughtfully went to Brighton to do it. I cannot believe that the house is haunted.

Well, my dearest, there you are. The house really is very good & I can see you in it (& I should have you fairly near me) but I don't like the village & the villas. I wish you had been with me – but it's simply silly to say that because I always wish you were with me.

I dont mind what you write your letters with or on, even a lithographic stone, if they're like the one I got this morning at breakfast. It *was* an amazing morning here yesterday & still more lovely this morning. It's no good your saying that you *may* create a wraith out of yourself which will haunt the garden, because that's just exactly what you have done. I never go into the garden now, I think, without it. It walks by my side, feeds the goldfish with me every morning, notices the new flowers as they come out. Sometimes I see it painting in the orchard or eating a mutton pie under the fig tree. I even hear it laugh or say: 'No, Leonard, I do *not* agree with you'. And the other night when the moon was up & I went out on the terrace before going to bed, it walked by my side in a long golden dress & was so beautiful that I realized that the penny novelette writer is quite true to life when he works up to the grand crisis with 'Her beauty was such that he caught his breath, a lump came in his throat, & for a moment his heart stopped beating'. It even follows me up the village street when I go to post a letter in the new box on the main road for the other day the wraith of a bus appeared & your wraith let me hold its hand & got into it saying: 'Well, goodbye Leonard'. And don't you know that this evening & last evening after tea your wraith came out with me into the orchard & gathered the apples with me & I wasn't at all nice to the wraith, being depressed because it was not you but the ghost of you – for that is one of the things you've never done here & ever since you began to come I've looked forward to the September evening – sunny, absolutely still, with the first chill of autumn in the air, & the mist beginning to creep up out of the water meadows – when I should see you in the orchard gathering the apples – for I think it's really the most beautiful moment of the year here.

Dont you know all this, dearest tiger? If not, I think it's rather disgraceful. For if you create a wraith of yourself, you oughtn't really to let it wander ab— (this is Peat's interference – I flung him off, whereupon he has leapt on the table & upset a large bowl of flowers & the floor is swimming in water) about with me here out of your control.

This morning Duncan[1] rang me up & asked me whether I knew your husband's name. I said: 'Ian'. He said: 'is that all?' I said : 'What do you mean?' He said: 'He must have a surname'. Then I gathered he wanted your telephone number. I hope it means the Committee want your work.

I felt in my bones you weren't quite satisfied with the illustrations. Of course you're right to do them again.

Goodnight, my dearest

Your devoted

L.

------------------------

The wraith walking in the garden has suddenly given me a brilliant idea. It will sound fantastic to you, but dont dismiss it out of hand – common sense always sounds fantastic at first. Why shouldn't I let you ¾ of Monk's House? After the war I would do what I've always wanted to do – convert all the attics into another room like my work room. I will live up there & I will let the rest of the house to you, except the outside bedroom. The

1. Duncan James Corrowr Grant (1885–1978), painter, spent his early years in Burma and India where his army father was posted. Thereafter, he was largely brought up by his father's sister, Lady Strachey. He was educated at St Paul's School, the Westminster School of Art and the Slade. In 1911 and 1912 he shared 38 Brunswick Square with Leonard Woolf, Virginia Stephen (as she then was) and her brother Adrian. In 1913 he founded the Omega Workshops with Roger Fry and Vanessa Bell, with whom he lived and painted after World War I. Their daughter, Angelica, was born on 25 December 1918. The committee was probably the War Artists' Advisory Committee which Grant had done some work for.

only thing we should have to share is the kitchen & bathroom until I got a second one in the attic. I would undertake to treat you like Dorothy Woodman if you required it, & when we met on the stairs, would only speak if spoken to. I would give you ½ the garden for your own (which will, I hope, show you what I think of you, if you haven't believed it before – for there's no one else in the world to whom I'd give a square yard of it) & when I saw you digging potatoes or planting eucryphias[1] on the other side of the imaginary fence, I would pass the time of day, as gardeners do, but not the boundary between our gardens unless specially invited. Why not? Of course, it would be heavenly for me for I should see you painting in the garden instead of the wraith & the oasis might even be bigger than the desert. But though I admit I'm terribly prejudiced, I think there is something to be said for it apart from this. You like the house & garden & the country & you know you can paint here. And it would be so odd & there is so much to be said for odd things. So dont dismiss my brilliant idea out of hand, dearest.

I think it is possible that you might be able to get Rodmell Place after the war – I'll tell you about it on Thursday. But I can thoroughly recommend Monk's House.

I'm sure you were right about the German man.

*Sunday morning*
　　THE BAN HAS BEEN LIFTED
Will you be able to come?


99:　Sunday 19 Sept [probably 1943]　　　　　　　　*25 Vic Sq*

Dearest Leonard – I am enclosing a copy of a letter I have written to Lehmann. I am greatly against the idea of printing them backed two & two together. It would really look wretched. Green arranged it with [John] Lehmann on Friday, after I had decided to redraw the seven which gave Green an opportunity to discuss the business of how they were to be bound in. As you know before that Lehmann hadn't really gone into it at all. I have two to do tomorrow & then the proof on Tuesday. I am so very glad I have redone them. I think I must have got them too heavy because I have been doing exclusively colour ones all these last months. They look much nicer now on the stone & I don't anticipate an unpleasant shock

1. A small, tender Australasian tree with white flowers.

when I have the proof. I have been painting all day – that is when I haven't been catching fleas on Rose. Isn't it awful. We are both appalled but the truth is she has heaps. I have caught about twenty I should think. It is my fault that they have multiplied so because I haven't been combing her regularly. Should I Keating's[1] her? She hasn't had the kind worm pill yet because her appetite is better and she says it was starved affection that was the matter, because of my bounding to Arnos Grove every day. This letter is very blotchy because I have a new bottle of ink. I am sorry that you addressed Messers Pounce & Havem's letter wrong. Their offices are of course at Old *Screw* Lane. You needn't think I didn't see that the Ban is Off. Shall I come next week end then in case they clap it on again instantly?

> Love from
> T.

100:   [Monday] 20 September 1943                              *Chiswick P[ress]*

I am thankful for your sake that I am not an adventuress. Really my dearest Mr Woolf have you *no* sense of self preservation? (I call you Mr Woolf because I am talking very gravely to you & want you to realize it, not because this is anything but a straight letter). Can't you see what you might let yourself in for if I was foolish or selfish enough to snatch ¾ of your house & ½ your garden? You imagine me being there & think it would be nice & you perhaps just admit a shadowy & surnameless Ian at times. Do you realize Mabel would walk on your lawn, & a whole collection of our liabilities roar around the place? So if it is (as it is) proof of affection to offer half a garden – believe me it is also proof of affection to refuse it. Besides I don't want half your garden. I want it all & you to bring me mutton pies. Have you thought I could never come & stay with you, because I think even such imaginative creatures as we are could hardly remove an imaginary fence & carefully taking all the food from the shelf that belonged to you & none from my shelf, say 'now this weekend you are staying with me'.

We read your admirable description of Denton together at breakfast this morning & felt we had almost seen the house. It sounds very nice but I believe the jumble of shoddy village right under its nose wouldn't do. It is extraordinarily good in you to go there & take so much trouble. This

1. A flea powder.

sounds very formal & distant, but I must thank you for it because it *is* good.

When shall I come, are you staying in town on Thursday night. Shall I come back with you or what? as the lady said in the bus.

Rose and I are in a fever. I caught 30 fleas on her yesterday. Gran[ville Coghlan] says I must put a powder called Pulvex on her. He will try & buy me some to-day.

Duncan [Grant] wanted to know Ian's name because Miss [Caroline Byng] Lucas[1] wants to come & see the Press & prints.

The supernatural is so terrifying to me that I got quite jumpy reading about that wraith.

Love T.

It is bad to waste a half sheet but I can't write more. Mr B[ishop, a printer] is already asleep on his stone & I must curl up on mine. P.T.O.

While I was asleep I thought of a story for you to write so can use this after all. Suppose I *did* take ¾ of your house & the amiable wraith still hung about the place but the real me turned absolutely hateful to you & made your life a burden so that though you were still penetrated by the amiable wraith you were annihilated by the beastly real one?

101:   [Monday] 20 September 1943                    *Monk's House*

Dearest tiger, I agree entirely about the printing. I don't think I had better interfere unless John gets his hackles up. Since the war or rather since the Press moved to Letchworth, I have left day to day management entirely to him, as I cant deal with it from here. But if the hackles go up & he says no, let me know at once, will you?[2]

1. 'Mouie' and her sister, Mrs Frances Byng Stamper ('Bay'), had opened what came to be called Miller's Gallery in Lewes in July 1941. Lectures, exhibitions and concerts were held there and Caroline Lucas, herself a sculptor, got Vanessa Bell and Duncan Grant to start a (short-lived) art school. Now she wanted to learn about lithography. She soon installed a press and had Bell and Grant working on it. In January 1945 she and her sister published a volume of lithographs printed in the studio, and in May 1946 put on an Omega Workshops exhibition.
2. TR's printing problems further strained LW's relations with Lehmann, who wrote in *I Am My Brother* that his disagreements with LW were becoming 'more frequent and more difficult to resolve'. In October he wrote LW: 'I frankly despair for the future.' Their Hogarth partnership ended (ostensibly over whether to expand the press) in January 1946 when, on the 24th, Lehmann sent LW a letter invoking Clause 15 of their agreement. This allowed LW three weeks to buy him out; if LW did not, then Lehmann would have the right to buy LW's share of the press. In two days LW had arranged with Ian Parsons for Chatto & Windus to take Lehmann's shares, and for the Hogarth Press to retain its independence under his own editorial guidance.

How on earth did you see that the Ban is Off? You must have contracted a secret vice of listening surreptitiously to the wireless or looking at newspapers. Shall you come next week end, then? The answer is *Yes*. But I hope it does not mean a very skimpy week end. The weather has turned utterly beastly today.

Keating's is quite effective, but I don't much like it, partly because if it gets on my skin it gives me a rash.[1] The best flea killing powder I've struck for dogs is Pulvex & it would do for cats I should think. I will leave a tin at 25 V.S. tomorrow evening when I come up – in the basement, as you'll be at the Press. I have one or two.

I shall see you Thursday, dearest – I suppose you couldn't come back with me here that evening? Love from your
     L.


102:   [Monday] 27 September 1943        *37 Mecklenburgh Square*

You are so adorable, dearest, & so extraordinarily good to me that in the misery at parting with you I forgot (a) your canvas (b) my spectacles. I am so sorry about (a), but I hope you took it yourself out of the major filth-packet of that room. The lack of (b) allowed me to dream about you all the way from Lewes to London. In my dream I had another 'brilliant' idea – will it bring another grave letter from you? It is this. I will sell you the whole of Monk's House & garden, the important terms being these:

1.  The vendor (L) undertakes to buy another house in Northumberland or elsewhere to be approved by the purchaser (T)

2.  The purchaser (T) undertakes to stay with the vendor (L) in the new house whenever she wants to & can, & in any case *not less than* 3 months & 2 weeks in any calendar year, the period being divided as follows: (a) A continuous visit of 3 months or two visits of 2 months & 1 month (b) Two visits of 1 week.

3.  The vendor (L) undertakes to provide the purchaser (T) during such visits with an electrically heated mattress & not fewer than 3 full sized hot water bottles completely covered in good flannel the colour of which is to be chosen by her.

I suppose the remainder of the week is desert (though I won't complain after the most perfect oasis). I think I shall go back tomorrow though I

1. Along with a familial tremor of his hands, in adulthood LW suffered from intermittent rashes and skin eruptions. Doctors tried treatments of tar, paraffin, ointments, solutions, tinctures, vitamins and antihistamines, with varying success.

have the most annoying things which will bring me up Wednesday & Thursday. I am doubtful about next week. I know I shall be up on Thursday morning Oct 7. Would it be possible for me to come to a girl's lunch that day & perhaps snoop another gallery? Or I would come to a girl's lunch or dinner any day that week. I love you, dearest, & repeat it, at the risk of boring you, for the pleasure it gives me to write it.

> Your devoted L.

103:    [Thursday] 30 September [1943]                    *Chiswick Press*

My Dearest Leonard. I wanted to write to you yesterday – but the day filled itself up with endless jobs. Mary Ann is away with her Autumn throat. Poor thing I think it is a Quinsy. It wasn't only jobs. I finished the picture (on the huge canvas) that I was doing in the fig tree garden. It was horrid after you had left for your train. I worked all the time but didn't like it.

I shan't let you go to Northumberland – the whole point about going to such places is that you would sever all connection with London & so you would have to sever me & I won't have it. When I think how often I would like to see Fuzzels & how seldom I do, I doubt if even that electric mattress would be certain of getting me to your peak far from the world in distant lands. I must go on with this jacket.[1] This is no letter at all & its dirty too.

> Love T.

Will you have huge quantities of apples sent to London with your furniture, on a strictly business footing? I went to see Mr Viney[2] & perhaps may get another lithographic job through him, I am to see another man who is away for a fortnight. Perhaps in the end I shall be rich & famous.

104:    [Thursday] 30 September 1943                      *Monk's House*

I had had the secret hope, dearest of tigers, of a 2 minute oasis this morning on my way from Victoria to the New Statesman Board meeting. But at the last minute they rang up to say that the meeting had had to be

1. For *The Three Rings*.
2. Oscar Vaughan Viney (1886–1976), master printer, of Hazell, Watson & Viney, printers, Aylesbury.

postponed until next Thursday, & though I would go to Durban to see you for 2 minutes certainly, I hadn't the courage to go to London for the mere possibility of seeing you for 2 minutes. Now next Thursday is full, but if you are free any time Wed. let me know as I have nothing that day.

I did not after all go up yesterday either, as the same thing happened – they rang me up at the last minute to say that Kingsley's libel case had been postponed & I should not be wanted to edit.[1]

There are rumours here that the ban will be reimposed next week or even this Saturday. Did you go to the Chief Constable on Tuesday?

Hsiao Ch'ien,[2] the Chinese, is coming for the week-end – the thought of it rather depresses me.

Next time you come here, tiger dearest, you must be your own enchanting self at first, but in the last 24 hours must deliberately turn nasty. I cant imagine how you'll manage it, but you might grumble at the eternal pie, nag me, paint your finger nails, & eat like Kingsley. Then perhaps I should not miss you quite so much when I returned from London & found you not here. Even so I doubt it. You need not be afraid of ghosts – they are not terrifying but irritating – at any rate when they are the thin blooded wraith of the one living person whom one wants to see.

This is Nancy's third. Ought I to reply
> Dear Mrs Nolan,
> I dont want you to write
> Yours sincerely
> Leonard Woolf[3]

---

1. LW edited the *New Statesman* for short periods when Kingsley Martin was away, for 8 weeks in all, in 1943. He had been on the Board from 1931, when it amalgamated with the *Nation*, of which he was literary editor (1923–30). The libel charge had been brought against the paper, its printer and Kingsley Martin by Captain Bernard Ackworth RN, who claimed that certain words in an article published on 25 April 1942 made him look 'an incompetent naval strategist and disloyal'. The paper's counsel argued that expressions of opinion were fair comment and not defamatory; Ackworth won £300 and costs.

2. Chinese journalist Hsiao Ch'ien (b. 1910) had known Julian Bell (1908–1935) in China in 1935. He came to England in 1939 at the invitation of the Chinese Department of SOAS. Dorothy Woodman and Kingsley Martin arranged for him to lecture for the China Campaign Committee, and he sent dispatches to his paper *Dagongbao* (*Ta Kung Pao*). In 1942 he studied the work of E. M. Forster, D. H. Lawrence and Virginia Woolf with Dr George (Dadie) Rylands at Cambridge, and in 1944 established an office for his paper in Fleet Street. Soon after, *Dagongbao* sent him to the Continent, then back to China to head its literature supplement.

3. Nancy Nolan began this third letter with a timid belligerence reminiscent of Abraham arguing with God over Sodom and Gomorrah: 'It was so pleasant to hear from you again that I am emboldened to write yet a third time.'

I am haunted not only by you, but by the C# minor quartet
Did your painting here go well?
Goodbye, dearest – ever your
    L.
I have two tickets for Margerie Few's concert on Tuesday, Oct 12 at 6.15
Wigmore Hall. I hope you'll come.


105: Friday 1 October [1943]       *25 Vic Sq.*

Dearest Leonard. I have scrubbed the kitchen the bath room & two
lavatories, we cannot blink the fact that I am in some ways a good woman. I
am now on my way, nearly, to the Chiswick P to do the other stone of the
jacket. My dear Chiswick P has sold itself to Eyre & Spottiswoode. I am so
sad about it. Ian says Douglas Gerald [sic][1] is not nice at all. What will
become of all those old men I wonder. Until the war is over they will leave it
as it is I suppose. Mr Bishop has been with the firm 48 years & there is one
who has been longer. And most of the men are over 60 I should think. I don't
trust the directors of the Chiswick P to have done well by them, they aren't
I think very good to their employees at least not in the way of pensions.

 I must go. Wednesday will be quite all right. Will you come to a girl's
lunch on the clean mat & won't you have dinner here too. I won't cook a
grand one, & Ian is apt to be home by eight now. *If* we came to Lewes on
Tuesday & went to snoop around the outside of Rodmell Place would
you like us to come & say hullow to you or not? The only cure for Nancy
[Nolan] is for us to go to Ireland. I can't guarantee to be horrid after three
days at Monk's House. It makes me more than unusually nice you see – I
suppose I could gobble my food.

 Has Percy given notice, I picked myself some parsley?
  Love T.


106: [Saturday] 2 October 1943      *Monk's House*

Dearest of Creatures, Your two letters by one post gave me more than
double pleasure. I daresay you will think me more than usually idiotic if I
confess that I had got it into my head that I *might* have annoyed you.

1. Douglas Jerrold (1893–1964), author and publisher, was managing director of Eyre &
Spottiswoode.

*I* should be annoyed – & very much so – if you & Ian (or Mabel or any roaring liability even) came to or near Rodmell without walking on my lawn.

I mean to have apples & onions sent up with the furniture. Dont you think you might be sufficiently an adventuress not to insist upon paying me for what comes out of what I should like to be your garden? I always knew (& said) you were a good woman.

White will not say when he is going to begin painting. I think I shall move in & let him paint with the furniture there.

I will come to lunch on the clean mat Wed. unless it breaks into your work when the time comes. Wouldn't it be a bore for you & Ian if I returned for dinner?

I wont go to Northumberland if it means severing you. But I thought it might be just worth while to sever you for 8½ months if I had you to myself for 3½. But like my compatriot, I should require it to be 'nominated in the bond'.

It is horrible about the Chiswick P. I have the greatest suspicion of E[yre] & S[pottiswoode]. It is the usual thing – big business everywhere swallowing & destroying any decent thing. They will probably sack right & left. If I belonged to the working classes, I should be a bloody revolutionary.

Dearest tiger, I do hope I shall see you here Tuesday, though it will be very strange your not being alone. And now for Hsiao Ch'ien who arrives by the next bus.

      Love from your devoted
      L.


107:   [Friday] 8 October 1943        *Monk's House*

My dearest of tigers, I have so much to say to you, but I will try not to, partly because I don't want to become a Nancy letter writer & partly because I simply must work tonight. So I will be business-like with (1), (2), (3) . . .

(1)  The agent sent me the enclosed this morning so I rang him up & went to see it this afternoon. Kingston – the old village – would have been ideal & I knew there were some very nice houses & cottages there. This is quite a nice cottage, but not good enough, I think. The rooms are none of them big & there are only five – what could you do with your liabilities? It is on the village street. The garden is a rectangle with a

pleasant little lawn & flower garden petering out into a few apple trees & vegetables. Mabel, when she stayed with you, would have to use a W.C. in the garden which seems to me contra naturam. I suppose one could build her one inside. The garden on one side is flanked by a building which is part of the premises of the village shop. I'm afraid I think it is again No.

(2) T. Ritchie Esq (I suppose he was christened Tiger Ritchie?) wrote & offered £5.5.0 for the watercolour. Is that mean? I felt I simply could not give £8.8.0 for that, when you had first insisted on £10 for your picture. If they accept, as they almost certainly will, would you mind sending them a cheque & let me pay you back? If I pay, they might just possibly find out & I feel she would not then be so likely be encouraged into sanity.

(3) Dearest, your letter was an infinitely greater reward than my offer to be your housemaid deserved. I yield to no man in what I can say & have said about your eyes. But I'm one of the few people of plain, prosaic common sense who knows what things are really pleasant (& what not). And I know I should get much more pleasure cleaning your grate from 10.10 to 11.10 than being Secretary to the Labour Party Advisory Committee on Imperial Questions or acting Chairman of Board of Directors of the Statesman & Nation Publishing Co., Ltd., which is what the rest of the day is devoted to. After all, if I were your acting housemaid I daresay you would look in once during the morning to see whether I was doing my work & you might leave me a pot of tea & a bun on a tray as you do for Mrs Whatshername. Also at your next Saturday dinner with Mabel you could tell her that you've got a new housemaid, a perfect treasure, the only thing against her being that sometimes, instead of doing her work, she sits in an armchair smoking (a pipe – I should omit this) & looking at your pictures. If you want a kitchen maid to help whenever you have someone to dinner, & the wages are an enormous kiss & any remains of the dinner to take home, I apply for it too as a permanent job.

The truth is that if we live side by side until 1980 in V.S., you will still underestimate your own value & my love of it. Provided that I can still get down on my hands & knees & up again, I shall still want to clean your grate & say things about your eyes. For I shall still be your devoted

L.

108:   [Friday] 8 October 1943                    *Monk's House*

This came this morning, my dearest of tigers. Is it worth pursuing –
asking whether it is obtainable post war? I doubt it as in any case it is in
Halland again.

    I bought you the last tube of flake white in Lewes today & that only a
small one, but they 'expect' some more. You must come & use it. I also
bought 5 Midgets which I have never really seen before. I do like them. If
you had known me then, would you have made me sit for the infant
Jesus?[1] I hope I look like him.

    I do wish I had been allowed to do your grate. The amount of drudgery
you do rather horrifies me. I don't mind a little housework, though I find
it rather jarring to have to do it immediately before even the diary writing
which I do. I cant imagine how you can go straight from it to your
painting. But I expect if I live to a 100 next door to you in V.S. you will
still surprise me by having all the gifts & all the charms, ending in being
the best of women & a perfect cook. Is it surprising that I love you? I shall
begin living next door on the 20th.

        Ever your
        L.


109:   [Friday] 8 October 1943                         *Vic Sq*

O my dearest Leonard. I gave you an enormous kiss in the kitchen last
night when I went in there to prepare Harold's[2] dinner. I thought of you
standing there the night before & of how much I preferred having you to
dinner to Harold. I thought it even more when he went. He talked in an
even measured voice never getting louder never getting quicker from 10
o'clock until a quarter to twelve. I don't mean he didn't talk from 8 to 10

1. For *The Birth of Jesus* Midget Book.
2. Harold Raymond OBE (1887–1975) was IMP's partner at Chatto & Windus. He was a partner in the
firm 1919–53 and chairman in 1953–4. He and Charles Prentice, whom IMP had succeeded as
typographer, acquired an unrivalled list of authors in the twenties; in 1926 he invented the Book
Tokens scheme. When Prentice retired (1934), John McDougall replaced him and with IMP and
Harold Raymond guided the firm's re-entry into journal publishing. In 1935 they launched the
successful *Geographical Magazine*, edited by Michael Huxley, and in July 1937 the brilliant weekly
*Night and Day*, which was closed down after six months when eight-year-old Shirley Temple sued for
libel over Graham Greene's review of *Wee Willie Winkie*. After the war McDougall went to Chapman
& Hall and the partnership was reformed to include Norah Smallwood and Raymond's son Piers, who
moved to Methuen in 1960. Harold Raymond retired in 1956. His wife was Vera Everett.

but we talked a little then too, afterwards we were like oysters on rocks. When he went I stood on the girl's mat & stamped & screamed & even Ian screamed a bit.

I went and had my blood counted in the afternoon & think Tooths [Gallery] must have been in the gap, because I couldn't see it going down Bond Street in the bus. I told the Blood man that you didn't believe a word of it & he was very scornful & took me into his laboratory to see how he did it & it is quite easy to do. They mix that exact measure of your blood with that exact measure of salt & water, then they shake it up & put a drop on a slide with a tiny trough in it & a minute square ☐ that size engraved in the trough & the square is divided into 200 small squares. They put it under the microscope & count the dots of blood in the squares and multiply by the amount they had diluted your blood with water & that is it. He said the proof was that if I had mine done at any other good clinic the answer would be the same to within a very small number of corpuscles.

What am I to do about the enclosed. I didn't ring up because I didn't know if that was right? Fisher's wife is scouring your house. I gave her a bottle of ammonia, a cake of soap, my brush & pail so you are fearfully in my debt.

Your offer to do my housework touched me much more than your offer to come to Durban for 2 minutes. No man has ever offered to do my housework before in spite of the things he may 'have said about my eyes'. So thank you dear Leonard. It will be lovely this weekend I think at Rodmell. The light is coming very softly this morning 'wrapped in tissue paper'.

Love T.


110:   [Saturday] 9 October [1943]                    *Vic Sq.*

Dearest Leonard. The electric man came to join you in holy matrimony to the service, this morning at 8.30. But though he was all prepared for the ceremony & very neat in a dark suit he could not after all carry the service through. There was no wire from the main to you. You will see that this was a very vital part of the business. The neat man of course wasn't the sort that puts wires there. He only joins them when they are there. I asked who *did* put them there & he said the contractors. So the long & the short of it is that White promises to put them there on Monday. I gather that though essential they are slight.

I have been standing upside down pouring jugs of water over my hair, perhaps for the last time for I shall start to use your elegant hose at once.

Would it be making too bold to ask you to bring me a lily on Tuesday? It does not need an immense stem & will not matter desperately if it is rather over. I have one in the painting of the window & would like to have another look, mine is now only a stem. Yesterday & to-day were very nice. I didn't go out of the house except as far as a loaf of bread & have been working all the time. As well as washing mine I have combed Rose's hair so we are both soft & beautiful.

     love T.

111:    Sunday morning [10 October 1943]         *[Monk's House]*

1) Shall I be an adventurer if I dont offer to pay for the ammonia? Because I shant & only thank you. It looks as if I shall only be allowed to add to your drudgery.

2) O my dearest why why aren't you here this morning? I never wanted you more. The softest & gentlest of October suns, & when I went out to feed the fish I became entranced watching a humming bird hawk moth methodically dipping his long nose into one flower after the other of that blue Salvia. I watched him for ever so long (with your wraith, of course, watching too) & five minutes later he was still there. It is incredible that wings should be able to go at that pace without a pause for so long.

     L.

112:   [Thursday] 14 October 1943         *Monk's House*

Dearest of creatures, I have no excuse for writing to you except my desire to do so. The phantom tiger has so interwoven herself into my everyday life & thoughts that every now & then I feel I must sit & talk to my tiger, the real one, & as I cant I boil over – like all my saucepans – into a letter.

When I got back here, I looked at my diary of last year. It was Oct 20, 1942, that you dined at the Wellington & came back for the first time to M.S. It is right, I think, that it will be on Oct 20, 1943 that I come to V.S. It is true, as you said on Wednesday, that it seems only the other day – in some ways only, in others to me it is almost a lifetime away. For you have changed life for me completely from a kind of dingy resignation to the most extraordinary happiness whenever I see you or think of you. Oct 20, 1942, was for me the turning point. I remember exactly the impression you made on me in Feb. the first time I came to tea. Your beauty & the beauty of your room & pictures, & your mind & moods appealed enormously to me, but I felt too that you were aloof from me in another world & that I had nothing to offer you. But you haunted me, for some reason particularly in connection with the flowers here & garden, & that, I suppose, was what made me suddenly lay freesias on your doorstep – a thing I had never thought of doing to anyone else. Then I dined with you and Ian in July and then one day in August I had an irresistible desire to see you & came to V.S. between tea and dinner. I was still more haunted after that, but still looked on you as someone infinitely far away from me & above me in a world in which you would think I had no part. So it was with considerable nervousness for I knew you even then to be a gentle tiger, but very much a tiger – that I asked you to come to the Wellington. And when we walked to Russell Sq for your train home, I knew that it wasn't simply your beauty & charm which attracted me, but that hard kernel, the sinews of your heart & mind, and that there was nothing I couldn't say to you, that I could go on talking to you forever, & that perhaps some day you might come to Monk's House. So Oct 20, 1942, means a lot in my memory. I have some other memories of the intervening year which amuse me now. Usually I think when one is in love with someone, especially when one sees her for short periods at long intervals, one's imagination outruns reality & one expects too much so that meeting is not quite as good as one expected. Sitting in bus No. 11 coming to see you, I used to say to myself that I must be absurd, that you couldn't be as beautiful & adorable as I had imagined you in the past week or fortnight. But you always proved me wrong (or is it right?). At any rate the real tiger is & always had been, whenever I see her, more beautiful, more adorable, more tigerish than the imaginary. Now when I come down Victoria St in my No. 11, as I did on Wed., I know that I'm not absurd and that, when you open the door, I shall find reality once more infinitely better than what I could imagine it.

I think that that is why I never say the things or ask you the questions, when I see you, which I meant to say or ask. The real tiger carries me away into an entirely new world in which I forget everything which seemed to matter before the door opened. As soon as the door shut on Wednesday, I remembered all the things I had meant to ask you – not that they did matter, for it is true that the only things which matter are you & your world.

Good night, my dearest, I shall see you in the real world on Monday.
     Love from your
          L.


113:   [Saturday] 30 October 1943                    *Monk's House*

Dearest (I suppose I mustn't say & most beautiful) of creatures, I think
these two cuttings may please you. The second[1] is from a magazine of the
Association of Girls' Clubs. I am not a subscriber – they sent it to me
because they wanted permission to quote Virginia.

Rodmell is again full of troops who come & ask for apples. This
afternoon, helped by your wraith, I planted a Eucryphia & a white
fuchsia. But life leaves one little peace. My sister rang up this morning to
say she was in Brighton & could she come over for the afternoon – she left
at 7. Then I discovered that Ann [Stephen], husband, & child now
propose to arrive here tomorrow (not tomorrow week) & stay 'as long as
you can have us'. I am very fond of Ann, but – but there is only one
person whom I really & always want to see on my Rodmell lawn & that
is Mabel's daughter-in-law. (I do hope that took you in).

The real excuse for this letter is the enclosed. I saw a house advertised
'3 miles from Lewes' & wrote for particulars. They sent me this & I have
arranged to go over & see it tomorrow afternoon. It might well be worth
your while to see it on Tuesday – three people were going over it today.
It is in a very good position on a narrow road running round Caburn – it
*might* be lovely. I am afraid I will not be able to let you know what it looks
like before your Tuesday post.

I have tried to keep this letter severely practical. I began it nervously
lest I should seem to you absurd & romantic. I don't think I'm really
romantic, though if I am about you, I have a good excuse. It is not
romantic, though it may be dangerous, to love anyone like you as much
as I love you. It is romantic to love someone passionately who isn't worth
a passion – it's dangerous to love passionately someone worth a passion –
& the more worth the more dangerous. If ever anyone was worth a
passion, dearest, it's you. Sometimes when I leave you, a – I daresay
unreasonable – terror comes over me, that I shall weary, bore, annoy you
& that next time I see you I shall find that you cant tolerate me. I don't
really know why you should, particularly the appalling insistence &

---

1. The first was of 'bosoms' (see letter 117).

persistence which I know I possess & cannot control, which is due to some horrible fire in my entrails & must be a weariness of flesh & mind to other people. I had hoped that age would put it out but I dont really think it does. It makes things obsess me. But only once before in my life has it made a person obsess me. And it's because you are in every way so worthy an obsession & passion, that my terrors are not unreasonable.

I should like to write you another four pages on the subject of female beauty, but I feel I had better not, if I dont want to weary you. But I may say this, mayn't I?, that your self portraits show that even a painter has no idea of what she herself really looks like. I could give good reasons for this which are not invalidated by the hairdresser's mirror.

Your other pictures gave me extraordinary pleasure.

If I love you, dearest of tigers, it is because you are so lovable, so that if I weary you, you must forgive me, since the Prime Cause is you.

Your devoted L.

I am beginning to enjoy Don Quixote. I like 'damsels there were in times past that at the end of fourscore years old, all which time they never slept one day under a roof, went as entire & pure maidens to their graves as the very mother that bore them.'


114:    [Saturday] 30 October 1943                    *25 Victoria Square*

My dearest Leonard

I am still writing letters in a city garden. The crysanthemums [sic] have hung their leaves a little, I ought to have watered them last night perhaps? I have now & I am holding their hands from time to time and do hope they will stiffen up. I was ashamed last night when I saw all you had given me & think perhaps I am an adventuress after all. After Mary had gone & I had painted on until the light went, I went downstairs & cleaned the downstairs bath room & then laid out the apples & hung up the onions. It looked so lovely I nearly fetched the crysanthemums and sat there. I went into 24 to get my cleaning stuff & after I had gone to bed I suddenly thought I'd left the key in the door so I rushed down stairs but it was safely in the hall drawer.

I enclose you the P.S. from the African Aunt's[1] last letter – the flowers she is talking about are the same family as the Stapelias.

1. Mary (Faanie) Ritchie (1869–1962) was a leader in the teaching of Nature Studies in Natal and author of *The Drama of the Year in South Africa* (1915), a book for children which served as a model for TR's 1949 Nature Study text, *Come and See*. She had often sent LW South African seeds, at

I shall be so glad when the last moving is over for you next week. It is so horrid. I thought you seemed rather miserable yesterday. I am sure such upheavals increase the desert feeling because it is the ordinary continuity of days that prevents it, and when you are properly settled I believe it will go altogether. I do really think it will Leonard dear. I am thinking a lot about the painting and am longing to start on it. I wish there weren't three dark months ahead.

I shall see you on Thursday morning & you must come to a meal that night too please.

Love T.

I think this must be the dullest letter I ever wrote you. I'm glad I've got Faan's nice P.S. to enclose.

115: [Sunday] 31 October 1943                                    *Monk's House*

My Dearest tiger, I think you probably should take a look at the house on Tuesday. I have arranged with Lady Forbes – a dear old creature – that you may come & see it if you want to. I don't much like the house or the rooms either, though I think you could do a good deal with them. But the position & view from every room, almost, and from everywhere in the garden are magnificent. And there is nothing you could not do with the garden. There are 3 superb greenhouses & a vine loaded with grapes. It is well worth considering, I think. I have just got back. I got so friendly with her & him, a retired Civil Servant, that I was there for nearly an hour & a half. If you go on Tuesday, the best way to get there would be to take the Eastbourne bus & get off at the top of the hill which leads down to the Beddingham level crossing – then walk by the road which branches left along Caburn to Glynde. The house is on the right – stucco & tiles – about ½ mile before you reach Glynde. I dont think you can walk on Caburn now – otherwise that would have been the best way.

I may be wrong about the house & it may be better than I thought. It isn't the kind of house which I like but one could live in it & you would make the rooms yours.

---

first through Alice Ritchie. She retired to Britain in 1947 and lived with the Parsons, regularly accompanying TR to Monk's House. She and LW shared colonial interests and experience, extensive botanical knowledge, and love for TR. Her PS is not in the Archive. Stapelia is a genus of cactus-like plants of the milkweed family, which contains more than a hundred species. In March 1945 TR and LW published 'The History of the Strange Stapelia' in the *Geographical Magazine*.

Goodbye my dearest.
   Your
    L.


116: [Monday] 1 November 1943       *Monk's House*

My dearest, You are an angel to me. Your letter was the opposite of dull: by bringing you into the room it seemed instantly to sweep away the clouds & cobwebs that menaced the breakfast table – rain, a grim grey day outside, the responsibility of two guests for six days, a baby who never cried but was unaccountably crying, the background of food problems & mutton pies which for some reason are for the first time in history non-existent in Monk's House. I felt ashamed of the letter I wrote you on Saturday night. I am not miserable when I get a letter from you & feel you have a glimmer of affection for me & that my 'terrors' are unreasonable. As for moves, guests, food, & rain – they dont really trouble me except on the thinnest surface.

If you are an adventuress, you are an inefficient one. All you get is a few onions & apples after missing your chance of getting ¾ of a house & ½ a garden. I doubt whether you'll ever learn to be an efficient adventuress.

What a nice P.S. from your aunt.

Goodbye, dearest of creatures – I end as I began that you are an angel to me.
   Your
    L.


117: [Monday] 1 November 1943      *25 Victoria Square*

Dearest Leonard. Is it so bad then to be called romantic? I only called you it anyway as a tit for tat because you said I had a fickle heart, which I don't really think I have at all. So you need not fear that I will have ceased to tolerate you next time I see you as you must know I have a quite major affection for you.

I do hope we shall go to see the house to-morrow, but Ian is working late to-night so I haven't been able to tell him about it yet. It sounds very well worth a visit. I had Irene [Hawkins] to sit this morning, & got on well. I took a canvas to Mr Drown to varnish to-day and he will have it done by the end of the week.

I got out Gilbert White's journals from the London. I had not looked at them before. They are edited by a maddening man who keeps on explaining that G.W. wasn't lazy & calls him 'the gentle old naturalist'.[1] I liked both the cuttings you sent particularly the bosoms. I think I shall buy mine a black lace brassiere. Ian must work late on Thursday so if you decide to have dinner with us it would be just with me.

      Love T.

118:    [Thursday] 18 November 1943          *Monk's House*

My Dearest of creatures, It was wretched having to leave you. But I am sure you will be all right if you stay in bed for the week. And lie like a log. You are too full of life for a patient. So dont sit up in bed like a Jack-in-the-box whenever you think of something – which is what you do. Otherwise you are a perfect patient.

    The bitch is being sent direct from Scotland with *her* name on the label. She will probably not arrive until Sat.

    I can just catch the post, but I felt I must tell you that I love you though I think you know it & that it is a twilight world without you.

      Your
      L.

119:    Friday afternoon 19 November 1943 [postcard]       *London*

Dearest L. I am in 3 Wilbraham Pl[ace, SW3] it is a good big room but sideways so I don't see much sky. & I don't feel that I am in a gold fish tank either. Mabel has been to see me. She came instantly. I had barely got into bed. She was very kind, saw no reason in my being here. I should have come to her, *she* would have nursed me – etc. I am going to have a slightly tricky time not going there when I get out of here. I think I feel a bit better to day but was very low yesterday and raved to Ian last night against all so that he said most pathetically *Please* eat don't turn on all. He hoped he hadn't been unresponsive about our abortive revolution – but said, I think truly, that I would never forget the three flights of stairs between me & the kitchen.

    Irene came to pack & said she would be perfectly prepared to take me

---

1. Walter Johnson FGS edited the 1931 edition of White's *Naturalist's Journal*, hitherto in manuscript since 1793.

on with you. So out I come in a week willy nilly.[1] This is a card because I couldn't get envelopes on the way here. I do look forward to seeing you.

Love T.

I will try & be a log.

120:   [Saturday] 20 November 1943                    *Monk's House*

Dearest of tigers, I have just fetched Flip as she is christened – but I think I may call her Merle – from Lewes, & she is sitting by my side watching Peat – who growls incessantly from a chair. I think she will be a perfect dog; she follows beautifully already & settles down quietly at one's feet in a bus. She is beautiful, Sally's colours, one eye brown & the other half blue & half brown.

I do hope you are better & fairly happy & the place not too bad. I shall come about there on Monday – how I look forward to it, my dearest. It is so cold here that I can scarcely write. Again I can just catch the post.

Thank you for Merle.

Love from your devoted
L.

121:   Saturday [20 November 1943]

Dearest Leonard.

I was just about to start this letter when you rang up. And now as I have told you about the bump on my neck I can't think what else to write about. *How* Ethyl Smyth[2] runs on. I get a very good idea of her & it entirely corresponds with the one you gave me. As for the Duties of Women (which has one of the prettiest title pages I've seen) I'm not right in a single particular. Except perhaps that I don't show great vanity in dress & house hold display. Chiefly I fail I think in not trying to make Mary Ann & Ian better Christians. Did you know that young ladies were dangled from their chins to make their necks longer? He didn't think this a good

---

1. TR was on the verge of pernicious anaemia (a vitamin B12 deficiency) and had been ill in varying degrees for several months before going to the Wilbraham Place nursing home. LW took her back to Victoria Square on 3 December. Irene Hawkins was going to share her domestic help with TR and LW, but this became impossible.

2. Dame Ethyl Smyth (1858–1944), composer, author and feminist, was one of VW's most intimate and demanding friends. She was not one of LW's favourites.

plan. It is astonishing how long he takes to say anything. He could make my lecture[1] into a book quite easily.

It is perfectly maddening but Irene's woman now says her husband says she is doing enough & mustn't come to you. Mabel is trying her source. I am told I must try & get a better daily for myself so as to do less – How I shall do so I can't imagine, because the only ones allowed must be ancient or have young. The operation on the other side of the partition has been very quiet all day. I hope she will keep it up through the night. It is curious how nurses always seem to wear iron shoes. Perhaps they wear horse shoes for luck. They are very superstitious. I look forward to Tuesday.

      Love T.


122:   [Thursday] 2 December 1943          *Monk's House*

Dearest of creatures, You must, I know, be sick of being asked how you are, & I don't want to bother you, but if it wouldn't, I should like you to send me just a card on Sunday to say how it had been. When I'm not with you, I think of you so much & continually that I'm sure you would tell me sternly that it is *wrong* & *silly*. But I cant help it – which must be even *wronger*. O Lord, how difficult it is to be good.

You gave me more pleasure than you know in letting me fetch you this morning from that gilded & gothic prison – & to see you again in V.S. If I hadn't loved you before, you would have made me by the way you have stood the last two weeks with a sweetness which I shouldn't have thought possible. I don't think you've anything to learn from Mr Gisborne.

It was absolutely lovely between Redhill & Lewes, sky, clouds & sun, but then suddenly turned to rain & wind.

Merle is always tremendously admired in railway carriages which is bad for her character & rather annoys me.

I forgot to tell you that Louie told me that in the winter she finds that milk will go solidly sour if she puts it in a really warm place e.g. over an oil stove. Wouldn't yours do so if you kept it on the gas heater? Louie & all her family have flu.

Good night, my dearest, dearest tiger. How I look forward to Thursday, wrong or right.

      Ever your
        L.

1. TR was going to give a talk to the Rodmell Labour Party on the duties of women. She may have been reading *An Inquiry Into the Duties of the Female Sex* (1797) by Thomas Gisborne the Elder. This would identify Mr. Gisborne in letter 122.

123:   [Sunday] 5 December [1943]                    *25 Vic Sq.*

Dearest Leonard,

This is just to tell you that I am much better. It is very nice indeed to be back home. All yesterday Rose lay on my bed in a drowsy ecstasy, whenever I moved or spoke to her she at once broke into her high quavering purr, and when Atkinson stethascoped me she even did it in response to my deep breathing so that I thought he might imagine it was coming out of my chest. He said I was better but until Monday must stay in bed until six. Irene is very sweet & does everything in the least fussy way, & also gets on with her work.

My fuchsia cuttings have green fly how *can* they have?

I have gently straightened out John's orchid with my fingers & now I have a tissue paper orchid – the shape quite perfect.

Nellie Neale Margery's ex-help is coming to see me on Monday so I am very hopeful that she may 'consider' us. It will be very hard to tell Mary Ann. If N. Neale will consider us perhaps she will consider you too.
    Love
      T.


124:   [Thursday] 16 December 1943 [left in 24 Victoria Square]

Dearest Leonard.

Thinking about you after you had left I thought (and I hope you will see what a crashing compliment this is) how very like Fuzzles you are. You are the only two people I have ever known who are entirely unselfindulgent. And who shape your lives down to the smallest detail according to your not at all ordinary convictions. The almost equally astonishing thing is that I have managed to stake a claim in both of you. It is curious that while Fuzzells has shaped her life on God & you have done the opposite you should end by being in many & in such important ways the same.

When I come back I shall force you to work down here. I have been as warm as a pie all morning & it is nonsense for you not to be so until evening. What a change Gotham [the Coghlan's farm] will be. I am attached to them all and I disagree on almost all ideas.

I think we should go & visit Fuzzels in April? I leave you this not very reluctantly as I had it in the spring so it is gone. I have no idea where to put in any stops.
    Love T.

125:    Tuesday 21 December 1943        *Gotham [Farm, near Cooden]*

Needless to say I entirely disagree with your ingenious theory of reflections. You are much too positive to be that.

Dearest Leonard.

I could hardly hear you last night. I was ringing up in the pitch dark in the dairy because the house telephone is out of order, it wasn't the dark that made me deaf, the receiver crackled like a machine gun all the time. We have been lucky in having only one dreary day & by lunch time it had cleared & we had a good walk in the marsh under a beautiful mussel shell coloured sky. While you battered your way back in pouring rain & dark so did we from the Dr where we had gone to get my liver pushed in. I was tired by the time we got home but no worse for it.

We had a wonderful day yesterday when the landscape looked simply heavenly. We walked all over & around the village of Hooe. A particularly good one with some very lovely old farm houses. One especially good one we wove a fantasy life about. We asked who owned it and were told 'Miss Sparks'. As we could see a man through the window we thought we might put a note through the door saying 'Sell us your house or we will expose your shameful maison'. We have since heard that there is a Mr Sparks so will have to think of something else. The village lies along a ridge with a full cup horizon all around & soft ups & downs between.

I am going to give a cabbage leaf to the bull. He is in a small shed & quite friendly & will accept cabbage leaves & likes his nose to be scratched. I would not like to be a bull. I would rather be a cow & have a calf every year until I was beef. There are four calves very sweet with tear stained faces. One had huge tears splashing out of its eyes while I watched it yesterday – I suppose it was the cold & not grief but it was very touching.

We went into Bexhill because Ian had a hole in a tooth. It is desolate – more than half the shops boarded up & very few people. The emptiness & down at heel look show up more than ever the appalling hideousness of the buildings. There can be no uglier anywhere – even in Polegate.

I have just heard from Nellie this morning. What heart beats I have had waiting for the post every day. She will come & all is well. Nothing is explained. I think there has been a letter astray from what she says.

Thank you for the tip about portraits, I shall have to make a new start on the one of you – how do you fancy to be done? It will cost you more of course than being done 'straight'.

Fuzzels has sent me two pale pink wool vests. I shall never be cold again & will always be barrel shaped.

Love T.


126:    [Friday] Christmas Eve 1943                    *Monk's House*

Dearest, What a fool I am! I left the key of your house in the door or on the hall table or it fell out of my pocket on the floor at lunch or I have just lost it. If you find it will you give it to me again? Or ban me as a punishment? What a fool I am! I have lost a knife & a pencil & now a key all in 7 days.

I got a seat in the train but most people didn't & the carriage & corridors were solid humanity. Human beings solid are not pleasant – a certain amount of air between them is desirable.

I wish you had let me go to Chatto's. I do hope you sleep well tonight. I am so romantic that I would rather go with you to Harrods than walk anyone else to Heaven – which I suppose is merely to say that I would rather go with you to Hell than with anyone else to Heaven.

Love from your
L.


127:    [Saturday] 8 January 1944                    *Monk's House*

[Advertisement taped to letter] 'Cocker spaniel puppies by Windfall of Ware (Challenge Cert.), 8 weeks, black, 9 to 15 gns. – Ferguson, 66 Warwick Park, Tunbridge Wells.'

Darling tiger, Last night I wrote you a letter of only one sentence. It was *not* 'Dearest T, I have come to the conclusion that for your (and/or my) sake it is better that I should never see you again; love L.' It was 'Dearest, the enclosed was in the Times; love L.' And then I didn't send it, but wrote, dearest in your name to the man asking him to send particulars to you at V.S. So if you get a card from him, you will know why. Windfall of Ware is probably a relation of Sally's.

I also heard from the cats-meat woman of a cocker for sale at Newick & have written for particulars.

I don't admire your rival.

When I've seen you every day for 10 days & turn the corner of V.S. knowing that I shant see you for 5, I almost wish you were less lovable.

> Love from your
> L.


128:   [Sunday] 9 January 1944                                   *25 Vic Sq.*

Dearest Leonard

Atkinson came very late yesterday not until 8 o'clock. I had quite given him up. The answer seems to be that it is better but not yet good enough. I kept the two blood counts which he had brought with him − & if he doesn't demand them back on Tuesday will show them to you. I asked had I really got Pernicious Anemia & he said I had been on the edge of it when I was last done but am better but must still go on having 2 beastly injections a week & eat 4 hogs' stomachs a day. The satisfactory thing he says is that I have no abnormal cells & it is improving, from my look he would have thought it should be a better count. I'm all right on the white c[ell]s now but seem to need about a million more red. As for the other things on the sheet I don't intend to try & make any thing of them. Their names are highly putting off & I doubt if I've got any such things in me at all.

Mary Ann is attacking 24 this morning. I took her in & explained what she was to do on Friday. This morning when I was seeing Ian off I saw her wildly sweeping the insides of the window of the front ground floor room. I went in & remonstrated with her & I hope she is now doing what she was asked to. It seems Mr Woolf has no brooms nor no floor cloths nor nothing. Rose eats her fish roll with the greatest reluctance. There is a sultry gleam in her eye to-day & I think she is dreaming of Wave. This is a very bloody letter isn't it − but you asked for it.

> Love dear Leonard,
> from T.


129:   [Friday] 14 January 1944                               *Monk's House*

Dearest of creatures, Is it foolish, having seen you framed in the kitchen at 12.40, to find it impossible not to write to you at 10.15? To have had you at the back of my mind ever since, when talking politics at lunch or reading in the train about Rabbi Jacob ben Makhir ibn Tibbon & Rabbi Levi ben Gershom, the two Jews who invented the quadrants which have made your Hakluyt possible? To have had you there actually in my mind all the time so that when I have to do something (give up my ticket), or say something (about Roosevelt to Herbert Agar),[1] or think something (about that damned article which you ought to have secretarially told Kingsley I couldn't write), I feel you, almost see you shadowly standing at the back of my mind, smiling your severe tolerance at what you rightly know to be just nonsense, & so that when these things fall away from me & I am merely conscious, I sit & think consciously of you? To have, too, nothing in the ordinary sense to write to you about? Of course, it's foolish – you so often say I'm foolish & so often about you. Well, I'm not really ever afraid of being it, you know; I don't mind being it. To be in love makes one necessarily foolish in the ordinary sense & way. But I don't think it's foolish to be in love, not with you. If there's any reality in the universe – of course, if you drive me into a corner, I'll disappear down the mouse-hole shrieking 'Probably none' only to pop out of the hole at the other side of the room to whisper to you 'You are reality', & then you'll say I'm 'shifty' – I say if there's any reality, you – my you – & my feeling about you are real. For you are one of the very few things in the universe which matter. That sounds absurd, but it is not absurd. The number of things which matter are infinitely small, & they are never the things which are ordinarily expected to matter, but strange, unexpected things which one stumbles across in infinite space or in Victoria Square – like you. I felt this overwhelmingly in those few moments this morning when you left me to look at your pictures. More than ever I felt & saw something real & remarkable in them. It's not what you saw in Lefevre's window because it's you & the way you see things. I think that when one sees your pictures now as they are ranged together, it's extraordinarily impressive the calmness & uncompromising statement of what is beautiful.

I must stop though I could go on forever, but if I do I shall expose too much of my 'folly' (which is really just truth & wisdom) & it's nearly 12. I have just looked into the night & garden with the usual result of saying to myself if only you could be here, dearest tiger. For it's the strangest & most beautiful of nights with a dying moon low down in mist & haze & a quite clear sky & brilliant stars immediately overhead. If only you could be here – & then too I wouldn't be writing a 'foolish' letter.

1. Herbert Sebastian Agar (1897–1980), author, special assistant to the US Ambassador in London (1942–6). He was literary editor of the *English Review* 1930–4 and editor of the *Louisville Courier-Journal* 1939–42. He was director of Rupert Hart-Davis, publishers, 1953–63 and of Independent TV (TWW) 1957–68.

I had a curious & characteristic lunch. Desmond[1] had been coming but rang up to say he couldn't at the last moment & I took his place. And then after all he came without ringing up to say he could. Herbert Agar is a nice American. I used to know him well years ago before he became a best seller but had not seen him since, & it was pleasant to find him unchanged (except in the elegance of his clothes) by success.

Goodnight, my dearest, dearest tiger. I am not ashamed of anything in this letter because I love you & nothing which even you may say to the contrary will convince me that I am wrong or foolish about you.

      Your L.

The man from Chailey who had a spaniel for sale rang up this evening. But it was a dog, so I said No.


130:    [Sunday] 16 January 1944

Dearest Leonard. This is simply to tell you that there is a dense fog. There was one yesterday but not so dense and if there is one to-morrow I shall give up. But what do people mean when they say they will 'give up'. I mean how do you know they have? Really you should find something delightful to do in a fog because it has such a curious way of making everything last longer. It gives me a nervous horror of dirt & I clean the house, & it all goes on forever. Do you notice it has made my paper paler? I shall be lost taking this to the pillar box. Which I must do because I am really making a drawing.

   I hope you are better. It is probably a sparkling day at Rodmell. How awful it would be if they had not thought of the sun & we always had to live in a fog. You must admit in some ways the Lord is a good artist if he had been badish he might have only managed fog, & yet have got us alive to live in it. This is hardly worth a good 2½p stamp let alone the valuable sticky label.

      love T.


131:    [Tuesday 18 January 1944, left at 24 Victoria Square]

I am at home. I have found my flowers, are you buying pies? I have real

---

1. Desmond MacCarthy (1877–1952), literary journalist, editor and drama critic. He and his wife, Molly, were old friends of the Woolfs. Dorothy Woodman was also at lunch.

girls to lunch Gypsy [Lucas] & Irene [Hawkins]. I want to wash my hair this afternoon. Come in if you come back before lunch. Or come in anyway. I don't suppose you mind seeing real girls, they won't be here until 1 ish.

   T.


132:  [Friday] 21 January 1944        *Monk's House*

Darling tiger, I am slightly excited & at the same time apprehensive of your saying that I'm once again wrong or foolish or both. I went in to Lewes this morning to buy some horsemeat for Merle, but what I actually bought was a Rembrandt etching for you. It is No. 27 in the enclosed catalogue. I sneaked in at the back of Miller's & found no one there at all. So I broke into the Gallery & had it all to myself for ½ an hour. I was just congratulating myself on being able to get away without seeing anyone when the two sisters caught me.[1] I was fascinated by No. 27 & when I found that it could be bought could not resist the pleasure of seeing it on your wall. You've put so many beautiful things on my walls that you must let me put one on yours. That is if you think as I do about it – I do hope you do. The show ends tomorrow – isn't it a nuisance? I should have liked you to see it.

 I do hope you won't be very tired by all your visitors. I love you, dearest, more than ever.

   Your L.


133:  [Friday] 4 February [1944]     25 Victoria Sq, S.W.1

My dearest Leonard. This is not a formal closing of our acquaintance – but a formal thank you for my etching. It simply must be written down, how much I love it. I cannot get over it at all. It is not only that I think it is so lovely but the great pleasure I get out of owning it. I don't as a rule have a strong feeling about possessions but this is quite different. And I think I will never come to the end of it.

---

1. While supporting the often distinguished exhibits, concerts and lectures held at Miller's Gallery, LW regarded its owners, Frances Byng Stamper and her sister Carolyn Byng with mild amusement, and he was not alone. The ladies of Miller's, as they came to be called, were of aristocratic background; among other eccentricities, they travelled weekly to London to spend their food coupons at Fortnum & Mason's.

I drew Minnie & Winnie[1] on the stone yesterday. I drew them sleeping so soundly and restfully I wished I could creep into their shell too & put my head on their frilly pillow.

I have taken the liberty of lighting your boiler for Mrs Crooms. I will turn it out when she goes in & starts drawing it off. I also have readdressed a letter found on the mat. The Christmas card man:[2] came last evening & says could I please try to do something brighter as his committee thought the ones I did gloomy & I may have three colours or even perhaps four. So I will try again. He is an amiable man you would hardly have guessed it was Christmas cards that kept him straight with his Bank. And perhaps they will keep me straight too and you might not guess that either. I had breakfast surrounded by snow drops.

      love T.

134:   [Friday] 4 February 1944          *Monk's House*

Darling tiger, I *can't* help thinking of last week end & the difference you make to life, a house, the garden, me. I was melancholy yesterday at the thought of not seeing you, until you were in the room & I saw you & then everything was different all the way up Grosvenor Place until you disappeared into the Tube as you used to aeons ago in Russell Square when I had the greatest difficulty to prevent myself throwing my arms round your neck. And all the way down Grosvenor Place I meditated on the incredible stupidity of human beings. Peter [Brooker], for instance. He must be the most stupid person that has ever existed or has ever been imagined, except Othello – & does he now, I wonder, sit & mumble to himself: One whose hand, like the last Indian, threw a pearl away richer than all his tribe? It shocks & enrages me.

Then I had to meet two 'politicians' at 1.30 at De Hems. Walking back through Leicester Sq. I looked in again at the Sadler show.[3] If I could choose, I think I would take the Renoir. Dare I say that, looking round, I thought that your pictures would stand up for themselves in

---

1. Alfred, Lord Tennyson's 'Minnie and Winnie' (from *Child Songs*) was one of the poems in *Bells Across the Sands: A Book of Rhymes with Pictures* (Chatto & Windus, 1944), which TR illustrated. Some 15,000 copies of this book, which included many of her own rhymes, were printed. The sisters were sleeping in each other's arms on a Giant Clam shell.

2. TR designed several Christmas cards, and continued to make her own long after she stopped doing so commercially.

3. Michael Sadler's collection of art at the Leicester Galleries included paintings from Constable to the present. TR and LW had seen it together on 19 January.

that room? Please dont have the usual conversation with yourself – 'The silly fool, it's only because he's in love – so he & it can be dismissed.' Or I shall again have to remind you that I'm intelligent. The reason why I so often have to do so is that intelligence is the only asset remaining to me, now that I no longer have any green flannel collars. Then I looked in at the National Gallery. The new picture is Daphne & Apollo by Pollaiolo – is that the name? I had not seen a picture like that for years.

Here Peat greeted me in a lamentable state – quite lame of one leg, completely dishevelled, but indomitable. All night I woke up at intervals to hear an alert, an all clear, or guns or bombs. I do hope they didn't keep you awake. There followed the grimmest day – a bitter NW gale. At one moment it became quite dark & everything was blotted out in a wild snowstorm. Five minutes later the sun was shining on a white landscape. I spent the whole afternoon with Percy carrying 2 tons of oak logs from his gate & shooting them down into the cellar. The middle hinge of my body is now rather stiff, but at any rate I can have a good fire for you when you can come again. When—

That will set me off again & I mustn't be set off again, I know without your severely telling me, my darling tiger, so that I will only say goodnight, & that there is something in you of which I am really fond, as you even admit, which just means that I adore what is adorable.

> Your
> L.

135:    [Saturday] 5 February 1944                    *Monk's House*

Dearest of creatures, My legitimate excuse for writing to you yesterday I forgot in the end to mention. So today I will type it. It was to say that Peter Jones's man came and I showed him the sofa in the studio and he said he would communicate with you. I suppose it was the studio sofa? For a moment I thought I might have made a mistake and that it was the one downstairs.

It was sweet of you to write the letter I got this morning.

I wish you could have seen Peat this morning when I roused him from his bed in the frame (he refused to stay in the house) – he came out on three legs, one eye closed up, and wauling good morning at the top of his voice. He ate some bread and some haricot beans, drank some milk, and hobbled off again into the garden on his three sound legs, and throwing me a cynical glance over his shoulder from his one sound eye.

> Love from your
> L.

136:  [Friday] 11 February 1944                    *Monk's House*

Darling tiger, Our walk to the London Library disproved your theory that it doesn't matter much with whom you go into the garden or walk to St James's Square. I enjoyed it so much that I was as good as intoxicated when I staggered into the tram at Victoria. It wouldn't have been like that if you were a [squirmy?] or not you.

I sent you the story. I had not read it for ages. I'm afraid it is not very good & certainly *not* one of the six best. The cover design, which I didn't like, was by Carrington.[1]

I read the enclosed in yesterday's Evening Standard. She, Lina Cavallieri, agrees with you & I imagine, like you, is not a [squirmy], though she is probably not like you in many other respects, to judge from the list of husbands. Your taste in husbands seems to be slightly different.

How I wish I were pushing the pram with its kettle & saucepan.

I love you, Dearest
> L.

137:  [Friday] 11 February 1944                    *Monk's House*

Darling tiger, Is it wrong, I wonder, to write two letters to you in one day? I expect it is, but there are one or two things I meant to tell you & didn't & there are always so many things which I want to say, when I see you, that time is not long enough. This for instance first. I do want to have one of your major works here. I should like it to be the great still life on my wall now. But do you think the rooms here are so low that they will spoil it? If not, may I buy it & if so, will you tell me its price? Could I have it sent here or would that be foolish before the show? I am longing to have one of your pictures here. You said, remember, that you would let me buy

1. Dora Carrington (1893–1932), painter and devoted companion of Lytton Strachey. In 1921 she married Ralph Partridge (1894–1960), writer, but after 1926 he lived in London with Frances Marshall (b. 1900), whom he later married, and she with Strachey, after whose death she shot herself. She did the cover for LW's *Stories from the East* (Hogarth, 1921).

the other still life, the flowers, & you must let me know its price too. I might have that here, but it looked so superb, I thought, where we hung it at 24, that I want to have it there again.

On the whole it is perhaps just as well that we did not make today our first day's tramp with the kettle & pram. The wind from the north was wicked, as they say in the village – it cut through one like a knife. I had to go to your room & borrow the leather jerkin I lent you. (I knocked on the door before I went in, & said: 'The bathroom is empty, Trekkie', & nearly burst into tears).

The other thing I want to say is many things on the subject of happiness, but I mustn't, I see, after all at this hour, because I still have some work I should do, &, if I once begin, I should probably go on deep into Feb 12 & cover too many sheets for you to be able to read them. You will be as sensible as possible in the malestrom of next week, & you will summon me if there is any donkey work I could do for you, dearest?

Goodnight, darling tiger.

L.

Peat's eye is now ⅜s open, his leg is rather better, but he has a violent cold in the head & his voice is ridiculously husky & wheezy.

138:   [Sunday] 13 February 1944                                     *25 Vic Sq*

Dearest Leonard, I like the middle story best. Which was the one that so excited the glossy agent? Can people really fall in love without knowing anything about what is inside the other one's head?[1] Perhaps you are right & I don't know anything about it but that will make it all the easier for me to write with authority on how to avoid it. I think you should write some more stories. I am on the glossy agent's side, but I can't offer to supply you with plots or promise if you put yourself in my hands that you will earn 3,000 a year.

Everything about glow worms is nice. They have a passion for glowing & do it even as eggs inside their mother. They glow through her inside. They glow in mid winter if you dig them up & boys glow too only not so wildly as girls do in the marriage season. *They* know so much about

---

1. The middle story, which TR likes best, in *Stories from the East* is 'Pearls and Swine'. LW refused to rewrite it for American readers. The first, which TR questions the wisdom of, is 'A Tale Told by Moonlight'. In it an Englishman travelling in Colombo falls deeply in love with a native woman to whom he cannot even talk. They live together until he gets to know her; when he leaves she kills herself.

love that then they light up two great bands around their stomachs & in the dusk climb a grass stalk and swing their hips about like Mr True's exercises,[1] shining their light this way & that until he sees it (he has eyes especially made to see it quickly) and then it is very poetic for when he comes she puts out her lights and they do with a little candle. She spills her eggs anywhere on the grass or earth. The grubs & grown glow worms live on small snails which they first anaesthetize & then mumble up into a sort of soup. I am mad to have some & will write to the Times in May. I can't think why the marsh isn't full of them. They like it moist.

This is an extremely interesting letter for I have now something else exciting to tell you. The [Rembrandt] etching is there. It is true. A reproduction, John says not done from such a good print as mine, with an account about it. It is apparently very late. There is also a drawing from which the etching was done. Most beautiful composition, but without the superb mysterious drawing of the nude figure in the etching. I long to show it to you.

You wilfully misunderstand me. I never said it didn't make any difference to me if I walked to the London with you or Harold Raymond. I said if I had to have Harold I'd rather be walking to the London or pottering in a garden, that I would irk quicker & more if I just had him boxed up in a little furnished flat.

I have washed my hair & am drying it now in front of the fire. I felt I must have it respectable for Tuesday for fear the King said afterwards 'we must take care that *that* man doesn't get another step, did you see his sister's hair?' Or converting the advertisement in the Tube: 'Men whose sister's hair is lank never reach the topmost rank'.[2]

The Paragon is coming to see me at 3.30. I think I would go mad with the poetess if I go from my studio to the basement thinking about my grey stone. She crashes into my head bawling about stuff to get the grease off gas stoves. She says it is terrible for you to be on your own. 'Men aren't much good without a woman', but I daresay Crooms would rather manage.

Cavallieri had a very varied assortment I agree but I wonder if she ever had such a queer one as Peter?

Is this the longest letter I have ever written you?

I must stop now at any rate.

Love dear Leonard,

T.

1. Mr True gave TR exercises for back strain from printing.
2. Pat had been made Air-Vice-Marshal on 18 November 1943 while retaining command of his bomber command group. The Paragon was TR's help.

139:   [Monday] 14 February 1944                          *Monk's House*

Darling tiger, I ought not to be writing you; I ought to be working. But I must tell you that there are glow worms here. According to Louie & Percy, they have never seen them in the gardens, but they see them on the side of the road all the way to Southease & Piddinghoe. So it will be your duty to spend May & June here & we must collect them every night & stock the garden. Your description of the loves of the glow worms was wonderfully poetic; you know what their love is, I admit.

After I had told you that Peat was recovering he sallied out again & returned 12 hours later in a disgraceful state, blood flowing down his leg & his face. I don't know what to do with him; I can't keep him in.

I must walk. Your trials begin today & I keep on thinking of you & longing for Thursday when I shall really see you again. Your letter was a lovely beginning for the day. Goodbye, darling creature.

   L.


140:   [probably Wednesday 16 February 1944, left at 24 Victoria Square]

Dearest L.

I shall look in this evening about seven in case you aren't either feeding politicians or having dinner out with journalists. I shall see you tomorrow anyway.

      love T.


141:   [Saturday] 19 February 1944                        *Monk's House*

Darling tiger, I haven't done anything about Hamlet, partly because I couldn't communicate with my sister to get an answer before Tuesday, but even more because I see it begins at 6 & I have to interview a young man (who wants to join the Press) with J.L. & I may not get rid of them before 6. I *am* sorry; I should have liked it.

Today has been a fiendish day here with an icy wind from the north & everything drab, dirty grey from sky to grass. Except for ½ an hour cutting up wood I worked solidly all day & then just before dinner thought I must get the cobwebs blown out of my brain & so heroically went out on the watermeadows with Merle. She enjoyed it at any rate, but I was frozen stiff inside & out. They have begun to cut up & remove the fallen elm.

I thought of you – but when dont I? – at lunch today. It was a man's lunch – a large shoulder of mutton & a steamed pudding! I had meant to have them for dinner but Louie for some reason 'put them on' before she left. I haven't eaten a meal like that for years – but I prefer the girls' lunch any day. What should we have done if you had been here?

When I said goodbye to you yesterday, you so bemused & bewitched me that I didn't know what I was saying & said what wasn't, I think, true. It comes of looking straight into your eyes – which I still think the most beautiful I've ever seen, perhaps because I feel that when I look right into them I do see ever so far deep down in them you, the you which I think of now as the tiger or even – is that wrong & presumptuous? – as my tiger & which I once described to you as Trekkie, when you were Trekkie. And now I suppose I ought to explain the 'because' four lines up, because I think you are too sceptical about yourself to admit the casual connection, which is that that you is the most beautiful person I've ever known. And that, dearest, is *not* nonsense & it's no good your saying it is – I am talking of the you which I see in the depths of your eyes, the you which paints pictures & thinks poetry & never misunderstands & is fiercely serious & laughs divinely & makes one laugh divinely & changes by being with one the whole colour of one's day or life, which one thinks one has for a moment caught under one's stupid Pierrot's cap only to find it so often aloof on the other side of the universe – the you which, you will now admit, is not the you in the hairdresser's mirror – it is the real you. You made me say, as my head went round & round, looking into your eyes 'intently', that I hadn't the faintest idea of what goes on in your head. I don't think that's really true. I do know something of what goes on. But I'm the exact opposite of the base Indian. I even believe when I'm with you that you have some affection for me. But that's just why it's heaven to be with you, wretched to leave you, & why when I don't see you, I get the terrors that it cannot last. The mere fact that I love you so much gives me the terrors that I shall bore & irritate you. For it *is* boring to have someone really in love about the house. For when one is in love all one can do is go on saying 'I love you' which is practically to creep about the house all day really on one's belly whauling, like Rose. If I weren't in love with you I might even be quite entertaining, like a man of the world – though you won't admit that, I know. It certainly would be odd to talk like a man of the world to you – I know I never shall.

Now very deep down I lose nearly all belief & the deeper the more sceptical. But I do believe in one or two things – the value of art & of people & of one's relations with people. You combine all 3 values for me

& as I said the you which I know to be you is the most beautiful person I've known. You mean therefore a great deal to a sceptic, I mean to me, & it may be foolish, but it's natural, if you're the opposite of the base Indian, to be occasionally terrified that the pearl will quite reasonably throw you away.

This is the longest letter ever written – but it isn't a whaul (I wonder whether there is an h in this word), it's just plain truth. And it's a good thing to tell you the truth every now and again, my darling tiger, even though it was with the eternal 'I love you'. And now it is past midnight & I suppose one must face the horrors of leaving you & the fire & go to bed.

The enclosed on size of families may amuse you. It is interesting that aristocrats have the largest & artists & actors the smallest. He talks some bosh at the end. There are also a few stamps enclosed.

Good night, dearest and most beautiful of creatures. It does end with the eternal

I love you.

L.

142:    [Sunday] 20 February [1944]                    *25 Vic Sq.*

Dearest Leonard. This isn't a letter it is to let you know that they choose not to give an evening performance of Hamlet on Tuesday. Mondays Weds & Fridays appear to be the days it is on, and Ian can only do Friday of those which I suppose is hopeless for you. I printed the grey yesterday & have spent to day correcting all the stones & am now ready to start printing when the way is clear before me.

How miserable this cold is. I believe it is as well we aren't behind the pram. I am afraid I would be whingeing.

I shall miss the post if I don't run across with this.

love T.

143:    [Saturday] 26 February 1944                    *Monk's House*

Darling, darling tiger, I have been sitting here the last quarter of an hour looking into the fire & thinking of you & now I can't go to bed without saying to you, not that I'd go to Durban to see you for 10 minutes (because you wouldn't believe it or, if you did, would disapprove with that austere gravity which I love), but simply that to see you here for 10 minutes was happiness, but it was wretched to walk back down the village street without you. How I wished I could have kept you here – I hate to think of you harrassed & trailing out to a dinner you don't want to go to & I'm worried that you should have so much thrust upon you & that you don't sleep. I don't want the following conversation to take place between us (it's the quotation from Two on a Tower[1] I told you of): I (in a sudden accession of anxiety as I turn to look more closely at you) 'But how you have watched! The orbits of your eyes are leaden, & your eyelids are red & heavy. Don't do it – pray dont. You will be ill & break down.'

You (cheerfully): 'I have, it is true, been up a little late this last week.' O my darling creature, how I look forward to next Thursday, though I warn you I shall be an old granny to you & make you eat, rest, & go to bed early.

Fussells is one of the nicest people I've ever seen; she seems to bring with her an envelope of goodness like the envelope of air round the earth & yet she has none of the vices & horrors of good people. But I cannot say that I like Mabel & I don't think she really likes Woolf or Leonard, as you call him. We had a curious conversation; she wanted to find out where I was & as it amused me to be completely noncommittal except about the time of your arrival, she eventually had to say: 'So you're staying in London over the weekend?'

Goodnight beloved tiger. You will look in & see me Monday evening? I did a lot of work before I began staring into the fire. I was doing the Political Quarterly yearly accounts & they were £1 out & I eventually found the error.

> Love
> L

144:  [probably Monday 28 February 1944, left at 24 Victoria Square]

I have made bold to open your window for you. I will look in this evening when I get home from the Press.

> love. T.

Leaden orbits must *not* be mentioned.

---

1. Thomas Hardy wrote that in this slightly built romance he wanted 'to set the emotional history of two infinitesimal lives against the stupendous background of the stellar universe, and to impart to readers the sentiment that of these contrasting magnitudes the smaller might be the greater to them as men'.

145:   [probably Monday 6 March 1944, left at 24 Victoria Square]

Dearest L.

   I was quite right to dread turning my nose homewards. This morning I asked Mrs Wheately to sweep the hearth rug and she said she thought we wouldn't 'suit'. I asked the bread lady & she may know someone. How fruitful life is. I think perhaps I should not ever come to Rodmell. You spoil me so for the hard world. I am coming on Thursday all the same.
                Love T.

146:   [probably Monday 13 March 1944, left at 24 Victoria Square]

Dearest L.

   Am doing the shopping. Will be back in ½ an hour & come in. Ian is home. I have seen the news about the ban.[1] Life is really just like a dream; you never get the thing your hand is stretching out for.

147:   [probably Tuesday 14 March 1944, left at 24 Victoria Square]

I fell asleep on the mat unintendingly after I parted from you. Was waked by the bell & it was the real Miss Harris the grey one I saw was someone else. I enclose the note she brought. Then in came Ian who said Harold had found he had made so much money out of the Midgets he was going to give me £100 more & would I do 6 new ones. And he Ian thought I should go to Rodmell this week-end as it was my last chance. So all is clear. This is not a dream I *was* waked by the bell. I shall almost be able to get into Lewes on the grounds of being a regular member of your household.        T.

148:   [Tuesday] 21 March 1944 [left at 24 Victoria Square]

I answered the telephone, Lehmann must go to a funeral and wants to postpone your usual meeting & will ring you later on.

1. From mid-January to mid-April there was a mini-Blitz of fifteen major bombings, thirteen of them on London. By March troops were being massed in preparation for D-Day; just before 6 June there were over one and a half million American troops in the UK. The ban was reimposed around Lewes and, as LW reports in mid-April, there was a control on local movements once or twice a week.

Dearest L.

I have arranged a small picture exhibition for you & bought you a loaf of bread. I have had a cable from Ian. I think he may be home at the end of the week. I think I may come to Rodmell as Pat says he (Ian) might have to hang about so I have cabled him to ring Rodmell on arrival in Scotland. If I hear no more I will most likely come. My nose is bad my cough is better my rib is the same.

      Love T.


If a small party comes & asks to be let in here it is Eddy the fire Brigade one.


Have heard through the Ministry that Ian expects to leave on Saturday so I shall come home early Sunday morning.

      Love T.


149:   [Thursday] 30 March 1944                   *Monk's House*

Darling tiger, You left this passionate paper here & I feel I must write to you on it. I have been trying to obey you, but it is difficult. There is too great a difference between existence & life, & between life & love. But I know I must 'be brave', sensible, silent. Do you think I have the makings of a 'strong, silent man'? That is what I shall have become by Monday.

To add to my cheerfulness I found 3 officers of the Manchester Regiment already installed in the bedroom downstairs where they will be until Saturday. It is characteristic of the Captain, Colonel, Hon. gentry of this village that they contrive with their large houses (¾s empty) & servants to avoid taking in three officers & put them into Monk's House in my absence!

I worked until 3 & weeded your garden until 4 & very nearly finished it.

I think that, unless you forbid it or wont come to it, I shall take a furnished house in the country for the next 6 months. Would you come to 'Stourbridge, Worcs. Detached, modern well furnished house: 2 recpt, 3 bedrooms, usual offices, garden. 4½ guineas per week'? And could you paint in Stourbridge, Worcs.?

I continually think of my room full of your pictures. (These [3 ink] blots are yours, not mine) If you had the slightest doubt of your achievement or if anyone had, the answer is there. It is remarkable how they reinforce one another & show your power & intensity. They are the pictures of one person & yet each is an entity & there is no repetition or sameness – no just painting for painting's sake & therefore the same picture all over again which is what so many artists seem to me to do. And they are gay, as I told you, & the beauty of them all together there was astonishing. You said the other day that you gave me nothing. The pleasure your painting gives me makes anything I can give you – breakfast in bed or a scuttle of coals – well, there you are! *Nothing at all.*

I think I had better stop or I might begin to crawl on my belly & whinge & *I have* been brave, haven't I? And, dearest, dearest of creatures, it's not really very easy, for, as I remember you, you are just as gay, serious, & beautiful as your pictures – which isn't strange for your pictures & your painting are you. In fact I love you because I love your pictures & it isn't because I love you that I love your pictures – that's why I'm right both about your beauty, your character, & your painting. Goodnight, my darling.

    L.

150:   [Wednesday – Friday] 29–31 March 1944    [*25 Victoria Square*]

My Dearest Leonard.

I am like Louie writing in the kitchen – it isn't quite in the kitchen but the breakfast is still not cleared away. I have nothing to tell you except that I haven't started printing. As I was going down yesterday to begin, the clivias & Arums & daffodils all yelled at me at the tops of their voices so I spent the day painting them & shall go on as soon as the chores are done.

Rose whose clamourings [sic] had reached a surprising pitch of throaty longing went off yesterday morning. This is B[lue] Waves last chance. I wonder if they have been stinting his meat? The alert last night kept us awake an hour but we didn't get up as the guns were so far off. I went to sleep again.

[Cheaks?] haven't any left of those roses for this season, isn't it disappointing.

I must go & see what that sour daily of mine T. Ritchie is up to.

As you see this isn't a letter. It is instead of crumbs for the fish.

      Love

       T.

These are all your letters.

151:   [TR to LW] midday [Saturday] 1 April [1944]

This came just as I was taking the others to the pillar. So that is rather what we expected isn't it?

152:   [Friday] 7 April 1944                                   *Monk's House*

Darling tiger, Luriana.[1] I think that even your *toe* (& even *your* toe) would have softened if it had been able to look into my heart when I turned the corner into the garden here on Thursday. For it would have seen how I missed & wanted you. It was as if a magician had waved a wand over the garden in the three days & completely changed it. All the daffodils, crown imperials, & hyacinths in full bloom. The plum trees white. In the greenhouse the freesias a mass of flowers & the great red buds of the great lily bursting the sheath. But you've become so great a part of the garden & of me – no, not a part, but the whole (I can see you disapproving of this true statement & changing from the smiling to the extra serious polyphoto) – that I feel it's wrong when the flowers come out when you're not here. I simply dont want them without you. I picked a great vasefull of freesias – I do hope they will not all open before Tuesday, because I do so want to give you a good bouquet of them.[2]

I am profoundly depressed – by the Gardners.[3] The whole family (except the mad Major) i.e. Diana, Paully, & Lilian (or Lily-Ann), his wife, descended upon me after dinner & have just left. There is nothing

1. 'Luriana', a poem by Charles Elton, had been given to LW years earlier by Lytton Strachey. It runs through *To the Lighthouse*. LW and TR must have discussed the poem, and LW was inviting her to 'Come out and climb the garden path/Luriana Lurilee/The China rose is all abloom/And buzzing with the yellow bee'. At the same time, LW had first written 'Lurium' here in large, heavy script, then corrected it to read 'Luriana'. Since in the letter he equates TR with his flowers and both 'ium' and 'iana' are suffixes of the names of flowers, LW may have been playfully adding Lurium (an invented specific English name – meaning perhaps 'enticer') to his usual generic name for TR, 'tiger'. A Latin scholar, he would then reasonably change the neuter ending 'ium' to 'iana', and so TR became 'Darling tiger, Luriana'.
2. Freesias were the first flowers LW gave TR, in a box he left on her doorstep at Victoria Square just over a year earlier. A genus of South Africa, they had special significance for although she never returned to Natal, TR remained attached by strong memories especially to the flowers, warmth and colours of the place of her birth.
3. The Gardners lived in Thatched Cottage, two doors from Monk's House. Virginia Woolf encouraged Diana's art work and writing, and, although they were not close, TR corresponded with her. Diana Gardner's woodcut of German aircraft flying low over Rodmell (first published in the *Sussex Express & County Herald* on 9 January 1942) has often been reprinted in books about the Woolfs.

wrong with them except that their brains are like Merle's & that they therefore talk as Merle would talk if Merle could talk. Merle's conversation would obviously be intolerable & the reason why I – &, I may add, you – are so fond of Merle is precisely because she can only talk with her paw & her tail. Three Merles talking with their mouths about the war, about Katherine Mansfield, about books reduce one to profound depression.

I believe Southease Rectory is for sale. It is worth considering. I shall try to find out about it before Tuesday.

There was a full control on at Lewes station last night. I don't allow myself to think of the possibility of your being here for 2 months. God would never allow that. That's why he has put the control on at Lewes station. I'll tell you tomorrow how it was done, but it's so late now that I think I had better not take another sheet (there is one) but go to bed, Darling creature, you make even a world of Gardners worth living in.

Saturday 8 April 1944
I tried to find out about Southease Rectory. It appears to be for sale, but it is said that Lady Reading is 'after it'. The parson has left for Tooting where he proposes to live for the rest of his life. I have written to the agent who is said to be dealing with it.

This is how, I think, the ban came. I told you that Heaven is really an enormous switchboard. We are each connected and the switchboard registers our happiness or unhappiness. The angels in charge have to report as soon as anyone registers 'happy' or 'too happy' so that a 'Higher Authority' (H.A.) may take steps to make him unhappy. My angel reported:

'Woolf, L., Rodmell, Sussex, Too happy.

Cause: Ritchie, T. (alias Parsons, alias Brooker) Victoria Square, London'

H.A. minuted: 'Eliminate Ritchie, T. (alias Parsons, alias Brooker)'

Such orders of the H.A. are carried out by Arch angels who are allowed a wide discretion subject to the general directive that the max human effort & disturbance are desirable in order to produce the most trivial result. For instance, they continued the present war in order to make an unhappy Corporal happy & then still more unhappy than when he began. So they contrived the ban to eliminate Ritchie, T. from Woolf, L. & Rodmell, Sussex. The war & the ban also have the advantage of making so many other people besides Woolf, L. unhappy. I'm sure that all the metaphysicians & priests & prophets are quite wrong & that God works in a mysterious way in his government of the universe & that his way is more or less as I have described it.

I thought I might have heard today from Nan Kwell, but I suppose they've forgotten all about it.

Darling tiger, I shall see you on Tuesday at any rate (unless they ban that too) & we shall 'go out to dinner' to Dr [William] Robson. It will be terribly boring for you – you don't know that kind of bore, probably, – but very strange. I would go with you even to the Ritz or the Dorchester. Goodnight & sleep well, dearest of creatures.

Love  L.

153:    [Friday] 7 April [1944]                                        *Vic Sq.*

My dearest Leonard

I can't think why this paper has gone so narrow, but what I am writing about is not that, it is to tell you that I think you will have to leave no. 24. You are making me *dependant* on you Mr Woolf. I hate it when the house goes empty. There is nothing from the Redfern [Gallery] this morning, only a bill from the Electricity I think, and a letter for Mr Evan Evans one of your aliases I suppose.[1] You can say what you like about my present daily, she is splendid. She has cleaned the drains, she's the only one I've ever had who did that.

Rose & I are sitting on the mat eating an apple & reading Lear. She is in a golden mood gently purring if spoken to & stretching her furry middle out towards the electric fire. The blackbird is here again & was last evening. He is the greatest addition to the square. I am going down now to print my pink very bravely I hope. Lear & this letter are turning me from a daily into a printer. If there is a narrow blue belt in my drawer will you bring it next week & my little jewel box. The Rembrandt won't get into the tin box. I have looked at it again what do you think? I think it should stay there unless we move into a villa.

Have you the Rousseau confessions here or there? Rose is now lying in a superb ballet dancer attitude. I wish you could see her.

Love T.

---

1. LW had been to the Redfern Gallery on 23 March 1944 on TR's behalf. Acting as her 'P.S.' and 'tough', he sometimes used aliases when trying to arrange for her paintings to be exhibited.

154:   [Monday] 10 April 1944                                        *Monk's House*

Darling tiger, Before the laburnum blossom precedes the lilac or vice versa, I should like to bring to your notice the following from 'Two on a Tower', Ch. XXIV: 'It was mid-May time . . . Among the larger shrubs & flowers which composed the outworks of the Welland gardens, the lilac, the laburnum, & the guelder-rose hung out their respective colours of purple, yellow, & white . . .'

I will bring the jewels but I can't find the belt.

I shall write to the Leicester Galleries.

The only compensation for not seeing you is your letters & the greater (I suppose) pleasure of seeing you again. Love

                L.

I have a Rousseau, I think, in every house. There will probably be one even in the Polegate [Village] Villa.

There are possible alternatives to my leaving 24 V.S.:
a)  Never leaving it when Ritchie, T. is at 25;
b)  Ritchie, T. at Rodmell;
c)      „       „ & Woolf, L. in the Polegate Villa.


                ? [sic]


155:   [Thursday] 13 April 1944                                      *Monk's House*

Darling, darling tiger, I rang you up tonight unsuccessfully about a letter from the Leicester Galleries. I will ring you again tomorrow morning.

I sat in the train until halfway to Lewes saying to myself 'I am a fool, I am a fool' – just like St Paul. Why did I leave V.S. when I might have seen you for ten minutes tomorrow? There is nothing I care for but you – And then I really did about Horley stop saying it, simply because I hate the futility of regretting, & dejectedly but doggedly read Tolstoy's Polyushka. And also because I had had a perfect day with you & felt that for 5 or 6 hours I had cheated God & his switchboard. Beloved, for that's what you are, I wish I could say what you are to me. You laugh when I say you're good to me; you are that just by being yourself, but you're something infinitely more which I can't find words for. That I love you is nothing for anyone can be in love or for that matter be loved. But you make me feel for you an affection, a kind of adoration – I can't find the right word – perhaps there isn't one – which goes deeper down into me than I had thought possible, & makes loving you something above love. And it's you that does it & draws it out of me & makes it not foolish but right & inevitable. There is something extraordinarily beautiful in your mind, heart, gaiety of spirit & with it the seriousness, even melancholy in the depths which, the beauty, I mean, I see – & see so foolishly, you say – in your eyes & face, too. As we sat on the grass at Kew today & talked about art & the 3 periods & the great works of art, I thought, but didn't dare say, that you are almost the only person I have ever known who are yourself a great work of art. (I think of the Lord's second period). And I've never known a human being so perfect a work of art. I've been five or six hours with you today & a good many – but how much too few – the last months & you've never said anything or made a movement which did not seem to me beautiful & give me the feeling of ecstasy or satisfaction mental & physical which one gets from a work of art. I know you'll say this is foolish – but it is not. And I think you really know what I mean, badly though it may be put. That I love you, adore you, passionately for something which is really there in you & worth a passion. That is why you *are* good to me, darling creature.

And now before I go to bed I had better say what I started to write to you about. *There was no control tonight.* And I asked my friend in the parcels office what they were doing about it, & he said they very rarely had one on – only once or twice a week. If that is so, I believe it would be worth risking at any rate for a long week end.

Goodnight, sweetest of creatures & fiercest – I love you because you are.

    L.

156:   [Saturday] 15 April 1944                 *Vic Sq.*

My dearest Leonard.

There are times when I detest Rose and this is one of them. I have just got back from Westbourne Pk[1] with my pictures & with my change in my pocket very prosperous & satisfied. Rose greeted me slightly subdued in the passage. I stroked her & found her hair was wet. I instantly guessed that she had broken a vase. Went into the sitting room to find complete chaos. She had got up on the Rickety table to drink the freesias water. The leg had finally broken off taking everything to the ground, smashed the

---

1. The Robsons lived at Westbourne Park, W2.

large white wedgewood tureen which is one of the few sizable things I have for flowers, smashed the smaller wedgewood dish & the strainer I had inside & the whole room was a lake. It is really my own fault. I should have chopped up the Rickety table years ago & so I would have if I hadn't painted the top & liked the result.

I was led into W. Robson's bedroom to see the Balcony picture which was sheltering behind a colossal chocolate brown wardrobe. I agreed it didn't really look its best there and so though rather reluctantly he has decided to have only the Freesias. There seemed no alternative except getting another house.

I took the final colour of the marsh lithograph yesterday. Quite successfully. I shall now start thinking of Adam & Eve.[1] But I can't think of anything except flowering trees. Every year I boil up into a frenzy about them. This year it has brought a spot out on my elbow. I ate a huge amount of the mutton last night while reading Rousseau and washing my hair.

We couldn't take that flat. They would be sure to ask us if we were related. And I believe the other people would keep us pretty hard at it. My friend who I told you was 'The Darling' came to tea yesterday. She is getting more & more genteel. She keeps on talking about 'ladies'. Their governess it seems isn't one. I wouldn't be her governess for all her silver & all her gold. It is strange when a friend tells you long accounts of her situation & you are on the wrong side all the time. I was heart & soul on the governess's!

We are off at 5 o'clock D.V. And now I am off to Penge, perhaps I shall give Rose to them. One way or another let us have a meal on Wed. But I expect it will be you having it here. On the back of this is the poem about being married to Peter.

I send on two things from 24.

    love dear Leonard

        T.

It isn't on the back I had written all over it.


A rat tooth gnawed
At my conventional felicity
Like a sea-anemone my heart contracted.

My startled sleepy ears
Identified the grind of
Tooth on dry despair

1. For the Midget Bible Stories series.

But hid, and would not hear
Nor spread the news
To the brain or the heart's city.

With stifled breath
And shaking heart beats
I lived in card house safety.

I dared one lidless serpent glance
Across the acres of my days
And saw the huge bare fields
And knew my grey horizon.

157:    4 o'clock [Saturday] 15 April 1944                    *25 Vic Sq.*

Dearest Leonard
    I must be off in a few minutes so I cannot answer your letter properly.
I found it on the mat when I got back from Penge. The real truth is that
everyone knows the insides of themselves too well to be able to believe
very well of themselves. It doesn't matter really how hard they try Tolstoi
or Rousseau or anyone, it isn't possible to remove the last skin. Or really
it isn't removing a skin but turning the whole organism inside out so that
your outside eye can come inside & see from my inwards outward.
    Well I must find a taxi. The case which has nothing but bare necessaries
& toilet requisites in it weighs like lead.
    Could you buy me bread – white & brown on Tuesday & light my
circulator if you can without being blown up.
    Love Leonard dear
            from T.
I wish I was that lovely person you describe

158:    [Thursday] 20 April 1944                            *Monk's House*

My Dear Trekkie
    I got back here to lovely weather &, despite the unsettled & somewhat
disturbing conditions in the great world – there is evidence of this in the large
number of troops in my field & they have broken my fence in three places –
I feel that one has a great deal to thank God for. It is in fact our duty, I feel,

126

to be happy & that is why of course I am, particularly because in addition to all my other blessings – a nice house, a pleasant garden, & a reasonable income – I enjoy, for my age, good health, eating & sleeping well. It is good therefore to be alive & be privileged to enjoy so lovely an evening.

I also enjoyed seeing you in London & it was good of you to give me not only dinner & lunch, but 2 tins of pilchards & what you so humorously call a huddle. By the way there was a heading in my Evening Standard this afternoon: Hitler goes into a Huddle on his Birthday. My happiness is increased, if that is possible by the thought that perhaps I may see you next week.

The real object of my writing is to say that Gorringe[1] was not in but I left a message & will try to get in touch with him tomorrow. But it may mean some delay in your getting the permit to view.

Hoping that this will find you as it leaves me

     Yours,

      L.


Tiger Darling, Is this the kind of letter I *ought* to write instead of telling you that you are adorable & that I miss & adore you?

     Your

      L.


159:   [Friday] 21 April 1944                   *Monk's House*

Darling, I hadn't time to explain fully as I wanted you to know the main fact by tomorrow morning in case the catalogue instead of a permit to view reached Ian. I could not get Gorringe on the telephone all day as he was always out. The home itself is not in his hands – in fact it is not yet up for sale. The Ecclesiastical Commissioners are to inspect it on Friday & decide about its sale, but it is practically certain that they will sell it. Gorringe will be in the house on Tuesday getting the furniture ready for sale & said you can come & look over it. I think it would be worth while & if you thought it possible you could write at once to the E.C.'s asking about price & I will meet you at Southease Halt if you decide to come.[2]

The control is practically never on. But there are signs here which make me think that the invasion may occur at any moment now.

---

1. The estate agent.
2. The Parsons looked at the house on Tuesday the 25th and returned to London.

Tiger, darling tiger, I tried in London to see that you are not – as you say 'that lovely person' & I have tried hard since I came here. But it's no good – you *are*. And its no good pretending that I don't miss you, long for you – because I do. The only remedy, as I once said before, is for you to turn nasty, – & that's no good, because you cant & even if you could, I should still love you.

   Your

   L.

160:  Friday 21 April 1944             *25 Vic Sq.*

My dearest Leonard. I'm sure there must be large notices up saying write fewer letters – and it means me. There is nothing to tell you except that I have had my hair cut & the hairdresser gave me a shell pink Camelia 'from my garden at Weybridge'. Though this sounds ardent I think we would be wrong to take it as *positive* proof that he is in love with me, the wretched thing being that there were several other camelias on a little glass tray & I can't help thinking he destined them for other bosoms. Even so it is pleasant to be given a Camelia when one has one's hair cut. Rose is in a dream of love for me. She looks at me with swimming eyes & purs continually.

One of the little boys at Granville [Coghlan]'s school overhearing them talking about something said 'was that in the last Peace.' A fairly sobering remark don't you think.

We shall have to come home by the earlier train on Tuesday – I am going through the hoop & having the Raymonds [Harold & Vera] to dinner – I shall get all ready before we leave but will need about ½ an hour or an hour. Will you come & have coffee with them I'd like you to see Harold. I do hope you are conscious of a soft blanket just this colour around you?

   Love dear Leonard.

   T.

161:  [Saturday] 22 April 1944        *Monk's House, Rodmell*

You say, tiger darling, that you write me too many letters. But what about me? Is it a hint? This is the fourth in 40 hours. But my excuse is this: 'House to let furnished. 5 gns. a week. Apply Brenton Coward, Rozel, Otford, Kent.'

I do hope you can come here on Tuesday. The difficulty will be to get you back in time. The 4.54 via Haywards Heath would get you to Victoria at 6.23 but you would have to walk to Lewes. If you went by the 5 bus from Rodmell you would not get to Victoria until 7.22. Is that too late? If so, I think I had better order a car to take you to the 4.54. I should like to come in after dinner & meet H[arold] R[Raymond]. I hope I don't disgrace myself & you.

Shall I really be allowed to take a house with you in June. Or is it a dream?

I love to get your pink letters, though there are, you must admit, holes in the blanket.

> Love
> L.

---

162:    [Sunday] 23 April 1944                                   *25 Vic Sq.*

Dearest Leonard. It would be terrible if that was what your letters were like. I'd much rather have a real whinge. Ones like that don't suggest a blanket at all. This is to tell you that I dreamed about you. We were going 'out to dinner' together but they wouldn't let me sit next you because you were a lion (I mean (I cannot at all spell meterophorically [sic])) and so you had to sit near a lady lion.

Peter [Brooker] came yesterday and depressed me dreadfully in every way. I ached all over when he went & found I could hardly move my eyes or arms, but could only sit & roll my eyes dismally round the room.

I must post this. I shall ring up on Mon. night to ask & tell you about coming down. If I don't it will mean we are coming as fixed.

Love dear lion – but no I won't have you one or they will make you find a lady one. I'll have you as a private blanket.

> from your loving
> T.

---

163:    [undated]                                        [LW, *Monk's House*]

To possess all of you, body, mind, and soul,
For in love there's nothing between nothing and the whole:
'I love your eyes, your mouth, your hand, your foot, your ear—'
'Not quite so fast, not quite so fast, my dear,
You have no locus standi, no claims, I fear,
No place or rights or privileges here.'

'Darling, of course I know
That this is so;
Mine was a cry
For what's beyond the sky;
On this low earth my claim is pretty low,
You must allow,
Only a toe.'

164:    [Thursday] 11 May 1944                          *Monk's House*

Darling, I cannot go to bed without writing to you. I keep on seeing your
face as it was just before I left you. You were sad, I know, & worried by
the nag & fret of day to day life. And I hate myself because I feel I may
have added an ounce to your worries by that stupid poem. And, darling
tiger, I hate the thought of your not being happy for you are an embodied
happiness to other people. You know that your merely being in the room
with me makes me happy – gives me the kind of deep happiness, an
assuredness of beauty & rightness, which one gets from a sunny day in the
garden. And I notice that it is not only I who feel this; it is everyone –
except people like Harold & Vera. So that there is something horrible in
the thought that you should not yourself be happy.

As for me, you can dismiss me from your head. I get more happiness
from an hour with you than from a year away from you & it really
outweighs all the longing for you & missing you when you aren't there. I
can't pretend that I don't miss you & long for you – here more than any
where. But you have turned a passive, neutral existence into life of
passionate happiness. To know you & love you has been the best thing in
life, & if it has, as it must, the other side to it which crept into that silly poem,
it isn't worth thinking about in comparison with you & what you are to me.

I won't say what it's like here today because, if I did, you might think I
was contradicting myself in the last paragraph – though really I shouldn't
be. Only I must tell you that the Echinocactus is in full flower & is not a
large white trumpet, but a smaller magenta trumpet, very strange, & the
Rebutia[1] with the small pink flowers in the white fur muff, which I think
you saw last year, is out – & I looked at them with the wraith.

1. A member of the National Cactus and Succulent Societies, LW grew many varieties in his
greenhouse, where vines dangled from the ceiling and TR felt immersed in her South African past.
Echinocactus (Hedgehog Cactus) is primarily Mexican, Rebutia is South American; by 1600 both
had been imported to Europe, and later to South Africa and Australia.

I am afraid you'd never be as fond of me as Kingsley is. He rang me up this morning & asked me to come & lunch with him. I refused. As soon as I got back here, the telephone rang – Kingsley. Would I lunch Monday? No. Would I write an article on the I.L.O. [International Labour Organisation]? (You don't know what that is.) Would I review a book by Elspeth Huxley? If you say two nos, you feel you must say a Yes instead of a third No & so I said Yes out of sheer weakness. I don't want to write about the I.L.O. or review Elspeth – & now I shall have to read about the I.L.O. all Friday & Saturday & write about it all Sunday morning.[1]

Darling tiger, I must begin on the I.L.O. at once & say good night to you, (Peat as I wrote this put out a paw & gently smudged the word 'say' to show, I suppose, that he said it too. He was on the sunniest patch of the flowerbed by the front door when I arrived). And say that I love you, adore you, & kiss your toe – I mean, my toe.

Your
L.

165:   [Tuesday–Friday] 9–12 May [1994]                    *25 Victoria Sq.*

My darling Leonard – You will see that everything is wrong about this letter. I started it as far as the darling on May 9th but as the person I was writing to was the manager of the Tannery I thought perhaps darling wasn't right & so I started again on a new piece & now I am using it up on you. I should not be writing at all but drawing a most ravishing Poppy. I went to Selfridges on my way home yesterday to buy some of your sacred biscuits (the nice Jewess at the Kosher is religious & disapproves of me having them, but I would sell her church wine if I had any). Coming out through the Flower Dept I thought 'I wish there'd be a nasturtium & a Poppy' & there in front of my eyes was a bunch of poppies. Pale pinky white. White. Vermilion & golden yellow, crimped petals yellow centres & rather stronger material than sheer legs. Do you think they are your Papavar Pilosa? If so we must always have quantities of them as they are enchanting. They were 2/6 a bunch but I beat them down to 2/- because one was rather dead. Pat told me yesterday that two women had been jailed for a month for going into a banned area – I now see in the paper

1. 'Choppy Seas for the I.L.O.' appeared (unsigned) on 20 May 1944; the review of *Race and Politics in Kenya: A Correspondence Between Elspeth Huxley and Margery Perham* was published on 3 June 1944.

they were camp followers so perhaps they wouldn't jug me, as they are always so very hard on prostitutes I expect it was just a part of the old thing.

The sun is pouring in, my balcony is in a drift of light & I would like to start painting it once more but I cannot & must do poppies & Moses.[1]

    love dear Leonard.

        T.

166:   [Thursday] 18 May 1944                       *Monk's House*

Dearest Trekkie, darling Marjorie, sweetest of tigers, You are all these to me & my faith is this that I worship you in Trinity & Trinity in Unity, neither confounding the Persons, nor dividing the substance. For there is one person of Trekkie, another of Marjorie, & another of tiger; but the lovableness of Trekkie, of Marjorie, & of tiger is all one; the Glory equal, the Beauty coeternal. Trekkie beloved, Marjorie beloved, & tiger beloved. And yet there are not three beloveds but one beloved. And in this Trinity, none is afore, or after others: none is greater, or less than another. But the whole three Persons are dearest together: and darling: and sweetest. So that in all things as aforesaid: the Unity in Trinity, & the Trinity in Unity is to be worshipped.

I never understood Saint Athanasius & his Creed[2] until tonight. It is now quite clear to me & why at last I feel secure of everlasting salvation. It is entirely due to you.

Having known Saxon[3] for 45 years, I feel quite sure that the enclosed letter means that he *did* fall in love with you. At any rate it is just the kind of letter which he would write if he had fallen in love with you & wanted to tell you so.

It is a strange thing that 2 weeks following in the hour before leaving you I have said something to depress you. Is it because though I really try not to be I am subconsciously depressed by having to leave you? I didn't mean what I said quite in the sense you took it, I think. At any rate you

1. For the Midget Bible Stories series.
2. The Athanasian Creed explicitly avows the doctrines of the Trinity, as opposed to Arianism, in which Jesus is the best of created beings but not of the same substance as God. Athanasius and Arius were 4th-century Alexandrians. Although its authorship is unknown, the Creed is supposed formerly to have been drawn up by Athanasius.
3. Saxon Sydney-Turner (1880–1962) shared rooms with LW at Trinity College, Cambridge. He was an Apostle who took a double first in classics but was said by his friends to lack drive. He worked in the Treasury. The enclosed letter is not in the Archive.

know, tiger darling, that I'm not so foolish as to believe that life with you in it is over.

Do you like the enclosed Congolese?

The red lily is fully out, the oranges have grown perceptibly, red cockscomb cactus is flaming.

Goodnight, beloved Trinity – I worship you with an adoration which Saint Athanasius had no notion of.

> Your contrite
> L.


167:   [undated, left at 24 Victoria Square]

[Dearest Leonard – crossed out] Dear Woolf.

*If* you are going to Selfridges would you buy me some coffee beans – I have great quantities of coffee so it isn't urgent. Are you dining with me tonight[1] or with the person you kept on confusing me with in your last letter?

I am off to the Tannery have washed my hair & put on silk stockings. I do hope darling Mr Hare will like it.

> [love – crossed out] ever your
> [T. – crossed out] Marjorie Ritchie


168:   [Friday] 19 May [1944]                                   *25 Vic Sq.*

My dearest Leonard. This is not a letter – in fact you don't really deserve one at all.

Time frightens me & you must not shake the bogey in my face. It is no use telling me to face it. I can face some things but now I don't seem able to face that. It is much worse since the war. But I do not intend to be physico analylised [sic] in fact I mean to let it rip & simply to make you not do it. So there is your lecture & I must also tell you that Ian's motorbike has cut you out as being the most interesting thing to watch in the square.

He came home on it last night & we dragged it into the hall & he went off on it this morning. The old Scots skivvy was so thrilled she watched

1. LW's diary shows that he and TR lunched together in London on 17, 18, 22, 23, 24 and 25 May, when they went to the Army & Navy Stores to buy a bicycle, which LW took to Rodmell for her to use. They also dined together most of those evenings.

like a little animal from its hole half up the area steps just the top of her white cap showing motionless above the street level.

I drew Murr[a]y's rose after you left & now I am off to get the tools if I can. I shall go straight to Euston Rd. It must be heavenly at Monk's House this morning, a tissue paper day.

Love from
    T.

Mrs Osborne's[1] friend's sister has sprained her ankle so Mrs O's friend may be sometime as the sister is 'heavy'. I think you should ask Dorothy [Woodman].

Love T.


169:    [Thursday] 25 May 1944                           *Monk's House*

Tiger Darling, I can't help it, I must write to you. I had meant not to because I still have a lurking fear of boring you. And why on earth you don't think me an intolerable bore, I don't know. For I always do and say the same thing & feel like an old dishevelled fowl now singing away its everlasting single & solitary tune over & over again in the apple tree outside the window. Every Thursday night I sing it to you & I simply cannot go to bed before I do. Why? Because, I think, when I have left you in V.S., I cannot stand the abrupt break from you & you come with me here & in a way by writing to you I keep some part of you still with me. The last days were in some ways the best I've ever had with you in London – right up to the last second when I saw your dear face at the window & went round the corner feeling that I hadn't this time depressed you. You will laugh at me, of course, if I can say what I am trying to say, but I don't mind that. Twice in the last few days I had a more than usually divine illumination* of what you are & are to me. Once when I walked away from [Sybil] Colefax[2] with the dusty grit of her conversation in my mouth & though I knew I shouldn't see you that evening, the mere thought of you as I walked down Victoria Street seemed to blow all the Colefaxes away & leave in her gritty place something of extraordinary freshness & beauty. And again in that 5 minutes last night when I sat by you on the sofa. I am really very fond of Maynard [Keynes], Desmond [MacCarthy], Morgan [Forster] & all the old Bloomsburyites. But we're

1. TR's daily help.
2. Society hostess at her home Argyll House, Chelsea.

terribly bony & brainy, I think, & practise a kind of bleak intellectual ruthlessness upon one another. I again got from you an extraordinary refreshment of spirit & as I could see you there & hear you, it was ever so much the more vivid – & I knew what it was most clearly – you have in you always the very stuff of which poetry – lyric poetry – consists. It is a part of you – & none of us have it at all – it's in your face, your laugh, your thoughts, your feelings, your words, & above all, your pictures. It's what I saw without realising it that first time I saw you – when people *still* turned to look at you in the streets – & made me never forget you. And I saw it again in 1943, even though by then only I turn[ed] to look at you. I dont think I realised exactly what it was until the evening I walked back with you from Fleet St to Mecklenburgh Sq. But it is just pure poetry & it's in the picture there on the wall. It is in 'one small flame upturning seems to his discerning Crocus in the shade' & 'with their palm leaves & cedar sheaves' & 'Alas now for the flowers that you let fall'[1] – & in flowers themselves & your extraordinary personal love (which I love) of flowers. It is cool & fresh & clear & beautiful, & though you can be just as intellectual & ruthless as we are, it means that you are never bleak & bony as we are.

Laugh at me, dearest, as much as you like, but all this *is* true. It is one small part of the many reasons why I love you. I should like to write another page but I suppose you'd say I was foolish & I should like to tell you about the garden & the cactuses & the orange trees now with four leaves & Peat, but I suppose I mustn't & must end Darling, darling tiger, I love you & that is both the beginning & end,

Your L.

* I looked up apprehensively at all the apple trees when I got here, but I could see no illumination or images of the Virgin, thank God.


170:  [Friday] 26 May [1944]                                        *25 Victoria Sq.*

[Across the top of the letter is a delicate tracing of a man in a canoe]

My dearest Leonard. Mars must have been shining specially near the earth last night I think. There was a fine Randan rumpus in the Butcher's shop

1. From: 'When the World Was Burning' by Ebenezer Jones ('One soft flame upturning/Seems, to his discerning,/Crocus in the shade'); 'Luriana' by Charles Elton (see letter 152 and note); *A Winter's Tale* by Shakespeare ('For the flowers now that, frightened, thou let'st fall').

when I went to get my rations this morning. A dreadful old Rat trap of a dame whom I see about in all these shops. She has a right to the best. It began by her refusing to have any pork, others might have it but not she. In a fine tirade she told the butcher what she thought of him & how she must have beef. My attention was slightly distracted by my own hopes & when I listened to her raging next it was directed to & returned by a French woman also shopping. This lady's voice rose higher & went faster than the Rat traps but she didn't put the Rat trap off at all. The fight went deeper & deeper, old wounds to do with the milk man were revived & flicked. At last the French one left but the Rat trap went on & is probably still there. There seemed no reason to think she could ever say all that was souring on her bosom about butchers & meat & the tradespeople who longed to serve her.

Then I went to the Public Library & was flanked by a drawn thread of a man reading his morning paper – and it didn't please him, every two or three minutes he snorted like a horse. I thought at first it was to do with his nose & not his spirit but he would also burst out furiously saying 'Yes but *how many* people – that's what I want to know' & such wild questionings. *I* was in a very different humour for the Encyclopedia Britannica had a real photograph of a girl (I think Japanese) feeding mulberry leaves to silk worms on trays. I could hardly believe it. I found it under silk. I wonder now I think of it if we would have found anything at the Lon Lib under Japan?

The enclosed tracing I made for you when looking through the Encyclopedia for Boston. It had written underneath 'Canoe woven from rushes by the natives of Bolivia'. I think the landscape looks a little bit bleak don't you? There was no view of Boston harbour.[1]

It turns out that Monday is Bank Holiday so there is an extra day for me to get the tracings in to the Chiswick. I shall draw a Petunia for the other garden flower as I have a good drawing of one. Irene was whistled at by sailors in the street & when she walked straight on they yelled at her 'Ya Vicars' wife'.

I had a real old fashioned bad night last night so feel rather more limp than vital. Do you sometimes feel that you need it to rain almost as much as a plant does? Now I must do those shoes. This is a very long interesting letter isn't it?

How I wish I could walk round the garden.

Love dear Leonard.

T.

---

1. For *The Story of Your Cup of Tea* in the Midget Books How and Why series; the petunia was for *In Your Garden* in the First Pictures series.

171:    [Saturday] 27 May 1944                    *Monk's House, Rodmell*

Marjorie darling, Your letter with the rat trap woman & the man in the library made me laugh. Shall I write you the second sheet which I didn't write to you on Thursday at midnight & was going to be about you laughing? Perhaps I had better not, for it might end in my weeping. I nearly did when the 3 tubes of flake white came & I went into your room to put them in your drawer & saw your white woolie on the back of a chair, the Rembrandt, iodized throat tablets, turpentine, & your shoes. There *is* something terribly personal in shoes without the owner (& with *the* toe too not there). I shall be off again in a moment if I don't get away from you to hard facts – & I can't because the truth is, tiger dearest, that I've got you not only on the brain but on the heart.

Well, to facts, which here are always you. The cactuses – O I do wish you had seen them. One with eleven bright orange flowers all out & absolutely covering it in a brilliant crown & next to it another with four orange red flowers. And two of those cardinal's or bishop's mitres, one with a great flower on top white with delicate mauve lines & the other the palest of lemon yellow.

Thursday when I got here was fiendish – a sea fret almost on the meadows & cold, damp north wind. Yesterday not very pleasant but today hot & heavenly. I work & put out plants & think of you. I met Clive [Bell] waiting for the 4.45 on Thursday & we talked with the greatest amiableness & all the time I thought of you, & when I discussed Merle with a man in the carriage, all the time I thought of you. Because I have got you not only on the heart but on the brain.

This evening frenzied barking by Merle when I was eating a tinned steak & kidney pudding. Mrs Collins, the policeman's wife, at the door & with her 2 children: 'Would I sell them one of my goldfish, as they have made a pond in the garden & cant get any fish anywhere?' I gave them 2 fish & thought that Mr Collins might perhaps some day turn a blind eye on Marjorie Tulip Ritchie. Cactuses, Clive, flake white, strangers in railway carriages, goldfish, policemen, turpentine, & shoes – it is always you. Because I've got you not only on the brain but on the heart.

There was a control on Thursday night, but none yesterday. And now as I near the bottom of the page, I know I must stop & get back to my book. I am silly, I know, darling tiger, & this is a silly letter, but you're in my heart & in my brain & I love you.

        Your
        L.

The Ecclesiastical Commissioners consist of 2 Archbishops, 40 Bishops, & various laymen; but 3 of the laymen – a Baronet, an M.P., & a Peer – deal with Church property.


172:    [Saturday] 27 May [1944]                              *25 Vic Sq.*

Dearest Leonard. This is irregular, most. I haven't made the beds. But I have traced six drawings & I find tracing so stupefying I have to stop every so often & I think of other things, dishevelled fowls or anything like that. I wish I had time to do a drawing of you finding a radiance due to an image of the Virgin in one of your apple trees. It would make a good pair to Gabriel & you on the lawn.[1] I am not sure that all the nice things you tell me don't have a very good effect on me. Perhaps I shall really by degrees become what you say I am. Like Lord George.

I have just looked out into the Square & watched a father very carefully comb his little son's hair and with smiles & looking their best they have gone off. It is a treat of some sort from their looks. Humans are so nice when they are like that. And so beastly when like the Rat Trap. Though she was funny too but one could only have laughed with a quite easy mind if one had never lost one's own temper. Alas not T.R.'s condition.[2]

I don't know why that 'crocus in the shade' is so powerful it always gives me a throb. I connect it too with you & remember the evening you read it to me at Monk's House. You never add up all the pleasures I owe you. I should have missed my Thursday night letter very much.

          love T.


173:    [Thursday] 1 June 1944                               *Monk's House*

Darling, tiger darling, I told you I always think of you in the train on Thursday & how I did tonight & how I longed for you to be sitting by me & watching the absurdities of men & things. For it was absurd. And I kept on thinking of the delight it would have been to watch you watching, to see the serious disapproval which you, as a dog critic & dog-lover critic, would have had to show & to have caught the delighted amusement in your dearest face which I know so well, & which you couldn't have

1. With LW saying: 'I don't believe a word of it.'
2. TR had a quick temper. She often told Anneliese West she wished she could control it better because then she would not have to apologise so often – which she always readily did.

helped showing. I got a seat with a table in front of me & then there entered & took the seat with the table on the other side a young man & woman & with them was a dog. He had a lot of beagle blood in him, though perhaps not pure beagle. He was rather old, heavy, & wise. Round his back, waist & chest he had a considerable lint bandage. The young man carefully & solemnly opened a handbag in which meticulously & neatly folded was a very large piece of thick brown paper. This he slowly unfolded, smoothed it out, & laid it on the table. The dog was lifted up & gently laid on the brown paper. He sat up & took a look round & having satisfied himself about Merle & me he lay down flat full length on his side & the young woman put her handbag for a pillow under his head. He slept. The young woman then put her head on the young man's shoulder & slept. Before she fell asleep, I asked them what was wrong with the dog. She answered with such voluble animation that I could not hear what she said, but I think she may have said that wartime diet had led to impurity of blood.

It was sunny when I got to Lewes & there was no control & I said to myself you might have come. It seems almost impossible to believe now that you may really one day come again or that there were days when you really, when we really, did come. And bicycling out the wind blew the scent of the bean flower into my face all along the road, & again I thought of you &

The beanflower's bloom
And the blackbird's tune
And May & June

And there were roses out in the garden, & two enchanting pink blooms on your Church Farm geranium, & the yellow cistus which I bought after seeing yours at Church Farm all over flowers. Is it any wonder that I have thought of you & seen & heard you every second since I left you?

When you told me about how you felt about the earrings, darling tiger, I felt that you were absolutely & perfectly right, as you always are, & more sweet than ever I had imagined. It is because you feel things like that that you make me love you with something deeper & more overwhelming than just common or garden love, though you'd say that's just nonsense. I don't think it is. In the last weeks I have got to love you deeper, more passionately than ever before, & at the same time I have felt that by some miracle there was something which bound you to me as well as me to you. I used to feel desperate when I left you, desperate because I couldn't believe that I had anything to give you, so that I always expected that the next time I saw you you would find me out as a nuisance & a bore.

The last weeks that desperation & the terrors have gone; it is miserable to be away from you & there is the longing for you, but also there is a kind of incredible certainty, of something divinely solid which I shall come back to find among the cups & plates in the kitchen at 25. If you were not you, I could not say that to you, because it is, I know, presumptuous to say it, but being you you'll know what I mean & that I say it with infinite humility. I think there is a curious wave length system between minds & hearts so that we either can or cannot (in infinitely varying degrees) tune in to one another. But I see from the time & this being page 4 I must really not embark on this. Perhaps tomorrow night I'll continue.

Dearest & sweetest, you know what I mean & that I know that I'm not worthy to kiss even your toe. Yet I kiss it – humbly. I think of this afternoon & you & Phillip IV & Rubens – how glad I am we went to see it – & the extraordinary pleasure it is to look at pictures or listen to music with you. I do hope that it & Tim [Ritchie] & Athene [Ritchie] & the flies in the Green Park & the flies of life did not make you still more tired & that you sleep – are already sleeping – soundly tonight. Schlafe, mein Kindchen, schlaf ein – I wish I could sing you to sleep with Mozart.

Your

L.

Do you think one ought or ought not to answer a letter like the enclosed? I find it very difficult to know.

174:  [Friday] 2 June 1944                                   25 Vic Sq., S.W.1

My dearest Leonard

I asked [George] Devenish [a lithographic printer] just now if he could find you someone for three hours a week & he says he can. He says for certain but certain is that certain does. He says he might even fix you up with his old missus. There was no letter for you last night or this morning. I am in a, if not the, wilderness so cannot write you a good letter. Don't think it is a worse wilderness than perhaps it is, there may be some succulents in flower behind one of the borders.

Davis & Ian are really meeting at 10 o'clock. They are coming here to look at the pictures & then going to lunch at the Boring Goring. I shall not go to lunch, but must wash my hands now to look respectable. Athene was friendly & playful but what do people do who have it all the time?

love dear L from

T.

Dearest, darling tiger. The most perfect life would be to be *always* with
you &, after your drawing, the more I think of it, the more I favour
Bolivia, in the canoe. For there would be absolutely nothing to distract us
– I should just contemplate you eternally & we would talk & talk & talk,
only now and then dipping the paddle into a motionless sea. As far as I am
concerned I should not only have perfect happiness, but should,
according to Plato, be living the highest possible form of mortal existence,
continued contemplation of the good & beautiful. But I know you'd never
take me to Bolivia. The second best, I think, might be to be with you all
Monday, Tuesday, Wednesday, & Thursday, & then come down here &
spend the whole of Friday, Saturday, & Sunday entirely alone writing a
gigantic unending letter to you. The only thing which I *want* to do when
I'm away from you is to write to you & I've had a desperate struggle all
this evening to read proofs & I said to myself I would read proofs until
11.15 & then write & that's what I've done. If I wrote all day for three
days, you would get about 130 pages every Monday. I'm afraid you
wouldn't be able to stand it. Why is there always something which makes
even the second best impossible?

That of course is not really quite true. I suppose the best thing in life is
to be an artist & to create as you do. And if one isn't and can't, the best is
to get what I get from you. I am sure, as I said last night, that minds &
hearts have different wave lengths & one can 'tune in' perfectly to some,
whereas with others it's hopelessly impossible & if one attempts to do so
you get the most appalling jars & discords. What is so heavenly with you
is that everything about you seems to be always in perfect tune with the
vibrations of my mind & heart – you are always saying things or doing or
looking so that I get a thrill or vibration of complete harmony, the kind of
answering thrill which one gets from some divine phrase of Mozart. And
I think my terrors have subsided & I have felt more sure the last weeks,
because by some miracle you do seem to be able to tune into me without
feuding jars, discords, & atmospherics. It does sound presumptuous to
say that – conceited. But it all really comes from you.

Darling creature, I must post this – its midnight. I suppose I shant see
you on Monday morning as you'll be off to the Chiswick. And I have a
meeting at 5.30 which I'm pledged to go to. I shall come in & see you as
soon as I get back if you are alone. How I hate not seeing you.

I think your Church Farm geranium one of the most enchanting of all
small flowers. And the pink cistus near it is covered with blooms in the

morning. I have planted out some of the other geraniums from the Hort. Society seed near it.

O my darling tiger, the longing I have for you.

Your L

176:   [Thursday] 8 June 1944                    [*Monk's House*]

Darling, This is not a Thursday evening letter for I told you I wouldn't write one. But I find it would be too bleak (for me) to go to bed without a word to you. And I know now that you will like to hear that I haven't been knocked down by a bus or anything else & am in my usual (ailing) health.

It seems singularly placid here & the train was emptier than usual & it positively rained when I got to Lewes & I was quite wet when I arrived here. In the garden roses chiefly, but the cactuses are wonderful. One of the Echinocactus which has never flowered before has bloomed fully out. They have the long upstanding trumpets like the great white one I gave you last year, but this is smaller & a pale yellow, rather the colour of the mesembryanthemum[1] that was out last time you were here.

I rather hoped you would ring me up again & tell me to come & lunch in Arnos Park. I let Mrs Osborne in & left some dregs of rather old milk in your kitchen.

I have been looking several times this evening at the empty chairs opposite to me (occupied, it is true, by Peat & yet empty) & I say to myself: 'If T were sitting there, she would be exactly what she has always been, & I have that anchor & therefore it is just the same & I just as happy as if she & not (or as well as) Peat were there.' But somehow or other, you know, it simply doesn't work, & when I go round the garden as soon as I get back without T & yet always with T, it isn't the same. The trouble really is that if one has known the best, the second best loses its flavour completely.

There is no doubt that 'On love, Affection, & Marriage' written & illustrated by T Ritchie, with Notes, Collections, & Appendices by L Woolf must be written & published.

Peat has been fighting again & is bleeding & limping. I wish you would send Rose to him. But perhaps as she has had a family by Wave that would be wrong.

---

1. Mesembryanthemum is a large genus of South Africa's succulent plants many of which can only be grown in England, as here, in a greenhouse.

Don't rush yourself too much, dearest, & don't let cats or anything else disturb your sleep.

This is the quotation which William [Robson] sprang on me. I daresay you will get it right:

> Should the corvette return
> With the anxious Scotch colonel,
> Escape would be frustrate,
> Retention eternal.[1]

This has almost turned into a letter. The truth is, as you see, that it is impossible for me on Thursday evenings to conceal, repress, or forget that I love you.

L.

177:  [Friday] 9 June [1944]                          *25 Vic Sq.*

My dearest Leonard.

I finished the day off by falling flat on the way to the Arnos Grove Station bursting both stockings & one knee. I had been working on the red stone & it was as if I had decided to run the red printing over my knee. I had to sit all the way in the tube & watch the dull faces opposite each go through the same steps of deep reasoning. She's bleeding – she's torn her stockings – she must have fallen down. And some times the same one did it all through again.

There were no proofs only something from the Aboriginie Protection Soc. & a letter from the Labour Party.

I must go & try to win through to the Chiswick P on my own & buy the meat first. Rose was shut in last night so I had a good one. She is in the state of Edith's children & can't bear me out of her sight.

Love dear L.

T.

178:  [Wednesday] 14 June 1944 [left at 24 Victoria Square]

Dearest, It's all right about this evening in so far as he found the other one, but wrong for today, because there was something wrong with its

1. LW no doubt means Robson's ditty to refer to IMP's return.

clip which needed repair & he will take a week to do it. So I haven't after all any claim on your ears on your birthday. I must try to catch my train & will write tonight & will try to say what is not true about you in order to win your *serious* attention & possibly respect. But, darling tiger, what is delicious & true is what you have become to me.

L.

I am putting another drop of milk in your kitchen.


179:   Your birthday, [Thursday 15 June] 1944          Monk's House

Beloved tiger, I know already that I can't write you the extremely amusing letter which I had planned to write you. This will be dull, pedestrian.

First, the Lion of Judah. I was immensely flattered, though I tried to pretend to myself that I wasn't, in order to flatter myself still more by pretending superiority to all that, because as soon as I came in he left an inferior gentleman to whom he was showing rings with a curt 'One moment' & came over to me. He found the second imperial earing at once. Then I told him what we wanted with the other. At first he was horrified at the idea of turning it upside down & it was impossible & would spoil it. Then we seized a girl assistant & her ear & clamped the earing to it first one way & then the other, the abandoned inferior gentleman glaring, as I suddenly observed, over her shoulder at me indignantly. Mosheh was at last, rather grudgingly, convinced by ocular demonstration on a female ear that we were right. He then became quite excited & said it must have a tiny piece added to it above so that it would hang more beautifully. I had to agree to his doing this. Do you think he can be trusted?[1]

I got down here with no adventures – the trains are almost empty. I went to Gorringe but he was out & I shall ring him tomorrow morning. It was sunny but very windy & has now clouded over with a kind of leaden orbit thundery hue in the sky. The garden full summer with pinks & roses, but not one cactus bloom in the greenhouse.

1. LW bought TR brooches, ear-rings and rings for birthdays and Christmases. The jeweller, Edward Good, had a shop on Museum Street. He was a friend of TR's, and the author (pseud. Mosheh Oved) of *For the Sake of the Days* (Faber, 1940), in which she appears as a beautiful young Englishwoman who drives him from London to the Downs, and to visit Lullington Church at Wilmington. His other books, several in Yiddish, include *The Book of Affinity* (1933) and *Visions and Jewels* (1952).

In the train I tried to compose the 'amusing' letter which I had planned which was to ignore truth & describe all your (imaginary) faults, spots, & blemishes. How do you explain it that I simply couldn't do it? I couldn't produce a la Bruyère 'character' of a faulty T. Ritchie. 'She has a spot on her chin' was as far as I could get & even then I had to add 'it is a very small spot.' So I must end this letter for if I go on I shall be like [Balven?] and then you'll laugh at me. When we are separated, I can only think of you as I remember you, & when I see you again, I know now, as I told you the other day, that the miracle will happen & I shall find you more sensitive & understanding & fiery & amusing & lovable & beautiful & simple & complicated & harmonious – it is extraordinary harmony & harmonies in you dearest, that make you so different from everyone else – & direct than I remembered. There you are, darling creature, you can have your laugh at that & me, but not even your laughter can alter the truth.

I do hope that after all you enjoyed your birthday dinner or at least bits of it. Dont do too much & if you have business letters to write keep them for me to do on Monday & sleep well, tiger darling.     Your
L.


180:   [Friday] 16 June 1944                                     *25 Vic Sq*

Dearest Leonard.

What an unpleasant night. No sleep at all. I have swept your little hole out & taken two mattresses into it so that one can go in & say well tant pis I've done all I can & go if possible to sleep.

The dinner party was in some ways less fearsome than I had expected. Everyone was talkative & cheerful. I thought Pat [Ritchie] might be dumb & Nora[h Smallwood][1] argumentative.

It is not you I laugh at. I thought going in the tube what it really is. I laugh to see myself put so high. Mind it really is partly due to a shadowy sardonic character called Fish. I don't know when or why Alice & I created him but whenever either of us seemed to the other to be rated too high by a third & be blown with pride the other said rather sourly 'Fish *would* laugh' and I think Fish would you know at nearly everything you have told me.

1. Norah Evelyn Smallwood OBE (1909–1984) was from 1945 one of Ian's partners at Chatto & Windus, which she had joined as a secretary in 1937, and from which she retired in 1982, two years after IMP's death. Her husband, Peter Warren Sykes Smallwood, was killed in action in 1943. She was very possessive of IMP, with whom she had a long affair.

I have never been so rich. I was given three cheques for £10 yesterday. If they stop this absurd shelling I shall have my studio repainted. I must be off to the Chiswick. The cemetery was looking delicious last evening all the huge half wild rose bushes full out & up to their knees in grass. I think of my earings a lot & long to wear them. I miss you too.

      Love T.

181:   [Saturday] 17 June 1944           *Monk's House*

Les étres nous sont d'habitude si indifférents que quand nous avons mis dans l'un d'eux de telles possibilités de suffrance & de joie, pour nous il nous semble appartenir à un autre univers, il s'entoure de poésie, il fait de notre vie une étendre émouvante où il sera plus ou moins rapproché de nous.[1]

      L.

182:   Monday morning [probably 19 June 1944]

Dearest L.

    I am going to the Chiswick. I will not be late back & will come in & see if you are with politicians. Ian is going to work but will not I think stay late. You will have dinner here won't you.

    I printed the green grey yesterday & now have only the crimson which should be an easy printing as it is straight colour. The g. green went well. I didn't go to sleep until 2 because I stupidly had turned off the gas circulator & it took hours after I had re lit it stretching itself & feeling its joints & cracking them & sighing to find itself hot again. It was a quiet night for bangs. I only heard about four & none so very near.[2] I would

---

1. 'People are usually so indifferent to us that when we have instilled in one of them such possibilities as freedom and joy, he seems to us to have become part of another universe, he is surrounded with poetry, he creates a touching extension of our own life in which he becomes more or less connected to us.'

2. A week after D-Day the first V1s (commonly called doodlebugs, flying-bombs, robots or buzz-bombs) landed in England. On the night of 15 June, 244 were aimed at London; 73 reached the target. Between 19 June and 3 July an average of 100 every 24 hours were reported, about half in London. They came at all hours, interrupting work, parties, sleep. Only one V1 landed near Lewes and no V2s, which began on 8 September. Travelling at 4,000 miles an hour and moving in a parabola through the stratosphere, they were fewer in number but silent, while the flying-bombs warned with a spluttering noise.

have rung you up but we had dinner with Mabel so I couldn't. I wore my earings. I thought it rather a shame to wear them there for the first time but they felt comfortable & slightly like a blanket so I wore them. It is no use telling you I am not what you say. I didn't feel sweet at all but had a nasty bitter taste to myself. Ian couldn't have gone down on the Friday he was really too stiff. He could have on the Saturday, but I think it was 'all for the best' so I hope you now don't feel the slightest enragement?

    love

     T.

If you get Brown bread will you get some for me. No white.


183:   [Friday] 23 June 1944                                *Monk's House*

Darling – darling tiger, I can only say I love you, I love you, & again I love you. And you won't get this, I suppose, until Monday morning, when I shall be there to say it instead of writing it. O my dearest, I have never hated leaving you so much as I did this morning. Yet I felt it was no use to stay. And – in spite of all the laughter of all the Fish – I have never felt so certain as this week of the lovableness & loveliness of your character. Everything that is hateful, enraging, irritating, worrying, exhausting, terrifying, exasperating rained down on your dear head – I have never known anyone meet that sort of accumulation of little & big horrors with your sweetness. You made me ashamed of myself (a thing which has very rarely happened before because having no conscience one is inside without shame). There you were with pilotless airplanes perpetually falling about your ears, perpetually making beds, cooking meals, looking after people – & then Ian ill on your hands – & all your work brushed aside – & except for one minute flare up after sleepless nights always just your adorable self as if you were walking in the garden after breakfast. Whereas I after 4 days of it with no one to think of but myself was already on the point of becoming enraged.

How I wish you were here – but you know that. The only consolation is that there was a Control on today at Lewes & if they had sent you back, it might have dished us completely for July. When you come, you must come in the middle of the week. You *must* get away from London. Though there are moments of terrific barrage of guns (mostly pretty far away) punctuated by explosions which I take to be the shooting down of one of the beastly things & though a pane of glass has been blown out of the kitchen window & all Mrs Ebbs's ornaments have been disturbed & Mrs Charnes's house is

in a lamentable state, the peacefulness here is extraordinary after London.[1]
It makes it the more hateful that you aren't here.

Your easel, canvases, box have already arrived. Your room is ready.
But you make me so happy when I'm with you now, dearest, that I think
it really is true that it gives me something to hold on to when you aren't
there, something which makes even the wretchedness of being parted
from you negligible in comparison.

Laugh, Fish, laugh, with all the other fools.

Sleep well, darling creature, I love you,

L.

184:   [Sunday] 25 June 1944                    *25 Victoria Square, S.W.1*

Dear Sir,

Last week I informed you that your cistern overflowed & dripped if no
water was being used in your house. I was amazed to find it doing the
same thing this Sunday & could not understand how at a time like this of
acute water shortage and National Effort you could so neglect the
ordinary duties of a citizen and fail to have it attended to. I broke into your
house & left your bathroom tap dripping.

Yours truly
*Marjorie Tulip Parsons*

The Occupier

185:   [Tuesday] 27 June 1944                              *Monk's House*

Dearest, sweetest, loveliest of employers, I am a bad secretary.
We never wrote the letter about Church Farm. It should be

'Dear St Paul, I am sorry to say that I shall not be able to continue renting
Church Farm & must therefore give you the formal notice terminating
the lease at the end of the December quarter.

Yours truly,  I. M. Parsons'

1. Reverend and Mrs Ebb lived at the Old Rectory where she directed the fête dramas which may
have inspired the pageant in *Between the Acts*. Charnes Cottage was between the Rectory and
Monk's House.

Merle is distinctly better, though not entirely recovered. She was rather bad on Monday & it was probably a mild attack of distemper. Peat resisted arrest when the vet called to take him off in a basket. He bit & scratched Louie & successfully escaped. He turned up out of the most sheltered spot in the garden as soon as I arrived, frightfully pleased with himself, & greeting me with an extra loud meaowing.

I don't know that this can be called exactly a peaceful place today. I had scarcely sat down to my correspondence when there was the zoom of a fly bomb straight for the house. It really was rather exciting. The beast appeared low down with a Spitfire on its tail. Unfortunately the pilot did what I, being a bad shot, have done only too often. He got excited & instead of waiting until he had a complete certainty (after all he had all the way to London before him) he opened fire just before they got over the garden. He missed (I think luckily for Monk's House) & they streaked away over the meadows to Lewes, he firing (wildly, I thought) all the way until he had exhausted his ammunition & had to give it up. I hope the beast didn't reach Victoria Square. An hour later the same thing happened again, only this time there was no Spitfire & the guns blazed away at it with the same result.

You will be extra careful to get to shelter, darling tiger, won't you? I have one claim on you which even you cannot deny me. I know I have no positive claim, locus standi, rights, or privileges. I know you love me exactly as you do

(1)  Willie [Robson]
(2)  Saxon [Sydney-Turner]
(3)  Mr [George] Devenish
(4)  Harold Raymond
(5)  etc.

But I have this negative claim: that you mean more to me than you mean to anyone else. I believe it to be true though it may sound presumptuous. For you mean & are absolutely everything to me. Without you life is nothing, meaningless; with you I have everything. So that though I'm sure you would say 'Of course, I'll be careful, Leonard dear, for your sake – & for Devenish's', you might be just a tiny bit more careful than ever seems necessary – for my sake. And rest on the sofa occasionally even when I'm not there to tell you to. O my dearest, you can't know how horrible it is to come down here now & leave you in that turmoil.

I have written this rather earlier than usual with a blazing setting sun just going out behind the down, rain, a leaden sky & rainbow in the east which makes me think of you twice & thrice over – do you remember the rainbows & hanging out of the window to look at them? But I will say as I always do goodnight, darling tiger, I love you.

>Your
>L.

186:   [Friday] 30 June [1944]                    *25 Victoria Sq., S.W.1*

Dearest Leonard.

Nothing to tell you except that I have just finished getting the picture into its frame & the lithograph in a portfolio & labels written & the Bible found to quote about Adam & Eve & a sample colour enclosed for Stiles to tint the flat and the whole lot put among the dustbins in the area for S[tiles] to collect. He says he will take all to the Nat Gal before eleven to-morrow. So that should be all right. Owing to mistaken zeal on the part of the owner of the litho stones Miss [Caroline Byng] Lucas has been sent *two* glazed rollers instead of one. Will she keep the one she prefers & return the other. She wouldn't want to. Will my P.S. write call or phone about this please?[1]

I had a good night & am just off to the C[hiswick] P. I finished the midget colour stones but hadn't anything left inside me to draw the little what not drawing for Doddy[2] so must do it to-day.

I must buy the MEAT & go.

Love dear L.        from T.

187:   [Thursday] 6 July 1944                          *Monk's House*

Darling tiger, I have arranged with Gander that he will call for your trunk next Tuesday & bring it here. It makes me begin to believe that it is possible that I might hope that it is conceivable that you may possibly at some uncertain date really be here. I can see you shake your head at such a rash statement, give me one of your serious looks, & say firmly: 'Perhaps.' I have never, dearest, never looked forward to anything so much as to this. It is, therefore, I agree foolhardy even to begin to believe

1. TR was sending a painting and lithograph to The Artists of Fame and Promise exhibition at the Leicester Galleries, which she, LW and Irene Hawkins would view together on Wednesday 5 July. Stiles was painting Victoria Square. Acting as her private secretary, LW was to write to Caroline Lucas, whom TR had helped with lithography, to get the roller back.
2. Dorothy Moir, over whose fireplace TR would paint a decoration in 1950.

TR with God always waiting round the corner ready to knock one off one's perch.

It is hot here, & has been sunny but too much wind. Another pale yellow echinocactus in bloom. The garden has settled down to summer. I hope it will be a bit more peaceful when [crossed out] if you come. I was rather amused – I had barely left Lewes station when there was an alert & as I toiled up the hill to Swanbourgh a bang & column of smoke about 2 or 3 miles ahead. I was just at the moment level with the deaf man who does the roads there & is the most typical of Sussex yokels. 'That was at Southease', he remarked, 'or maybe Rodmell. (He was quite wrong). The last was two minutes ago over yonder at Firle. I always said he'd do this when the time came for him to pack up. He knows he's got to pack up & so he's sending them things over. He knows he's got to die.' I agreed with him. One of them things has taken part of the roof off Berwick Church but has not damaged the paintings.[1]

At Lewes station was waiting Duncan [Grant] for his mother who came by the same train as I. She lives at Twickenham & is rather unnerved by them things & Maynard has let her go & stay at Tilton.[2] It seems to me that if Mrs Grant can go to Tilton Mrs Parsons can go to Monk's House.

Merle is distinctly better & leapt about almost in her old ecstatic feather haired way. Her eyes are still rather bad & her hind legs even more disconnected from the brain & fore legs than before.

I thought, dearest of creatures, that you had the right to be encouraged rather than depressed by that show. There is no doubt that your two pictures stood out as different from any of the others in that room & I'm sure that the difference is something valuable & important. It is always dangerous to compare especially from art to art, but what we were saying about tricks of the trade is true of Wordsworth, I think. It gives your pictures a directness, simplicity, even a kind of nakedness which I expect is frightfully difficult to use. But you have already learnt to use it in a remarkable way & I'm certain that in your case the buds have barely

1. Begun in 1941, the Berwick Church murals were painted by Vanessa Bell, Duncan Grant and Quentin Bell on plasterboard in a barn beside Charleston and fixed into position in January 1943. Some direct painting connecting the decorations to their church setting was completed that summer and a service of dedication was held in October. Vanessa Bell later painted three more panels, which were destroyed by vandals and repainted by Duncan Grant, who, with Quentin Bell, also added further decorations. Angelica Bell and several Charleston neighbours modelled for the murals.

2. John Maynard Keynes's farm adjoining Vanessa Bell's house at the northern foot of the South Downs.

begun to open. I say this with the greatest humility but I must say it. The fact that your pictures grow on one the longer one has them on one's walls instead of dying on one (& them) as so many do & that the longer one has them the more they grow in depth & complexity – so that oddly they seem gradually to lose or modify the initial simplicity & nakedness, which I think they do possess – must mean that they do have a trick of the trade, in the good sense, & I expect you're one of the people who have to develop their own trade tricks. I don't think that really means that in some subtle way they haven't learnt something from the tricks of the trade of other painters. It isn't really true that you couldn't tell from the picture of yours I'm looking at now – & it is lovely & very remarkable – that you had looked at the great masters, just as one can really see that Wordsworth had read Milton.

I was thinking as I sat upstairs this afternoon opening my pile of letters that I lead rather an odd, dissociated life & I owe it as I owe everything to you. On Mondays at 11 when I find you in the kitchen or sweeping the floor I suddenly enter a kind of dream of 72 hours of complete happiness whenever I see you. Then at 11 on Thursdays a knife descends & cuts the thin-spun thread & for 96 hours I live an entirely different life immersed for the most part in what is ordinarily called reality, the thing for which everything must be sacrificed – work. But I'm quite certain of this – that the dream is reality & the reality is just bunk. I am inclined to think that I did more good to the world on the only two occasions in which I succeeded in kissing your toe – & certainly to myself – though as a matter of accuracy it was your shoe – than in all the hours & days of 'work', sitting at a typewriter churning out pompous nonsense. I should like to go on to a 3rd sheet, but you would probably disapprove & tell me to 'work'. I despise work & love you, my dearest   L.

188:   [Friday] 7 July [1944]                                    *25 Vic Sq.*

My dearest Leonard.

I don't think you will get this letter before you leave on Monday. I went to the Leicester at lunch time with Ian & looked at every picture & was quite moved by the presence of two pictures by T.R. and thought they looked quite well really. How stupid emotions are. Why be shaking from head to foot on Wednesday & cool & rock like on Friday?

Ian thinks his removal fairly likely within the next three weeks – more & more likely I mean.

I have absolutely nothing more to tell you because I am very stagnant inside & no one has thrown stones into me from the outside. Irene came home full of triumph & had bought [Enid] Marx.[1] It must be catching because to-day the picture above & below were sold. And whose painting turns out to be next but one do you think? Texhures'? [probably Jean Texcier] is that how you would spell it. Probably not. I must post this or it won't even start off today.
     Love Leonard dear
       T.


189:   [Friday] 7 July 1944               *Monk's House*

[typed insert]    In demarcating the affecto-symbolic substrate underlying the behavior of man, we have attempted to contrast the incitements that pertain to this condition reaction-segment, and thus segregate the organism's epigenic behavior-reactions from the motivations of man's organism as an orthogenic whole.

    This may seem a large order. Indeed, from the narrow viewpoint of the conditioned part-brain of man, it is a large order – so large, in fact, as to appear quite beyond the possibility of fulfillment. But from the viewpoint of the organism's basic orientation this position becomes infinitely simpler than the position maintained by psychopathologists today in respect to man's disorders of behavior.

Tiger dearest, We thought the Chimpanzee book jargon. What do you think of the above from a pamphlet sent me this morning.

    Here is an interesting fact from my book on geology. Burton ale has a very fine & peculiar quality due to the salts in the water used in making it. The salts were deposited in a kind of Dead Sea which covered that part of England when it was more or less a desert about 100 million years ago. God works in a mysterious way & obviously has an ingenious mind. It is rather like Saxon [Sydney-Turner]'s. It would be like him to take the trouble to create a Dead Sea & then cover it up with

1. Enid Crystal Dorothy Marx (1902–1993), designer and a friend of TR. Perhaps best known for her London Transport zoo posters and 1937 fabric, she worked in almost every form of graphic art, designing luggage linings, hand-blocked textiles, wallpapers, calendars, Christmas cards, labels, hook-it-yourself rugs, stamps and book jackets (for Penguin and Chatto & Windus). She was elected Royal Designer for Industry (1945), and headed the Department of Dress, Textiles and Ceramics at Croydon College of Art (1965–70). She was the author of *When Victoria Began to Reign* (1939).

rocks for millions of years in order – 10 million years later – to give a peculiar flavour to beer.

Do you remember in Proust that Swann always thought the same as the Princess in the unimportant things? I think the marvel is that we always think the same about important things. It sounds conceited for me to say that – but I felt it at once as a miracle & the miracle has persisted. And you said the other day that from the first you felt you could say anything – & everything? – to me. Aren't the two things connected? Isn't it therefore probable, dearest, that this accounts for my passion for you – in part & a large part – & that there is something in you which covets it? Not just a phantom in my mind. Nor a fortuitous fixation, as the jargonists would say.

I am getting to not being able to go to bed without writing to you. How I wish, dearest, I could give you a bulls-eye, a hot water bottle, & say it to you. Perhaps, perhaps . . .

    I love you,
      L.
I think persiafolium can only mean Persian leaved but what that can mean I don't know.

190:   [Wednesday] 12 July 1944         *Monk's House*

Dearest & darling, I posted your letter & also sent the airgraph, though you did not instruct your P.S. to do that. I hope he did right.

I do hope you're all right. It is very odd here today. Perpetual noises of every kind, a continual thunder of guns north & south, the roar of aeroplanes in the sky, explosions, flybombs quite a lot, bangs as they are brought down, but no alerts & no all clears. It has never been like this. I saw three of the things brought down in less than ½ an hour, one on Iford Hill, one on Caburn, & one a good way off over Glynde way. I hope it doesn't mean they're getting through to you. I think they must have a new range of guns in the weald & that most of the noise comes from them.

If Ian goes over the week end, you will let me come & be with you in the evening – it is so dreary being alone after a departure like that &, even if I were no good, I could play you Mozart who would be. As for me, I sometimes think you still don't realize that I love you & love to be with you always whether in a 3rd class carriage to Marlow or in Mrs Gwyn's little house or in the kitchen or the greengrocer's shop or the area or

Monk's House. It is almost incredible that next time I come down you'll come with me.[1]

Merle, who is much better – in fact recovered except for her eyes – is trying to prevent me writing to you by pushing the paper off my knees with her paw.

The mystery of your keys in my pocket was solved. I remembered afterwards that when Irene took her new leather box away, she dropped the keys on your doorstep & I picked them up &, I suppose, put them absentmindedly in my pocket.

Do you think Mabel would write me the enclosed letter? If she would, it would be the best hand of legal evidence that you were ordinarily a member of my household. For she would be what is legally called 'a hostile witness'.

I have put up The Annunciation in my lithograph gallery – it looks superb.[2]

After 3 days with you, you leave me at the Hyde Park Corner tube intoxicated by you like the bees hereon the lime flowers. What will my condition be after 2 months? There is nothing about you which is not adorable & which I do not adore. And that is what my answer will be to Mabel if she sends me the letter – I wish she would. 'Dear Mrs Parsons. Many thanks for your letter. There is nothing about Trekkie that is not adorable & that I do not adore. Yours sincerely Leonard Woolf.'

Goodnight, my sweetest tiger. I love you.

L.

[Enclosed, undated, typed spoof]

Dear Mr Woolf,

It is only after great hesitation that I am writing you this letter, but I

1. IMP was about to go to France, where he remained until demobilised in 1945; when he did, TR was to live at Monk's House with LW. IMP thought this the best arrangement; whether he knew the strength of LW's attachment to her is unclear, as is whether he would have objected had he known. He and LW were on the best of terms and had met alone the previous day. To say that such a wartime living arrangement was irregular would be wrong, but the spoof supposedly from Ian's mother and attached to this letter shows that LW and TR enjoyed anticipating how it might be interpreted. On 9 January 1945 Vanessa Bell wrote to Jane Bussy: 'Well, this young woman came to stay at Rodmell when London was being fly-bombed in June and there she still is, and that's all I know about it. But L. seems to me far happier and better and I myself think at any rate her feelings are fairly clear . . . he really looks more rested than he has done for years. But I tell you this gossip for what it's worth. I know nothing and have heard nothing' (*Selected Letters of Vanessa Bell*, Regina Marler, ed.).
2. A copy of 'The Birth of Jesus' from the Midget Bible Story series.

feel it my duty to do so. Ian tells me that during his absence abroad Trekkie will, for two months, at least, be living at Monk's House and that he approves of this arrangement. I must say that I think the whole thing most peculiar and ill-advised. I know of course that during the last year you have allowed Trekkie to make a home of Monk's House and do her work there whenever it was not necessary for her to be in London. But at least Ian was then in London. Now that he is out of England I do not think that this should continue. No one could be fonder of Trekkie than I am but, like all of us, she has her faults; she has what is called the artistic temperament and is very impetuous and has what to an old-fashioned person like myself seem dangerous views on marriage and the duties of a woman. She is perhaps too much influenced by admiration and even flattery. There are reasons (which you may not know about) which make it particularly necessary that she should be careful of her reputation. Her reputation and, I should think, yours must suffer if she continues to live at Monk's House alone with you. She should come to me or go to one of her relations or Mrs Bashwood at Gerrards Cross might take her.

I have not told either Ian or Trekkie that I am writing to you. I am trusting that a man of your age and experience will see that I am right and will find some way of putting an end to a most unfortunate situation.

Yours sincerely

[unsigned]
P.S. I always thought, if you will allow me to say so, that you were ill-advised to take 24 Victoria Square.

191: [Thursday] 13 July [1944]                         *25 Vic Sq*

My dearest Leonard
I shall probably ring you up this evening as I may know definitely about Ian by then. He still knew no more yesterday. I have my sheet of proofs of the three colours & they look very successful. I think they will be much better than the last ones, there is no doubt that doing them this way is infinitely better. The black goes where it is wanted & doesn't need to get too heavy. The 16 Century garden prayer is also done & you are going to be in a fix because of course I shall be wondering if you don't frame & hang it up and how are you to hang up a prayer? Mr Herbert is a jewel. He printed the prayer in the morning which meant he had to 'come out of Black' and washed down three times in the afternoon so as to print

me the whole three midget colours by last night. Mr Bishop said he wouldn't have done it for anyone else so you see it pays to be friends with a printer. I am just about to draw in the black on the proofs & then go up to the Press & start the stones. If Ian goes on Saturday I shan't go up tomorrow.

I have put all the bowls of Petunias on the window sill & have practically a bed of them there. I slept very well last night. This is an awful letter dearest Leonard. The catalpas are full out in St J[ames]'s Park, very lovely.

    Love T.


192:   [Thursday] 13 July 1944

Darling creature, As I've written so many letters from your relations to myself, I think I had better complete the series. I enclose Pat's. I think my answer would have to be an invitation to Tim for the 2 months.[1]

Two of the tiniest tubes of Flake White have arrived for you.

Today has been absolutely quiet here – no guns, no bombs, no bangs.

I had to go into Lewes this morning & Merle insisted upon coming too. She seems to be completely recovered. I've been writing letters ever since & must leave you & go back to them again.

I kiss your toe.

    L.


193:   [Friday] 14 July 1944           *Monk's House*

Darling tiger, Your letter did come this morning, & now I am writing to you instead of beginning my work. Isn't that disgraceful? I am so glad the proofs are going well – I meant to ask you about them last night & we rang off before I could. Of course Mr Herbert will do for you what he won't do for anyone else, but it isn't because you are friends with a printer. It's because Mr Herbert is in love with you, like (1) Mr Bishop (2) The Jewish gentleman going to Marlow (3) The red faced gentleman coming from Marlow (4) etc (5) LW.

I was reading another Mr Herbert in the bathroom this morning & came on these lines

1. There are no such letters in the Archive. LW seems to have written spoofs to all TR's relatives about her imminent move to Monk's House, and his preferred hypothetical chaperone was Tim, Pat Ritchie's wife.

Love took me by the hand, & smiling did reply:
'Who made the eyes but I?'[1]

Whenever I look in your eyes intently, I shall think of that, though Herbert didn't mean it quite in my sense, I suppose.

I love you more than does even Mr Herbert & all the others.

L.

194:  [Saturday] 15 July 1944                                   *Monk's House*

Dearest of creatures, It is 10 to 1 & I have finished all my 'routine' work & it's no good beginning to write so why shouldn't I write to you? You see I am learning only to think of you when there is nothing more important to do. I know you'll approve that.

Your box arrived this morning; also the small roll of paper. Can it really be true – that you'll be here in exactly 101½ hours?

I suppose I shant see you Monday morning. I have a 'politician' coming at 7.30 & Mrs Bamford[2] possibly at 6.30; but I expect they will go by 8 or 8.30, so that I might see you later in the evening & for a moment before 6.30 if you're back. Will you come in when you return &, if you won't face the possibility of Mrs B, make scrabbling noises at the door?

I may go this afternoon to Millers [Gallery] to the opening of Religious Art by the Bishop. I don't want to, but it's disgusting weather, cold, grey, drizzly, windy. If I had only seized the one opportunity to seduce you to Bolivia I should never again have gone to any party, lunch, tea, dinner, political meeting, picture show, concert, theatre, film. Why is one never wrecked on a desert island with the person one loves? I'm sure when my turn comes, I shall find there not you, but Tim or Mabel or Sibyl Colefax or Mrs Bamford or Caroline [Byng] Lucas. 'Howl, howl, howl, howl!'

101¼ hours now, darling tiger.        L.

1. From George Herbert's 'Love'.
2. Mildred Bamford typed for LW.

# Letters 195-215 (July 1944-January 1947)

The flying-bombs caused so much damage in London that by mid-August 275,000 people had been evacuated. Although Victoria Square had not been hit, Trekkie moved to Monk's House at the end of July just before Ian was returned to France. The next three letters (hand-addressed spoofs) were written while she lived there. In October 1944 she signed a ten-year lease for a house at Iford, two miles from Rodmell; when Ian was demobilised in the autumn of 1945 they sold 25 Victoria Square and shared the first and second floors of number 24 with Leonard.

Monk's House had on its ground floor a drawing room, dining room, kitchen, and Virginia's bedroom, which had been added to the house in 1930 and had to be entered from the garden. Upstairs were two bedrooms, the bathroom, and a sitting room. Leonard's study, set into the roof space at the other end of the house in 1937, had a dormer window and a small balcony. In these early years Trekkie slept in the small bedroom upstairs. After 1947, when her Aunt Mary (Faanie) Ritchie retired and came to live with her, she used Virginia's bedroom for her own, leaving the inside upstairs one for her aunt. She had a printing room near the garage, and painted in the wooden garden shed Virginia had called her writing lodge. In February 1949 Leonard doubled it in length for her and added long windows; thereafter, it was named Trekkie's 'Blue Ark'. Eventually a heater was installed.


195:   [spoof to LW from TR, undated]

Dear Mr Woolf

I am writing to you as the Rector of Rodmell, as your neighbour, and as a man, and I ask you in all fairness to read this letter in the spirit in which it is written. I will write frankly as I believe that is what you would prefer. Well, Mr Woolf are you being quite fair? Ours is a simple community, we are country folk not thinking perhaps very much for ourselves as taking our standards of behaviour, our code of morals, from those set above us to guide & lead us. That I think expresses the point of view of the villager, and Mr Woolf it is *our* sacred trust to guide & lead these simple folk in the paths of duty & righteousness. And believe me – to renounce something which gives us pleasure, in God's service brings us to a deep and lasting joy which passeth all understanding. Do not deny yourself this joy for the sake of a paltry passing pleasure. Finally as a neighbour I must ask you to think of the children. Your house stands very near the school, these little ones must pass your door each day, must they pass with downcast or averted eyes?

The answer to that question rests with you, and I am confident, nay certain that the answer will be 'Never more.'

Believe me yours most sincerely
W. Buham

196:    [spoof to TR from LW]
        [Thursday] 3 August 1944                *Monk's House, Rodmell*

Dear Miss Ritchie,
   I am taking the liberty of writing this, as I have not courage to say it to you. I have served you in my capacity of secretary to the best of my ability for a considerable time. I do not think that you can complain that I have ever attempted the slightest intimacy of any kind with you and you have always treated me with cold and often or perhaps usually severe politeness. I have never presumed upon my knowledge that your attitude towards many other people is markedly and surprisingly different. Nevertheless my service to you has been, if I may say so, faithful and devoted, and will continue so. You have never called me by any name but 'Miss Webster'. I do not presume to ask you to call me by my Christian name Leonora, but in view of the fact that in Beethoven's opera Fidelio Leonora when she disguises herself as a man calls herself Fidelio, it has struck me that perhaps you might reward my faithful devotion to you by occasionally, at any rate, calling me Fidelio instead of Miss Webster. I trust that you will not consider this letter a liberty.

   Yours truly
      Leonora Webster

197:    [spoof to LW from TR, undated]

My Dear Leonard

On Monday last when Herbert[1] and I were returning to town from Marlow as our trains passed one going towards Marlow I thought I saw you. You were (if it was you) in a 3rd class carriage. Herbert thinks I should not write to you as he is sure I am mistaken in what I saw, unfortunately the trains drew apart before he could see what I am convinced I saw. And I am writing this letter because I could never forgive myself if a word from me could save you from much regret & I will tell that word. I know you have never been fond of receiving advice, but I am your sister Leonard and I feel very strongly about this. And I think what mother would have felt.

Perhaps I have not made myself quite clear. I saw you in the carriage sitting with a young (or youngish) woman, you were holding her hand & she was resting her head on your shoulder. You must forgive me if this is all a ghastly mistake, but I do think all this sort of thing so trite.

      Your affectionate
       Sister


198:    12 o'clock [Thursday] 9 November 1944                    *Vic Sq.*

My dearest Leonard. What a long time since I wrote you a letter. I have almost forgotten what our letter terms are.

It seems a great loss to have reared me in S. Africa & not taught me to carry heavy weights on my head. I have just got back from the L[ondon] Library bearing on my stomach a large vol of Lichtensteins travels in S. Africa the II vol of Burchill in case someone else snoops it & a huge vol of Pinkertons travels in which is imbedded Thurlwing. I have been & tried on my new coat which looks most respectable. I slept well & haven't got a headache. From all this you will understand that Ian hasn't yet arrived. But I think he will to-day as there doesn't appear to be any major natural disturbance.

I miss you even in Vic Sq. I keep on waiting to say things to you. This that I found in Mr Corry for instance when I was reading him yesterday afternoon. He had had a fever 'on the windward coast' & the black ladies

1. LW's siblings were: Bella (1877–1960), Sidney (1878), Herbert (1879–1949), Harold (1882–1967), Edgar (1883–1981), Clara (1885–1934), Flora (1886–1975), Cecil (1887–1917), Philip (1889–1962).

looked after him so well that the following paragraph burst from him 'In this situation I was attended with every tenderness & solicitude by the females; some bringing me a calabash of milk, others spreading me a mat to repose upon, and all uniting in kind offices: it is from them alone that man derives his highest happiness in this life; and in all situations his sorrows are soothed, his sufferings alleviated, and his griefs subdued; while compassion is their prominent characteristic, and sympathy a leading principle of their minds.'

I am going to begin quite a new note book & keep a proper note of reading. If I do that & keep a proper note of sales & expenses for Income Tax the balance in favour of 'proper' in me will be so great that whatever else I may do connected with chairs & nightgowns & bedsocks won't be able to push me over into the 'improper' category.

      love dearest L.

      from T.


199:    4 o'clock Thursday [9 November 1944]
      [postcard of Correggio's 'Mercury Instructing Cupid Before Venus']

This is one of the few large size pictures that I know which has successfully something witty about it. Ian arrived at one. America has blown over. He will get 7 days leave for sure & is going to try for 10. We go to [Murray Hicks] 29 Kingsgate Rd [Winchester] tomorrow morning. Come back on Monday & to Monk's H on Tuesday. They have the small & superb Rubens landscape on show at the N. Gall. A[nthony] Devas should not mind the critics abuse, he has sold almost all his pictures at the Leicester Gal. M[ichael] Rothenstein has also sold a lot. E[thelbert] White very few. T.R. sends love.


200:    [Saturday] 11 November [1944]      *29 Kinsgate Rd., Winchester*

Dearest Leonard.

O how cold & grim it is. This house is more or less an ice box. I shivered all night even though I added a cardigan to my usual night arrangements. We went for an icy walk yesterday after lunch. It was beautiful but so cold that for the first time I could hardly draw a breath that wasn't a whinge. Ian developed a sharp sore throat last night & is snugly in bed now. The Dr has been & injected me & says Ian's is just dead tiredness & the icy wind combined. He had a fantastic four days before coming over & really I'm not surprised he is done up. I shall send this to London as I think you may leave Monk's House before post time. We shall be at 25 after lunch I suppose. I had your letter this morning. Isn't it strange how writing suddenly whirls us back to last year or was it this year? Whirls us anyway.

Love Dearest L from

    T.

201:   [Wednesday] 15 November 1944      *Monk's House, Rodmell*

Mr Woolf presents his compliments to Miss Ritchie. He encloses some letters which were addressed to her here. He is quite well, at least physically, & Miss Ritchie knows indeed that he always is. Mentally he has suffered from a kind of manic-depressive disorder lately, in which periods of great exhilaration alternate with those of deep depression. He thinks himself that there is an adequate & perfectly natural cause for this disorder & he has noticed that the depressive stage immediately is alleviated, in fact vanishes, if Miss Ritchie is with him. He is quite well & probably rather more sane than most people & he loves Miss Ritchie rather more than most people love Miss X or Mrs Y. Miss Ritchie is much more worthy of love than Miss X or Mrs Y. Miss Ritchie told Mr Woolf, he believes, that she is inclined to regulate her conduct not by asking 'What do I want?' but 'what ought I to do?' Mr Woolf cannot deny that he is inclined to regulate his life & conduct by the answer to the question 'What do I want?' He is compelled, if he is to be truthful, to answer the question by admitting that he wants to be with Miss Ritchie, that he wants always to be with Miss Ritchie, & that he does not want to be with anyone else but Miss Ritchie. He suggests that perhaps Miss Ritchie might consider whether the consideration what she ought (rather than want) to do might not cover being with Mr Woolf. The fact that she alleviates the manic-depressive disorder of what is called a fellow human being might adequately change want into right.

Mr Woolf had a cold & rather dark journey here. He was received with enthusiasm by the three animals, including Miss Ritchie's kitten [Pilly], all together in the kitchen. Miss Ritchie's kitten is not making the writing of this letter easy. She is, like Mr Woolf, quite well.

Mr Woolf has purchased some new records of Beethoven & Mozart which he would like to play to Miss Ritchie.

Mr Woolf adores Miss Ritchie. It is because she has something of great, rare beauty in her. It is always there when he sees her & it is in what she says & does as well as in her pictures & her èyes. It was very clear this afternoon when he was eating cheese on the floor in front of her fire. It remains with him now & that & the thought that he will see her on Saturday at 4.15 alleviates the depressive stage. He would like to say 'Goodnight darling tiger'.

L.

202:    [probably Wednesday 24 January 1945, left at 24 Victoria Square]

Dearest L.
Have nipped out to buy bread & envelopes
T.
If I should not see you now – I don't think it possible that Ian will go, he says he won't know for certain until 12.45. So I shall stay here to-night. Won't you stay too & not go back in this fog. I shall be back after lunch etc before four
     Love T.

203:    [Wednesday] 24 January 1945                          *Monk's House*

Darling Tiger, I feel that I am back to a Wedneday evening – only it was more often Thursday – in the middle of last year – with many differences in between – & I simply cannot go to bed without writing to you – that you are the best (I dare not say loveliest, most intelligent, sweetest, nicest, or x-est, though you are, for you would say I'm silly, but you *are* the best) of all creatures & that I love you. The house is melancholy without you, the cats are melancholy without you, the dog is melancholy without you; the owner is – is, well, shall we say, as merry as a grig? But he sympathises with house, cats, & dog.

In a way I was almost glad you did not come tonight. It was ferocious travelling. Out of London thick snow, thick fog or mist, bitter cold. The same here & what with snow, icy roads & fog, I thought at one moment we might end up in a ditch outside Iford Grange. However we crept onto Rodmell. So cold here that there was ice on Merle's bowl of water.

I found photos & proof of your illustration for the GM[1] here sent by

1. In March 1945 TR and LW co-authored 'The History of the Strange Stapelia' in the *Geographical Magazine* (no. 1, vol. XVII). TR's large illustration of the cactus showed a pot of its short fleshy segments with a flower and twin-seed pods, one of which exposed the arrangement of seeds.

Express & wanting captions by Friday. I shall send them but don't like doing so without your approval. I propose for yours 'Drawing of Stapelia Variegata by T. Ritchie'. I shall do them finally tomorrow morning & send you a copy so that if you disapprove you can ring up Ivy on Friday morning.

Pilly is well & hungry. She came up here, leapt upon me & tried to find an abundance under my waistcoat, but was disappointed.

O dearest, how I hope it's Friday. I almost wailed & howled when I saw the fondant hanging in the bathroom. Whatever you may not be, you are certainly the most lovable of creatures & by me the most loved. Even you, dearest, cannot deny that.

L.

204:    [Thursday] 25 January 1945                    *Monk's House*

Dearest collaborator, Here are copies of the captions which I am sending to the G.M. today. I hope you approve.

The thermometer went down to 12 last night – 20 degrees of frost! The water would not run out of the bath and the waste from your basin and the overflow from the main tank froze. The garden is deep in snow and every twig of every tree is covered in frozen snow. There were still 15 degrees of frost after breakfast. But it is now bright sunshine and in it the snow has begun to melt. When I posted your letter at midnight last night in bright moonlight shining through a fog – it was an astonishing sight – I went up to the Club to try to find Peat, but he wasn't there. He appeared after breakfast shrieking with joy. I am working by the fire in the sitting room and all three animals surround me – Pilly a little disconsolate as I cannot type with her in my bosom.

I have had a letter from the Rural District Council asking me whether I will agree to sell them part of my field for cottages. I shall say no. I am not much concerned. A card from John Lehmann saying that he would like to buy the picture.

I went in to the Army & Navy yesterday to buy a toothbrush and a little old woman seemed to be hovering all round me. As I turned to go she seized me by the arm and I saw that it was Pippa Strachey.[1] I hadn't seen her since the war and it suddenly seemed to me that I hadn't seen her

1. Philippa Strachey (1872–1968), one of Lytton Strachey's sisters, was secretary to the London and National Society for Women's Service, and an active promoter of women's rights.

since she was a brilliant, brighteyed young woman vehemently and not very successfully trying to teach me to dance a Scotch reel.

Come back, come back, come back; I cant do without you, dearest.

L.


205:   Tuesday morning, 10 April 1945        *North British Station Hotel,*
*Edinburgh*


Dearest Leonard.

No Pilly – no snuggle. A cup of tea and a biscuit from a soothy but secretly sharp attendant. And now I sit in glory Lee in the large dining room of the North British and it's solid worth rather than beauty that's on the faces around. Two identical fur coated sisters & a little boy came along in the lift from the train. One of their suitcases opened & instantly two identical fur behinds were raised in the air as they stooped to fix it.

The N.B. Hotel's porridge is not as good as Monk's H porridge. I believe it to be made of quick oats. I slept a lot in the night & would have slept all the way if I hadn't been slightly cold. They have cut down the heating & *no hotty* started me off chilly. The best looking person in the room (apart from you know who) is the fur coat little boy. He has the incredibly blooming cheeks & brilliant eyes that some children have whatever their parents are like, for the fur coats are very plain but this hasn't stopped someone from cramming diamond rings on their fingers.

It's already a hundred years since I was at Monk's House & I feel as if it will be a hundred more before I'm back.

I like to hear waitresses talking pure Edinburgh, and its the one good thing to be said for this temple of respectability that all the servants are very nice & friendly. I am now full of porridge – sausage egg & weak coffee, I must gird up my slightly whistly loins & get myself to Balerno.

It's no compliment to say I'd rather be at Monk's House with you. But O I would.

> Love dearest L
>> from T.

206:   [probably early autumn 1945, left at Vic Sq.]

Darling L

I had meant to write a note & now I am between the lunch & the coffee so can't. Sauce was spoilt, Hailsberry tart was good. I kissed you in the kitchen.

> Love
>> T.

207:   [Sunday] 16 September 1945                          *Monk's House*

Dearest queen, I meant to say that I had fixed Friday Sept 28 for that Labour Party meeting here which you address. But now Friday is not your evening. Would it be impossible & shall I change it to a Thursday? I don't want to & waste one of our evenings.

I could write you a long long letter, but I won't for it would almost certainly change into a long long whinge. So I will only say what I used to & always will say – I love you.

> L.

208:   [Monday] 17 September 1945
       [large picture – black ink & wash on pink paper]

Dearest

I ought to be drawing the Horny Goloch[1] or some such creature & not morning glories but I can't take my eyes off the Glory. I carry it round

---

1. The Horny-Goloch was for *Scottish Nursery Rhymes* (Hogarth Press, 1946), selected and edited by Norah and William Montgomerie, which TR was illustrating. 'The horny-goloch is an awesome beast,/Soople an scaley;/It has twa hornes, a hantle o feet,/An a forkie tailie.' It was, in fact, a tiny creature.

with me & Merle walks behind like a procession. Do you notice the date at the top? methodical you see even if it is only about a blue convolvulus, but really could anything be more important?

Kinnie has sent Golden Ball Zinnia seeds this morning.

I have nothing more to tell you except that we must write a book.[1]

I shall look forward to tomorrow evening. I'd rather have you & [Murray] Hicks than just Hicks.

   love T.

209:   [Tuesday] 18 September 1945                    24 Victoria Square

Darling queen, It was a queenly act to send me morning glory & when I saw it lying on the hall floor my pulse bounded. Dearest, you are always like no one else in the world – that is why to me there is no one else.

But now I have to go to them all – Alymer [Vallance], Dick [Crossman], Norman [MacKenzie], Willie & Juliette [Robson][2] with

1. The title of this book, which was never written, was to be *On Love, Affection and Marriage* (see letter 176). She and LW had lived alone at Monk's House for the better part of a year. With the end of the war and IMP's return from France TR divided her time between Sussex and London. She and LW saw one another almost daily, but this sentence and the title of their proposed book suggest the strain of her new life. Her Midget Books had been singled out for favourable mention in the catalogue of the Fifty Books Exhibition at the Churchill Club in March; she had been asked to do another 8 (1946) and was drawing for *The Treasure of Li-Po*, her sister's posthumously published book of which 3,500 copies were printed in September 1948, 1,250 in November and 1,500 in January 1971.
2. The *New Statesman* staff met on Monday or Tuesday to decide on the contents for the week. Kingsley Martin edited the paper from its amalgamation with the *Nation* in 1931 until 1960. Aylmer Vallance had previously been editor of the *News Chronicle*. Richard Crossman (1907–1974) was a Labour MP from 1945 to 1947 and a cabinet minister in Harold Wilson's governments. He was assistant editor from 1938 to 1955 and editor 1970–2. Norman MacKenzie (b. 1921), author, was assistant editor 1943–62. Other Board members were G. D. H. Cole (1889–1959) and Raymond Mortimer (1895–1980).

whom I have to dine tonight – Damn them. And whatever is the opposite of damn – not bless which is an abominable word – you. I suppose it is once more just I love you.

      L.

Mrs Moir is buying chrysanthemums off a barrow.


210:    [Monday] 3 June 1946                              *Monk's H*

My dearest.

    The whole upheaval of the kitchen is worth it, you will be the first to agree when I tell you that I have found A BRAND NEW COFFEE PERCOLATER. large size. I have just finished helping Louie clear out the things & found it in an old picnic basket. I shall hope to see you at Vic Sq tomorrow but will tell you now what we have done. All daily things are on the table in the apple room, coffee tea & teapot & coffee pot are in the green tin cupboard. All not used things are over against the wall in apple room. It is a good thing dearest to get it done as the dust is very deep. I wish you would come & sleep & eat at Iford until it is over.[1]

    Dearest I must be off in a rush of chickens kittens & milk bottles. It was very much best to take Merle off. Sapho doesn't mind it at all & has been trying to catch the tit.

    Your – what am I? it is so long since I wrote to you I forget what my name is

      T.


211:    [probably Tuesday 4 June 1946, left at Victoria Square]

Dearest. I shall look in to snatch up this auricula [primula] before catching the 6.45. I shall not have finished at the C.P. today so shall have to come to town for the day next Tuesday. The proofs[2] are very satisfactory, but it takes a long time to draw the black.

    love T.

If you had time to go into Gorringes by the most west door opposite is the

1. Although the Parsons had moved into Iford Grange in January, TR had stayed at Monk's until IMP was demobilised and, as evidenced here, continued to play a large role in its domestic life. Sap[p]ho was a cat.

2. For the jacket of Tom Hopkinson's *Mist in the Tagus* (Hogarth, 1946). The white cover was printed in blue, light purple and black.

chemist or 'beauty counter' which sells oddly enough thermos flasks. Last week they had some thermos jugs for 37/6 if they still have would you buy one? It isn't open yet.

     T.

And if they have it Plain chocolate at Myers for both books.'

212:    [probably Wednesday 5 June 1946, left at Victoria Square]

Dearest,

   Here is your ration book. I have had a romantic meeting with W. Robson who was pale & fatigued. I did not lose or break the glass thing which should be under the coffee mill. I can't find it anywhere. If you loved me you would keep a box of matches in some secret place that only we would know of. I had to go & ask men who were removing Q[uintin] Hogg's effects for one.

    love your

     T.

213:    [probably Thursday 6 June 1946, left at Victoria Square]

Dearest

   Will you ring up me at the chiswick P to tell me how long a run Quentins[2] book will be & what size. They can't tell Krue until. It was queer here last night.

    love

     T.

214:    [Tuesday] 7 January 1947         *Golden Lion, Ipswich*

O my darling I wish you were here – it does feel so strange & queer. I am sitting at a long table with a plush cover & all round it are commercial

---

1. Food was rationed in Britain from 23 September 1939 until July 1954. The tightest rationing was in 1945 and 1946, at the end of the war, which for Britain lasted one day short of six years and cost one-quarter of her national wealth.
2. *On Human Finery*, Bell's humorous essay on clothes and human behaviour (Hogarth, 1947). In July 1946 TR and LW spent ten days in Dorset. This would be the first of many holidays together; in the next few years they drove to Weymouth (1947), Cornwall (1948) and France (1949).

gentlemen doing their accounts. The hotel doesn't really take 'ladies' but made a special gracious gesture & took T.P. The com gentlemen are very surprised to see me sitting amongst them but after a momentary pause in their accounts as I came in they are all scribbling away again. I have spent a somewhat desolate day. Waiting about at the works where as usual though they knew I was coming nothing was ready.[1] Like all works it rambles all over the place – all over the town nearly. You are always going through those push doors out of rooms full of roaring machines into back yards full of snow. I was almost in tears at 5.30 it all seemed so lowering. However the usual kind sweetness on the part of one of the lithographic draughtsmen who has obviously got the same sort of Mr Bishop nature, restored me. I have to have my large last meal at this hotel at 6 o'clock, which does leave a long cold dark evening to spend. I shall I think be forced to the pictures by Thursday or Friday, a thing that I have never done (I mean go to them alone). At any rate there seems to be no wireless for the gentlemen, which is one great mercy.

*Later* I have been sitting round the minute fire with the commercial gents & must go to bed before the extreme chill sets in again.

Good night darling, from your

T.

215: Morning 8.30, Friday 10 [January 1947]        *Golden Lion*

Dearest – how many shall I put?

I was so glad to have your letter this morning. It is so queer here I feel as if·I were living in exile & had been for years. O I shall be glad to be home. The table I draw at is too low & my back has quite given out. This morning I must find some bricks to put under the legs. The back ached so when I went to bed last night I was quite frightened & wondered if I would ever get home from that queer little box of a bed room. It is not so bad when I'm up & I have done Mr True's exercises. In the night I said

---

1. In 1946 W. S. Cowell, printers at Buttermarket, Ipswich, introduced Plastocowell, a transparent plastic plate which produced more faithful reproductions of original drawings in long print runs. Although TR had difficulty with it at first, it was easier for artists to use than zinc plates or lithographic stones. The Nature Study course, which Chatto & Windus began to publish in May 1949, was printed at Cowell's using this method.

It's true
I wanted you
But more than you
I wanted True.

I have asked Ian in a letter posted with this to try & make an appointment for me on Tuesday.

I must be off now & see if I can get the table raised.

I was reading Flaubert's love letters in the commercial room last night, strange reading in that place. Poor Push.[1] I don't blame her. I feel just like that but having a repressed nature don't express myself so freely.

I shall see you soon after you get this dearest.

your Tiger.

1. A cat.

# Letters 216–246 (June 1949–October 1950)

After January 1947 there are no letters for over two years. Trekkie was writing and illustrating the first unit of 'A Junior Course In Nature Study', three thirty-page books published by Chatto & Windus between May 1949 and January 1950. In 1947 the school-leaving age had been raised and changes made to the curriculum, especially in the teaching of science. The three volumes of *Come and See* were reprinted seven times in the next twenty years in runs of up to 25,000. Trekkie had always excelled at catching the nuance of the stories she illustrated; in these books her drawings were an integral part of the text. She began her first volume by inviting young readers to walk with her out of her back door and through her garden gate. As she described everything they would see, her bright and inventive illustrations poked underneath leaves, opened seed-pods, explored burrows and nests.

Just before publication in 1949, Trekkie began a diary. Keeping it was 'like being a secret collector only it is oneself one puts the pin through, one's own wings one spreads out in the little glass case'. In May Ian had a sinus abscess which required surgery. Waiting at University College Hospital, she wrote that '27 yrs or so and 500 yds or so away from the Slade & Peter I am now treated perfunctorily as Mrs Ian Parsons & TR has melted off somewhere'. Although the second and third volumes of *Come And See* were turning out well, Trekkie felt 'very confused about painting'. She was drawing from life at the Brighton School of Art and, 'hidden and secure' in her studio at Monk's House, was trying to put 'the huge cloud of human despair & disillusionment under which we live now' on to canvas. 'I cannot quietly paint somewhat New English or London Group pictures. I must simplify tone. I must be more positive in shape and colour & out of this arrive at atmosphere.' Experimenting with 'a penknife into the paint' she was soon 'covering all with simple clear colour, no radiated shadows & expressing the form with a clear precise line & very slight lights & darks worked into the mass of colour'. It freed her 'from the burden of gradated shadow without removing the beauty of solid form in space, keeping the design clear and definite and colour much more personal & independent' (Diary 7–14.5.49).

Faanie had retired from Natal and come to live at Iford Grange, and in June 1949 Ian's mother arrived for two weeks. In self-defence Trekkie took to her studio where she drew the curtains 'secretly across the door' and read Countess Tolstoy's diaries. In her own she wrote: 'I would put up with the crippling tedium of having [Mabel] willingly, if I did not also have to put up with her barely concealed animosity.'

*Oil painting by TR of Anneliese West.*

216:     [undated, left at Monk's House]

Dearest Leonard. How queer it is to write that & plunge back to about two years ago.

It is so hot we have spent all day sunk in your chairs & I have taken all my clothes off & washed them. I have bought a pink felt hat in that bag there on the table. I like the cat pictures but not the one of you at all.

We are now leaving with John to meet Ian & have dinner.
I shall ring you up on Friday.
    love T.


217:    [undated, left at Monk's House]

Darling
    We mean to catch the 2.30 bus & go to see Ronald Colman in Lost
Horizon. It would add to our delights if you were in the bus & come too.
If you can't face it & we get out in time we will stay in the returning bus
& come to Rodmell & catch the next one back. My sting is very sore. I
wonder if it was because the wasps had been breathing in cyanide. I am
feeling thread bare.
                    Love.


218:    Saturday [undated]                    *The Glen* [*Balerno*]

Dearest
Have just had your letter this minute, and it confirmed that there was a
you. It is so queer and remote here that everything becomes unreal, and
people shadowy and it isn't so much do you believe they love you, as do
you believe they are there at all.
    It grows sadder & sadder up here. Everyone gets older and has
worse calamities and it is like a long slow story, and the wind blows
and the leaves scatter down and 'Ah me the years O', is almost the only
thought one has. We went into the gallery this morning but it was so
dark & I would rather have been alone so that it was something of a
negative visit. Except that there is a very fine show upstairs of
Rembrandt etchings. They hung them up for the Festival. I had no idea
they had such a splendid collection. Mine was there. Afterwards I
bought myself a winter vest – there was only one good one so I shall
be warm one week & cold the next all through the winter. The journey
up was very comfortable. The 3rd sleeper is just as good as the 1st
really. It was sunny & delightful when I arrived, and we went for a run
in the car & had a short walk in the afternoon. The country looked
most beautiful – today it is the usual thing – dark, wet & windy but
mercifully not cold or not so cold. This place seems to grow gaunter &
harsher every time I see it. Fuzzells looks well & is jumping about as

usual. Being Saturday afternoon there are already about a dozen people around the place.

The party was much what you would expect. I was the only lady not in black except Vera [Raymond] & her's was a dim colour; so I looked very bright & sugary in my pink dress. I am very distressed to hear about Philip. I dreaded that it would be that. How awful for them. I do hope tomorrow will pass safely.

I long to be home again. It is all so spectral here, & I feel spectral too, or like one of the last leaves hanging on the tree. I had better stop before I turn into leaf mould.

> Your
> T.

219:    [Sunday 18 September 1949]

Dearest.

There was one other thing. I asked the insurance people to write to you & let you know what the additional premium was for taking one or two rings etc away & that you would pay it. It will only be about 7/6 I should think.

The foot is the same. I put a Phlog poultice on last night & I think each night I shall put one of Fuzzells famous cold water bandages on. I had forgotten about that.[1]

I have on my new suit & I look like those pictures in Vogue of ladies going up the steps of some large public building; ladies who will never sit down. I do hope all the apples won't be picked by the time I come back.

> love your
> T
> As she loves
> Thee
> That should be in a ring

220:    [Tuesday] 20 September 1949                    *Monk's House*

Dearest, dearest, dearest. It is 24 hours since you left but I don't know how many times I haven't caught myself muttering in a burst those three

---

1. The Parsons were about to leave for France. The cold-water bandage was a common cure for sprains and swellings in Fuzzells's generation. You put a cold or tepid wet cloth around the afflicted joint and covered it with something to keep the moisture in and at body temperature.

words which are not three words or three persons, but one word & one person – T. And half, if not wholly, aloud, so that old ladies in the train look askance at me as if I were not all there. And they're quite right; I'm not there, but ever so far away with you.

And at the same time the corporeal unimportant. I have taken Percy [Bartholomew] to Brighton. He is really much better but says he will never recover. And I saw Tory & Frank – very red & brown & having eaten & enjoyed themselves enormously, & travelled 12 hours in busses yesterday. And I saw Leslie [Humphrey] & called Dorothy Bussy & Janey & Simon [Bussy],[1] muttering occasionally to all three dearest, dearest, dearest. And a girl with a young man & a large bouquet of flowers asked a crowded railway carriage what one of her flowers was, though it was not actually a flower at all but a branch with black berries. I listened to them all say that they did not know, except one man who said it was honeysuckle. Then I said with some emphasis that it was hypericum or St John's wort & he with greater emphasis said 'no, no, St John's wort hasn't black berries' & he drew a picture on his newspaper of the seed box of the low growing hypericum. So I muttered dearest, dearest, dearest, & was silent. And when we all got up at Victoria, he said to me: 'I believe you're right – it is St John's wort!' And I again muttered at him dearest, dearest, dearest.

I have been to Carvells & arranged with them & cancelled Hammond. I was concerned about you & the devaluation & whether it would land you in difficulties. Did you see the Italian dictionary I left for you on the table?[2] Perhaps you had one? I found that the big one was not here but in London. All the animals are well. On Sunday night Push brought the kitten downstairs & deposited it under the sink. Yesterday she removed it to under the green cupboard & it now sleeps on the brooms.

Dearest, dearest, dearest. It is late & I must do the fire. I love you even more than when I saw you five years ago.[3] And in 5 years I have discovered nothing in you & I include toes – which are not adorable.

> Love your T
> Says T
> As she
> Loves thee

1. Tory and Frank were the cook and gardener at Iford Grange. Dorothy Strachey (1865–1960) and her husband Simon Bussy (1870–1950), a French painter, lived mostly in France. Their daughter Jane (1906–1960) was a painter; in 1934 she gave VW French lessons.
2. On 19 September the Parsons left for France and Italy, where IMP had publishing business. It was the fifth time TR had crossed the Channel since April, the last two being with LW to France and back 8–18 July. The pound had been devalued on 14 September from $4.03 (US) to $2.80.
3. At the end of July 1944 TR had gone to live at Monk's House for almost a year.

> But I love T
> To infini -
> T.
>    Yr
>    L

21/9/49
I have the a/c from Heath & will pay it today. A cold windy rainy autumnal day here, but I love you.

221:   Reims, lunch, Tuesday 20 September 1949 [postcard]

This is not in lieu of whether you may get it sooner as I have yet to buy envelopes. I have arranged a wonderful system for curing my foot. I keep on wrapping cold water bandages with Meron Wilson's scarf over all & so doing a Fuzzell's compress, & so I believe I am curing it. We have so far done well & comfortably & had a good night at Compiègne & didn't sign anything.[1] T.

222:   Thursday Morning [22 September 1949]                    *Basle*

Dearest
     This will still not be a letter proper as it is being written double quick at the hotel we have spent the night in just outside the Swiss barrier into Basle. We came across the mountains of the Vosges yesterday in a perfect afternoon. And they really looked extraordinarily beautiful. We had spent the night at Nancy & then motored to the obscure village where Ian had made his famous war time forced landing & where the man gave him a bottle of mirabelle plums. They were so pleased to see him, & made us have lunch. The man is the sort of Mr Dean of the place.[2] We were given a very good meal & loads of drink & told the prettiest route on. Lunch lasted 2¼ hrs so you can imagine my French was wearing fairly thin &

1. Compiègne: where German officers signed the articles of surrender in 1918; and where Hitler famously performed a little dance of triumph following the defeat of France in 1940.
2. TR's diary says they had been 'where Ian had his "adventure" in the war, with forced landing & Costa Ricans and where the local bicycle shop man befriended him and gave him a bottle of mirabelle plums to bring home' (22.9.49). According to the personnel management agency of the RAF, rules prevent the release of information about this. Frank Dean, the Rodmell blacksmith, was part owner of The Forge Garage.

there was a marked tendency for me to begin every sentence with Je . . .
& then a long pause.

Almost the biggest excitement – no *quite* the biggest has been fields &
fields of colchicum.[1]

My foot is very much better. I go on wet compressing it every night &
also in the car when I am not driving.

Now I have to stop.
>           love
>               T.


223:    [Friday] 23 September 1949                          *Monk's House*

Dearest, dearest, dearest. I had intended writing to you & trying to get it
to you by airmail but it is too late now to write a real letter as I had a Parish
Council meeting & after it Denny Botten sat on talking slowly about the
moon, bombs, bricks, Nelson, crops, Miss Ratledge & Miss Emery,[2]
houses etc. until past 11 – & then the cats had to be fed & the fire stoked.
So I can only say again that I love you & that I miss you & that you have
become so much a part of my mind that it does not work in Rodmell when
the part (or is it parts?) are or is in Venice.

I had your card this morning & do hope you really have cured your foot.

I did the bees yesterday & prepared all the hives for feeding. Yours
were quite quiet but my white hive was angry & stung me twice through
coat & trouser.

O dearest of creatures I count the days.
>       Your
>           L.
There has been a thunderstorm all the evening


224:    Monday 26 September 1949                      *Pensione Seguzza, Venice*

Dearest,

We arrived safely here last night. Having spent 24 hrs in Verona. Last
night it was really a thrill, just dark as we got in to the gondola, nothing

1. Colchicum, a Mediterranean native which bursts into flower with the first autumn rain, looks
like a crocus but has six stamens instead of three.
2. The Botten farm was opposite the Rectory. Miss Ratledge was a nurse called 'the rattlesnake'
by some villagers. At one time Miss Emery lived next to Monk's and bred fox-terriers.

could have been more lovely & I quite understand how people go dotty about Venice, like Ruskin. So far we have only seen it at night as I am now writing in bed at 8 o'clock having had coffee. This is a lovely room, mercifully unlike hotel rooms. It has a stone flagged floor light green & white walls, a huge gold mirror and a superb carved chest of drawers.

Everything has gone with great care & comfort all the way. We have had perfect weather, very hot these last four days & the landscape has been, nearly always, very good. Grapes are hanging on the vines & they are just beginning to pick them. I saw one string child standing with his feet spread and a huge bunch held in both hands to his mouth, exactly like hundreds of Poussin cherubs and cherubs from friezes.[1] I think Italians are the best looking people in Europe. They are lovely. The girls walk about in graceful groups with their arms round each other & such slim & shapely figures. Especially they seem to have beautiful feet, they all wear healess sandals & clatter along in them showing very pretty heals & toes – I cannot tell you anything else about the toes – their religion I suppose will be Catholic like the rest of the body.

I hope I shall find a letter from you at the Post Office to which we now go. I have spoken to every Italian and French cat that I have been able to – but of course there is the difficulty of being understood in a foreign tongue.

I hope all house cats are well – O I had an awful dream about Merle. I dreampt that I hit her on the nose, twice spitefully, and after the second time she snarled at me and almost bit me & I thought how awfully I have spoilt her temper. It was my fault, now I must make it up, but she wouldn't she went on snarling & not coming near me. & I thought how grieved you would be & woke up.

This no doubt means bad things.

Must go.

love T.

If I buy some sheets I shall send same to me at Monk's H. Will you please pay duty – and will you buy the tea – Mrs Bermet's will do. love T.

1. In her diary TR wrote: 'It is very difficult to know what one is looking at when one sees a thing for the first time. I find it almost impossible. I think when one's eyes are all the time secretly looking in terms of painting it is hard to see objects . . . [they] become like part of one's secret peering' (27.9.49).

225:    Saturday 1 October 1949 [postcard]                    [*Venice*]

Leaving Venice Thursday 2.30. Sitting in the fearsome garage waiting for Ian.[1] I had your second letter to-day. I never thought of asking for more at the P.O. but heckling Ian went just before lunch & there you were sitting side by side with Mabel in the niche. It has been lovely in Venice wonderfully beautiful all the time. I cannot answer your letters so you must guess.

Friday.
We are now in an odd half-finished station hotel in a small manufacturing place near Mantua darkness fell before we could reach the latter so we decided to stop. This is a place where the huge lorries pull in and black faced men sit bolting ham rolls. But we had a good meal & comfortable beds & very friendly people. Now we go to Milan & Ian sees his publishers. T.
Foot quite recovered.


226:    Tuesday 4 October 1949 [postcard]                 [*Aubenas, France*]

[encircled at top] Darling Athene[2] How do you like these French Cats?

As you see there has been some mistake here. I took two together. We are to be in Paris tonight and home on Saturday. We have been round by Roquemaure.[3] I may have to go to town to fetch Faanie on Tuesday so will take Percy [Bartholomew] on Monday if that is all right. It was wonderful in the Ardèche.
        Love T.

1. TR waited in several places for Ian; earlier at the Basle French frontier her feminist irony won through: 'All the cars are the same, the anxious male half produces carnets, passports etc, changes money and shows the engine no. – the female sits silent and sack-like with glazed eyes while all is doing & then when the car is passed through she smiles softly with pride that the car & man have passed & she is mother as it were to both' (Diary, 22.9.49).
2. Athene Ritchie and her mother Tim were staying at Iford while the Parsons were away.
3. TR had been to Roquemaure with her first husband and was remembered by Plantin, the owner of the hotel they had stayed in. She and IMP talked with him for some hours and 'it did not seem at all strange, my past & my present go on together in side me all the time so that there was no jolt once the visual difference of twenty years in Plantin's face was assimilated'. While Ian saw publishers in Paris, TR bought 'two enormously expensive soutiens gorge and a hat and decided "I am sick of being inside myself, and it seems to be work alone which has a door heading outwards"' (Diary, 3–5.10.49).

227:    [undated, left at Monk's]

Dear Leonard.

I have left behind the study I made of the cyclamen, it was wet & I shan't need it in town so it can wait until next time, there is no obligation not to look.

I am sorry about the M.ss but only in a slightly perfunctory way as I cannot tell you how much I enjoy being here. The landscape, music & talking. I hope I shall be able to make a picture.

    T.


ACCORDING TO TR'S NUMBERING THERE ARE 9 LETTERS (NUMBERS 131–139) MISSING FROM HERE.


228:    Thursday [probably 26 January 1950] morning at the breakfast table

Dearest dearest,

O it is not at all nice without L.W. 'O lantern of which shent is the light' – I can't do more Chaucer without the book but it feels just as he says. All is well. Animals very pleased to see a deputy but most delicately expressing that it *is* a deputy.[1] Everything is icy. We are unstuck but only just.

I am going to rush to the post with this so as to catch the 9.15 one & now it is 9.10.

Darling I will write a better letter during the day.

       your
        T.

Will send on letters by the afternoon post


229:    Thursday 11.30 [26 January 1950]        [*Monk's House*]

Dearest

I am in the blue room now, having been up to the top of the village with all the Political Quarterly post and with those I sent on to you. I thought it best to do them all at once & post them even though they won't go until afternoon. It was partly to give Merle a run that I decided this. She is the

1. LW was in hospital with a prostate problem which required surgery. The quote is from Chaucer's *Troilus and Criseyde* and should read: 'O thou lantern, of which queynt is the light'.

only one enjoying this horrid frost. 10% on Tuesday night & 9% last night, & freezing all day. The cistern in the loft froze but Ted [Warner][1] unstuck it. The lav is still frozen. I have hung the car lamp on it. It is still as in a trance, not a movement in the air. The cisterns are holding their breath & so am I for them.

Everyone in the village has enquired for you. Louie says a lot telephoned and everyone I met going up the street stopped me and asked with real affection in their faces. Push is well but a little sulky. I think she is about to come on heat as she yelled for a bit last night. Merle shows that I am only a deputy when we go up the street by running much further on than she does with you & when I call her she is apt to say 'shucks' though if I insist she comes back in a token way.

There will be a lovely cyclamen for you when you come home. And a blue hyacinth. The aconite buds are above ground but seem doubtful as to the wisdom of this move, & are arrested with their noses still in the earth. I shall try to get another coconut for the tits. This freeze makes me stupid and dull as a stone. My mind feels as my body looks, a great lump all swathed up in heavy layers of wool. Ian has given me Lauren [van der Post]'s M.SS.[2] to read. I have only read a little but like it extremely.

I rang up Charleston[3] & got Quentin [Bell] who is always very dim & distant on the telephone, very different from how he is when here at a meeting.

I am afraid the page has a sort of yellow spotted fever. It has gone over the imaginary line to the painting side of the table.

I have been looking at my paintings & hanging them up in my mind beside those I was looking at in London. It is salutary.

Darling I will ring you up to-night.

How often I think of you you can guess.

> Your
>
> T.

---

1. A gardener.

2. *The Face Beside the Fire* (Hogarth, 1953) by Sir Laurens van der Post (1906–1996), South African-born writer whose first novel, *In a Province* (1934), LW published when no one else would. Van der Post's wife, Ingaret, told TR and LW 'how she worked over Lauren's book. He leaves all the cutting to her. She took I don't know how many 1,000s of words out of the novel & he wouldn't even look at what she had done' (Diary, 12.11.52). TR did the jacket and was particularly upset when Norah Smallwood wrote: 'so nice – but change the colour and make this a little & that a little different. IMP agreed that you should say no it won't do or accept it, but not fidget people who produce work for you with these niggling alterations' (Diary, 29.11.49).

3. Vanessa Bell wrote to LW the same day: 'I gather . . . that one of your worst troubles is the skittishness of the nurses. Don't be too severe with them for you are completely at their mercy and I'm sure they'll think nothing of murdering you if you upset them too much' (*Vanessa Bell: Selected Letters*, Regina Marler, ed., Bloomsbury). VB had had a mastectomy in August 1944.

230:    Friday [January 27 1950]

Dearest.
  All the household pines for you
  Me
  Merle
  Push
  Louie   Ted
and finally the house itself. I have never before known of such sympathy between a house & its owner, almost neurotic you might call it. Whatever you call it the fact is that this house is suddenly suffering from a weakening of it's ball-cocks. We had to have the dank Frank Dean yesterday. The cistern in the loft had to have a new one altogether & the lav had to have something welded. Now all works again so I take it as a good omen for the Master. Yesterday Merle chased that unfortunate black cat of Mrs Chisholm's so viciously all up the road from the garage & round the lane to the school that she has torn the dew claw of both her feet on the gravel. I have bathed them with Detol & put on Boracic. Push's cold is better. She was sneezing so much on Wednesday evening that I wouldn't let her out yesterday to her chagrin. I don't think she's coming on heat after all as she seems tranquil. I think the shrieks were because you hadn't come back.
  It is white frost to-day & there were 10% last night. But the forecast says it is going. The gutter at the corner of the house above the road overflowed & froze as it trickled down, & has made an ice parrot cage in the fuschia bushes.
  I rang Octavia[1] up this morning, and she was glad to hear the operation had been sucessful. She said that the not being able to pass water at once was not at all unusual especially if the person was like you unused to having operations & being handled by other people. And that M & B often had a depressing effect on people. After they cut us off last night (inefficient switch board I think) I rang matron up & she said too that putting the tubes back was quite usual. O dearest how I want you home again. All the hierarchy does. Ted & I have long talks in the potting shed. He is really attached to you. Louie & I have ours at the tops of our voices

---

1. Dr Octavia Wilberforce (1888–1963) had been a friend of the Woolfs since 1928 and was VW's doctor for a few months in 1941. She practised medicine at the New Sussex Hospital for Women & Children until she retired in 1954 to oversee Backsettown, the rest home for overworked professional women and tired housewives which she had set up as a charitable trust in 1927 in her 15th-century farmhouse.

with most of the house between us. I think that the remarkable thing about Louie is her appreciation of the individuality of people's characters. She would never be a Nazi. Miss Emery called yesterday. The Parson & half the village I met in the street. Only two complete days & I shall see you.

*Afternoon* I have rung up your matron & she says you are better to-day & that Dr M[illin] is quite satisfied with you.

     Your longing T.

All the household also sends love & respects whichever is suitable.


231:    [Spring 1950, left at Monk's House]

Dearest

We have won through. All news when we meet.

    I flung the bottle of green ink over my shoulder last night. Over House-coat and carpet. As you see there is still a mark on the carpet. It was just pure idiocy on my part – or epilepsy – the bottle came away from my nerveless hand. I have bought stuff for the chairs – *quite different* linen with a Vanessa design I think very pretty indeed and I'm sure you will like it.[1]

    love

     T.


232:    Friday 11 August 1950              *Monk's House*

Dearest of creatures, It seems years since I saw you yesterday & centuries since I sat in Monk's House with a pad on my knees writing a letter to you at Victoria Square or the Glen. And I can only say the same thing now as I used to 100, 200, or 300 years ago: That I want you here & that there is no consolation when you aren't. The wraith still walks, but now to the blue room from a pink house. Only my love has grown.

    Much has happened in the last 36 hours, but of no real relevance without you. First London where I only saw Norah [Smallwood] who told me in a Norahesque way of Hetty Lowes Dickinson's funeral where she had met Morgan, as she calls him, so that I felt like saying

1. TR was redecorating Monk's, which she painted pink outside. In July she and LW drove to Blakeney on the edge of the Forest of Dean, for a holiday.

Mr Forster.[1] Then the Lanchester returned this morning, driven by the little garage man to whom I gave lunch of pie & beer. A nice little man who obviously finds it hard to make a living at Kelvedon. The car, he said, went perfectly, but it seemed to me to run a bit rough, with a noisy & smoky exhaust. But it is a blessing to have it & also my shaver which I got mended in London. Now I only want my wireless & my T.R., both mended (but not, I hope, rough with a noisy & smoky exhaust) & I shall be back where I was.

Then I drove in the car to the Allens[2] at 5.30 & was shown round the garden & tried – I dont think successfully – to talk like a gentleman. They are very nice, but I wish there was just a little more grey matter in the brain. The poor old admiral (I did him an injustice – he is Vice – not Rear) could do with a good deal more.

The cats have behaved much more reasonably. The kitten eats like a grown cat, voraciously & smacks his lips over rice pudding, refusing to be pushed off the saucer by his mother. I think they have about as much grey matter in the brain as the admiral, but talk to me about different things & in a rather different way. Merle seems to me about the same. She was delighted to see the Lanchester & hopped into the back seat at once. I think her brain is more or less Mrs Allen's.

Dearest, I do hope it is not too boring at Dorton.[3] And that you'll soon be here again. You know I love you, but I repeat it. Goodnight, dearest.

    L.

Without you, as I daresay I show, my brain is of the order, not of Merle's & Mrs Allen, but the Admiral & Bang.

---

1. Edward Morgan Forster (1879–1970), novelist, read classics at King's College, Cambridge, became a member of the Apostles, and was influenced by G.E. Moore and Goldsworthy Lowes Dickinson. He was a close friend of LW's and a member of the Memoir Club. His novels include *Where Angels Fear to Tread* (1905), *The Longest Journey* (1907), *A Room with a View* (1908), *Howards End* (1910), and *A Passage to India* (1924), which he stopped midway to write *Maurice* (posthumously, 1971), about homosexuality, which could not be published in his time.
2. Mrs Ruth and Vice-Admiral John Derwent Allen lived at the Old Rectory, Southease.
3. Dorton House was a school for the blind near Aylesbury, Buckinghamshire, where TR's uncle John M. Ritchie OBE, PhD, who was himself blind, lived. He was honorary superintendent and secretary of the Royal London Society for Teaching and Training the Blind for 35 years and author of *Concerning the Blind* (1930). He had been injured in a car accident on 3 August. His recovery was slow and TR's letters show her irritation when the increasing burden of family responsibility she shouldered seemed unnecessary. Because of the accident John Ritchie resigned in October, remaining on the Council, of which IMP was also a member.

Dearest,

What sort of a letter can I write to you from here, suspended as I am between being and doing. You've no idea how odd it is, as if you took a seedling out of one of [Ted] Warner's pots and put it in the desert trough. Though physically perhaps the reverse would be more exact. For maids in white caps wait on us. Wonderful little tables are *laid* at eleven o'clock with tray cloths & chocolate biscuits and coffee. Tea time produces the same tables with grander cloths (they have lace edges at tea) and an astonishing array of food. Two sorts of sandwichs cakes, fancy cakes, biscuits. And Faan & me sitting as solemn as owls picking at it. Breakfast is pleasant being a tray in Faan's room with toast and tea & no nonsense. Lunch is 'dinner' joint veg and pudding dinner is supper with fish or egg & bacon more pudding & cheese. Lunch or 'dinner' has a cup of tea after it supper has coffee. The coffee is astonishingly good. The two cooked meals we eat in the dining room the others come up on trays.

We got to Aylesbury at about four yesterday leaving at about 11.30 & having a picnic on the way. It was a pleasant drive, very slow almost all the way as the road is so very windy and we had to read sign posts.

We came by Guilford Bagshott Marlow as you said. Marlow looked entrancing, the light had become most beautiful by the time we reached Twyford. I like that country just as much as I dislike the Bagshott Bisley part.

John continues to recover but no dates are given yet. I am in hope that we shall get him back next week-end. He has had nearly all the stitches out & has ceased to be so dizzy. He is still kept lying flat, but looks noticeably better than when we left.

Matron has left, she went off to Devon at 7 o'clock this morning. It is much better without her. Though she is extremely kind & has lent me (you will be glad to hear) a nightgown. I brought a petticoat by mistake. The size of matron's nightgown makes me feel a girlish sylph; so much room there is for what I haven't got.

I have been all round the garden. There is a splendid walled garden that wants a clean sweep & new trees put in all round the walls. It is a great waste. Except for the apricot it is mostly plums.

Aeroplanes make a great noise at night which is tiresome. There is some training place near. I wish I was at Monk's House, I wish I were not suspended, I am so conscious of my physical self when suspended, I wish you were here – no I'm not sure that I do, you would be so miserably suspended, not cosy as on Victoria Station. I think of you a great deal.

    love your

     T.


234:   Sunday 13 August 1950                *Monk's House*

O Dearest, dearest, I wish you were sitting over there & we were listening, as we used at this hour, to a Beethoven quartet or a Mozart Concerto. Shall we ever again, when you return from your crucifixion on the cross of boredom, which has claims to be the worst of the many unpleasant crosses?

My brain is a puddle tonight. I have sat down to myself for the first time today when it is almost time to go to bed. First the Hort. Sy meeting which dithered on interminably in its usual way. Then I had to go to Frank Dean & Freeth to try to make arrangements for getting the sideshows materials. More dithering conversation & no means of getting them. So I drove to Lewes to try to get hold of Collins. No Collins.[1] Back to Rodmell. Dinner. Drove once more to Lewes & at last Collins. 'Well – er – yes – er – Mr Woolf – er – we must see what we can do – yes – er – well – yes – it is – er – rather awkward – well – er – yes – well, Mr Woolf, we must see what we can do – of course, there's Burchette – yes, & then of course there's Moon – well, er, we must see what we can do – yes.' So we are seeing what we can do.

Louie returned today in time to do my breakfast. She enjoyed herself enormously in the Black Forest – gives a most entertaining account of her adventures. She obviously was a great success with the Germans & behaved with the greatest common sense. It astonishes me how she manages to combine 80 per cent of real intelligence with 20 per cent sheer imbecility. She cant stop telling you her experiences. Her conversations with cemetery keepers, police men, Americans, restaurant keepers are fascinating. I don't think she liked Anneliese's[2] people very much. She stayed with them for 3 days.

1. Chip Freeth, general handiman on Janson's farm; Collins, the village constable.
2. Anneliese West (b. 1931), Louie's sister-in-law. Her husband, Harry West, had been at Dunkirk, where he alone jumped from a lorry carrying about twenty men just before it was blown to bits. A small boat rowed him to the larger one that evacuated him to England, after which he returned to his regiment and fought until the end of the war. Anneliese was born in a small town in Pomerania from which her family was evacuated in 1945 before the Russians arrived. Harry West met her there and returned for her birthday in 1949; he brought her to England, where they married. She was indispensable to the Parsons and much loved by TR and their friends.

The wood warbler came & settled on my ladder today within a few feet of me.

Dearest, you see how puddled is my brain.

But puddle or not, I love you.

Your<br>L.

235:    Monday [14 August 1950]

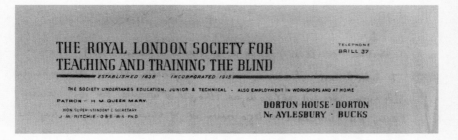

THE ROYAL LONDON SOCIETY FOR
TEACHING AND TRAINING THE BLIND

*ESTABLISHED 1838 · INCORPORATED 1915*

TELEPHONE
BRILL 37

THE SOCIETY UNDERTAKES EDUCATION, JUNIOR & TECHNICAL · ALSO EMPLOYMENT IN WORKSHOPS AND AT HOME

PATRON · H M QUEEN MARY
HON SUPERINTENDENT & SECRETARY
J M RITCHIE · OBE · MA · PhD

DORTON HOUSE · DORTON
Nr AYLESBURY · BUCKS

Dearest does all this on the top of the page sober you? It does me, but I think it is a good thing to use it as it will give you the same feeling of not being natural, as I have, sitting eternally in this building. It is idiotic really & shows a weakness in myself that I cannot do anything but look around as if across a gulf at the lovely landscape. It *is* lovely & I remember now why it makes me feel – ah me the years O – It is because when I first started to paint landscape it was in something the same sort of country near Pinner. Smallish fields & huge plumy elm trees and wide cup views from small hill tops. Yesterday I drove Faan & one of the house staff, a young highly respectable creature from Glasgow. (She is doing a holiday job here as under under matron, her usual occupation being superintendent of the canteen of a Theological College in Glasgow, and I should think she is well placed.) (I did not realize that I had made that long bracket, & now must have another before I can go back to the comma at the house staff), I drove them to Blenheim. It was an extremely pretty drive and a superb afternoon. We did not go in, as I thought it would be too much for Faan, but I would like to go over it if I can manage to before coming away. As to that, John continues to do very well, he has been raised upon three pillows now & the surgeon thinks he should get home to-day week. If he is really well Faan & I will return to Iford on Friday, picking up Ian on the way, & come back to Dorton on Monday morning,

I would see him in, & if all was well come away that day. He is to have the nurse for a week but may not need her more than a week.

There is a magnificent old magnolia on the wall at this window with a dozen great blooms out on it. With money and three gardeners as good as Ted one could make a superb place of this.

Your letter came this morning, how long since I had a letter from you. I like them so much I think I should go away oftener.

I have only met one cat here, a small disconsolate black one at the front door one evening, too small a cat for the house, and with a look about him of being more at home at the back door than the front. Very different from the look of the blue eyed owner of Monk's House.

I have finished this vol of Clarissa, she has bought her coffin and is all but in it.

Love your T as she loves Thee.


236:     [Tuesday] 15 August 1950                           *Monk's House*

Dearest of creatures, This is not a proper letter. One thing & another has made it too late. It is only for the pleasure of saying a word to you, if only on paper, & to say that I have not cooled even though my pulse is sub-normal.

I went to London today. The usual routine & an American woman, Mrs Stebling, sent to me from New York by the mysterious Rosinski with 3 vast MSS. I saw Ian & heard from him that you will return for the week end. I wish it were here. But at least I shall see you, if I don't touch you except by accident – which we both so much dislike.

It is raining now here quite a bit. The turmoil of the show is already engulfing us. The garage is now full of sideshows & the jumble sale adds appropriately to the normal jumble of the apple room. Though Collins assured us there were enough show cards, Ted with a white face announced early this morning before I left that there are already over 500 entries & only 350 cards. I sent him in to Lewes to get more printed by Farncombe & they are promised for tomorrow.

My treat for tomorrow is Burch & her friend to tea!

I bought 4 faggots[1] at the Army & Navy. I unpacked my bag in the kitchen taking the faggots out first. Before I had got the last thing out of the bag Bang[2] had devoured a faggot.

1. A faggot is seasoned minced liver or other offal and bread which is shaped into a sausage or ball for cooking.
2. A cat.

Franz Joseph, Emperor of Austria & Apostolic King of Hungary, loved Frau Schutz [sic][1] for 30 years. At the age of 70 he began putting a few crosses at the end of his letters which he wrote to her continuously. I think my love for you is different from that of the Emperor Franz Joseph for Frau Schuatz [sic]. But it is love (& affection) but not just affection.

Your

L.

237:   Wednesday morning early [16 August 1950]          *Dorton*

Dearest, I have found a bit without the heading, perhaps we will both feel more at home on it. I was so glad to have your letter yesterday morning. John continues well & is sat up to-day with a back rest, so I think we shall be able to drive home for the week-end, and I shall be able to do a bit to help with the show. It is a shame how you have been left with all to do, chasing Collins & so on. Is your exhaust still smoky & dirty? It is not my exhaust that is in that condition but my heart & head. I feel exactly like a plant potted up in the wrong earth, and I may be getting green fly.

I met a drenched little black cat in the front porch last night, (not the same one as I saw before) this was all black except for a white parting line down the middle of it's face. It rushed at me yelling with an awful raucous voice, it was in despair, the rain streaming down, it in the wrong part of the house and no way of getting round to the back but through the rain. It dashed round my feet in the way cats do when they are beside themselves so I picked it up & comforted it & carried it through the house & loosed it in the back kitchen. I had no authority for this but the cat's, so I hope it is all right & that it hasn't eaten to-day's dinner or made a mess on the hearth.

It was a fearful night here, really torrents of rain but is all blue & white this morning. John appears to be building himself a house here, he says nothing about it, but there is a house being built just beside the stables and we are told it is his. How queer Ritchies are.

I rang Philip[2] up to ask if he could recommend a place for John to go to near here after the children come back. And he has told me of one

1. Frau Katarina Schratt was an actress in the Burg Theatre, Vienna, who was a long-time companion of Emperor Franz Joseph. She had a house behind his summer palace, which he visited daily, as sometimes did the Empress Elizabeth. Everyone thought their friendship platonic, but historians say that Frau Schratt's son was the Emperor's.
2. Philip Woolf, LW's brother, was from 1922 to 1952 manager of James de Rothschild's nearby Waddesdon Manor in Buckinghamshire.

which I shall go & see to-day or tomorrow. He asked me to come & see them. I will try and go in, perhaps to-morrow evening. It is absurd how this fetching & carrying of nurses & Faanie to John, leaves no day at all except long unusable lumps to gloom in which can be used for nothing else.

I am waiting for Faan to dress & then I take her in to sit an hour with John. I haven't heard from Ian yet, but I imagine I shall have dinner with him to-night.

O dearest, one day I suppose this will all be over & I put in the right & the lice removed.

Love your T.

238:   [Wednesday] 23 August 1950                    *Monk's House*

Dearest, I don't know whether this will reach you before you leave, but I feel that I should like to write to you once more before I go to bed. And now I can imagine exactly what it looks like in your vast three-sided Hall. For they sent me yesterday the Annual Report 1948-49 of School for the Blind, Dorton, Buckinghamshire, with two large photographs of Dorton House. Whether the Hall is the house or there isn't a Hall at all I am not quite clear.

Yesterday my bus stopped in Whitehall, as usual, outside Cables Via Imperial & in the window is a large placard something like this

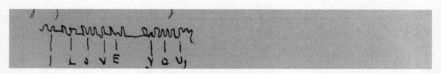

And I thought instantly of ↑, T. R. Strange, isn't it? And I see the look of misprision on your face when you read this.

Nothing has really happened except that Ted has taken out the leaning laburnum tree. Miss Emery can now see more of the garden, but it is, I think, an improvement.

Dearest, how I long for you to be back here for you know ∿∿∿∿∿ TR (Via Imperial)

        Yr
        L.

239:   Wednesday morning August 2[3 1950]          *Dorton House*

Dearest – I was in a flaming fury last evening, when we arrived here. Because really we need not have come, at least until to-day. John had friends from London yesterday, is having another this morning, & the nice acting principal is back with his car & can transport the evening nurses. It is ludicrous. We arrived at 4.30 sat with him for ten minutes & then drove the dull little man who was with him (he had come from London to see him & had spent an hour with him) here to Dorton for supper. This morning a dear friend from London is coming down to see him so we are not going in, so *why* are we here? I burst out to Faanie last evening that John was a blood sucking octopus, and she was very sweet & sensible & entirely agreed with me. It is so difficult with people. John is very unfortunate & very brave and so one feels softened and the blood sucking tentacles fix on before you notice it. But I shall slice them off on Friday, matron returns on Saturday & he can fix them on to her ample sides. I feel I have been made a fool of sitting here with my life oozing away while I drink morning coffee & am agreeable to relays of under matrons.

I went in to the Wallace collection yesterday & made some drawings of armour for Kenneth [Moir]'s fire place. It is very beautiful, but nothing could demonstrate better the idiocy of men; fixing yourself and your horse into cumbersome tin boxes that weigh a ton in order to lumber up to another tin box & crash a great sword on it's head – or have it crash one on yours. And what good came of it at last said little Wilemine. Little Wilemine must have asked that question since time was, but more particularly in the time of armoured knights I think.[1]

I did not sleep well last night, first there were mosquitoes, then aeroplanes. Between 3 and 4 in the morning my head is like a great empty house full of musty rooms. I rush up & down it opening this door & that but the rooms are always mouldy & full of old stale junk.

The best thing here are these great elm trees, they are like people elm trees in summer. Writing at the window I get the sensation of some one standing still outside & looking in & I glance up & it is a huge elm tree. They rise up so straight from the ground & hold out their branches like

1. This letter is a fine example of TR's spirited temper and feminism. Painting the decorations over Kenneth and Dorothy Moir's fireplace later in the year gave her 'a great taste to paint on walls. A dangerous taste to have at this time. First there are no walls to paint, second there is no tradition left for painting them. All the same I would like to do something more. I would like to do something real – not a "decoration". However the Moir one really looked very good I think. I prepared the wall by scraping it & laying a gesso & size ground & painted gouache. It was lovely to do, the surface most appetising & the colour settled on to it deliciously' (Diary, 12.12.50).

arms. There is a young horse in the field galloping underneath them in a most beautiful & primeval way. Horses galloping by themselves always make me think of the beginning of the world.

Dearest, dearest, I shall come away on Friday, and I shall never come back if I can help it. I forgot to tell you that Faanie chose your bouquet for the best arranged prize entirely without knowing it was yours, so I was very pleased with her. Clarissa is now dead but Richardson not done.

Love your T.

240:   Monday 25 September 1950 [postcard]     *Nonancourt [France]*

A very rough crossing until near to this side, but neither of us was sick, or even felt sick. We spent the night here, a very nice little place, with a river running through it. Comfortable beds – and a good dinner last night. Who should be waiting on the Quai at Dieppe but Norah [Smallwood], 'it was a great surprise to me.'[1] Will write a letter further on.

Love T.

1. Exactly when IMP's affair with NS began is unclear but by now everyone knew of TR's antagonism to her. She was gracious and hospitable to NS but did not like having her around, especially when she and Ian were on holiday. In her diary TR wrote: 'There was no wait for cars at Dieppe . . . but there was a major shock in the form of Norah's sandy face and the rest of her (sandy too because in one of those semi camel coats) waving & grinning at us as we came out of the custom house. The shock was so great I must have shown it as she said "There was a look of consternation on your face when you saw me". Ah well, I behaved very well after the shock & after about half an hour of having a drink together in the little place on the quai we got off' (26.9.50). Not so when in May 1951 she discovered IMP had told NS she was trying to wear contact lenses. TR 'roared off' at IMP and then wished 'to God I had not such a violent passionate nature. . . . It is absurd to mind so much,' she wrote, 'but I do. She is like dry rot in a house. She seeps into everything. It is only by removing myself altogether that I feel I have any privacy from her. I hate her & that's a fact & I despise myself for doing so.' A total rationalist, TR nonetheless felt 'like a river into which a drain has been discharged' (8–9.5.52). Her concern here was also for Chatto & Windus. Paper rationing had ended in March 1949, but with devaluation and a scarcity of skilled printers and binders, production costs had risen; by 1950 there was a perceptible decline in Britain in the sale of new, more expensive, titles. Booksellers were concerned to protect themselves; publishers were also concerned to take their share of expanding overseas markets. As Chatto & Windus sought solutions, TR thought NS used IMP to get her way; according to Max Reinhardt, who owned the Bodley Head, which joined Chatto & Jonathan Cape in 1973, everyone in the office was terrified of her.

241: [Monday] 25 September 1950      [*on*] 37 *Mecklenburgh Square*
                                                    [*letterhead*]

Dearest, dearest, You see where I creep back to when you leave me. When you come back, I shall expect you to a supper of Dublin prawns.

I thought of you continuously all day yesterday. What a day! I am afraid you must have had a horrible crossing. Frank told me the boat seemed to roll terrifically as you went out. It poured & blew all day here. Today has been better, but equally with heavy showers. And tomorrow they promise us strong north winds & cold.

I fed the bees again yesterday & today as all the hives still empty the feeders in 24 hours. I have fed myself full of ducks, rice pudding & pears. The duck was the tenderest I have ever eaten & cooked to a turn. Perhaps, when you come back, I'll give you a duck instead of Dublin prawns.

I asked Mrs E[dwards] how they came to set up with the S[aunder]'s. They met in the war when Mrs E was evacuated to North London. She lived at No. 1 & Mrs S in No. 3 of a road of villas. Mrs X who lived at No. 2 told them of the Ridge Hotel & they all migrated there. 'I can't keep pace with Mrs Saunders's inside,' said Mrs E. 'Her back is cured, but now her bowel has dropped & she has to wear a permanent truss'. When Mr S goes & plays golf with Mr Rayner, which he does too often, they all know they are for it. Some friends paid a call on Mrs Rayner the other Sunday. She sat in front of the fire & ate her tea at a small table in dead silence, offering them nothing. Then they went away. You can imagine Mrs E's face when she told me this.[1]

Dearest, such is Rodmell – without you

Only my love remains

             L.

1. TR's diary elaborates that Mr S. was 'a good fellow, but with a business heart & the taste of a designer of bedside lamps – which is what he is' (8.11.50). A year later Mrs Saunders told her she should not have taken him back after he abandoned her earlier and asked for a divorce. 'It is the usual story of female misery,' TR wrote, 'and as usual the crux of the thing is money. It is extraordinary that mothers who know so well what dependence on a man with whom one is out of sympathy means should not by now have broken the myth of "happy ever after". Until women are women first and wives afterwards 75% of them will be unhappy exactly in the Mrs Saunders way . . . what nonsense it all is, the saved family' (2.11.51). Mr Rayner was an optician who was said to drink too much. Mrs Constance Edwards worked as a secretary for LW at Monk's House.

242:    Tuesday night after the first hot bath since leaving.
       [26 September 1950]                                    *Le Puy, France*

Dearest.

We have done a burst here & have a room and bath room & as you see
I have just had a really good hot bath. The water was so hot I thought it
dangerous to leave it until the morning when perhaps it would have been
stone cold. We spent last night at Aubusson, a very nice little town, but a
gaunt rather dirty hotel. Everyone in Aubusson seemed very gay &
merry. Jokes in the Patisserie & jokes in the Boulangerie when we bought
our picnic. The road from there to here over the Puy-de-dôme was really
lovely. One climbed up the other side & then saw over into a vast light
blue valley with Clermont Ferrand merely making a pleasant salmon &
white scramble in the middle distance. The sky a wild rumpled mass of
white & grey & blue. All the little mountainy fields were full of Autumn
crocus. What happens in the summer when they make their huge leaves —
I mean what happens to the cattle who are pastured in the fields?

Wed.

We go on to Largentière to-day, if we like it we will stay there rather
than Aubenas. It is not far from Aubenas & I will go in for a letter I hope
to find there.

This morning is grey again but I think may improve as yesterday did.

I must dress. The water is just as hot as it was last night so I am going
to have another hot bath.

I will post this though it isn't much of a letter, because moving about
there is not much opportunity to write a better.

What a shock to see Norah on the quai at Dieppe — I showed it I am
afraid very clearly. A nicer shock was to see a Siamese cat at a little
mountain village on the top of the Puy-de-dôme. It tore across the road.
It was Pushkin's colour but had only half a tail, no chance to gaze in its
eyes.

There is a chance to send this off so it must go.
        Love dearest
         Your
         T.

243:   [Wednesday] 27 September 1950      [*on*] *37 Mecklenburgh Square*
[*letterhead*]

Dearest of creatures, I am still, as you see, here & without you. And I'm writing at an odd time before lunch, because I forsee not being able to write after dinner. For I have John [Bullard][1] here until Thursday. I found him at Victoria Square yesterday having returned from France & with three days on his hands in a gasless cold house. He was thinking of going to Salisbury, so I brought him down here. Today he is walking over the Downs while window cleaners stamp about the house. Bang glowers at them from the asparagus bed.

I was so glad to get your card this morning. Norah told me that your crossing had not been as bad as I had feared. It was a nasty day again here yesterday, but fine today, only bitterly cold with a ground frost last night. The walnuts fall in showers; I gathered about 200 on Monday – I wish you could telescopically help.

Yesterday I took dahlias to Russell Square [to T. S. Eliot] but no answer to my ringing, so I left them on the doorstep. On my way back I walked down St James's Place & at the end leaned over a wall of a bombed site adjoining the Green Park looking down & meditating on willow herb & the autumn leaves, when two jays flew squawking out of a bush into the Park. I have never before seen a jay in the Green Park. The garden here today is full of goldfinches.

I took your books to the school this morning to show to Mrs Donnithorne.[2] She was enthusiastic about them & will, I think, order them.

There is some hope of my getting the gramophone next week so if you come the week after, you may find it slightly less boring than usual. O dearest, dearest.

L.

244:   [Friday] 29 September 1950      [*on*] *39 Mecklenburgh Square*
[*letterhead*]

Dearest, It was nice to find a letter from you on the breakfast table this

1. John Bullard (1903–1961) was educated at Trinity College Cambridge. He entered the Treasury in 1926, transfered to the Unemployment Assistance Board in 1934, and became under-secretary of the National Assistance Board in 1947, resigning in 1954.
2. The teacher at the village school. Two of the *Come and See* nature books had been published in May 1949; the third in the series, January 1950.

morning & to know you were all right. I only hope you have better weather than here, where it is grey & drizzly. I have gathered 10 bushels of apples & don't know how many of walnuts which rain down all day long. I have finished feeding the 60 lbs of sugar to the bees. The hives are beset by wasps, but, though Ted & I have searched everywhere, we cannot find a nest.

John left after dinner last night as he had to meet his godson today & advise him about the future. John is a nice man, but too low in tone. They tuned him a little flat at birth, while a person like Mrs Edwards, I suppose, was tuned on the sharp side & not quite in time at that. John is in tune all right from one side to the other, but it is a bit flat & always in a remote minor key. We discussed Peter a good deal; he seems to bore John by talking incessantly of Roman Catholicism.

Tomorrow Cecil[1] comes & we go to Tunbridge Wells & Brighton. Dearest, will you ever come again or have I merely dreamt your existence? It must be at least a year since I saw you & even if you substantially exist, it will be over a year before I see you again on Monday week. At any rate, wraith or real, I love you.

L.


245:  Sunday, [1] October 1950                              *Millau*

Dearest. It was so good to get your letter at Aubenas. And to learn the inner history of the Saunders Edwards union, & the latest of Mrs Rayner.

Yesterday we drove away from Aubenas in pouring rain. It was a great disappointment as it was market day & I did want to walk round the market. We had two delightful days there though, sunny & perfect. We spent them ambling on the superbly beautiful little hills. It really is the most entrancing landscape. Like the landscapes in Books of Hours. We drove through the astonishing Gorge de Tarn – huge walls of rock with absurd little ruined toy castles on pinnacles. In some places the rock actually overhangs the road in a terrifying way [large sketch] like this. We have driven so long on perpetually turning roads I don't think we shall be able to keep straight along a road any more.

We arrived here at 6.30 & had a stroll round what looks like a fascinating little town – watched the most accomplished boules I have

---

1. Cecil Day Lewis (1904–1972), poet laureate (from 1968) and detective novelist, was literary adviser at Chatto & Windus, and later a director. In 1951 he married Jill Balcon. The Parsons were godparents to their son, Daniel. Among his final books, which contain some of his best poetry, are *The Room* (1965) and *The Whispering Roots* (1970).

ever seen. Indeed it didn't seem worth while their playing, as each seemed able to do exactly what he intended to.

My arm is still not right but does not hurt so much and I expect it will go as Octavia [Wilberforce] says. I don't think much of her little white pills. I still wake with a bang at 4 o'clock & only get the small change of sleep after.[1]

To-day is fine though not yet sunny, but it looks like hopes of sun.

Please will you buy my tea from Mrs B if it is not bought in my books. I am bidden away. dearest love your

T.

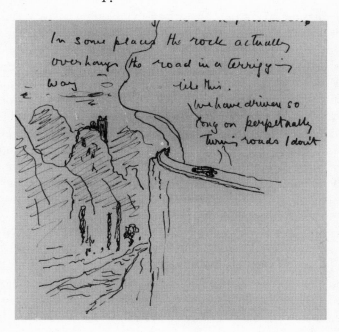

In some places the rock actually overhangs the road in a terrifying way like this. we have driven so long on perpetually turning roads I don't

246:    Monday 2 October 1950 [postcard]    [*Albi, Tarn, France*]

We got here last night & like it very much. What an incredible cathedral. We saw it in the evening light when we arrived last night and are going now to see it properly. I can soon have enough of the inside of Churches & Cathedrals but I much enjoy their outside. Rodez was a very interesting old town. We go late to-day to Montauban. It poured on Sat. as we drove through the Cévennes but is warm & bright now.

Love T.

1. TR had increasingly bad neck, shoulder and back pain, which Octavia Wilberforce called printers' occupational disease.

# Letters 247–259 (2–12 July 1951)

In a vain attempt to get rid of her glasses, Trekkie went to a contact-lens centre in Cavendish Square at the end of November. Unlike today, the process of fitting lenses was lengthy, painful and in her case, unsuccessful. While she subjected herself to six months of eye drops and fittings, she filled her diary with menopausal despair. 'How can I learn to control my idiotic fits of gloom', she wondered. 'Yesterday I was in the depths all day, & all day I argued with myself. My reason could not alter the flavour of my thoughts; it is as if some gland discharged an inky stream into one's mind . . . The worst of it is this curious feeling of isolation – not a nice isolation but a miserable forlorn one . . . The humiliating thing is that one's body should control one's mind even for a moment, except pleasantly. The other bad thing is that one's mind, such as it is, is positively less active than it was. I fight against this continually – it must be kept going like one's legs.' She couldn't sleep and there was 'the awful boredom of one's own mind. You have it with you all day & then you have to be awake & have more of it at night' (8–15.12.50).

At London parties she and Ian were admired for their dancing, but she felt increasingly old among the fresh faces of publishing, and family obligations continued to bear down. 'When will I work again?' she asked herself at New Year 1951. 'It seems always that I just begin to climb up the glass side & have my fingers over the rim when bang down I go again. To refuse to be discouraged is the thing, but it grows harder and harder. It is easier to believe in the future when you are young & there is more of it in front of you.'

By the end of January the crocuses were out at Monk's House and the bees had returned. She was grateful for Leonard's comments about her painting. Ian 'is good about me wanting to paint, and as sympathetic as he can be, but if I stopped he would soon not miss my pictures at all – and not just my pictures but all pictures. So it is for me, as it would be for a writer living with someone who never of their own accord read a book' (3.4.51).

247:    Monday night 2 July 1951                                    *Valence*
       [postcard of 'Le Triptyque du Maître de Moulins']

I have to use this as I have nothing else to write on. Please keep it for me.
We have had a lovely run so far. We were (owing to bribery) the second
car of 80 off the boat & so got away at 3 o'clock. Last night very
comfortable at Orleans. Tonight Valence which is drenched in the smell
of lime flowers & we are full of a superb dinner. It has been a lot of sun all
the day & everything looking extremely beautiful. Moulins where we had
lunch was a delightful little town with this V good painting. love T.


248:    [Monday] 2 July 1951                                   *Monk's House*

Dearest, It is rather late to begin a letter, but this is only to say goodnight.
Rodmell, Sussex, London, England, Great Britain, the Commonwealth,
& English speaking Union are very dreary without you. (I have, as you
will see, been listening to speeches by Eisenhower, Salisbury, Attlee, &
Winston at an English Speaking Union banquet. Eisenhower was rather
impressive.)

   I went to London today, lunched with Willie [Robson] & a Russian. I
got into a carriage at East Croydon & after the train had started found that
it was labelled LADIES ONLY. I apologized for my intrusion to 8 ladies
& 6 of them assured me that it did not matter at all. Two in the seats at the
further end looked resentful & started a conversation at the top of their
voices absolutely incredible. One looked & dressed exactly like Mabel.
The other gave an account – obviously to impress us – of the dinner she
wished to order but could not get at her club. 'No champagne cocktails,
my dear. How can one give a dinner without champagne cocktails?' The
rest of the carriage dissolved in laughter.

   It has been heavenly weather. Laurens's[1] strange plant opened a flower
as I came into the greenhouse tonight. It is green of a slightly yellowish
hue & later developed a darkish streak. I suppose it may change to red
later. I went into the garden for a moment at 11 & the scent of the
honeysuckle – which is a sheet of bloom – was amazing. The little
hypeastrum which I got from South Africa is most beautiful, bright red

1. Laurens van der Post and LW occasionally gave each other unusual plants. TR and LW bought
others from especially South Africa; LW kept careful records of their growth and flowering.
Crinum is a genus of bulbous tropical plant of the amaryllis family with thick strap-like leaves and
large trumpet-shaped flowers.

with a white centre. One of the crinums has shot up its flower. Two flowers opened on the pear.

All my news, you see, is of flowers. But they are of no value if you are not with me – for, though you don't approve of the word, I love you.

       L.

The only other news is that Dr Rickman[1] is dead. This is news for Ian.

249:   Wed [probably 4 July 1951]

Le Moulin is very nice indeed. Balcony terrace wide sea view no houses in front. Sanary is awful. Crowds of people – but I think we can lead a life of perfect seclusion & bliss. Cicardas [sic] a tortoise & a little cat seem to be here with us. The bonne very amicable but hard to understand – Spanish Marseilles & no teeth. I have to go and see the shops now. I will write a proper letter at once but I wanted this to go. Sea deep blue.

      love XXXX  T.

A mimosa tree in the garden, aloe, saponaria in flower also the same prickly pear. It is a really nice mill.

250:   [Thursday] 5 July 1951             *Monk's House*

Dearest, It was nice to get your card this morning & hear that all was going well. I spent a night once in Moulins. I long to hear from you from & about Le Moulin.

I have done a lot of beekeeping the last two days, putting the new excluder on & also the extra lifts. It all went quite well except for a silly thing I did at the orchard hive. I had to take 2 lifts off to change the excluder, & thinking it would disturb the bees less, I lifted both off together quite successfully. But they were so heavy that in putting them back I jarred them & they got shifted. The bees were very angry, but I got them back all right with only one sting through my trouser. There is a lot of honey in that hive.[2]

Laurens's lily has fully opened. It is very beautiful, most graceful petals

1. John Rickman was in charge of publications for the Institute of Psycho-Analysis. *A General Selection from the Works of Sigmund Freud*, which he edited, was the first in the Hogarth Press series Psycho-Analytical Epitomes.
2. LW had been keeping bees for several years and was a member of the Sussex Beekeepers' Association.

twisted back now red with a yellow centre – the style is at right angles to the ovary which is queer.

Duvalia radiata has flowered, small, quite black, with a mauve centre. The auratum is superb, like yours, with broad yellow stripes & heavily spotted.[1]

The Lewes Water Co. rang up to ask who had done the WC at Paddock Rd as it was not right from their point of view. I gave them Dunstall's telephone no. & they said they would tell him what he should do.[2]

This is the dull letter of a dull man – dull, as usual, when you are not here. If only you were. Love from us all three.

L.

251:    Thursday [5 July 1951]                    *Le Moulin, Sanary, Var*

Dearest,

Now I can write a proper description of the place.[3] You must imagine that we are on a high spit of land with the bay town & port on our left & on the right the spit runs on & ends in a rocky point. On the other side of it is the awful bit – it was more or less destroyed by the Germans & now butter coloured villas are rushing up among the ruins. But the town & port are very pleasant & one need never go the other way. We get down to the town by a path that is half path half steps & this brings you down to the little port. The shopping is easy & pleasant, but everything is frightfully dear. You must bring all the money you can. The bathing is perfect. Yesterday afternoon we bathed from a 'dique' in the harbour only about a dozen children & ourselves. (I got involved in remonstrating with a little French girl who was being cruel to a crab). To-day we went in off the rocky point to the right. There is a lot of wind to-day so it was quite boisterous but heavenly. Unfortunately Ian put his foot on a sea urchin & got it full of prickles. I have got most out but will have to poultice it tonight. Until to-day it has been absolutely still – but (inspite of Miss

1. Both cacti.
2. See also letter 252. In March 1951 the Parsons bought a small house in Paddock Road to rent to Irene Hawkins. TR worried that living in the country would make it difficult for her to keep in touch with London publishers, but the move was medically necessary. Hawkins soon got a job teaching painting, which provided a more steady income; then she contracted TB and from July 1953 was in a sanatorium for six months.
3. LW would join TR in 10 days when IMP returned to London.

Edge) I am writing in nothing but my bathing suit & a cotton skirt & am perfectly warm.

The house is very nice – perfectly quiet – you come in at the front door to a round hall & through to a terrace, below which the little garden rushes to the cliff's edge. On one side of the hall is the kitchen and living room on the other the bath room & lav. Upstairs is a round room with another round balcony & above a round lighthouse room with windows half round it but no balcony. Mrs Thevenet's English blood has come out in green & brown paint, so that it is not pretty – but the view is simply lovely & being on one's own just as good as I thought it would be.

The old bonne is very amiable if difficult to understand.

You must buy a pair of bathing pants from Mr Percy Haines & you must bring the thinnest trousers you have. All the French wear the shortest shorts ever seen regardless of the bottoms they contain. They are all made to the same pattern from tiny babies to fat old mens or womens.

We are about to set off for another bathe. The only thing that is even relatively cheap is drink so we are drinking a lot.

I greatly look forward to your arrival.

We are writing side by side at the long table like children doing homework.

> love your
> T.

252:  [Friday] 6 July 1951                                      *Monk's House*

Dearest of creatures, I thought I had better go into Lewes this afternoon & see what was happening at Paddock Road. I had rung up Newhaven & they said that I would find Mr Dunstall in the house. He was not, but it was full of men & I eventually sorted out which was Dunstall's & which Davey's. The Water Co. had objected to the pipe to the WC having been put above ground. A trench has now been dug & the pipe will be laid in it underground. It will be finished next week. The wiring was being done & will be finished today. The Rayburn [heater] had arrived & will be fixed next week. I went to Davey's office & they said they hoped to complete the work by the end of next week.

On my way back I went to see Push. The kittens are still within her. She was in a wooden hutch in the cage, asleep I suppose. When I called her, she came out very pleased to see me. She really is a charming beast. She seems extremely well & looks as if she should be delivered in the next 24 hours.

I had a letter from [Hugh] Dalton's P.S.[1] saying that he was sorry to inform me that the Chailey RDC had now made the order compulsory & the Minister would hold an enquiry. It is rather a nuisance.

Tomorrow I am going to see Mr Thornton Smith's roses; Sunday I go to tea with Mrs [Elizabeth] Robins;[2] Monday Quentin is bringing me his MS. You see how I enjoy myself.

I had an odd letter from Sir Ambrose Heal of Tottenham Court Road about his grandfather & my grandfather, both of whom apparently lived in Woburn Lodge.

The echinopsis has opened its white trumpet. It has been unendingly fine & warm & the garden is a sea of pinks. There are now two toads permanently installed in the garage.

Why do all pens refuse to part with their ink?

Dearest, I love you.

> L.

I have found a fascinating scientific book 'Individual Differences in Colour Vision'.


253:   [Saturday] 7 July 1951                              *Monk's House*

Dearest, On my way back from Lewes this morning, I looked in at Iford to see how things were. Everything looked very well & I saw Tory & Frank. I also saw Pilly & the kitten which was born on Thursday. It is, I think, almost the best kitten produced by Pilly, very light grey, sturdy, & well shaped. Pilly greeted me quite affectionately. The greenhouse & garden looked flourishing.

This afternoon I went to Mr Thornton Smith to see his roses & took the Nolbandovs[3] with me. We were shown all over his house. I wish you

1. Edward Hugh Barol Dalton (1887–1962), a Labour Party leader and the author of three volumes of memoirs: *Call Back Yesterday* (1953), *The Fateful Years* (1957), *High Tide and After* (1962). He became Minister of Local Government and Planning on 1 January 1951. His private secretary was Jack Beddoe, to whom LW had written about a long controversy with Chailey District Council over the location of a pumping station for the sewage works.
2. Elizabeth Robins (1862–1952), American actress and author who played Ibsen on the London stage. She lived with Dr Octavia Wilberforce in Brighton. The Hogarth Press published her essay *Ibsen and the Actress* (1928), and in 1936 accepted *Raymond and I*, about searching in 1900 for her brother who had joined the gold rush in Alaska. Colonel Robins objected to the book appearing in his lifetime and LW, who with Octavia Wilberforce was Robins's executor, had to wait until 1956 to publish it.
3. Sergei Nolbandov, film director, and his wife Grace lived at Alley House in Rodmell. His films included *Ships with Wings* (1941) and *Undercover* (1943), both made at Ealing Studios for United Artists.

could have seen it. It is of unimaginable horror. Every room is Tudor, packed with objects so that you can barely get through. He collects china, 80 china dwarfs ranged in a glass case facing 50 shepherdesses in another case. It is Fortnum & Mason, the Tottenham Court Road, & the V & A museum inextricably muddled. The garden is not much better. I have never seen a business man so much enjoying the business of being the squire. He even insisted on showing us the church which he restores, decorates, patronizes, though, I believe, a Jew.

Lewes is full of acquaintances. Outside the White Hart I ran into Oliver Strachey, James Strachey, & Duncan [Grant]. I had a letter from Joe Ackerley[1] saying that he was coming for four days next Wednesday & would I dine with him. I have told him that he must dine here on Friday.

Laurens's lily is, I feel sure, Gloriosa – either Gloriosa superba or irridescens. It is a most elegant & beautiful flower.

I had my first dish of raspberries tonight.

I long for you, dearest.

L.

254:    Sunday 8 July [1951]                    *Le Moulin, Sanary, Var*

My dearest. I begin to feel ill used or else the posts are very bad here. I have been gone a week to-day & have only had your letter written after being in London.

Yesterday we went in to Toulon & Ian has succeeded in getting an air passage home on Monday next. Really Tuesday, because he could only get on the 2 A.M. plane. The afternoon one being full – So he booked a seat on the 2 A.M. one. We will therefore both meet you at the aerodrome on your arrival. We will take an early meal with Ian in order to get back here before dark if possible. And he will have to fill in a few hours by himself at Nice. It is a pity he could not get on the afternoon plane, but it is at any rate better than having to go by train.

To-day is the first poorish day we have had. There is a strong East

---

1. Oliver Strachey (1874–1950), musician and mathematician; his wife was Mary Berenson's elder daughter, Rachel Costelloe (1887–1940), an active feminist, author of *The Cause*, a history of the woman's suffrage movement, many articles and two novels. His brother James Strachey (1887–1967) was married to Alix Sargent-Florence (1892–1973); both practising psychoanalysts, he was the leading translator of Freud. Joseph Randolph Ackerley (1896–1967), writer, was literary editor of the *Listener* 1935–59. His books include *My Father and Myself*.

wind blowing & though it was sunny in the morning the sky is now slightly obscured. Up to now the weather has been perfect. Wonderful sun & though it has been hot there has always been a fresh breeze. Nothing could be more agreeable than the way we pass our time. Bathing, sitting on our terrace reading 'The Small House at Allington' aloud. Going down & buying food for the day – and yesterday taking a little drive into the extraordinary hills behind. We found an ancient castle all in ruins & owned by goats & swallow tail butterflies. In an angle of the wall was a thin brown faced woman sitting on a sheet of canvass and beating out lentils by hand. Exactly like 'le Vanneur de blé'. She had a round black hat on & was extremely friendly. Everyone is very friendly & kind, our only lack at the moment is the bonne who has not turned up for three days. I am listening for her now it being nearly 4 o'clock which is her hour.

I do think you will enjoy it here, it is so heavenly having a place to oneself. And the terrace & view is perfect.

The laundry is a bore & I wish I had brought our own linen. They take an enormous deposit off you & charge fairly steeply for the hire of not very good linen.

If you can bring two table napkins & a hand towel it would be an advantage. Also if you could without difficulty bring another lb of coffee it would be useful. We shall have finished the large tin I brought by the week-end, and I doubt if one lb will be enough for you & me for our fortnight.

The tortoise is becoming very friendly & especially likes bits of tomato. The little cat continues her discreet attendance. She is minute but I believe her already to have been a mother. What of Push? Tory tells me in a letter written on Wednesday that Pilly has still no kittens.

Now I do hope to-morrow will bring me a good letter.

It seems a very long time since we left.

Dearest love your

    T.

Prickly pears both amber & lemon are in flower here.

I could not read the name of the Dr someone whose death would be news for Ian

255:  [Monday] 9 July 1951                                    *Monk's House*

Dearest, This is not a proper letter but an exclamation of pleasure at getting your letter of Wednesday & hearing that everything is all right & that you like it.

I went to Elizabeth Robins on Sunday & on the way back looked in on Sappho. Miss Breeze[1] was in. Five kittens had been born on Saturday. Three appeared in the morning all right, but there was then some difficulty & 2 more were born in the evening dead. The 3 were still with her, the same black vigorous little creatures as before. As soon as she heard me, Push hopped out of the box & came to the bars explaining everything in a low voice. She seems very well.

Quentin came to tea bringing another MS. We played bowls, but were driven in by rain, the first rain since you left. It is pouring now.

I cannot write as Bang has inserted himself between my knees & the paper. He disapproves of my writing.

I wish it were Monday evening, but the 16th, not, as it is the 9th. Love from your
  L.


256:  Tuesday [10 July 1951]                    *Le Moulin, Sanary, Var*

Dearest, All your letters have arrived in more or less of a bunch. Two yesterday & the one about Thornton Smith this morning. Posts seem to be very strange – because I cannot see why you had not had mine posted on Wednesday, by last Saturday? I wrote at once. Missed the morning post which goes at 7.30 but caught the evening one. Then I wrote the next day to tell you how nice it was & it was because we had only seen the back side bit that we thought the place awful. In fact it is perfectly delightful.

The little port with the small boats in the water & the boule players on the shore is delicious, & our own view & terrace absolutely heavenly. The shop people are all kind & helpful & though food is dear it is very good. We get a joint of meat eat it hot & then go on with it cold. Figs are 'plentiful & cheap'. We have had one Langouste [lobster] at a very high price, but very good. We have still not tracked the bonne down who had not appeared for five days. I don't really mind as it is pleasant being quite on one's own – but the house is getting rather dusty. The tortoise likes tomatoes & figs stumps. The cat is in regular & discreet attendance. I am so delighted to hear of Pilly's kittens. I have already written to say we will

1. Mrs L. Breeze MRCVS, the local veterinary surgeon. Sappho, Pilly and Push were TR's cats, Bang was LW's, half Siamese and coal-black.

both be at the aerodrome to meet you. Don't eat lunch we will all have it together as we will have to stay a little with Ian to help him pass his time. We will bring a picnic with us. Don't forget to put cotton wool in your ears so that you don't feel deaf when you arrive – Ian calls out that the best thing is to take something to suck – boiled sweets. He says he doesn't know about cotton wool, so perhaps it isn't a good thing.

One of the bad things here is flowers. Nothing but dull carnations – and huge juicy gladiolas.

I am sure you will enjoy it and am greatly looking forward to your coming. I will send a card to Vic Sq too about our meeting you in case the letters don't arrive.

> love your
> T.

257:   Tuesday 10 July 1951 [postcard]                    [*Sanary sur mer*]

Incase you didn't get my letter this is to say we will both be at the aerodrome to meet you, with a picnic lunch. Ian has got a seat in a plane back but not until 2 A.M. We will stay some time with him & then drive off to get here before dark.

> love
> T.

258:   [Wednesday] 11 July 1951                         *Monk's House*

Dearest creature, I am concerned to see from your letter which came on my breakfast table that you think I am neglecting you and cooling and all that. So I am writing at once in the morning and on the typewriter to make all plain. I wrote four times last week and posted them all as soon as written, the last letter yesterday in London. I suppose the explanation must be that letters take a long time. The letter which I got today was written by you on Sunday three days ago.

I am glad you'll be able to meet me on Monday. I will bring coffee and towels. It all sounds very nice. I went to the Army & Navy Stores yesterday and bought myself what they call a swimming suit. I tried it last night and see that it is impossibly uncomfortable, clinging to one's bottom like the drawers of Nessus. I shall now try to get myself a pair of shorts in Lewes. I must try to look as smart as possible.

The weather has broken here too. More rain last night and this morning, but the sun has now broken through. Joe Ackerley is coming to dine here Friday. Otherwise I have no news. Yesterday was rather unpleasant in London and I had to go to a Fabian Executive meeting at the H[ouse] of C[ommons], so I came back by the 6.45 train.

Dearest, I not only write you letters, but continually think of you and love you even in typescript.

> Yr
> L.

The dead man was Dr John Rickman, the psychoanalyst.

259:    [Thursday] 12 July 1951                                   *Monk's House*

Dearest, This is the last letter before I see you & I don't suppose that even this will reach you before Monday morning – to judge by your letters. I had yours today by the afternoon post, mirabile dictu, & was glad to see that you had had 3 more of mine.

Not that I really have anything to write. When I don't see you, a kind of suspended animation settles upon me & I know exactly what it feels like to be a hibernating toad or tortoise. The days pass like a slow motion film, writing in the morning, tinkering in the garden of afternoons, reading in the evening.

Today it began to rain after lunch & has not stopped since – in fact, the last few hours it has been a deluge with the usual horror of blocked gutters.

Gloriosa has 4 flowers out. I wish you could see her & I hope you will, as the flowers last a week or more. I have had some fine morning glories facing gloriosa. The opiontia microdasys is going to have several blooms, but I'm afraid we shall not see them.

Bang, who is on my knees, refuses to allow me to write, making dangerous grabs at my pen. The pen itself, even without his attentions, refuses to pass its ink. Like all my fountain pens, it ought, I am sure, to have its prostat[e] gland removed by Mr Millin.

Dearest, only 4 days now before I see you.[1]

> Love from yr
> L.

1. LW arrived on 15 July. Their 'complete seclusion . . . the sea, sun, bathing, warmth, being able to wear nothing all day but a cotton skirt & blouse (no underclothes at all) or a bathing suit' made TR feel 'at home in [her] body'. She read Gide's journals and painted. (Diary, 28.6.51).

# Letters 260–281 (September 1953–Spring 1957)

Ian's mother stayed at Iford during all of August 1951. She had lumbago and had burned her back with hot-water bottles. Trekkie was 'truly sorry for her physical decrepitude . . . [but] old lady bed room smells' made her sick, 'and they are worse when over laid with talc powder'. By month's end she felt 'that the tide is right out to the limit and the bare rocks of my nature are exposed, and pretty bare they are' (27.8.51). Mabel died in late November; Trekkie sorted her belongings and returned to Sussex to work on *Living Things* (1952–4), a new three-part Nature Study unit written by Alice Gibbs, which she was illustrating, and *England Under Four Queens*, of which 10,000 copies were published in June 1953. She finished the canvases she had begun in France and 'without the usual turmoil of parting with them' took them to the Leicester Galleries to be sold.

In June Trekkie turned fifty: 'It is a dreary business make no mistake recognising age in oneself. I have reached that stage in my look's decay when it seems absurd to repine. And I don't much. In my youth I did not dig the mine of my beauty very deeply, at least now I need not become desperate because it is becoming exhausted.' She still had violent menopausal depressions and disturbing dreams – in one she was smothered with snow. In another she was really twenty-two and had been 'wrong in thinking I was fifty and feeling there was not much time to go'.

In mid-July she and Leonard drove to Balerno where they walked in the hills (for seventeen miles one day); Leonard, who had been 'rather depressed and in low-spirits' cheered up, and Trekkie felt 'out of myself like any easy female' and was determined 'not to give way to weak self-pity. There is not so much to us after all. We live a while & then we die & living we make a great fuss & dying are as if we had not been.' At the end of the month she was 'home again' at Monk's. 'How nice it is. The house, the garden, the animals and cooking one's own dinner. Aubergines fresh from the greenhouse – little marrows cooked in butter & the almost last raspberries . . . I have a curious double sensation: here I am back – & yet not back as I haven't been to Iford yet – and in a way – in a possession way, Iford is mine and this is not – and in another way I could not feel more at home than here' (14–31.7.52).

Iford meant visitors. She was working on the nature books in Slough, with little confidence in the printer. It was disappointing and time-consuming to get the drawings right on the plate and find in the proofs they had been 'messed about'. Finally, in October, she sent off eight packages of colour plates for the second part of *Living Things*. Leonard was cutting extracts from Virginia's diary for publication and Trekkie was absorbed by them. 'Being here the house of course increases their power over one,' she wrote from her studio. 'How hard she worked. And never let herself off. She notes the day as being her father's birthday, in one place – "he would be such & such an age had he lived" – thank god she says he hadn't – "I would have been able to write no books." That's true, this thought has gone through me too. And now I face it with Faan – too much of one's life has to be lived at an angle other than one's own . . . I do admire VW. She was a worker, and single minded. Nothing but her work mattered. It is interesting to see that she slightly altered all through at the change of life, not in her purpose but as in cooking you alter the whole flavour of a dish by throwing in – say – a pinch of cinnamon – so she had a slightly different quality. I imagine I perceive something of the same thing happening to me. But what is behind me – compared to what she had done at 50? I have struggled as single mindedly – and from a lower swamp – both as regards position & endowments – only better health, I have that' (20–27.11.52).

At New Year 1953 she sent the key plates for the *Four Queens* to the Chiswick Press and resolved to get back to 'serious painting, and to think of how fortunate I am to have a room of my own'. But it wasn't easy. Having never wanted children, she continued to be surrounded by nieces and nephews who came to stay, and whose lives she helped direct. Her aunts, especially Fuzzells, made her feel 'old & mouldery & sick of conversation that is mostly memories'; the thought expressed, guilt followed at having been unfair (1–8.1.53).

Iford Grange was wanted by its owner and where Trekkie would call home was once again uncertain. Leonard wanted her to build a house in his vegetable garden. She agreed that would resolve 'to a great extent this dual existence' (12.3.53). Ian had been made head of Chatto & Windus and would be spending most of his time in London. 'I am tied to him and to Leonard & to my Ark. Faanie is tied to me. Capital will be short at present. We have all got too much furniture.' These things, she reasoned, 'were certain'. She wanted to ' spend one night a week in London (Monday nights), helping Ian entertain. Spend the two worst months of winter in Cornwall with L. Have less household responsibility & yet still be able to garden.' The best thing would be 'that Leonard lets me make the sitting room & bedroom at Vic Sq ours. That is, put in our things etc. so that Ian feels at home there. That we take a large flat in Brighton for the next two years. Furnish it & sell the rest of our stuff. That L gives me a strip of garden at Monks House & I buy a small green house & have it at Monks H. The losses – Our own house & garden & domestic clutter. The gains – Less house responsibility. More freedom of movement – more cash in hand – possible escape from worst of winter.' These were her 1st April 1953 resolutions. On the 22nd she and Leonard went to Zennor, which was 'extraordinarily beautiful, remote and tranquil & no sound but plover & sea gulls calling'. On return, she finished the Nature Studies books quickly and took them to London, where on 2 June she watched 'the small shadowed bowing figure [of Queen Elizabeth] going, it seemed, to the sacrifice' – her coronation.

260:   Tuesday morning in bed still [29 September 1953]   *St Beauzire*

Dearest,

This is a lovely place, we got here yesterday at about six o'clock. The flight was very easy & only took 20 minutes when once in the aeroplane, but owing to the morning fog they were about an hour and a half behind hand. Anyway we were driving away from Le Touquet in bright sun at 1.15. Had lunch at Etaples in a little restaurant near the station where they had a tame rook. It squawked & hopped after madam who abused it but gave it tit bits. From there we drove to Nantes looking at Beauvais cathedral on the way. At Marites we spent the night in a brand new hotel, as clean & bright as can be & had a good dinner too – but no sleep owing to incessant motor bikes which made a noise like hornets all night long. We woke to a shower of rain but it cleared off & we had a lovely day's drive to Hérisson a little town off the main road and near Monluçon. It was a very good idea to go there as it was perfectly quiet and a really delightful little ancient place with a river half around it. The hotel was clean but ancient & had the usual lav hollowed out of a corner of wall with no window & no ventilator. Now we are here & it is perfect country for walking & a delightful little hotel – tiny & very clean, good food, and a very friendly owner – a little hump backed Mademoiselle. The only thing is the weather which was wet all yesterday, very cold air & looks much the same to-day. It is maddening as everything else is perfect. Admirable walking country all around, and you can walk anywhere, there are tracks & anyhow the fields are mostly stubble. Perhaps the weather will improve. The glass has risen slightly & Madamoiselle said the wireless said it would be somewhat better.

I wish you were here, you would like it I know. It is so entirely country, and we have our meals in a little room near the kitchen to ourselves because it's warmer than the proper dining room. There is no wireless, if one could be walking or sitting in the sun it would be simply perfect.

Now I must write to Faanie.

Dearest love your

T.

261:    Thursday [1 October 1953]                                *St Beauzire*

Dearest, I was so glad to have your letter this morning, but very sorry indeed to hear of the bee mishap. I thought you were going to leave that hive – I wish you had until I was there with you. It must have been awful. It upsets them more than anything a jar like that. I do hope you succeeded in finishing off yesterday without any further trouble. *And* the children. I greatly suspect that measely little Smith boy. When I saw him in the garden I felt sure it was a bad thing. And so God has had to thunder them out of the garden & now I suppose they are all wearing fig leaves.

The weather became lovely yesterday (Wednesday) bright sun but a fairly cold wind but not strong. We went all day energetically walking all up & down the gorges. To-day was even better, the north wind has gone & it has been much warmer. We had a perfect day walking up the valley of the Allier from near Brioude. A heavenly grassy valley & clear running river, we actually offed with our clothes & jumped in. It was very cold but I felt brave & invigorated, and indeed it was almost necessary as we have not had a total immersion since we left. Here the only draw back is that the hot water is off & all we get is a can. But it is a really delightful little hotel, & the people so friendly and kind. Mademoiselle la Patron is a splendid cook, & the only trouble is I eat far too much. Her idea of a picnic lunch is – Heaps of large slices of bread, a huge piece of butter, hard boiled eggs – saucisson – two huge slices of grilled veal each – two kinds of cheese a large piece of apple tart some grapes or apples or peaches. And all this she apologises for explaining that we did not warn her in time & so she had just to give us rather an impromptu affair. There is a large white chowish dog which belongs. He is very friendly & bounds up to one behind first – the trouble is he wears his tail twirled up to one side & then he wags it & then he gets in a muddle as to which side it should be on & so his behind becomes unsettled.

I wish you were here, it is really perfect country, and there are no tourists at this time of year, in fact it is extraordinarily empty. One old lady in a near by village told us that fifty years ago when she was a child the village had forty inhabited houses in it – now there are thirteen.

Thank you for the pictures of the bat, they are lovely. What beautiful creatures they are. Give all animals my love. Take more care of yourself dearest. And love your loving

T.

262:    Tuesday 6 October 1953 [postcard]                    [*Tulle, Corrèze*]

We came away from St B[eauzire] yesterday as a swirling mist came down. We are on our way to Lascaux and stayed the night here. It is a very nice absolutely untouristy little town & what is more it is boiling hot. We had the first bath since leaving home. It seems years since we came away. I hope all bee incidents are over. And that Belle has stopped digging up the garden. Much looking forward to seeing you – I wish you were here we are sitting in the sun drinking aperitifs.[1]

love T.

1. Belle was a cat. This trip was taken just after Chatto & Windus had been turned into a limited partnership company. On it TR read an advance copy of *A Writer's Diary*, LW's extracts from VW's diary, and thought of 'perhaps using part as starting points for drawing. . . . This can go along with painting, excellently. The great thing is to fight discouragement & not to allow myself to sink into the lost and abject state I have known so often since the war. I must try to recover the rich feeling I had at the end of August, I had the sensation of coming out of a long tunnel into an *expected* beauty . . . This has been an extremely good, real holiday. Tranquil happy feelings. Ian like his old self – calm & good humoured'. But on 15 October, back in Sussex, she felt: 'There is no continuity in oneself. A fortnight going about always with someone else – no painting no chores – and then shot like a bullet from a gun to work – hours alone in the Ark & chores . . . these last three days I have felt like a punctured motor tyre.' In November LW's *Principia Politica* was published to 'some very bad reviews. Bad & unfair,' TR wrote, 'and important ones . . . *Manchester Guardian* and the *Sunday Times*. Trevor Roper's in the latter was so obviously personally vindictive' that she thought it should not have been printed. *A Writer's Diary* also received some derogatory reviews. 'Bloomsbury is a red flag to a bull to most people. I cannot understand the violent animosity. LW says very little [but] it has depressed him to some extent – or rather he has had to draw heavily on his extraordinary reserves not to be depressed. It is difficult to say what those reserves are, largely a life long habit of not demanding anything for himself I suppose. It is partly that he sees everything against a large background in a way, and so the fears & sorrows & hopes are small against it' (Diary, 11.11.53). The autumn was made sadder by Push, who had gone blind and either walked around the kitchen in a vague way or stood dazed by the stove. LW had her destroyed in early January 1954.

263:   Wednesday 10 o'clock [21 April 1954]                    *Monk's*

Dearest

Here I sit deputizing for you with the animals. I have fed Clo till she should burst if her inside & outside were not made of the finest 'two way stretch'. The dogs are lying round in their usual way, Bang I have not seen. It is always the same when you are not here, I have a feeling of being suspended in time, as if a glass wall was put between one and one's immediate responses to sight & sound. Clo is putting herself between me & my pen which adds to the difficulties. I rang Vanessa who wasn't there, but Quentin was, so I told him.[1]

I got here at about five. Aubrey [Everest] had done the garage doors & also the pipe to the work room sink. The sun came out & the garden looked lovely, it is so neat & edged up that it almost needs a 'keep off the grass' notice. I did not go in the green houses.

I rang up all the builders & they have *never yet been sent a word of a specification* from D & knew nothing of it – this means that he has lied to us & so we shall break with him completely. Perhaps it is a blessing that it has come so early before money etc has become involved. But he has wasted weeks of time for us. He is a very odd man, I think he must have a secret vice perhaps.[2]

O dearest it is horrid without you. I shall go to bed. How I hope you will come home next week.

> Your
> 
> T.

[a blotch and arrow] that is Clo's mark. Pilly is progressing very well.

---

1. Fuzzells had arrived again in February. Her presence made it difficult for TR to work and, not for the first time, she felt she was a fool to spend her life 'not fulfilling myself but in aimlessly living around other people' (26.2.54). Then in April LW's rash erupted violently. When TR removed all the cineraria from the house it seemed to improve, but became worse again and, after three weeks of unsuccessful treatment with paraffin and a 1/8% solution of silver nitrate, he had to be taken to a nursing home and their trip to Greece the following week cancelled. On 21 April she sat alone and wrote in her diary, 'it is awful here at Monk's House without him'. Clo (Cleo) and Bang were cats.

2. In September the Parsons had bought a building site at Southease; in October the weed was burned off and working drawings ordered. They now discovered tenders had not been sent out; they asked their solicitor to retrieve the plans and left for Majorca on Sunday 9 May. In July, instead of building they bought Juggs Corner, just north and above the village of Kingston, and moved there in October. This large 1932 house had about two acres of woods and garden, and a wide view of the Downs. Aubrey was Louie Everest's son.

Thursday morning

I have opened this to add a line after having your letter this morning. I am so delighted that he goes on being pleased with you. I think you'll be back next week-end. All the animals go wrong without you – I mean morally wrong. Nig[g][1] has taken to chasing Bang. He came in this morning & is now asleep on my bed. Everyone moves around in a rudderless way without you. Ted [Warner] has found an extraordinary track all over the garden. He thinks it is a gigantic snake. It winds across the front lawn through the little gate to the big lawn all across it & over the asparagus bed in the veg garden across the top of his soft carrot bed & into the hedge. It looks exactly like bike wheels but there are no foot marks & I don't think a bike could be ridden so near to the hedge as it goes. So it is a mystery.

I will ring you to-night.

I am posting a packet with this. I have also redirected what I am sure is Gilbert's stuff so that you can show it to McKenna.

love dearest from T.


264:   Friday [23 April 1954]                              *Monk's*

Dearest

How nice it was to have your letter this morning, & also to talk to you last night, & O how nice it will be if I get you back on Monday. It is very cold & cheerless to-day – yesterday was bitter but also beautiful, to-day is only bitter. Clo has gone to bed under my counter pane. Bang has not been in yet, though I think he answered me from a good way off when I called.

The buds continue to come out, they must I suppose as now is the time, but they come out into an unwelcoming air. Everything is very dry & we want as always a 'nice growing rain'.

Evelyn [Pember][2] came to tea yesterday. She keeps on saying how good the small head of Marco [Enid Marx] is. Sometimes I think I'll burn it.

---

1. A dog.
2. Evelyn Pember, daughter of Sir Lewis Amherst Selby-Bigge, had gone to America and written books, including *Coucou* (1929), *Living One's Own Life* (1932) and *Building Heaven* (1933), before returning to her native East Sussex to live.

This must go – there is no point in it as a letter, it is simply to say come back[1] &

> love
> Your
> T.

265:    Saturday afternoon [8 May 1954]

Dearest, I send this to you just as I go. £1 12 is mine if you pay all & debit me please.

I simply do not know where I am. Do please take care of yourself. I do so hope the kitten will survive.

My dearest I hate going before you are well.

> T.

266:    [Monday] 10 May 1954 [postcard]                    *[Barcelona]*

2.45

We have arrived here & have to wait until 4.45 before going on. Brilliant sun superb light. Do hope you are 'going on' & that the kitten is still alive.

> love T.

267:    Monday morning [10 May 1954]                    *Casa Fornells*

Dearest

I am writing a note to you sitting up in bed while Ian washes.

This is a perfect place and the sun is shining. It is about 16 winding miles along the coast from Palma which is large & sprawling & whitish yellow & full of roses & villas & large hotels & yesterday all the population walking about in their Sunday clothes.

We got a small old taxi from the 'air terminal' ie a small office in a side street where the bus decanted us. The taxi man was very nice & friendly, & we seemed to manage quite a lot of conversation. The first five or six miles was all villas then they thinned out & finally up & over a high

---

1. TR brought LW home on Monday 26 April, better but not cured; by 7 May he was well enough to go to the Lewes Literary Club committee meeting.

mountain ridge we went came down the other side & here we are. It is a very nice utterly unpretentious new clean hotel & you are so near the sea you can hear it in bed.

The evening was cool & there was a wood fire in the dining room. Most ingenious, built in the centre with a chimney going up like a pillar in the middle of the room. There are stacks of flowers – the taxi went so slowly we could identify them along the way – cistus – asphodel –

We have just decided not to wash but to go at once & jump into the sea. I will close this so as to catch any post there is. I do so hope you are going on. How I wish you were here.

      Your
      T.

268:    Wednesday [12 May 1954]                           *Casa Fornells*

Dearest

I am wondering if there will be a line from you to-day & I shall not close this until after lunch in hope.

It is really delightful here, the sun is superb, the water not as hot yet as it was at Sanary, but delicious all the same. We bathe three times a day as a rule.

One never knows what will happen about one's preferences & dislikes – I am now absolutely enamoured of pine trees – but they must be these charming light & airy ones. The woods are entrancing. These trees have almost white stems & twigs & they hold the needles in little bunches & are a soft delicate green. Underneath grow masses of cistus, in the woods they are chiefly the small white, & on the hill sides the large pink. There are some huge lillie [sic] bulbs with biggish leaves that I have found. I can't think what they are, they look rather like the one Faanie gave me that hasn't flowered yet & whose name I have forgotten. I imagine these have flowered some time ago. I've remembered it now – Bruersoegia. The only bore at all here is the inevitable bad light in the bed room for reading, & that dinner is at 9 o'clock. We are gradually getting used to this. We get up at 9 bathe have breakfast, coffee (very good) & wonderful circular wound up dough nuts – made for each person as they are ready for them. We sometimes go out rowing in a round little boat. We walk in the woods & look for flowers & we bathe some more & sleep & eat. It couldn't be more tranquilly delightful. There are Danes as always & Germans & English in the hotel. The largest batch of English has just left. There is a young honey moon couple an old bore couple, & ourselves left to represent the Nation. My pen has got runny inside due to the sun I suppose, it makes my writing even worse than usual. We are going into Palma this afternoon. It is about 16 miles (very hoisty ones) off & more or less has to be got at by taxi as the only bus goes from a mile away at eight in the morning. I think I will post this as after lunch the post has gone.

    Love your
      T.

269:   Friday [14 May 1954]              *Casa Fornells*

Dearest

    I was so glad to have your letter last evening & to know that you were still 'clearing'. Very sorry about the little kitten but so long as the mother is well it can be born [sic] (this sounds very ambiguous) I feared it's chances were slight, & perhaps first kittens are always doubtful & that is why they say you should always drown a cat's first kits. They often seem to lose them themselves. We had one at Herstmonceux who had two dead ones like Push.

    It goes on being perfect here with always only two flaws – no light & far too late dinner. We are hoping to-day that a small sailing boat will arrive for us. We went to the Yaught [sic] (I can't spell it) Club at Palma & very kind Spaniards finally fixed us up with a tiny boat. It belongs to a young man called Miguel with extravagantly large black eyes & long curly lashes who mostly just stood breathing hard, at last it was all done & he is supposed to sail it round from Palma arriving here at lunch time – who knows if this will happen. It would be great fun to learn something about sailing & I look forward to it. Yesterday we shared a car & drove right through the island to some awful stalactites. It was worth it as we saw the cultivated part of the country & it was very beautiful; lovely red earth & yellow farm houses & country people in blue blouses & straw hats & queer hoes like large hammers. They were also going about a lot in lovely little mule carts in which they sat in a drowsy lordly way. The caves were as usual hideous but enormous, as big as the Albert Hall & had a lake big enough to be rowed about on. They also have a concert there twice a week but luckily not on the day we went. We had shaded lights and the dawn rising etc. Did I tell you we were staying on here so you can go on writing to me until next Wednesday & I hope you will.

    Much love as always from your
      T

270:   Monday [17 May 1954]                    *Casa Fornells, Paquera*

Dearest,

I was so glad to have your letter of the 11th followed the next day by the note of the 10th. Your letters seem to come fast but I can't understand why you hadn't had my card from Barcelona when you wrote. We have got our sailing boat – did I tell you? It is minute & we have been out four times – yesterday's was far too rough & I did not really enjoy it at all. We seemed to heel over almost underwater & the waves splashed in – however we survived & I had a brave feeling for the rest of the day. It is delightful when there is not too much wind, & I can see if you really knew what you were trying to do it could become a passion. Otherwise we go on eating & bathing & not sleeping very well if you're me.

There is a French trio here who are the object of our constant speculation – a middleaged man & two young ones. The middleaged one is extraordinarily like Quentin's Olivia[1] both in form & expression – the curious thing is that she is nice & he is not – or so I think – the one young man is tall & fair & the other very dark. They are all extremely dressy in the highest style of 'sport' wear. Every day they are in different pullovers – or shirts – or shorts & all look brand new. They speak to no one & very little to each other. There was a nice simple Danish couple who went yesterday. We shall miss him as he helped with the boat – rowing us out to it & coming to fetch us in – He is a baker & has bought a new shop in a suburb of Copenhagen. What odd people one meets on holidays. I think of you – & wonder about your rash – I do wish it was quite gone. You must have had a lovely day & show for the Garden[2] open – Poor Ted I am sorry about his eye – love dearest your
  T.

1. Anne Olivier Popham (b. 1916) and Quentin Bell had married in 1952. Educated at St Paul's School and the Courtauld Institute of Art, she was a wartime civil servant, and after the war a staff member of the Arts Council of Great Britain. She worked closely with Quentin Bell on the research and documentation of his biography of Virginia Woolf (1972) and edited VW's *Diary* (1977–82), volumes 2–5, assisted by Andrew McNellie. TR liked her enormously.
2. LW had opened his garden to the public. He was for years president of the Rodmell Horticultural Society, which now gives a cup in his name to the best display in their annual summer show. When TR returned on 23 May she wrote of the garden, 'What a moment this is when all the young greens are threaded with white. Glut of May, as Alice and I used to call it. It is the best moment of the year.' A month later she and LW left in his new Daimler for a two-week holiday, visiting Philip Woolf and his wife Marjorie (Babs), Bristol, Wells, Glastonbury and Salisbury. The following April they drove through France to Alençon, Rochefoucauld, Bergerac, Cahors, Albi, Arles, Aubenas. The weather was warm; they ate roadside picnics and from the carpets of wildflowers added to their already extensive botanical lists.

271:   Sunday [late June 1955]            *Gleneagles Hotel, Perthshire*

My dearest,

Contrary to all expectations there have been three heavenly days since we came North, And I have positively enjoyed myself.

Fuzzells was very much better than when she was in the South. We had a gentle walk round the resevoirs on Friday afternoon in wonderful warm sun & everything looked simply glorious. Ian fetched me at eleven yesterday in Douglas's car & we drove off at about 12 had a perfect picnic on the way on a small grassy knoll with curlews calling all round us. We got here at about 6 o'clock, and it is pretty well as expected – A vast hotel – extremely comfortable, absolutely luxe as far as bed & salle de bain etc. The booksellers are all off to-day on a coach trip, we did not join in & have had another heavenly day walking on the hills. O there's nothing to equal Scotland when the weather's right. Bright sun soft wind birds – springy grass little streams, I found a huge patch of Butterwort in flower, I've found the leaves but not the flowers before.

Now we are back in the gilt & plush & big Scottish families having big Scottish teas.

I was so delighted to hear the happy end of the Frankel trial – Poor Ben & Anna[1] it must be wonderful to have it done with. I imagine though that he will have huge costs – Ian says is there to be a hat round among friends as he would like to help.

The awful thing about all hotels is how theres never anything nice to look at. Here you can dance play golf squash tennis croquet & swim – but of course there isn't a library & because the booksellers have the smoking room I have to write at a marble table surrounded by the magenta & gold of the 'ladies room'.

I long to see you & look forward to Wednesday.[2]

love your T.

---

1. Benjamin Frankel (1906–1973), composer, and Phyllis (Anna) Lear (d. 1967). He had been sued for slander by Edward Clark, conductor and musician, who claimed Frankel had said he embezzled travel funds from the International Society for Contemporary Music, a charge of which Frankel was acquitted, but the substance of which he confirmed in court. The case came to trial mid-June and was widely publicised; both men had been members of the Communist Party and when Frankel resigned in December 1952 over the Slansky trial he had done so in an open letter to the *New Statesman*. The judge thought Clark had brought the slander charge, using Party funds, to discredit Frankel. By consent of both parties, no order was made as to costs. In July LW joined Anthony Asquith, C. Day Lewis and Gerald Finzi to raise money for Frankel's share.
2. LW joined TR and they drove back together. On 23 July Chatto & Windus celebrated its centenary in London with a gay, informal party at which IMP made a speech from a table top.

P.S. Could you possibly bring up my white coat from Juggs – it would be best in a parcel as it is so easy to mark it. Faanie would wrap it up. love T.


272:    Wednesday 4.30 p.m. 3 August 1955 [postcard]                    York

Dearest

This is just to say the money has arrived & been safely collected. Thank you so much. We are about to look at the minster & then turn southward. We had pouring rain yesterday from mid-day but it is fine to-day. I am longing to be home & to see you. Was it Evelyn [Pember]'s new [grand]son that you say is saturnine? I can't stand J[acquetta] Hawkes[1] if it was she?

Love your
T.


273:    6.15 p.m. Friday 16 September 1955 [postcard]                  *Vic Sq*

We shall come down on Monday I can't get hold of anyone so have written to Moser & Lucases & put all off. There was an incident in my carriage. One lady snapped at another, & the snapped at lady was very upset. The snapping lady got up & went out as soon as she had snapped. But the snapped at lady had to have a cup of tea to pull her to-gether.

love
T.


274:    Monday morning [23 April 1956]                              *Nantes*

Dearest L

We are here in the sun, which we have had brilliantly all the way, writing at a small rickety café table while they noisily mend the next door café so forgive a letter which may not be very well composed – I find the bangs disconcerting.

We meant to spend the first night at Alençon but found the French had already changed their hour so we couldn't quite make it & stayed instead at Orbec, a very nice little quiet town – had a room at the back but of

1. J. B. Priestley's third wife, married in July 1953, no children.

course it was provided with a howling dog & a striking clock. I stuff my ears with wax but still seem to hear a lot.

I woke up yesterday morning to find my voice had gone. I couldn't make a sound – it *is* a queer feeling, it's like *being* the lawn mower that won't go. It is a bit better to-day I can produce a sort of a croak but it sounds as if it came from the tomb. I don't feel at all ill which is lucky.

We had lunch yesterday at the Vatel in Alençon, do you remember the good sole we had there last year?[1] It is extraordinary, we are one week earlier than you & I were last year & you wouldn't believe the difference in the landscape. Hardly any flowers out at all – after Alençon there were heaps & heaps of cow slips & here the pear blossom is out. They grow rows of tiny trees, no bigger than goose berry bushes, between the vegetables & they look so charming standing stiffly with their white bunches of bloom along the rows.

We are about to look at the cathedral & then move on towards Bordeaux. We want to get down to places like Pau in the basses Pyrennes (can't spell it) if possible. We have all ready bought to-day's picnic.

Yesterday we stopped & looked at the chateau at Angers. They have a superb collection of very early tapestry really glorious. The story of St John in the Apocrypha all done in wonderful rose, deep blue, white & buff yellow, done in the 14th century. I do hope you & cats kittens & dogs are all well.

love your<br>T.

275:    Thursday [26 April 1956]                              *Libourne*

Dearest L

I write while Ian has gone to have his hair cut.

My voice is back thank heaven but I still cough & have a stuffed up face. If only it would warm up. The sun is splendid but there seems always to be a cold wind. You wouldn't believe how backward the spring is. The vines are black sticks & only now, when we are so far south (we are nearish to Bordeaux) are the leaves showing green on the trees. This is a

1. In her diary TR made unfavourable comparisons throughout this trip with the one she and LW had taken the previous year. That day she 'suddenly got quite sick of the guide book & its language & trying to make sure which object was the ancien couvent and which the ancien ecole etc' and threw it away. 'All this sort of looking somehow clouds one's real vision & I feel as if I were not looking out of my own eyes. Ian enjoys it more than I do.'

nice little town very comfortable & a lovely great river – the Dordogne joins the – I can't remember what – here & so there is a great stretch of water. We are going on to St Emilion as soon as Ian comes back & then on further South for the night.

In spite of the wretched bug that is in me I am enjoying myself, as I don't feel ill, & inards are behaving perfectly. The car is going very nicely & is light & easy to drive. The only misfortune so far (apart from the bug) is that yesterday when I got down into what seemed a dry grassy ditch in order – no *not* what you are thinking – but to throw our lunch refuse into a culvert, I found that under the dry grass it was liquid tar & I got it all over my sandals & feet. We had to clean me with the remains of the lunch time butter!

The first English we have seen were having dinner in our hotel last night.

I do hope all cats kittens dogs & the Woolf are well.

> love your
> T.

276:    10.45 a.m. Monday [30 April 1956] [postcard]            *Cahors*

We came here last night from St Gaudens (not far from Tarbes) We have had four cold wet or grey days but this morning is glorious, so we mean to stay another night & not do any driving except to get us out of the town for a walk. I am much better – in fact except for coughing still, I am all right. It is extraordinary how few flowers there are. I cannot get over it, after last year. I do hope all is well at home love T.

277:    Tuesday [1 May 1956]                                    *Cahors*

Dearest L.

We came here on Sunday night from St Gaudens, not far from Pau – We came via Montauban which acted in its usual style. We got there ¾ of an hour before the musée closed on Sunday afternoon. There were a few drawings out in cases in which one could not see them. I asked where the others were. O they were all behind the scenes & they changed the ones in the case from time to time – If I saw the director would he allow me to go behind to see them? Possibly but the musée was about to close – Tomorrow morning? Ah no tomorrow was Monday & from Sept until after Whitsun the musée always closed on Mondays.

It is wonderful how this happens invariably when one goes anywhere to see anything.

We decided to come on here as we took against Montauban. It rained all Sunday. Yesterday was better but cold & to-day is grey again. We had four brilliant sunny days to start with but since then the weather has been mostly grey with quite a bit of rain.

Everyone complains & says its never been like this before – and obviously the winter has been frightful. Huge bay trees stand dead in their withered leaves, and all yews and other evergreens have turned a bright awful burnt sienna colour & are dead too. Yesterday is the first day we have really found any wild flowers. We are staying here until to-morrow, it is an extremely nice little town and there is a lot to see round about.

I still cough from time to time, have all the symptoms of a cold in the head – but any glands have gone down now & I feel better. The curious thing is that I haven't felt bad, & inside has behaved in an exemplary way.

We have eaten a great deal of very good food. This hotel has a wonderful Broche on which chickens & bits of meat turn before your greedy eyes.

Ian wired Nora[h] [Smallwood] & he had a letter at Pau in which she said the weather was cold & wet at home. It seems to be so everywhere. People passed through here last night & said it had been so in Spain. I am longing to be back & to see you & all creatures again.[1]

> love your
> T.

278:  Monday morning 23 July 1956 [postcard]  *Portsmouth*

Have enjoyed it very much so far. First night was spent at Littlehampton last night here. Yesterday's was a lovely sail & last evening most beautiful. Not too uncomfortable but v bad for sleeping

> Much love
> T

---

1. In late June TR and LW took their usual driving holiday, to Worcester.

279:    Thursday 26 July 1956 [postcard]               *Weymouth, Dorset*

The beach kiosks immortalized by T.R. are still in place.[1] The weather much better than when we were here. It is a very strange life but I am enjoying most of it. Love T.


280:    [1956]                              *27 St [Bernhurits?] Terrace*

Dearest

   My pen is dry & the ink is lost.

   I am still alive. But it is a wonder. You've no idea what these last days have been like. Fuzzells has kept every paper that she has ever received & in the utmost confusion. Boxes cupboards – desks were literally crammed with letters, photographs, receipts notes for lectures and all higgle piggle. Photographs of my grandfather as a young man cheek by jowl with last week's electricity bill. Luckily they collect paper for salvage so I filled sack after sack. The flitting was yesterday & here for the first time am I sitting down – while men are laying a carpet in the sitting room. I think it is all going to be very nice. And Fuzzells (who is still with the Arrnets) is in excellent heart.[2]

   Do you recognize this somewhat serious looking child? [Photo of Trekkie and Alice Ritchie as children in South Africa, holding small animals.]

      love

      T.

It was very heartening to have your letter.


281:    Saturday morning [early spring 1957]                *Blackpool*

Dearest – I have just time to write you a quick note before being plunged once more in booksellers and their ladies.[3]

1. TR had drawn beach kiosks in *Bells Across the Sands* (1944). That autumn she and LW flew to Holland to look at a Rembrandt exhibition.
2. Fuzzells sold The Glen when friends convinced her to move into Edinburgh. She was still using candles in her bedroom and bathroom, had only two gas fires for heating the house, and in the kitchen an ancient gas cooker. She was 90.
3. Harold Raymond had retired as chairman of Chatto in 1954 and Peter Calvocoressi had become a director. Complicated trade negotiations which regulated the price of books and who could sell them occupied the book trade during the fifties and resulted in a new Net Book Agreement among

It is very queer – we are right out along the sands from B. Pool & it is not at all what I expected. I've just been for a walk on these sands & there I was with miles & miles of empty sea & sand, literally nothing but me and a few gulls, straight out from a dense hall full of how do you do's Mrs Parsons & hearty shakes of the hand (the gulls were not at the hand shaking party).

A long rather exhausting journey up. The Hydro is as awful as anyone could expect *and* uncomfortable beds. Hot water & own bath. Hideous beyond all telling & also grim, not luxurious like Glen Eagles. We had breakfast, however, in our bedroom & it was a good one.

I am determined *not* to be intimidated, but O how I do dislike this sort of do. Being a wife, I never wanted to be a wife from as far as I can remember. I suppose because of this I dreamed last night that I threw a green exercise book at Ian here in a public meeting, & woke feeling we had had a quarrel which we hadn't.

Dearest how I miss you & Monk's & Troy & Clo & her sore feet – the only thing that's the same is the 'gold' eiderdown on the bed. Love as always & love

      your T.

---

booksellers and publishers in February 1957. In June and July 1962 this agreement was successfully defended by IMP and many others – publishers, booksellers, librarians, accountants – in a five-week-long hearing before the Restrictive Practices Court. IMP was an officer of the Publishers Association (whose conference the Parsons were attending in Blackpool) 1955–7, and from 1957 to 1959 was the first person from Chatto & Windus to be elected president, a particularly important and, at the time, stressful job. TR may have disliked being 'Mrs Parsons' but she was an admirable one, especially in a domestic crisis; when just before the formal dinner at which IMP was to speak he discovered he had forgotten his collar stud, she and Nora David, whose husband Richard headed Cambridge University Press and succeeded IMP as president of the Association, rushed out into the Blackpool night to find him another.

# Letters 282–285 (September–October 1957)

On 25 April 1957 Ian put Trekkie and Leonard on the plane to Greece and Israel. Ian was not well and immediately Trekkie felt she 'did not want to go at all'. The sight of Athens 'hit by strong setting sun and marked by wild mountain shapes' restored her. If the hotel was 'absolutely hideous in every detail', in a new part of the city 'filled with sugar cube houses & flats all around', the Acropolis was spectacular. She had not at all imagined 'the great rising entrance, nor the scale of hill to buildings. That is the miracle of the whole thing', she wrote. 'Everything is the right size, & the right size for human beings.' Leonard had been an anti-Zionist in the twenties but, after the Holocaust and the establishment of Israel, felt that 'Zionism and anti-Zionism had become irrelevant'. His account of their trip in *The Journey Not the Arrival Matters* is more enthusiastic than Trekkie's. She shared his astonishment at 'the feeling of boundless energy' everywhere. Always visually sensitive, she wrote about the extreme utilitarian look of Tel Aviv, the 'wonderful Hagar landscape, Arabs cultivating little fields and energetic Jews gaining land everywhere by bulldozing great masses of marble off the ground', the beauty of thousand-year-old olive trees and new orange groves. But she thought 'the holy places awful' and the kibbutz where they visited a friend of Leonard's from the Rodmell Labour Party extremely depressing. As the temperature rose she worried increasingly about Leonard's health, especially when they got lost for six hours on a walk near Safed. Leonard returned with a cyst in his mouth which concerned them all summer; it was finally removed in late August and found not to be cancerous.

282:   5.30 Saturday [28 September 1957]   *Pensione Maria Adelaide*
*[Rome]*

Dearest L
    I scribble at top speed just to say we're here & have had a superb flight.

Brilliant sun all the way & the land stretched out under us as clear as a good painting.

Unfortunately Ian came in at eight last night having another violent inside upset. He had had a terrific chase over Cheltenham (which takes *four* hours to get to) & no proper meal & leaving again about 7.30 in the morning. I was completely in despair all night not knowing what we had better do – took *two* trips to Picadilly to the Boots to get soulagements. This morning he was better & well enough to set off & now he is really a great deal better & will I think be quite all right after a good night's sleep –

What a start. Rome looks glorious all rich warm yellow in the evening sun.

Will write a proper letter later

All my love. T.


283:    Tuesday [1 October 1957]                    *Pensione Adelaide*

Dearest

All is going well. I do hope you had the very quick note I sent you off on Saturday night. But Ian says it took ten days for a letter he sent to Vanessa to reach her, & ten days for her reply to reach him. Ian's inside is better & so is my ear – nearly quite cured.

We have wandered about & seen some of the sights. Best of all is the marvellous moment of light – that moment when we always say the flowers have their most brilliant & pure colour – just as the sun has set. Here it is really miraculous in these narrow ochre & red coloured streets which turn very deep & yet hold for that moment the whole truth of their colour. And the people passing are still clear & brilliant. The sky like in Claude's pictures is always a long way off up above the roofs.

There is fascinating cat life going on. We have a window which opens on to a little once-upon-a-time garden, which is now the home of about eight cats. A mother & her four large kittens & a few aunts & uncles. There is a pile of leaves in the corner where they make delicious little nests like Old Peat's in the frame. They look thin but not desperately & are by no means poor cat trash as they wash themselves a great deal & are always doing fine Leonardos on the ends of old columns & on the ledges of the ruins.

We had dinner with Aubrey Menen[1] last night & he & his boy friend

1. Chatto & Windus published several of Aubrey Menen's books, including *Dead Man in the Silver Market* (1954), *The Abode of Love* (1958), *The Backward Bride* (1961), *A Conspiracy of Women* (1966), *The Prevalence of Witches* (1970) and *Cities in the Sand* (1972).

are taking us to see some sights this morning. I like Rome very much indeed as a city – the best of any capitol city that I have been in. I mean that I like Paris now but didn't at all at first & I like Rome right away. We haven't looked at pictures yet – St Peters I think awful, and I don't like the fusionable Bernini & his baroc [sic] stuff.

    Much love as always & to all animals more particularly the Woolf
      love your T.


284:   Sunday 6 [October 1957]                    *Tarquinia*

Dearest
    We have arrived as you see at Tarquinia We came here last night getting in just after dark – train from Rome. The weather has been not at all good after the first two lovely hot sunny days. We've had grey sunless weather & two actually fairly wet ones. Each evening it has cleared to a hopeful glorious sunset & a sailing moon at night & each morning grey skies again.
    This looks a nice place, we had a stroll last night & are just about to set off this morning – no doubt to hear that the tombs are closed until next April. I am such a Jonah for seeing things.
    We have been leading a very social life in Rome – what with Aubrey Menen, an old acquaintance of Ian's called Kenneth MacPherson[1] – even a Lord – Lord Westbury – two Italians who are the guardians of Keats' House and Philip Davis daughter April who has married an Italian attorney.
    I need not tell you I suppose that Rome is full of cats – Very nice self possessed ones – but very small.
    We eat a great many delicious grapes & only twice have found perfect figs.
    Now from sounds I know Parsons is ready & so must stop.
    I miss you very much & think often of our Israeli trip – so different from this one.
      love your T
I had a letter & was very glad to hear news of Pilly & Faanie. Faanie has written twice – Pilly not at all.

---

1. Kenneth MacPherson lived on Capri with Norman Douglas, whom IMP had visited in 1933 with Charles Prentice (then a Chatto & Windus partner) and Pino Orioli, bookseller.

285:   Tuesday 8 [October 1957]                    *Adelaide [Rome]*

Dearest

I was so pleased to have your letter yesterday when we got back from Tarquinia. It sounds a very successful little jaunt. A charming old town still with its wall all round it. And the painted tombs well up to my expectations. We also had a lovely sunny walk yesterday morning all round the outside of the walls – & found heaps of wild cyclamen (I gathered seeds) & I think tiny wild larkspur. It has been fine to-day with a heavy shower after lunch. I like your letter very much & hope they put it in – I send it back as you asked.[1] Please will you do a little shopping for me on Saturday morning or Friday – whenever you do it for yourself.

1 lb butter
1 lb bacon (short back)
6 baps – loaf of bread if possible Nutrix
6 buns
meat – whatever he has that is good
    leg of lamb – pork – beef about 4 lbs.
some eating apples

I do hope this is not an awful bore

We walked through a street market this morning & bought Persimmons grapes & I think the last green figs – all delicious.

I look forward very much to seeing you – we seem to have been away for months.

            love your T.

1. LW had a letter in *The Times* on 7 October 1957 responding to that of a Mrs Lee. She had agreed with a 30 September letter from John Sparrow, the warden of All Souls, who had called for reform of the laws concerning cruelty to pets. Mrs Lee, whose letter was among many responses, thought people maudlin about pets; fat old animals, especially those lacking teeth and eyesight, should be put down. LW urged her to carry her argument 'to its logical conclusion'. Should 'fat old persons be destroyed with fat old dogs'? He was himself old, 'though, in the circumstances glad to say, thin'.

# Letters 286–300 (July–August 1958)

On 7 March 1958 Trekkie wrote in her diary: 'Painting still bad and depressed. Nothing inside me. I have tried to fetch it back by doing things like painting the new dining room table & now I am doing a panel on the kitchen door, but I am dead and lazy inside. It has not been a nice year though there have been nice things in it . . . I am more and more filled with a sense of failure – in a way, a failure to produce anything & failure in relationships.' At night thoughts fell like stones into her mind, 'dreary dusty ones like ends of cigarettes and old tin lids and hard useless iron objects, and sharp bits of glass all waiting in my head to be endlessly turned over and over – under old junk shop thoughts, layers upon layers of them, so much & yet creating a desert of emptiness'.

In early April she and Ian drove to Normandy. She looked forward to an Easter trip like the one they had made twelve years earlier. But it was cold and rainy and turned to 'driving wind and fast snow'. On the 8th she put Ian on the plane at Le Touquet and waited two hours for Leonard to arrive. The cold persisted, and they decided to return to England early. 'I said to L that this life of sitting, reading & looking around the lounges of hotels suspends one like a fish that has been taken out of the big round pond by L and put in a glass bowl in the apple room. It is still the same fish – but how different it's life, held in the bubble of the bowl.' Facing home she was 'still unresolved . . . I dither from emptiness to emptiness. I am/have not exactly fallen between two stools. I have sat with half of my behind on a different stool – painting & human relationships – both have collapsed because of being eaten away by wood worm.'

Here she cut about twenty-five pages from the diary. All she left in explanation is: 'I cry when I think of Ian and but for the tears feel like a dry river bed . . . I wish I could force myself not to think and think of what I hate to think of (11 & 12.4.58).

286:    Tuesday morning                          *Hotel Kummer, Vienna*

My dearest. I seem to have brought no paper so am having to use this form from my Italian exercise book. We caught our aeroplane & arrived in good order. Sir Malcolm Sargent[1] was in the same plane so we were met by batteries of cameras. The little motor car we had arranged to hire was duly there & after very little formality off we drove in it; Alas to a very nasty remote hotel. When I say we I am always referring to three persons as Mrs S[mallwood] is firmly pinned to us. Well this hotel might have been, as it were, at the far end of the Cromwell Rd. Newish clean, the hot water *not* hot & what had been called a bath room in our booking was really a niche with shower. After a tramp round next day we eventually found this. Near in, better class, very good hot water, & we are in a suite with Mrs S in the extra room.

It all goes on much as you would expect with moments of considerable languor and moments of feverish chatter and so far one pleasant expedition into the country, when I found quite a lot of wild flowers, including a tall branching harebell and a dark purple small delphinium. On Sunday Ian found on the edge of the pavement right in the centre of the town – a splendid convoluted hawk moth. I picked it up & we walked on until we found a little square with trees & so let it go. Vienna is a disappointing city – nearly all cities are I do believe – One feels there are so many streets & streets of Northumberland avenues. The people are very friendly & smiling but obstinately talk German – far fewer speak English than I expected. Weather is lovely, bright sun but a cool evening air. Last night we had on our best clothes & went to a wine reception at Schönbrunn which is the old palace. It, except for the rooms, and being announced as Herr & Frau Parsons – was very like a huge London cocktail party. This morning we go to see the pictures which from Dick David's[2] account are better than J. Ballard led me to expect. I wish to God

1. Sir Malcolm Sargent was then conductor-in-chief of the Promenade Concerts and chief guest conductor of the BBC Orchestra of which he was chief conductor from 1950 to 1957.
2. Richard William David CBE (1912–1993) was head of the Cambridge University Press. Educated at Winchester and Corpus Christi College, Cambridge, he had joined the editorial staff in 1936 and headed the London office from 1948 to 1963. He followed IMP as president of the Publishers Association (1959–61), and sat with him as an officer during the years leading up to the Net Book Agreement, which he also defended in 1962. His many publications reflected the other interests he shared with TR, LW and IMP, and included *Shakespeare in the Theatre* (1978) and a book on Cornish flora (1981). He was President of the Botanical Society of the British Isles 1979–81. He and his wife Nora (later, Baroness) David were close friends of the Parsons. Among James Ballard's publications is *Rolling all the Time: Stories* (1976).

I could go alone & so I will later on. I feel as if I'd been away a year & a day. I do hope all is well with you & all animals. We are going to have a day in the country on Saturday & I look forward to that.

Much fond love as always.

Your – your what?

Tiger it once was.


287:   Sunday 6 July 1958 [telegram]

ALL WELL ARRIVED SAFELY CASA PASA PLEASE TELL FAANIE. TREKKIE


288:   Tuesday [8] July [1958]       *Casa Pasa, Via R. Browning, Asolo*
                                                      *(Treviso), Italy*

Dearest L

Here we are – as I hope you all ready know for I sent you a telegram last night.

We had a fairly severe drive down to get here last evening at 5.30. The car ferry is all very well – but though you do save perhaps two nights on the way you have several hours of tedium which the Silver City abolishes. The embarking & the disembarking goes on for a long time. But the sight of the emphatic chalky finish of England in the lovely light of last Saturday afternoon was worth it all the same.

It is 20 years since I have seen that lovely chalky line from the sea. Boulogne was also bathed in a superb light & great modern blocks of flats had turned themselves & their reflections in the water into Venetian palaces.

We had quite a business crossing the Alps – we went over the Mont Cenis. It was boiling hot all through the mounting gorges on the French side – ugly rock faces on each side & sordid quarries making everything look very nasty. Higher up were beautiful grassy slopes and masses of wild flowers but we dared not stop because of time – until I fatally did where a lovely little stream came travelling down. I stopped & said to Ian who is always thirsty – well you'll get a lovely drink here & so he did – & I found a charming little Primula but alas the poor little car wouldn't start again. We had to reverse her round (luckily there was a verge & a man who helped push) & off we went down hill. She started fairly soon &

we turned & puffed back. After that there were no more stops until we were over the top & at the customs. There we found that the heat had melted the grease in the brakes & it had oozed out at the hub caps. When we got to Susa on the other side we had to wait ½ hour to have it all cleaned out & new grease put in.

We spent the night enroute at Vercelli just S of Turin & only just got there before dark. Next day we pressed on & were here by 5.30. This is a charming old town built into it's hill side. It has charming little arcaded streets. Our house is as it were a waterfall. You open the front door on the main street, and you are in a small hall & straight on down & through you see the garden in the bright sunlight. Between the front door & the garden are three rooms all on different levels. And up above are three more floors with an odd little one stuck in between. The bonne who is called Angelica is extremely nice. The house Vanessa was in is so near as to be almost one with Casa Pasa. It also belongs to Fossi. It is rather bigger & has a lot of things Pasa hasn't & which we seem to borrow.[1] At the moment the American who has rented it is away.

I left so much of me behind that as I drove off from Juggs there didn't seem anything of me to bring away on holiday. Now I have a curious suspended feeling. I am living the life I imagine to myself when I look through other people's windows after dark.

I long for a letter my dearest.
Your T.


289:   Sunday 13 July [1958]       *Casa Pase, Asolo* — I spelt it wrongly
                                   for you it should have been an e not an a

Dearest. *How* nice it was to get your letter yesterday afternoon. When there was none for me in the morning I was depressed and thought I could not get one before Monday, but there is a late afternoon post and yours came with that. I am glad to hear you have launched one kitten into the world, & that Wiz[2] is acting in such a bold way – is he any larger? There are hardly any cats here in Asolo. I have only talked to two. One a Tom who really needed me to wash his wounds as he had a bad bite on his face.

We lead an extraordinarily peaceful life. I am writing this at a large round stone table under a vine pergola on the little terrace, just after

1. Vanessa Bell and Duncan Grant had rented La Mura from the Marchesa Fossi in spring 1955.
2. A cat.

breakfast. Whether one will ever be able to do anything again is the question, for except for learning Italian & writing a few letters and languidly reading a few pages of Lavengro or Kilvert I do nothing at all. My hands are soft & clean & my brain if not clean is getting softer every day. Angelica, the bonne is rightly named. She is a small dark middle aged angel & does everything, waiting on one in the most useful & least obtrusive way. She washes everything we wear every day. She takes Ian's trousers & sponges & presses them & mends the pockets. She is going to make a skirt that is too big in the waist smaller round for me. She cooks us exactly the right sort of meals & all with true bonté. She has also found us a charming girl who comes each morning & gives us an Italian lesson. She is called Licia is twenty & has been to England for three months to a 'finishing school'.

We are going to Venice on Wednesday & are going to spend the night there as it is too hot to make great efforts. The last three days have been very hot but from what you say no hotter than with you. I can hardly imagine 96% in Monk's garden. This house & the next door one, where Vanessa was, are very much jumbled up together. Our little terrace & their back entrance join each other. At present we have it all to ourselves as the American lady who is tenant of La Mura is away but I rather fear is due to return next week. The only picture that we have looked at so far is the Giorgione at Castlefranco, a splendid work.

Write me a lot of long loving letters please – This brings all mine to you

> your
> T.

290:   Friday [18 July 1958]                                    *Asolo*

Dearest, How glad I was to have your letter. I found it waiting for me when we got back from Venice last night. We went off on Wednesday morning & spent the night there. It was rather bad luck as we had a thunderstorm & it rained all afternoon & evening. But all the same Venice looked gloriously beautiful. Yesterday we went in a boat out to Torcello as we had done before.

It was a superb day & though at this time of the year Venice is too full of people we enjoyed it very much. I am very much struck with the elegance and beauty of the Italian girls. If I were a man I would certainly try for an Italian wife but *not* an Italian husband being a woman. At least not unless he had something like the Villa Giacomella in his pocket. This villa is about five miles from Asolo & is absolutely wonderful. It was built by Palladio & though large is not enormous, & it is decorated indescribably beautifully by Veronese. You cannot imagine anything more perfect than the main salon or hall. It is this shape [drawing of an elongated cross], and I should think about 80 foot long. At each end is a fine great window one looking out onto the country & the other onto a fine fountain. But the great thing is the way he's done the frescoes. It is all white with standing figures in full colour. These figures stand in niches & between pillars all of which are done in fresco to represent marble, but done so perfectly that they don't look like real marble but are all the time painted marble. And the figures are as you would expect superb great warm standing females. The ceiling is barrel shaped & also painted & because it is not too high you can see it & it plays a part in the whole thing. I have never seen a more lovely interior. The family were in residence so we could not see quite all. I understand it belongs to the wife who is now some sort of Marchesa or whatnot but whose father got the villa by being a friend of Mussolini & whose grandpa was nothing.

I am glad you are selling off the kittens & hope the last one will find a good buyer but what is to become of Wiz? Thank you very much for going to Juggs and seeing to Pilly. I had a letter from Faanie & she was very pleased to see you.

I miss you very much, it already seems several years since I came away. Angelica who is truly a darling waits on me hand & foot. How shall I get back to all my chores again?

The storm has made the air fresher. It was very hot but I imagine not more so than with you. I forgot to say that the clever post office at Treviso *did* deliver your first letter, and only one post late.

I do hope the corylopsis will recover, I think it will, but it may have to spring from the bottom again. Poor Zin, it is hard on a cat to have heat inside as well as out. You do not say how Troy is?[1]

All my love dearest and to all the animals.

      Your T.

---

1. Corylopsis is a hazel-like deciduous shrub with yellow flowers. Zin, Wiz and Troy were cats. Troy, a Siamese, was one of LW's favourites. Pilly was TR's cat.

291:    Tuesday [22 July 1958]                                          *Asolo*

Dearest

I was so glad to have a letter yesterday. What extraordinary weather –
you are as hot and sunburnt as we are. We went last evening into the
country just behind Asolo, and felt exactly as if we were walking in the
background of a Perugino picture. Small green conical hills with tufts of
trees, delightful little round hay stacks with thatched umbrella roofs and
flower spangled grass. They are cutting their second hay & the grass is
thick with flowers. Scabious, knapweed, a beautiful branching carrot,
three different campanulas, a yellow marigold & a salvia like your smaller
blue one and many more.

We are going for a night to Ravenna on Thursday. To morrow
afternoon we are taking Angelica to Chióggia where she has a sister. I
have done a little painting of her head, she must have been very good
looking before age & a bad dentist had worked on her. She had fine great
eyes which she turns up like the Virgin.

Why won't Wiz grow in front I wonder? I hope poor Zin is over her
troubles. There are no cats in Asolo – but there is one fine one called
Stromboli. He is grey & belongs to the dentist's wife & sits under her
chair when she has an evening drink in the cafe on the piazza. When she
gets up to go she says 'Vieni alla casa' & he stalks off after her 'multo
bravo'.

Our teacher is arriving
All my love dearest
    your
     T


292:    Thursday [24 July 1958]                                     *Casa Pase*

Dearest,

How sweet of you to tell me the ear-rings have arrived my ears are
twitching to have them on.

We are going off this morning to Ravenna for the night & I am looking
forward to seeing the mosaics & going on to Rimini to see a Francesca
that is there. Yesterday we took Angelica to see her sister at Chióggia.
The old town is very charming, fishy smell & fishing boats – it is joined
to a gastly Lido crammed with hot people in every sort of beach get-up.
How terrible almost all the coasts of the world now are.

The American tenant of La Mura has returned – until now there has been no one there. We dreaded her arrival. She has a badly behaved boy of eleven. However I think she has twigged that we are not very sociable & we have only had one meeting.

This is not a letter but just a thank you dearest – for the earings & for telling me they had come.

All my love
  T.


293: Saturday [26 July 1958]        *Asolo*

Dearest, I must write in pencil because I have lent my pen to Ian. We had a very hot night in Ravenna on Thursday. It is a nice old town & the mosaics are truly wonderful. We went on to Rimini which has one Francesca, battered but beautiful. But the town is awful – at any rate in summer – like Brighton, crammed with summer visitors in every sort of undress licking ices as they walk along the street. The great plain of the 'sullen, something, something Po' is interesting country – miles & miles of fruit trees. Apples pears peaches & vines and all as flat as a board. Coming back we took small side roads & had a delightful glass of wine in a tiny place among a superb group of Thomas Hardy ancients. One walked round & round the car pondering on the G.B. At last he came & asked what it stood for & when we told him he said 'Ah well it's better to ask'. After that we had a courtly little chat & were directed on our way to a wonderful hand made ferry on which we crossed the said Po. & got back in time for dinner.

I am glad Wiz is placed – but would very much have liked to see him again.

This time next week we shall be on our way home.

All my love dearest
  Your T.


294: Tuesday [29 July 1958]        *Asolo*

Dearest
It was nice to have your letter yesterday – but I wish it had told of a good rain. We have had it here, a heavy storm two nights ago. You *are* being social, I have almost forgotten what it is like. We were in dread of

the American woman at La Mura – but thank God she twigged that we weren't 'social' and now she is in Venice for a week. She has left her truly awful little boy of eleven behind with a poor drip of a young Italian bear leader. The way the boy talks to him is horrifying & it is a good thing we have only two more days to go, as I feel something rising in me which is akin to Fuzzel's spirit – a mission to better him – I think however I shall get away without having given in to it.

To-morrow we are going to Padua on a picture expedition. It is only twenty miles off so we shall be back for one of Angelica's excellent dinners. She has taught me how to make a delicious 'torta' & I shall do it for you. It *will* be strange to be doing anything again, but O how nice to see you & all creatures & flowers – but most of all you

> Your
> T

295: Wednesday [13 August 1958]     *Londesborough Hotel, Lymington,*
*Hants*

Dearest

Here we are – and this is how the hotel spells its name. It is quite a nice little town & the hotel is comfortable & friendly. Really good coffee made freshly in cona machines & hot water to bath in. The room faces the main street which is noisy from 7 AM until 11 PM – when I say noisy I mean ordinary traffic not violent. We have got a little boat until Saturday at any rate. We went over to Yarmouth & found it there in the care of a charming boat builder. The father of the two young men who crossed the Atlantic & back again six years ago in a minute boat. We sailed it back last night to Lymington. It took two hours as the tide was against us & the wind from the wrong direction however we or rather Ian achieved it & we were in by 7.30.

I do hope Troy is better & I think of him & his loss very often. The 24 hours with Murr[a]y [Hicks][1] were very pleasant. He is looking well now & is much cheerfuller – never once asked me what my opinion of Euthanasia was.

The Gilbert Smith[2] family is well & cheerful – his little boy is what is called 'laughably' like his father. They may even get me on to a horse

1. In May IMP's old house master at Winchester had asked LW to write Hugh Gaitskell (1906–1963), then Labour Party Leader, to urge the Party to return the Elgin Marbles. LW wrote HG on 28.5.58.
2. Gilbert Smith and his wife, Daphne, were close friends with whom the Parsons often holidayed.

before I return to civilisation, as it seems the alternative to sailing is to charter a horse & ride about the New Forest.

There is nothing more to tell you – no amusing happenings or deep thoughts – just fondest love as always to send you and as always to say I miss you.

Your T


296:  [Wednesday] 13 August 1958                    *Monk's House*

Dearest,

It seems a century since you left and every kind of thing, mostly unpleasant, has happened. The weather abominable; I do hope it is better with you; torrents of rain and thunderstorms yesterday. Today some improvement, but it looks unsettled. Then a heron attacked the fishpond again and not a fish to be seen; I don't know how many he got, but yesterday I made Dan [Simpson] net in the whole pond.

Then the Dan situation is becoming acute. Louie thinks he may refuse to turn out of the house and that there may be difficulty in removing him. I was about to speak to him today when the Child Welfare woman you saw rang me up and asked me when they were due to move. She was very sensible and is coming out to see Mrs Simpson again this morning and will see me afterwards. I don't know what will happen and all I can do is to say to myself: 'Nothing matters'.[1]

Then Troy did not eat so I had Breeze again. She gave him another pill and said that, though he was certainly better, he had a swollen gland in the intestine which might have to be operated on – she thought it was due to what he had eaten. However next day he began to eat and is, I think, much better. Zin has therefore decided to come on heat.

The Welfare woman has just been here and I was present when she had a talk with Dan. She wants Mrs S[impson] to go into hospital if she can get the doctor to agree. Dan has agreed to her going if it can be fixed up – which is something. But I don't know what is to happen to him and the children.

The village is practically impassable. It will be quite impossible to get to the field down the village street and we shall have to get to it round by Princess Gap.

1. Dan Simpson had been gardening at Monk's House and Juggs Corner for about a year. His wife was exhausted from bearing seven children in eight years and LW had heard that he was physically abusive to her. He fired him and called in the welfare people to intervene on behalf of Mrs Simpson and the children. See also letter 299.

You see how lovely everything is here. I had a letter yesterday from a Mr Nathan which will amuse you. Also one from the Grahams.[1]

    Love from

        L.


297:    Thursday [14 August 1958]              *Londesborough*

Dearest

I have time for a quick line to say how glad I was to get your letter this morning. How wretched about the heron. I do hope the fish were mostly under the lilies, it is infuriating when they were so beautiful. I am relieved to hear that Troy has improved. It is terrible about the lustfulness of cats. Poor Mr Nathan, he certainly got a characteristic Woolf reply. It was rather nice of him I think. You might have asked him to build you a new conservatory just to 'show his appreciation.' I'm glad the Grahams have their baby.

Ian has gone down to the quay to see another boat which would be larger & a good deal better than the 'Jenny Wren'. I think he will take it we shall then sail the J.W. back to Yarmouth & return here on the ferry. The ferrys are to me one of the great disadvantages of this place. They are always coming & going & they always seem to me to be about to cut us & our tiny boat in two, but they don't seem to worry Ian – 'they must give way to us' he says but they show no sign of ever doing this & I feel we are like Pedestrians who are mown down by a bus on a Zebra crossing. In the right but dead. Yesterday was fearfully wet. We went out for about an hour & a half luffing about & drenched came in at 2.30 & ate our picnic in the bedroom (a familiar holiday experience).

We thought it was going to be hopeless today but the proprietor says it won't be too bad & he thinks we could take the J.W. back so this is no doubt what we shall do. I shan't be sorry to bid farewell, she is a poor little thing & very uncomfortable.

The place is rather nice. Not at all smart & a great many lovely 18

---

1. Mr Nathan was working on the village drainage system. Prof. John Graham and his wife Angela are Canadians who met LW in 1956, and lived in Sussex when Prof. Graham was writing about the work of VW. TR was kind to them, as she was to all visiting scholars, and they became friends. In 1966 TR and LW stayed with the Grahams in London, Ontario; at the end of a party at their house when TR had taken off her shoes and was relaxing during the clearing-up, LW was overheard saying to her: 'Who would have thought the colonials would be so interesting!' Prof. Graham published the holograph edition of *The Waves* (1976).

century houses down a fine wide hump backed street.

I do hope Saturday is a brilliant fine day to make up for this awful drain laying. How I wish I was going to be there to buzz round & perhaps help you a little.

What a trial Dan's muddle is. I am glad I went to the Child Welfare woman – that at any rate means they know about the whole thing. How I wish it was over & they gone & me comfortably settled with a steady good man —

I will go & post this to be done before Ian gets back.

All my devoted love.

T.

298:    Monday 18 August [1958] *Londesborough Hotel, Lymington, Hants*

Dearest,

I was so glad to have your letter this morning, and to hear the show had gone off satisfactorily. It is good to know that it is over.

We had a truly lovely sail yesterday. I can't remember whether we had secured the better boat when I last wrote? It is a great improvement on the Jenny Wren which we towed back to Yarmouth on Friday with me sitting in her trying to steer & feeling like Sir Richard Grenville.

The larger boat is called the Segan & has brilliant orange sails – it also has an engine very much wanted in this narrow muddy entrance. We sailed on Saturday round to Buckler's Hard in the Beaulieu River. The engine gave out & Ian had to do a very accomplished bit of sailing to get us in & that of course was very satisfying for him. We left the boat there & came back by car (it is only 8 miles) & yesterday Gilbert [Smith] mended the engine & we had a perfect sail home in sunshine all the way & not too much wind, the first quiet sail we have had. Now it is back to a steady drizzle. What a cat Troy is, one minute he is dying on his feet & the next he is hauling other cats down from trees by their tails. Thank you for going to visit my Pilly she would be very pleased to see you.

This is a curious holiday, I certainly don't have to cook & wash up – but I have to exert myself very strenuously. I am bruised black & blue & look like a fruit no one will buy.

The boats & water often look very beautiful & the little town is pretty, but so far what I have seen of the country is rather tame & dullish & much built over. I have had one short wild flower dawdle & found sea lavender

& sea aster, & I think, Dill, a yellowish umber with much cut aromatic leaves. I've put one in Gibbon to identify when we get back.

I wish I didn't have to go to Scotland, I try not to think of it.

I miss you & the animals & Monks very much – & in that order.

love your

T

299:   [Thursday] 21 August 1958                                    *Monk's House*

Dearest,

My cold is much better. I stayed in bed yesterday morning, and the temperature went down to normal (and has stayed so) so I got up for lunch. Torrents of rain here yesterday and a grey rainy morning today. What a year!

Patrick Dickinson rang me up last evening to say that they were still at Rye as their car had broken down, but they hoped to be able to get to Juggs tomorrow. I am to have the Quentin family on Sunday afternoon and will perhaps combine the Dickinsons[1] with them.

The Simpson saga continues. I rang up Miss Bishop this morning and have offered to pay for a nursing home for Mrs Simpson for two weeks from the 29th and maintenance of three of the children if Dan will go to his mother. She is going to do her best, but according to Louie Mrs Simpson is recalcitrant. A most unpleasant situation looms up.

All the animals are well including your dog. Troy has completely recovered. A woman in Brighton who has seen Monks Helen had written to ask whether she can buy Monks Dido,[2] who really is one of the most charming kitten[s] we have had.

The sun has just come out for the first time today so perhaps you will have a good afternoon. The garden is absolutely sodden and the state of the road is unimaginable. It is almost impossible to pass the various obstructions.

1. Patric Dickinson (1914–1994), poet, was the author of many books, poetry editor for the BBC, Gresham Professor at City University and a fine (Cambridge Blue) golfer. He and his editor wife, Sheila Dunbar Shannon, who were old friends of the Parsons, lived in Rye. Their children, Virginia (Ginny) and David, were the Parsons' godchildren. It was David who scattered TR's ashes on the Downs above Juggs Corner, in 1995. Quentin Bell and his wife Olivier had then two children, Julian (b. 1952) and Virginia (b. 1955). A third, Cressida, was born in 1959.
2. LW gave mostly classical Greek names to the Siamese cats he bred. Monks Helen & Dido were born on 1 August 1958.

I long to see you; shall I next week or will you just flash through from south to north?

           Love from
             L.

300:    Friday [22 August 1958]                 *Lymington*

Dearest

It was very nice to hear your voice – far off & telephonic though it was – last night. And to get your letter this morning.

We have done better here for weather than you have. Only Monday & Tuesday were really bad & Monday had part of it fine. To-day doesn't look too bad at all & we plan to take our last day in the boat, with all the Smiths on board. On Saturday we have to hand it over as the owner had already agreed to hire it to someone else before we got here. It has been nice in patches – in fact only the first days were fearsome when there was too much wind & a rough sea which made it all rather desperate. Yesterday we, Ian & I, sailed here alone to Cowes & back.

What a wretched business the Simpson one is. How heartily I long for them to be gone.

Poor Dickinsons. I will ring them up to-night to find out if they are there.

Yes of course you will see me. You must come to dinner on Saturday. I long to have been & come back from Scotland.

I have a swollen eye. A nasty holly branch gave me a switch when Ian & I took a damp & melancholy walk in the forest the other afternoon. I have not found many wild flowers but have noted down one or two.

We go from here on Tuesday & mean to stay three nights in Dorset somewhere and then home on Friday, which I look forward to very much and most particularly I look forward to seeing

    Woolf
    Dogs
    & Cats

       love your
         T.

# Letters 301–372 (April 1960–October 1968)

In 1952 Leonard and Trekkie had wanted to go to Ceylon but Ian said that he would 'dislike it'. At the time Trekkie wrote in her diary: 'I would dislike it if I were he so I cannot complain, but still I would like to go. But it is better not I expect. It is not worth it if it makes him unhappy; because I understand that sort of unhappy feeling I should not cause it – though I may have to bear it, as I have' [23.9.52]. She and Leonard finally made the trip in February 1960, just as *Sowing*, the first volume of his autobiography, was published.

On Wednesday the 10th they were greeted by the press in Colombo, where Leonard had arrived on 16 December 1904 with seventy volumes of Voltaire and a wire-haired fox-terrier to take up his duties in the Colonial Civil Service. 'How truly warmly they greeted L', Trekkie recorded in her diary. 'He is *their* writer and much revered.' The next day Shelton Fernando, permanent secretary in the Ministry of Industries, Home and Cultural Affairs, gave Leonard back the five volumes of diary he had kept as assistant government agent in Hambantota from 28 August 1908 to 15 May 1911, which the *Ceylon Historical Journal* was publishing as *Diaries in Ceylon*.

By Friday they were 'in Hambantota district, sitting on the veranda of a circular rest house built on a little promontory out into the sea'. On Saturday they got to 'the real place. L's bungalow, still there and still housing the Gov agent. It is right out on the headland with the sea on nearly three sides.' Leonard thought the car had radically changed the pace of Ceylonese life, but to Trekkie's eye 'the inland villages & landscape were lovely and still rural, the villages filled with softly walking people. What a lot is lost in poise and gentleness in the wearing of shoes. Everywhere they were barefoot & their feet moved at each step from heel to toe, instead of being planted down like a hoof.'

Everyone came up to them to talk, including several who remembered Leonard or whose relatives did. So different from his political analysis of their trip, Trekkie's account was full of sights, sounds and smells – of the scrub jungle, which reminded her of the bushveldt of her childhood; the animals in the reserve at Yala where she and Leonard were not allowed to get out of the car, which Leonard said was absurd because he had ridden all over it on a horse when there were many more animals; the residence at the King's Pavilion where they stayed in Kandy, 'with a number of servants & a bit of carpet up to the front door'; the 'old lady in the Kandian Chief's house [who] was like the old lady of any house in Scotland or France'; the furious rain in Tissa; 'the fishermen standing like posts in the shallow water' of the Indian Ocean, 'gazing in front of them waiting to see a fish to net'.

Trekkie kept her usual botanical record and listed the birds they saw. One morning as she watched through her field glasses, a boy of about seven suffering from a very runny nose joined her. 'He walked quietly beside me & in no time saw that I was looking at birds. He then pointed them out to me & having far quicker eye sight, he saw time & again when I missed them. Each time he pointed he made a small rather high pitched grunt & I timidly used my first Sinhalese – O – which means, yes.' She felt 'very at home in Ceylon' (9-27.2.60).

In April the Parsons went to America, in part to attend the celebration of the merger of publishers Alfred A. Knopf and Random House. With the successful defence of the Net Book Agreement in the summer of 1962, in which the problems of producing and selling books would be acknowledged as different from those of other commodities and needing certain protections, British publishers would settle into decades of similar mergers and acquisitions. For Chatto & Windus this would end in marriage with Jonathan Cape (May 1969), The Bodley Head (August 1973) and Virago (1982). Chatto itself had absorbed the Hogarth Press in 1946, leaving LW (a partner in the enlarged firm and a director when it was converted to a limited company) complete editorial freedom. This would be the cardinal principle of the other mergers, and the primary basis of their success. In 1954 Christopher's educational list had been taken over and renamed Chatto & Windus (Educational) Ltd; before the formation of Chatto & Jonathan Cape, the Scots firm Oliver & Boyd was acquired to become Chatto Boyd & Oliver. Chatto would later be associated with the Scottish Academic Press and Sussex University Press. In 1960, although few British books were published only for export, the proportion of overseas to home sales had grown to the point where international arrangements had become as increasingly important to book sales as mergers and computerisation would soon be to warehousing, distribution, accounts and stock control.

301:   Monday [4 April 1960]          *San Carlos Hotel, New York*

Dearest – This won't be a good letter but it comes with tons of love. We
got here all right but as from Colombo we left London 3 hrs late. We came
down at Newfoundland & my God it is just how you would think it would
be – miles & miles of fir trees & snow. The Airfield was white with banks
of snow on either side of the runway & a wicked wind blowing. We
stayed put. Yesterday Sunday was ghastly like Tissa only cold & cruel
wind & lashing rain. The bright spot was going to a truly glorious Monet
show somewhat spoiled by a banshee child who was also there & made a
noise that at first I thought was the central heating system letting off
steam. I thought of little Parkins!

My cold is beastly because of all the rain & cold. Thank God this
morning the sun is up and much warmer air

I will tell about N.Y. in my next

This is just to bring fondest love

from your

T.


302:   Sunday 10 April [1960]          *Stockbridge, Massachusetts*
                                       *With Bill & Dorothy Humphrey*

Dearest L

How glad I was to have your letter on Friday. The Humphreys[1] came
to N.Y. on Friday afternoon, stayed with us that night & drove us here
yesterday. This is lovely country & the whole drive from N.Y. was
delightful. This is New England & the houses are all charming white
weather boarding set in little copses. All is neat & tidy & not shacky at all.
We had two snow storms on the way (the drive took about 5 hrs which
included lunch eaten in the car) all the way it was on a fast fine road which
is called Parkway & on which no advertisements are allowed & which has

1. William Humphrey (1924–1997), American writer, and his wife Dorothy. He wrote stories for
*The New Yorker*, which were published as *The Last Husband and Other Stories* (1953); Chatto &
Windus published his first novel, *Home From the Hill* (1958), which was filmed by Vincente
Minnelli. The Humphreys and the Parsons visited one another and travelled together in Europe
and the US. One evening at Juggs Corner Bill Humphrey produced a ring he had bought his wife
and said it was supposed to be a diamond. 'Well, there's one way to be sure,' said IMP and carved
WH & DH (about three inches high and still there) into one of the three large drawing-room
windows overlooking the garden. The Humphreys were close friends of LW too and
corresponded with him regularly.

fine grass, not level but nice & rolling, all along its edges. This morning the air is cold but sun is out & it looks brilliant & rather like Switzerland. It is a charming little house very bright & pretty, and Humphreys are as nice as I thought they were. The only bore is that my cold is truly stinking. I suppose it is not surprising as there has never been any warm air except house air, so that when ever one goes out the change is violent.

I have seen some glorious pictures, and I think N.Y. a wonderful looking city. The skyscrapers really are magnificent, but like Ceylon they want the sun. When it is grey they seem grim & prison like but when the sun comes out they become airey & atmospheric & soar up into the sky like trees.

We go to-morrow from here to Boston for two days. Where I hope we shall have Mary to dine on Tuesday. Then back to N.Y. & this time will be staying at the Stephensons.[1] I rather regret it as I liked our little hotel – where we had a bedroom small sitting room & bath room – little kitchenette & cloakroom. The kitchenette had a frig & a sink & had we wanted to cook they'd have brought us a plug in electric plate. I do hope my cold will have cleared before we have to move in consulate circles – it makes one's face so shabby as well as how it makes one snuff & sniff.

All the time I wish you were here to see the enjoyable things – a simply superb Monet Exhibition & on Friday a very good Degas one at Wildenstein [Gallery]. There is a Piero della Francesca painting in Boston that I didn't know about.

Fondest love from your
    T

*What* a bore about poor Nig[g].


303:  Wednesday 13th [April 1960]   *c/o Lady Stephenson, 1 Beekman Place, N.Y. City*

Dearest L

Here I am back in N.Y. & in residence as you see. We flew from Boston this morning & I am now sitting in our room nine floors up & looking straight out across the East River which is very reminiscent of the Thames. I liked Boston very much. We were in the Ritz, the grandest hotel, & I must say it was delightful. Our room looked across the Public Gardens which are like a little St James's Park with ornamental water (on

1. Sir Hugh (d. 1972) and Lady Patricia Stephenson. Sir Hugh was Consul General in New York (1957–60) and Deputy Under-Secretary of the Foreign Office 1960–3. Like IMP, he had been educated first at Winchester.

which Mary was taken in Swan paddle boats when she was small.) She & Gavin dined with us last night. She was, as always, perfectly charming. She wanted to hear all news of you & she sent you her warm 'feelings'. She is too much of a Puritan to send you love outright! She may be coming to England this summer, but Gavin can't. It was lovely to find your letter waiting here for me — I wish I'd been there to shout Kingsley [Martin] down with your glories in Ceylon.

I have seen so many masterpieces I am truly stuffed. I go over them in my head when I'm in bed at night. I wish we had had longer in Boston. I simply had to gulp them down there. We left Bill & Dorothy early on Monday morning & took a cross country bus to Boston. It took 4 hours. The first part was nice as we had the front seat, but we had to change buses half way & were in the back & all the way an awful wireless was playing sobbing tunes. The country we went through was incredibly rocky & the soil seemed poor & thin all the way. Someone in Boston told me that all those little woods which we saw with Bill & Dorothy had once been cultivated land but poor. And gradually the farms have given up & the trees sown themselves. But you can still see boundaries of fields he said if you walk about in them — which would be hard to do as they are like jungle with a thick undergrowth of saplings.

I very much enjoyed being with the Humphreys and felt normal & like myself, but most of the time I have a very strange feeling as if I was a performing seal & doing it very well too.

The centre of N.Y., Manhattan, is extremely easy to find your way about in as it is ruled out in squares & the streets going from E to W are called streets & the ones from N to S are all avenues. I am greatly impressed by some of the sky scrapers & already have decided that some are good & some bad. They are doing some very good new ones. Things seem terribly expensive & I think they are, but of course we are living all the time in what would be the most expensive part of London.

I miss you — the animals — the gardens — music — very much indeed.

  Fond love as always

   from your

      T.

My cold is gradually going but was a perfect brute & finished up in one eye making me look like half a blood hound.

304:   Monday, 18 [April] 1960          *One Beekman Place, New York*

Dearest – It has turned to full Summer here and last Friday it was 86% in New York. The Saturday before there were two snow storms —

This morning is misty & muggy, but I haven't been out yet and it is very difficult to assess the temperature even by hanging your head out as they put the central heating under all the windows. We came back last night from a night with the Knopfs in the near country. He is a keen or keenish gardener & has been in this house for 30 years. All the shrubs were planted by him & a lot of conifers. He had two superb corylopsis in full flower, large shrubs and very beautiful, also some magnificent magnolias, some out, some just bursting.

But O the boringness of it. Americans seem to have *no* idea of conversation. You all sit round a long way away from each other & shout across. And one person holds forth & at the Knopfs that's Alfred, with Blanche making anti remarks from time to time. We had a lunch party & a dinner party and all was excitement about their that day announced merger with Random House.

Everything is bursting out now & trees turn green over night but it is at least a fortnight behind England. We whirl about & I am bearing up very well, the cold almost quite gone. We are going to Washington next week end with the Humphreys who are taking us in a borrowed car. I hope the cherry blossoms will not be over as this is a 'feature' of Washington but I now realize that things are *always* over or not yet out when one really wants to see them. The Knopfs have a black Poodle which made me miss my Belle very much. It does not take Knopfs or Poodles to make me miss you.

          Love your T.


305:   Friday [22 April 1960]          *1 Beekman Place, New York*

Dearest. I was so glad to have your letter yesterday. Yes the cold has gone & the weather is warm – 68% yesterday. It is impossible to count on it though, & I'm sure next week when we go to Canada we will find snow. This afternoon we go to Washington. We have to go by train & Bill was unable to borrow a car, but I am looking forward to the trip very much. Here the trees are bursting out & every day they change – not that there are many trees to see here – In Park Avenue are magnolias in large tubs – and of course there are good trees in Central Park. The only drawback to being here on the E. River is that we are quite a little way from Central Park. I wanted to get there early in the morning when I believe if you go over to the other side you can see a lot of migrating birds.

Yesterday we were driven out for the day to the Reader's Digest Establishment, given lunch & taken round & then had a good drive all up & down around the Hudson. Enjoyed this very much. It's not great landscape but it was interesting.

What annoys me is the snob business about pictures – even the Reader's Digest has to buy its Modiglianis & it's Roualts, what nonsense.

I must go – a week to day we should be flying home. I am longing to see you & all animals.

love your
T.

306:    [Sunday] 24 April 1960                                              [*Monk's House*]

Dearest, I shall see you, I'm glad to say, before I can write you another letter after this. How long it seems since you went. (My typing seems affected)

I have had a curiously busy week. Tuesday I drove to Rustington and had lunch with William [Plomer], Charles [Erdman],[1] and Morgan [Forster]. Charles had cooked a chicken and was terribly concerned because the legs had not cooked properly. William and Morgan tried to soothe him in voices appropriate to the reassuring that the young wife has produced a delicious meal. Then I went on and had tea with Octavia [Wilberforce]. The weather has been perfect spring all this week in the day at any rate, sun almost all day. But it is pretty cold at nights. Everything in the gardens has rushed out.

Wednesday I lunched with John Bullard and Dennis [Proctor] and went to the Cranium in the evening and found myself sitting next to Roy Harrod.[2] It was rather amusing as I had not seen him for ages and I knew

1. William Charles Franklin Plomer CBE (1903–1973), novelist and poet, lived at Rustington with his devoted friend Charles Erdman. Plomer came to London from Pietersburg in 1929 and succeeded Edward Garnett as literary consultant to Jonathan Cape, to whom he brought Ian Fleming's James Bond novels. He was awarded the Queen's Gold Medal for poetry 1963.
2. For John Bullard see p.197, n.1. Sir Philip Dennis Proctor (1905–1983) was Permanent Secretary at the Ministry of Power 1958–65. Educated at King's College, Cambridge, he edited Goldsworthy Lowes Dickinson's autobiography (1973). The Cranium was a dining club started by David Garnett, Francis Birrell and Stephen Tomlin to enable dispersed friends to keep in touch. Sir Roy (Forbes) Harrod (1900–1978) was joint editor of the *Economic Journal* (1945–61) and a member of the UN

that he knew that I had written what Lydia [Lopokova] had called a 'stinking' review of his book. However we got on quite well.

Last night I dined with Evelyn [Pember] as usual to meet Gerald [Norman]. It was as usual except that Mrs Maitland-Edwards, her daughter, and grandson were also there. Gerald asked if he could come and see me here this morning and I had him here for an hour or more. I meant to go and see Farney [sic] yesterday, but was prevented. She and Mrs Edwards are going to Juggs for an hour this afternoon, and I may go and meet them there to see that things are all right.[1]

I was rung up by Vanessa last Monday. She told me that Janie Bus[s]y had died suddenly. She did not know anything more than that she had been found dead in the bathroom. Vanessa and Duncan were going up to London and I have heard nothing more about it. I thought of ringing her up this evening.

O dearest, how I look forward to next week.

All animals are well. Love from your

L.

307:   Wednesday morning [27 April 1960]                     *New York*

Dearest L.

I am writing in bed while waiting for breakfast. We go off at 10 o'clock for Toronto. I can't believe that I shall be home in four days.

The strangest thing has been the violent weather changes – 94% in Washington. I liked Washington very much. It was delightful to be in a city with great trees again. And the pictures are really glorious. I don't think the Americans should buy any more, they really have enough here now. What they should do now is buy the picture but give it to the country of its origin – I somehow don't think this excellent and noble idea would appeal to them. Anyway the Washington gallery is quite enormous & simply crammed with masterpieces starting at the beginning & finishing with French 19 Century.

We had four hours in it on Saturday and a last hour on Sunday, not enough really to do more than have a flying idea of what was there. We also

---

sub-commission on Employment and Economic stability (1947–50). His books included *The Life of John Maynard Keynes* (1951). In an unsigned *Listener* article LW had said the book was a failure.
1. When the Parsons were away Faanie sometimes stayed with friends or in guest houses in Lewes, Piddinghoe or Kingston.

had a delightful picnic on Sunday with Richard Eberhart[1] and his family. He is a charming ebullient man – not at all as I had imagined he would be from his poetry. They drove us out & we had a picnic on the banks of the Potomac & were then taken to see George Washington's house. There were too many people to go inside & I didn't really want to – but the position of the house is magnificent on slightly rising ground looking on the river.

I don't know whether you'll get this on Saturday – but you may & the next thing you'll hear is me. How I look forward – love your T.

308:   Sunday morning 8.30 [9 April 1961]      *Hotel di Roma, Piacenza*

Dearest – Brilliant hot sun all yesterday & here it is again to-day.

Quite a good journey to Milan except for the rock like train pillow which pretty well dislocated my neck. We had a splendid lunch at [Giauniono's?] in Milan & then collected the car, & I think with great dash & brilliance found our way out of Milan. We decided to stay here as we were a bit tired & this seemed a good hotel. We got here at 6 o'clock. It is a very nice usual small Italian town – but they have as fine loud voices & motor bikes & also as splendid an ingenuity in making a noise at night as anywhere I've been. Though we were five floors up in a side street Saturday night went on until 2.30 & then someone started to mend something which seemed to need them to keep on lifting up & throwing down great iron chains.

We move on & hope to find somewhere for a sleepy mid-day picnic – to-night we expect to spend in Lucca. Everything out, poplar trees wisteria peach plum pear, these last were Switzerland. How I would hate to live in one of those long narrow Swiss valleys with the great boring menacing mountains all round.

We must go & buy an apple & some cheese for my lunch & a sausage for Ian as shops close at mid-day.

Fondest love to all animals & a special dollop for my Belle & my Jackson & the largest dollop for my dearest Woolf.

Your
T.

1. Richard Eberhart (b. 1904), American poet and professor who had contributed to *New Signatures*, edited for the Hogarth Press by Michael Roberts in 1932. Chatto & Windus were his London publisher. In 1966 he won the Pulitzer Prize for poetry.

309:  Tuesday 11 April 1961                              [*Monk's House*]

Dearest,

Vanessa died on Friday. I was going over to see her on Thursday if she was well enough, but rang up Quentin in the morning and we decided that I had better wait and see if she were any better on Friday. She had been ill with severe bronchitis only since Monday. I went over there yesterday; Angelica [Garnet], Quentin [Bell], and Duncan [Grant] were there. Angelica had only heard on Thursday that Vanessa was ill and arrived at Charleston after she died. Angelica and Duncan are coming here to tea on Friday. Clive [Bell] is getting on very well and will probably be able to come to Charleston next week.

I see in the Times today that Morgan [Forster] is in hospital in Cambridge, having 'suffered a slight heart attack on Saturday'. They say he is 'quite comfortable after a satisfactory night'. But it all sounds rather depressing.

Everything is well here. I fetched Nigg back yesterday. Breeze thinks her rather better and I am to take her back on Friday for another bath. Breeze was much impressed by her skill in getting out of the run in which she put her and escaping on to the road – opening two gates on the way. Breeze said she had never had a dog who had succeeded in opening the gate of the run. Belle is quite all right, but still scratches a bit. Ajax is also quite well, but rather worried because he has a fixation on Zin who now appears to be on heat again and has gone off for the day.[1]

I rang up the chiropodist who could not give me an appointment until April 29, so I rang up [Dr Raymond] Rutherford and asked him whether he could tell me of a chiropodist. He gave me the name of one in Lewes and I am going to see him on Friday.

We all miss you veryvery [sic] much. The Times says that the weather is hot in Italy. It is rather warm and muggy here.

I had a long albatrossy visit from the albatross[2] yesterday.

Love from all animals great and small.

> Your
> L.

---

1. Nigg was LW's dog; Ajax, Belle and Zin were cats. Mrs L. Breeze had moved her veterinary surgery to Hollow Barn on The Avenue, Kingston, just below Juggs Corner, on 1 January 1960.
2. Mrs Ebbs, the vicar's wife.

310:    Thursday evening 13 April [1961]        *[Brufani Palace Hotel]*
                                                                    *Perugia*

Dearest

Thank you for your letter which I had this evening. I am so very sorry to have your news. Why must people die? I don't like bad things to happen to you when I am away; & I am very sad to think of the loss Vanessa will be to so many people. I am very glad I knew her. I do hope Morgan will be all right.

To-night we have the news of Russia's space man,[1] after days of looking at ancient paintings on gold grounds & being plunged backwards & not forwards. It is too confusing being a human. Ants haven't changed in 30 000 000 (I don't know how many noughts) years, & I suppose we will also become fixed in a terrible mould & roll round & round in earth's diurnal course – or perhaps we'll change that & just roll. It is all very awful to imagine. 'Some men a forward action love, But I by backward steps would move'[2] – all I see here of ancient towns & ancient art seems so much more desirable rich & human.

We have had lovely weather, so far only one grey day – To-day heavenly & the Umbrian landscape superb. We went in the afternoon to Gúbbio a small ancient town in the hills about 50 miles away & the drive there was absolutely glorious. Soft hills & valleys & a dream like distant view. We must have a strong sympathetic magic because I *too* have a corn. I hope yours will be cured by Rutherford's man – Much love to all animals male – female & Woolf – I must tell you that Gúbbio had a huge terrible wolf that devastated the country side. St Francis went there & explained to the wolf how unpleasant it's habits were. The wolf immediately mended its ways – gave its paw to St F & lived ever after an exemplary life & was given Christian burial!

Fondest love dear Woolf
Your T.


311:    Monday [17 April 1961]                          *Montepulciano*


Dearest

I am beginning this here but may not post it until I get to Siena where perhaps I shall have another letter from you. Our weather has broken I'm

---

1. Yuri Gagarin circled the earth once in the spaceship *Vostok* on 12 April 1961.
2. From Henry Vaughan's 'The Retreat': 'Some men a forward motion love,/But I by backward steps would move.'

afraid & now we seem to get perhaps half a day fine & sunny & then torrents of rain. The usual Mediterranean spring behaviour. Annoying because as in England March was dry as a bone. All the same there is so much to see that rain is better here than most places. The Francescas at Arezzo seem to me very much less brilliant than they were 25 years ago. The Church was damaged in the war & though the frescoes were said to be all right I think they must have had something happen to them. They seem to have a bloom over them. I think they are working on them as there was scaffolding & Bill [Humphrey] says they can remove this bloom. To-day we go to Siena by evening, & on the way to Borgo San Sepolchro to see his great Resurrection which I have never seen. We had a picnic on a little hill yesterday where there were hundreds of cyclamen European pushing through the coarse grass. I found a sweet little bunch of flowers, two orchids, which I did not pick, because there were only one each of them. One pale lilac with white bracts & one very big spotted one with very dark bracts. Do you know what weight of luggage we are allowed to take in our aeroplane?

I dream of Jackson night after night, last night I was climbing a steep hill with him in my arms & he was very frightened. Faanie says Rutle's cat who is staying at Juggs has caught *two* mice. Please don't tell this to Ajax he may develop an inferiority. I do hope Nig[g] is better & that Belle is not still scratching. Fancy old Nig[g] taking herself off from Breeze.

I think I'll post this here. If you have written here I'll get it as we are coming back for the baggage this afternoon.

Much love dearest Woolf
from your T


312:   Wednesday [19 April 1961]                                    *Villa Solaio*

Dearest L

I was so glad to have your letter this morning. Our animals do seem to have got themselves into a sexual tangle & I only hope all will be calm before we go off.

This is an extraordinary house – Huge & decaying & rambling with a small decaying Signor and a very thin grey active intelligent Signora. She is also a painter & the house has pictures all over it by her & by friends – some not bad. A mixed company eat at a large round table every night. At the moment ourselves the Humphreys Signor Vivandi & the Signora – a strange dark son called Arturo & his very unbrushed American wife –

two deaf & dumb cousins from England & now a young American researcher in Virus diseases & his wife. There are two little girls who bubble about the house. One is the child of Arturo & his American the other of the Vivandi's daughter (who is in Paris) & a jet black Ghanaian. The daughter went to Ghana to paint & came back with this small memento. She is a very attractive child & very intelligent.

I have had a good eye-full of Francescas. The great Resurrection which I've waited more than thirty years to see came swingingly up to expectation. It is superb & *not* in a church so you can see it.

Weather is usually a hot sunny morning, cloudy & possibly a thunderstorm at mid-day & perhaps clear again by evening.

Much love this will be the last until you hear me on the telephone.[1]   T

313:   Tuesday 9 October 1961                    *Andennis, St Mawes*

Dearest L

Here I sit looking out on a very grey sea. We had a good journey down missing most of the rain & with superb great tossing blue & white skies all the way. We stopped the night in Blandford, the same hotel as we stayed in. It was full of parents with boys & girls. The boys from Bryanston & I suppose the girls from Cranbourne Chase. The children for the most part very talkative & stowing away large platefuls of food, the parents weary & polite.

Yesterday it blew all day & to-day the gale has abated and it is wet, but with either gale or rain it remains very soft & mild. The air is truly delicious. This house looks straight out on to the sea (unlike the hotel at Fos!) About an acre of garden slopes down to an unmade-up road & then there is the shore. The house is very comfortable with every modern device & so clean, & with pale fitted carpets all over it [so] that I am nervous that we'll behave like beasts in some way. The thought of our circus animals tumbling in is enough to make one faint. I'm glad to hear Zin has been safely delivered of all her kittens. I am very sorry I wasn't there to see them all & to help choose the best three.

If the weather improves there is a nice little sailing boat which the boat man has left out for us. St Mawes is a very sweet little place, I daresay it gets choked up with people in the summer time, but they can't spoil it

1. TR and LW left for two weeks in Greece on 26 April. *Growing*, the second volume of LW's autobiography, was published in May.

much by building as there are so very few places to build on. It rises up steeply from the little harbour, & wherever you can build a house one has been built.

We are to be taken in to Truro now so must put my shoes on.

Darling L I miss you v much

Fond love from your

      T.

I was v interested to hear the local news in Ian's letter – Could he really have had £500?[1]

314:    Saturday [14 October 1961]          *St Mawes*

Dearest

I'd have written before but it is rather difficult to do so as we are all boiling to-gether most of the time.

Monday & Tuesday were ghastly. Monday it blew a gale & Tuesday it poured. Wednesday was lovely & we all went off to Phil's motor boat. The idea was that we would motor about along the coast. However the engine wouldn't start. It was really quite pleasant all the same. We ate our picnic in the boat & looked at the wading birds & watched the sky & finally Ian & I walked home & they came by car. Thursday was glorious & Ian & I sailed all day long in a very nice little sailing boat. We went right round to the mouth of the Helford river, & I thought of the Ferry boat turn & that awful little man & his Ratty wife. Yesterday was lovely too. Phil & Ian & I went off to St Austel & they played golf & I walked round with them & found mushrooms. A nice little course high up with stupendous views & no other people at all.

Now two other people have arrived. Simple & pleasant but she has a fearful macaw-like Australian voice. He is a very special gardener & is a research plant biologist – I *think* that is what it's called.

I do so hope Zin has managed to feed her little cats. I long for one, I shan't be consoled for darling little Ajax until I have one in his place.

What glorious news about Aubrey [Everest]'s inheritance. Who was it who used to tell him he was going to be an heir one day?

My car battery has quietly died & I have to have a new one. They are getting it for me to-day.

---

1. Aubrey Everest inherited £500 when his father, Bert, died.

I miss you so much & think of you & darling Monk's. This house is in a heavenly position & is very nice but so much too clean.

Fondest love from your

T

315:     Wednesday [18 October 1961]                                   *St Mawes*

Dearest L

Thank you so much for your letter which I was delighted to have. Kat & Phil found us so entrancing that they stayed another day & did not go off until yesterday morning! We have had two wild stormy days. Magnificent skies and *dozens* of rainbows, but no sailing since Monday. We are hoping that to-morrow will be calmer & enable us to go out again in the boat. Yesterday we drove to Tintagel & it looked magnificent with a wild tossing sea, bottle green against the dark blue grey sky. To-day we went to Land's End. The wind was so strong it would not have been safe for a small light person like Gypsy to stand on the cliff. It is about forty years since I was there with Fuzzels, when I was a girl.

I was much distressed to hear from Elsie [Aitken] that Fuzzels fell, beside her bed, & has broken her femur. She has been taken to the infirmary but they are not going to keep her as they can't do anything for her. The sister says it may knit, but I cannot think that it will at her age. Elsie says she is not in pain but is very confused. She will go back to Morton Hall probably to-morrow. I shall ring up on Sunday when I get home. I have not told Faanie as I don't want her to worry when I'm not there. I'll tell her when I get back.

I had a good sensible letter from Gillian [Tulip][1] who has got a job with a solicitor in Hartlepool. She had not started when she wrote, but the letter was much the best I've had from her since all this started.

I miss you very much and all the animals; I do hope the poor skinny kittens are getting a little fatter.

Much love dearest from

your

T

1. Alfred William Tulip, TR's cousin, whom LW advised about the publication of *The Evolution of Matter* (1952), and his wife, Lydia, had three children: Gillian and John, who were twins, and Tony. Gillian was depressed and TR had been trying to help her.

316:    [Sunday] 8 April 1962                          [*Monk's House*]

Dearest,

I was so glad to get your telegram. It is wretched to see you go and I miss you all day.

My cold fulminated on Friday evening and yesterday I had a slight temperature and stayed in bed. I rang Rutherford in the afternoon and as it was his week end off he sent his assistant Dr Busk. He gave me antibiotics and the temperature went down to normal in the evening. It is normal today and he said there was no reason why I should not get up. I got up for breakfast and feel all right. It was really one of my fulminating colds. The only person who enjoyed it was Troy who refused to leave me all day. Louie of course was very good and did everything for me.

There is, I am afraid, nothing else to tell you. It poured with rain this morning, but is sunny now. I miss Belle very much.[1]

I had Angelica and Duncan to tea on Friday. I was rather concerned to hear from Angelica that last time they were in Rome they went as usual to stay in the Inghilterra Hotel and found it completely changed and not at all good. I hope you dont find the same.

Dearest, I love you.
            L.


317:    Monday [9 April 1962]      [*Hotel Inghilterra, Via Bocca di Leone]*
                                                                *Rome*
Dearest L.

All has gone well. The flight in a comet took an hour & 50 minutes but as always the comings & goings to & fro took much longer. We left Vic Sq at 10.15 & arrived at the Inghilterra at about 4 o'clock. We have a small dull & utterly quiet room, adorned by a large vase of superb white carnations sent in to greet us by the dear Humphreys. Saturday & yesterday were brilliantly sunny all day, with quite cold air in the shadowed streets & cold after dark. To-day is cloudy. We had meant to hire a car & go for a picnic but have put it off. Yesterday we roamed about in the Pincio gardens, lay on the grass, slept, and watched little Roman girls in their Sunday best picking fistfulls of daisies. Rome, in spite of motor cars, is a wonderful city to wander in, every little street seems to bend in the most inviting way, & usually the invitation is not an empty

---

1. Belle had eaten poison and died.

one, you come on lovely buildings quietly standing there with no fuss as they have been for four hundred years. But O why did they ever invent the motor-car. Except for designing lethal weapons they are the worst thing we have done. They spoil the look of every where with their nasty shiny tin & dreary shapes.

How is your cold? I do hope it is better. I can't stop thinking of my Belle, but I don't cry quite so much.

Fondest love as always.

From your

T.


318:   [Monday] 9 April 1962                          [*Monk's House*]

Dearest,

I'm much better today and went into Lewes to do the shopping which I could not do Saturday – in fact the cupboard was pretty bare.

Yesterday at 8.30 p.m. Tony Tulip rang me up and asked me where you were. He was in Lewes; with his wife he had taken a Sunday off and driven to Eastbourne and Brighton and had dined in Lewes. They had hoped to look in on you at Juggs. They came and had a drink with me and stayed talking until past half past ten. They were very nice; Tony seems to be doing well and hopes to be better off in pay soon. He is continually having to go for a week or two to The Hague and every now and again to Kuwait. Gillian, he says, is much better and likes her work. Myrtle has married an orchid grower and has or is about to have a child.

It is a bright day today, but still a strong cold wind from the NW. It poured with rain again last night.

I love you, dearest.

L


319:   Thursday 12 April [1962]                          *Napoli*

Dearest L

I was so glad to have your letter at the Inghilterra, but very sorry to hear that your cold had gone on developing. I'm glad you had the Dr & do hope it is now better, I worry that you had this very busy week on top of it.

The Inghilterra was just what we wanted. Our room dead quiet, bath room, loads of hot water & shabby, & very nice hall porters for a change. So

I don't know how it has fallen away from Duncan & Angelica's former visits.

Now we are in a slap up modern hotel bang on the water front, with all one wall of our room glass & a little balcony outside it. It is just the way to do such a hotel, but I wouldn't want to be here long. We go off this afternoon to the unknown villa. We couldn't go to the museum yesterday because of course it is closed on Wednesdays. So we went to the Aquarium which was very interesting & peaceful. To-day we go to the museo. The floor of the bedroom is made of some slightly shiny plastic, clean & I suppose cool – it is absolutely ghastly striped in yellow orange & black like a green wasp. But beds are comfortable & pillows soft. Heaps of Americans of course. The weather goes on being mostly sunny but still a bit cool. We had dinner with the Cacciatores on Tuesday who sent you their regards. The Humphreys are coming to England in June & will probably stay until October, & if they could get a place not too expensive in London would stay all winter. She is better from her awful Hepatisis [sic] (I've no idea how you spell that, but it does for your liver) she has to be very careful what she eats & no alcohol for a year. She thinks she got the bug from eating mussels in Naples, which I must say I think was a wild thing to do. I have been reading Mary Renault's new book [*The Bull From The Sea*] – but it is very disappointing. She has nothing to tell in it, it is just spun from bits of knowledge & her feeling for doing it.

Dearest take care of yourself I love you

> your
>
> T.

320:    Saturday [14 April 1962]        [c/o *Signor Domenico Savarese,*
                                              *55 Via Boffe*] *Anacapri*

Dearest L

We have arrived & are installed in this strange little house. It would really be perfect if the air was warmer. We have had it mostly sunny but always a really cool air.

The casa is small with a delightful tiny terrace which has a view through olive trees to the sea, & is absolutely private. The house is filled with extraordinary objects. Bleeding Christs, portraits of Cavalcanti's[1] mama, dead lizards, carved wood, plates & so on. The worst thing on arrival was seeing

---

1. Alberto de Almeida Cavalcanti (1897–1982), Brazilian-born director, set designer and scriptwriter, gained prominence in England when he joined John Grierson's GPO film unit to make *Coal Face* (1935) and *We Live in Two Worlds* (1937), with music by Benjamin Britten and verse by W. H. Auden. He then worked at Michael Balcon's Ealing Studios.

only one bed & it not very big. However they showed us round everywhere & in an outside room there I saw a metal camp bed & immediately asked for it. They carried it in. It is very narrow & rather bouncy & you have to be careful when you turn on it or it would buck you off. The first night lying on it's hard surface with rather heavy dampish sheets that smelt of camphor it made me think of the Glen. I've dried it out now & it's not so bad. We have two girls who come in alternatingly & clean up. We have breakfast & lunch here & go out for dinner. The house is also full of books. French English & Italian. I think it very kind of Cavalcanti to lend the place like this, as all his things are lying around. It is as if you walked out of Monks & just let someone else walk in. He has even got trousers hanging in the bath room! It's true his are in a cupboard. The first morning we couldn't get any water whatsoever & were very glum, but we've learned the method now. There is an electric pump which fills a tank on the roof from a rainwater well under the terrace. When we arrived the tank must have been all but empty, so that after the first couple of pulls the lav pulled no more & nothing came out of the taps!

I do hope you are better now & look forward to having a letter soon. I had one very welcome one on arrival.

Savarese is charming he is a carpenter & couldn't be nicer.

Much fond love

  from your

    T


321:   [Sunday] 15 April 1962                    [*Monk's House*]

Dearest, I was so glad to get your letter, though it took 4 days, and see that all was going well. I see that you may be having some slight warmth from the sun. Here it gets worse and worse. Today there is a bitter north gale and gloomy sky – I should not think anyone will venture to come to the garden this afternoon. Yesterday was sun but a piercing north wind with frost at night.

I have had one of the busiest of weeks and a good deal of what is called pleasure. Tuesday the office, and Peter [Calvocoressi] and I had a curious sandwich lunch with and at the Institute of Psycho-Analysis. Wednesday the Memoir Club – all fourteen members turned up and Denis Proctor and Bunny [David Garnett] read.[1] It was fairly amusing.

1. The Memoir Club was formed in 1920. Among its original members who read memoirs aloud to each other were Clive and Vanessa Bell, Lytton Strachey, Leonard and Virginia Woolf,

Thursday I had to go up to the New Statesman board meeting. Peggy [Ashcroft] meanwhile had asked whether she could come and spend Friday night here after being at Lullington all day. She came about six and the Cherry Orchard was on the BBC T.V. at 9.30.[1] She had always refused to be in a televised play, but had been induced to do this. Jeremy [Hutchinson] and Nicky [Hutchinson] had said that she ought to stay in town in order to see what the T.V. play looked like. 'You might learn something', Nicky said. She hated the idea of looking at it, but thought she probably ought to. In the end we went down and watched it on Louie's set. It was absolutely appalling. The whole play was made nonsense of by the way it was done – continual close-ups which made it impossible to follow what they were saying. Peggy was in despair and we couldn't stand more than one act. Yesterday I went and had lunch with her at Lullington and then she returned to town. Great excitement yesterday in the village; the vast mound of straw in the Chatfield's garden, which was to be used for thatching the roof caught fire at breakfast time. The fire engine came but it was impossible really to put it out – a certain amount was pulled away and the remainder eventually burned itself out. By a miracle it was a strong north wind; if it had been south or south-west nothing could have saved the house.

Last night I went to The Chalk Garden by Enid Bagnold[2] at the Lewes theatre and took the Albatross with me. She came out here when I was in London and then rang up to say she must come and discuss what should be done about the committee meeting. I felt I could not stand one of those unending Albatross meandering conversations and said that she had better come to the play and we could discuss the committee meeting between the acts. It was really not very successful; I had a good deal of Albatross and the play was even more appalling than the Cherry Orchard. If it had not been for the Albatross, I would have left after the first act.

Desmond and Molly MacCarthy, Duncan Grant, E. M. Forster, Roger Fry and Maynard Keynes. David (Bunny) Garnett (1892–1981), novelist and critic, had married Angelica Bell in 1942.
1. Peggy Ashcroft (1907–1991), actress, was a close friend of TR and LW and spent a good deal of time with them, especially after her divorce from Jeremy Hutchinson QC at the end of 1965. Her son Nicholas, a theatre director who formed the Mobile Caravan Company to take theatre into the Canadian Rockies, had worked with Michel Saint-Denis, who directed the *Cherry Orchard*. The RSC's production had been filmed at the Aldwych theatre in December 1961. Ashcroft played Madame Ranevsky.
2. Enid Bagnold (1889–1981), novelist and playwright, lived in Rottingdean, a few miles from Rodmell, with her husband Sir Roderick Jones, retired chairman and principal proprietor of Reuters.

In the morning I went to see Farney [sic], who seemed very well. She had watched the Cherry Orchard on T.V.

Dearest, three weeks is too long for you to be away.

     Your L


322:   [Tuesday] 17 April 1962                     *[Monk's House]*

Dearest

Your second letter arrived yesterday afternoon. I see from the Times today that you are at last getting hot weather and today here there is the first breath of spring. Yesterday and Sunday were about the most appalling April days ever known. I didn't expect two people to come to the garden on Sunday and I told Sargent not to come as it was quite impossible to sit outside. The sky was black; there was a tearing bitter north east gale; every now and then the rain streamed down. I sat in the conservatory. The really amazing thing was that 55 people came.[1] At six with the rain puring [sic] down I shut up altogether, thinking that no one could possibly come. However at a quarter to seven Ursula[2] suddenly appeared and I gave her a drink and she stayed talking until 8 – so I had a pretty severe doing. Norman has driven off in an immense army lorry to the marble quarries of Carrara, where he will stay several months. I said that you and I would dine with Ursula on May 2.

I am going up to London tomorrow Wednesday instead of today Tuesday as I have said I will go to the Cranium. And then I have the Lees on my back. I cannot think why one does it. The only relaxation from pleasure is filling up one's income tax return. I wish you were here.

The animals are well, but rather annoyed with me for fleapowdering them all. Zin pretends to be very near her time.

     Your
     L.

Farney rang me up to say that Anneliese had refused to take in a parcel which she (Farney) thought might have been for you so I looked in at

---

1. Once a year LW opened his garden to the public to raise money for the Queen's Institute of District Nursing. Before Malcolm Muggeridge interviewed him on TV in September 1966 he never had more than 100 visitors. Thereafter that number rose 284% in 1967 and 357% in 1968. 'It is clear', he wrote in *The Journey Not the Arrival Matters*, 'that Malcolm . . . increases one's notoriety (or the notoriety of one's garden).'

2. Ursula Darwin Mommins, potter, lives in South Heighton, near Newhaven. She and her first husband, painter and etcher Julian Trevelyan, divorced in 1950. Norman Mommins was her second husband.

Juggs on my way to get food this morning. I saw Anneliese and everything was all right and the garden looked quite gay with daffodils. The parcel was not for Juggs at all and she gave it back to the postman.


323: Good Friday [postcard of the Tempió di Nettuno      *Paestum*
      stamped incorrectly 20 March 1962;
      should be 20 April 1962]


I thought you would like a picture of Paestum. Ian says it is all very different from when he saw it 30 yrs ago. As they have been excavating a large town all round it. This means it is not so gloriously surprising as it must have been when you saw it – but it is still stunning. We spent most of yesterday there & ate our picnic in its shadows. There was even a wise Paestum dog. Like Odette's to look at, he lay fast asleep right over the far side of the Temple but as soon as we started to eat he arrived with ingratiating tail wagging. When we said 'no – you stay off,' he lay down & went to sleep & the moment we had finished & I looked towards him he sidled up for the scraps, very polite very friendly, & when he saw he had really had all there was, off he went with another tail wag to try another party. We missed our boat back to Capri so have stayed the night here (Sarno) just short of Sorrento. We hired a car in Naples. Now we are going up Vesuvius & back to Capri on the 2 o'clock boat. I miss you v much, love T.


324: Saturday 21 April [1962]      *Anacapri*

Dearest,

It was good to have your two letters when we got back last night. How awful the weather seems to be – and everywhere. We bought a Guardian in Naples yesterday on our way home & Warsaw seemed to be the only place with sun. We had meant to be only one night away but missed the boat back & so stayed at Sarno (I can't remember if I posted my Paestum card to you before or after this had happened). To-day the wind is blowing again & it is grey, but not cold. We practise away at Italian & sometimes I think I am improving & sometimes I feel hopeless. As usual we have involved ourselves in a fearsome project. The nice Custodo Domenico & his wife & two sons are all going to have Easter Monday lunch with us. This is going to be cooked by Mrs Domenico here at Casa

Gulba & is going to be, very suitably, kid which is already waiting in the frig. I can keep it up for a bit, but suddenly I wilt & can think of nothing I know the way to say. We return to Rome on Thursday afternoon. We have found two charming geckoes who live in the dining room roof.

I am longing to see you & seem to have been away for months.[1]

       Your T

I do hope Zin has had a successful batch


325:   Tuesday 18 September 1962 [postcard]       *Portscatho*

This is the view from the cliff wall which is lovely. We sailed yesterday, rather chilly but all right, & mean to go off again this morning. It is quite pleasant here, small & friendly. We had a nice evening with Murr[a]y [Hicks] & a walk along the river. He is walking much better. I drove Mrs S[mallwood]'s car – rather a trailing gear. I don't want a Jaguar. I think of you.

    love T.


326:   Wednesday 19 September 1962 [postcard]       *Portscatho*

We had a long day's sail & yesterday. Glorious sailing off & until 3 when we turned for home & had the usual sudden change to menacing grey sky & angry bouncing sea hitting one on the face – but all well. I think of cats – dogs & Woolf.

    love

     T


327:   [Wednesday] 19 September 1962       *Monk's House*

Dearest,

I was so glad to get your card. I'm afraid you must be having a chilly time particularly if you are sailing the wintery seas. It is really rather nasty here with a cold wind.

Everything has gone all right – the animals all well. Bess[2] had a slight lapse in the house on Saturday and though I only cursed her roundly was

1. On 10 May TR and LW would have a week together driving to Holford.
2. TR's sheepdog.

so contrite at once that she would not come into the house again for some time. She has been perfectly clean since and tends to wallow in a delicious sense of sin.

Octavia [Wilberforce] came to lunch on Monday and is going to send her book to Murray. I doubt whether they will take it, but you never can tell with that kind of publisher. Yesterday Ruth [Selby-Bigge] lunched with me at the India Club and we discussed the book all over again. She agrees that Murray was the right publisher to try. I met the Humphreys at the top of the village on my way back and they came and played bowls as they had on Saturday. I am dining with them tonight. I am also dining on Saturday with Odette at Evelyns [Pember]. She rang up and asked whether you, Ian, and I would come and meet a friend of Gerald's, called, I think, Barman, who is diplomatic representative of the BBC. I don't much look forward to it.

Love from your menagerie including

    Your

    L

328:   Thursday [20 September 1962]           *Portscatho*

Dearest

I was so glad to have your letter this morning. All is well here – our weather must have been better than yours for though it has been cool we've had a lot of Sun. We've sailed all of every day so far – but for to-day. *I* think there's too much wind & we may walk instead. Yesterday was exactly the opposite & we were becalmed. We sailed off on a falling tide, & when we were nicely out to sea it became Ancient Mariner stuff & we sat bobbing about unable to come or go. We did this for a while & then took down the sails & rowed home. The first hour was fairly stiff. Then we had a rising tide to help us & came in very easily & pleasantly. I enjoyed it. I'd rather have a calm than a gale any day.

This is a very sweet little place. Tiny & with the usual little stone houses mostly colour washed. All textures are good in Cornwall. The houses, the slopes of the land – beaches – sea & boats. They all have a fine quality, & if I lived here & forgot about Cornish painters I think I'd find it very stimulating for painting. Our pub is adequate. Very nice friendly people. The bedroom is tiny more like a cabin, if it *was* a cabin one would think it rather big. They don't like you to bathe in the morning as they need the hot water, which is rather a bore. We take sandwiches & come back to 'a nice hot meal'.

I am glad to say Ian agrees that to-day *is* too rough & so we will make an expedition instead.

I am very sorry Bessie made a mistake – but she is getting better isn't she – we will win through I do believe. More, all cats are blameless.

Fondest love from your

T


329:   Saturday 1 December 1963 [postcard]        *Stratford on Avon*

Last night was v good Peg[1] splendidly hateful & all went with ziz. The scenes changing done brilliantly with hardly any bits & pieces. All sh[r]ouded in dripping mist this morning, hundreds of ghostly swans.

Fond love from all T


330:   Thursday 23 January 1964 [telegram]        *Cairo*

GOOD JOURNEY LOVE = TREKKIE PARSONS


331:   Friday night [24 January 1964]        *[Hotel Semiramis] Cairo*

Dearest L

To-morrow we are off to Aswan. We had a good journey here in an almost empty Arab aeroplane. Hotel comfortable near the river so that we can take an evening stroll along the bank.

We walked this morning in a rather down-at-the-heel-quarter non touristique very interesting. The thing I wanted most was a very small tight asleep baby neatly composed on it's mother's shoulder. I wondered had I snatched it & brought it home would it have been twenty years hence a little Englishman? Then we went to Pyramids & Sphinx – very disappointing. In the first we had a long upstairs claustrophobic climb – Murr[a]y [Hicks] very gallant – for the second the light was wrong & so one could only see the face in silhouette. Slight irritation with M who is as you know inflexible. To-morrow to museum before going off.

---

1. Peggy Ashcroft was playing Margaret of Anjou in 'The Wars of the Roses' (*Henry VI*, *Edward IV*, *Richard III*) adapted by John Barton for the RSC, directed by Barton and Peter Hall. It played first at Stratford, then at the Aldwych theatre, and was revived at Stratford in 1964.

Hope you had my cable sent off last night. Please forgive calligraphy - hand very tired[1] & hard to write with upright ball pen. Cairo like all big cities is too big, too many long streets & high concrete buildings.

    Much love

     T


332:    Saturday [25 January 1964]                 *Aswan*

Dearest L

I hope I did not post your letter in the wrong box in Cairo but I may have done. I thought I was being clever in posting it in a Post Office box & not in the hotel one, but now I think it may never reach you. So I write a quick line here before dinner to say all is well. I'm sorry about the hand writing, with my hand it is hard to use a ball point & it's all I have. It hurts so I won't write much. Cairo was too big & concreted, there were nice things but as with every great city now there are acres of tedious boredom. Here we look down on the curly Nile, much narrower than I expected, & little sailing boats go by, some touristique, & some real indigenous barques. The desert really looks just like a desert with soft melting treacherous shapes of a lovely ochre colour. And the sunset over the river was just like the back cloth for 'Desert Love'. We had to spend half the morning before we left Cairo in Air Offices & Cooks because poor Murr[a]y managed last night to lose his air ticket home! All is now in the warm hands of Cooks & we hope they will have resolved the trouble when we get back to Cairo. We get up at *4* o'clock to-morrow to be taken to Abu Simbel by hydroplane.

It *did* rain last night in Cairo so I can even make it rain in Egypt. This morning was cool & faint sun there – but clear sun here – air quite cool at night.

I can't write more as it does make my hand ache. Will you tell Anneliese who may not have got the P.C. I posted with your letter in that yellow box. I also sent you a cable on arrival on Thursday evening.

    Much love  T.

---

1. TR had broken her wrist outside the Lewes post office a few days before Christmas.

333:   [Monday] 27 January 1964                    [*Monk's House*]

Dearest,

According to Rita's[1] statement I cannot possibly get a letter to you to Aswan in time so I must send this to Cairo and you wont get it, I'm afraid, until Feb 4. I was very glad to get your wire and hear you had a good journey. I hope your arm didnt worry you.

A lot seems to have happened since you left. There seems to be an animal on heat in every room. Zin shrieks all day in the apple room and I have to put her in the bathroom at night. Bess came on heat on Thursday but does not shriek, I'm glad to say. Coco[2] will be the next, I suppose, and I should think it will be my turn after that. Delos[3] is in great form; he got into the bathroom and pulled yards and yards of toilet paper off the rolls. I can see him at the moment in the garden; he has taken to spending a lot of time there, chasing birds, I think.

My X ray went off all right. On Thursday I was an hour and a quarter there, not very pleasant. I dont suppose I shall ever hear the result.[4]

Saturday I went up to Henry VI. I had not examined the ticket minutely and when I got to the theatre I found that they had sent me a ticket for the afternoon performance. It was impossible to get an[y]where near the box office for there was an enormous queue. I thought at one moment that I would never get in. However two minutes before the doors closed I got hold of a man. They had themselves discovered their mistake and had my ticket ready for me. I enjoyed the play.

I had a letter from Dorothy Humphrey this morning addressed to all of us. The climate is so perfect that Bill is inclined apparently to settle there after their two appalling summers here.

Grim grey weather here, but not really cold. I hope you have the scheduled amount of sun. There is an article by Osbert Lancaster in the New Statesman on a journey down the Nile. Rather critical especially of the Pharaoh's idea of art.

I miss you very very much. Love from all animals including your
    Leonard

---

1. Rita Spurdle, Ian's secretary at Chatto & Windus.
2. LW's dog.
3. A cat.
4. LW had his gall bladder X-rayed; the result was negative.

334:   Friday [31 January 1964]                               *Luxor*

Dearest L

No letter from you – but I think posts take a very long time. This will
be my third letter to you. One from Cairo one from Aswan & this, also a
cable from Cairo. I feel as if I've been away 6 months. First it was very
cold with a fierce N wind – now it is heavenly – even warm at night. Since
it grew warm I have enjoyed it. The curious thing is it is just as I
imagined. Early morning & evening light entrancingly beautiful, &
endless lovely groups of people with black faces in night shirts. Egyptian
art is truly dull. If they think of a thing they do it thousands of times for
thousands of years. And there comes an end to marvelling at the great
blocks of granite & how far they brought them.

My hand is a little stronger but goes on hurting in a wretched way. We
are comfortable on Ex King Farouks yaught [sic] quite a big cabin & easy
bath rooms & lavs. A poor black man sits all day near our three lavs seeing
that they are tidy. Near him sits a sad Greek lady mending mountains of
bed linen.

Are you well & all animals? I wish I could hear, it's as if you were on
the moon.

                    Fondest love   T
We shall be home on Friday
                    Friday week


335:   [Sunday] 2 February 1964                        [*Monk's House*]

Dearest,

Your letters were all right and arrived both here and at Juggs; I went
to Juggs Friday and saw Anneliese. Everything was well there, including
the cats and Jim with whom I also had a talk.

The Literary Club was a dreary performance. I gave dinner to the
Quigleys and Lilla[1] and took the chair. I didn't much like them. The room
was packed. He was terrribly up to date, contemporary, in favour of

1. Lilla Healing was honorary secretary of the Lewes (Monday) Literary Club, which met six
evenings during the winter at 8 p.m. at the White Hart hotel in Lewes. Invited speakers included
writers, politicians, musicians and artists. Together she and TR wrote (and TR illustrated)
*Cooking for Mother*, of which Chatto & Windus published 8,000 copies in 1958. This wonderful
cookery book for children came with basic recipes and advice 'for getting your mother *on your
side*'. The book humorously (and instructively) spelled out the 'DRILL': eggs were to be broken
one at a time 'in case you are unlucky and one is bad'; if your arm ached while creaming

antiart. He showed us slides of innumerable abstract and antiart pictures. Whatever the pictures may have been, his explanation of them was lamentably phoney. And whatever abstract art may be, it certainly has the power of producing the profoundest boredom and depression.

Tuesday I went up to the office and lunched with Willie [Robson], who sent you every message including an invitation to lunch when you return. So that we have something to look forward to.

Rutherford came Friday to report on the X ray. It was apparently entirely satisfactory. The gall Bladder was closed Wednesday and open on Thursday, as it should have been. It had a small stone in it, but that is of no importance as many people over 70 have harmless stones in the gall bladder. Vast masses of the Robins papers were delivered here by Vere, the landgirl. I have looked through some and ruthlessly destroy. I am in correspondence with [Charles Harold Noel] Adams in order to make you and Mrs [Mabel] Smith executors. We decided to make Mrs Smith a trustee of Backsettown and she is coming here to discuss things on Thursday.[1] I hope she wont prove to be as tiresome as the Hon Lady Burrell, O.B.E.

I am lunching with Nan on Tuesday and dining with Evelyn [Pember] on Thursday so you see how well I'm enjoying myself.

All animals are well. The brown dog lives outside the kitchen door but so far no accident. Zin is at last off heat. I kept her for 12 days in the apple room shrieking nearly the whole time. As soon as Bess has done, Coco will, I suppose, begin.

It is the most marvellous weather the last few days. Warm and sunny and snowdrops, aconites, crocuses bursting out everywhere. I suppose we shall pay for it later, as everyone says.

How I look forward to seeing you![2]

Your

　Leonard

---

sugar and margarine you were instructed 'DON'T GIVE UP'. TR's lively illustrations showed the right and wrong way to do things, adding a somewhat mischievous tone to the instructions, and providing good evidence of why children were so fond of her.

1. Elizabeth Robins had died in 1952, leaving LW and Octavia Wilberforce as her executors. Backsettown was the rest home for professional women to which Octavia Wilberforce had devoted herself after her official retirement from medicine in 1954. Adams and Remers were LW's solicitors.

2. From 28 April to 14 May LW and TR motored in France.

336:   Thursday 17 September 1964          *Newton Moor, Inverness*

Dearest

Scotland is really a heavenly beautiful country. It is so long since I was north I had really forgotten its glories. Lochailort was a very good place to be. A small inn, quite comfortable. Hot peaty water & a good fire in the sitting room. There is only room for eleven people & we were full. The others being a party of friends who were there to fish. Well off middle class Scots from Glasgow or near. One was a director of the Bank of Scotland. But the host, the man who had rented the fishing was a man called Nairn & he was extremely nice & instead of looking stuffily at us breaking into their occupation of the place he & his wife were very friendly & I think had almost the best manners I've ever known. Friendly & genial without a trace of pushing bruskness. We had a good deal of rain, but the air was warm West Highland air & we had glorious intervals of sun. The landscape is really superb. All the land was a rich gold colour with intervals of subdued grey purple for heather. The sand of the little bays was silver white & the water every shade of lizard green to clear cobalt blue. We went down on the Ferry to [Glen]uig & there had an enchanting walk along the shore & through small mossy water trickling glens. We went over to Skye & right across the Island to Elgol where Fuzalie [Fuzzells] & I went the first time I was ever in Skye. But the misty rain came down & covered the needle points of the Cuillins so that we could not see them. Yesterday we left & Ian planned a truly splendid route. We crossed W Skye again from Mallaig to Armadale [Bay]. Drove up to Kyleakin & crossed on the short Ferry to Kyle of Lochalsh & then drove down through Dornie & the Spean Valley to here. The last two hours through this great wide golden valley in the most superb light. And all the time this wonderful lack of humans & their spoilation [sic]. Miles & miles of pure unspoilt country with nothing but sardonic black faced sheep to stare at you. Here the air is colder & as I write I look out on a changing sun & shadow hillside with a strongish coldish wind blowing over it I fancy.

We should be in Edinburgh to-night & will I think stay at the North British (Waverley) Hotel. I *am* so sorry about your boiler. Why on earth has it done it again, it isn't so long since we had all that awful time getting a new one. Don't you think it would be a good idea to have an immersion heater put in your bath room tank against emergencies? It is easy to do & you would be sure of a hot bath what ever happens. I hope you enjoyed your dinner last night. And I hope Bess is not being a trouble.

    Fondest love as ever

                from your

                    T.


337:    [Saturday] 19 September 1964             *Edinburgh*

Dearest

    Ian had a line from N. Smallwood to-day telling of Clive [Bell]'s death. I am so sorry. Will you have to go to the funeral? I do hope not, it is so miserable. Death is the worst of many bad ideas the Almighty had in his scheme of things.

    It seems hundreds of years since we left exactly a week ago to-night. All has gone very well & Edinburgh has been bathed in sunshine ever since we arrived on Thursday evening.

    We've looked at the Old Town & the New & the Gallery. I tried to get you a copy of the sweet little Teniers of men playing bowls but it's out of stock so I had to order one. We go on to-morrow to Wall where we spend the night. Next night Thirsk next Cambridge – next home.

    I long to see you, & I love you

              Your

              T


338:    Sunday morning [4 October 1964]          *Bernay*

Dearest

    I am writing this leaning on the car in the hotel court yard in brilliant sun. This is a nice little old town, somewhat decayed in it's hinder parts. But a perfectly satisfactory hotel with it's window on to the courtyard. We got here at 6.30 & now at 10.30 A.M. are off to-wards Bordeaux & will probably stay to-night at Montmorillon. It all seems very familiar after our May trip. But we don't have lemonade for lunch!

    What a to-do about Bill & Dorothy [Humphrey]'s passport. We wonder very much what has transpired. I feel sure it will turn up & that he didn't really lose it. We came over from Lydd with a bus load of Day tourists all very merry & uninhibited & a great crush of ladies making jolly jokes in the 'Ladies'.

It was tantalizing only seeing you for such a short time & hardly alone at all. I hated coming away but as usual I like it now I'm here. I will post this here & will write later on.

Much love as always & to the Humphreys if they are still there.

    Your devoted

       T


339:   Wednesday [7 October 1964]        *Bordeaux*

Dearest

Up till now all has been glorious sunshine & delightful empty driving on yellow roads – but O how different was yesterday's last two hours. We were heading for Bordeaux, my turn to drive, when huge black clouds assembled, as big as a tar barrel. By the time I was driving over the bridge into the town it was absolutely pelting down & quite dark. We, luckily, had been fixed up in a hotel by Bruce Todd's wine friend. But how to find the hotel? We had a little map. We couldn't see a name on a street through the pelting rain & the traffic was literally hub to hub. Round & round we went and at last miraculously there was 'Hotel Continental', & a tiny place to leave the car while we took our bags out. More miraculously still we had room 'avec tous qu'il faut' & as I had been feeling very queer almost all the time we'd been driving since our lunch picnic it was the best sight I could have. I then had a complete explosion from both ends – how can one's body contain so much? It was very odd because Ian & I have eaten bite for bite the same, & really not at all glutonously & he is quite all right. I believe it was because I took a sleeping pill on Monday night & I am also taking pills [Dr] Busk gave me for my ring worm and they must have been deadly enemies. But thanks to my very quick reacting body & the vigour with which I expelled all, I think I am perfectly all right to-day. Better than the weather which is outrageous. We are now getting up & expecting a telephone call from Mr Barton about seeing wine made.

    Fondest love dearest Mr Woolf

       from your loving T.


340:   Friday [9 October 1964]        *Cahors*

Dearest

We came here yesterday from Bordeaux through the most terrific thunder storm. As bad as that one we experienced together above Montoire. We must have driven straight through the centre of it. The lightning flashed on either side & straight up in front of us & the rain fell in sheets. We were thankful to get here just before 7 o'clock. It only started at about 4 o'clock & the earlier part of the day was very hot. We had a pleasant picnic at the side of the Garonne among the usual charming willow & poplar trees. It looks I'm glad to say fine this morning. We had a thunderous time all together at Bordeaux, it was doing it on & off the day before when we visited the vineyards which was a pity as the poor pickers instead of standing with smiling faces among the vines were in rather despondent little groups holding up umbrellas & wearing macintoshes. However we were received into the 'Chais' [wine storehouse] of Leoville-Barton, Margaux & Lafitte. It was truly fascinating to see the vast great vats into which the juice was being pumped. It is then poured off into enormous barrels. These are rolled into the first year cave & then into the 2nd year cave where they remain until they are bottled. Lafitte was much the grandest & all, arrangements tremendously exact & perfect. We were shown (through an iron grill door) 'Le trésor' a cave of 48,000 bottles of every sort of wine. A wine museum. Some bottles as old as from the middle of the 18th century. They are carefully kept & recorked every so often.

Bordeaux, they say is a charming town, but towns as big as that must be lived in to be liked. To go to they are daunting. I'm not quite sure where we shall go to from here. We are in the hotel we stayed in some years ago. The restaurant not as good as it was, but we have a suite. It is very curious being very long, very high & very narrow so that it is like being in a very high railway carriage.

Fond love & I do hope all is well. It is not nice having no news at all.

as always

your loving

T.

P.S. My inside has quite recovered & can even accommodate garlicky crepes

341:  [Tuesday] 5 October 1965                    *Shipston-on-Stour*

Dearest L

We had a good drive here, except for about 25 mins at Cowley when all the motor cars were coming out of the works, & of course everyone there gives everyone a motor car for Christmas, so it was nasty. But here it is simply lovely. We are about 10 mins out of Stratford on the road to Oxford & it is quite a small place. The hotel *is* an old mill with the little stream running by the side of the house, & with a very pretty little garden. One can walk out & up a country road which we did first in the moonlight last night. This morning we set off & did a delightful four mile circle. Superb sun shine & great elms standing near & far quite motionless in the land scape. The land is rich warm burnt sienna loam & one has the feeling that there is *never* any wind. However we stopped & talked to two men who were bagging wheat & they said 'Oh we have our share' but from the light of the great elms I'm sure their share is less than ours. We go to Hamlet to-morrow night & I'm very much looking forward to it. I'd have telephoned you to-night but something has gone wrong with the telephone. This letter is terribly badly written because I'm sitting on the side of my bed & have only Pepys to write on, & he's too small for the sheet.

Ian was terribly tired after our non-stop Sunday, but I think he is already looking very much better. We had a picnic to-day, & lay in a stubble field, almost too hot. I don't remember two such October days since my first term at the Slade, when all the girls sat in cotton dresses in the lunch hour under leafless trees. I do hope Bessie is not being a trouble to you. I feel already as if I'd been away for weeks – what does one feel like I wonder if one really goes away for six months? I miss you & all the other animals very much. I hope Monk[1] is thriving, as I'm sure he is.

The intrepid Davids[2] are driving over to-morrow to come with us to Hamlet & will then drive back to Cambridge!

If the telephone is mended I will ring you on Thursday.

Fondest love from your

     T.          XXX

1. A dog, which TR took after LW died.
2. Richard (see letter 286 and note) and Nora David were close friends of the Parsons. Baroness David (b. 1913) was educated at Newnham College, Cambridge. She was Cambridge City councillor 1964–7 and 1968–74, and Cambridgeshire County Council councillor thereafter. Created a life peer in 1978, she is an active member of the Labour Party and has served as Government Whip 1978–9, Opposition Whip 1979–82, Deputy Chief Opposition Whip 1982–7 and Opposition Spokesman on Education 1987–97.

342:   [Thursday] 7 October 1965                    *Monk's House*

Dearest,

I suppose you may have telephoned and I may not have heard you. In fact the dogs did bark during the news last evening and I told them to stop it as they had been barking at nonexistent telephones, dogs, and ghosts most of the day, but afterwards I thought it may have been the telephone.

You must be having superb weather; it is perfect here. I don't think I have anything of interest to tell you except the death of Colonel Styles[1] which I saw in the Times yesterday. No one in the village had heard of it apparently. Nothing new in the office or indeed here. I had my photograph[2] taken a dozen or more times yesterday with and without the dogs and puppy. Monk wa[s] stung by a wasp in the middle of being photographed and raised a tremendous howl. We went to his assistance and immediately another wasp settled on his back and burrowed straight under his coat. We picked it out and it left its sting on the top of his back. He spends a good deal of his time pulling all labels and colchicums out of the ground.

I miss you very much. Love from your
                    L.


343:   Friday 8 October 1965                    *Shipston-on-Stour*

Dearest L

It was nice to hear your voice this morning, even though it was faint & far away. And it was nice to have your letter. I feel, as always, that I've been away for ever. But I do feel a bit better & I'm sure Ian is. He was tired after our first walk, but yesterday did 5 miles in good form. We are walking in the afternoon to-day as it is cool & grey this morning & the paper says will get better in the afternoon. After our walk & picnic yesterday we went to see Hidcote Manor gardens. It is really a lovely & interesting garden & I'd like to see it earlier in the year. God knows how

---

1. Col. Herbert Walter Styles (1889–1965) and his wife, Violet, lived at Old Farmhouse, Rodmell.
2. In the summer of 1964 *Beginning Again*, the third volume of LW's autobiography had been published, and LW awarded an honorary doctorate by the University of Sussex. In October 1965 he had formally resigned from the Hogarth Press (although he remained on the Board), and as director of the *New Statesman*. In early November 1965 he was to receive the W. H. Smith & Son Literary Award; these photographs were the beginning of the publicity which would follow, including a BBC interview on 26 October and another in November.

they cut all the hedges, as it's all separated up into small gardens with great yew hedges & cut specimen yews.

Ian says he's very unhappy about some novel that Hogarth has taken in called 'Voyage' [by Laurette Pizer]; he thinks the title impossible & that it would increase the difficulty of selling a first novel. The others agree. If you do, would you write to the author & ask her to suggest alternatives?

We enjoyed Hamlet. David Warner was very good indeed; & is the first *young* Hamlet I've seen. The King & Queen were awful. I can't understand *how* such bad actors get parts when there are always so many actors out of jobs. The intrepid Davids drove all the way from Cambridge & all the way back again afterwards *and* it was foggy. I'll telephone you on Monday evening when we get back. Much much love as always T.


344:    [Monday] 8 November 1965            *Dar Faiza Hotel, Djerba*

Dearest

Just look at that brocheur & you will see our bedroom in the corner at the top of the swimming pool. After a very inauspicious start all seems now to be going to be very nice. The aeroplane was full & very uncomfortable. Seats at just the neck breaking angle. The flight was extremely quick, however, we were only 2 hrs & 45 mins from London to Tunis – but at Tunis – we waited two dreary hours in a miserable little airport. This was because Djerba was covered in Mist! At last we took off & arrived at about 10 o'clock, the mist having more or less given way to sun. This hotel reminds me of a Ceylon rest house. It is very simple, but we have our own shower, basin & lavatory, & a good enough light to read by. The sun came out good & strong by mid day & we walked round the little town, & the harbour. It was all white & blue. White buildings & blue paint – white sky & blue sea. The evening light was superb, there are about half a dozen trading schooners in the harbour all in dilapidated blues pinks & greens & these brilliantly lit against the silky sea looked glorious. Every one talks French which is handy. We see the other visitors at meal times. They are not very interesting & look, though they are French, German, Swiss, like Bournemouth. To-day I think we shall find the bathing beach which is about six miles off. Last night after dinner we had a most entrancing moonshine (as Pepys would say) stroll. It was warm & balmy & brilliant. Slightly cloudy this morning, but I'm writing at 7.45 & I imagine it may always start like this at this season. The hotel is full of small whitey tortoise shell cats but we saw one black cat out walking which was so huge it looked like a puma. No dogs except one which was guarding some Biblical sheep. Lots of date palms, olives, tamarisks. Everyone seems very friendly & polite, & even small boys, who join one for walks, talk excellent French. We were very tired, but now after a good night I begin to feel more lively.

I miss you very much & I wish you were here; I think you'd like it. Love to all animals but most to that Woolf with the £1,000.[1]

> Your
> T

345:   [Thursday] 11 November 1965                                    [*Monk's House*]

Dearest,

It is very dreary without you and the weather does nothing to cheer one up. Yesterday was a fiendish day, rain, mist, and an east wind sweeping across everything. Today is not much better. Fred has been away for a week with pains inside. He goes to the doctor again tomorrow.

The animals are all right and in tearing spirits on the canine front. Everyone who saw the television says that Coco was far and away the principal actor and deserved the £1,000 award. I have to do another interview on Wednesday for the BBC television. It seems to me ridiculous.

Quentin's[2] next lecture is on Sunday morning at 10 on Nov 28. Angelica [Garnett] is coming to stay with me on the Sat night and go to the lecture. I am asuming that you and Ian will come too and I will make sure that this is all right as regards tickets if necessary. Duncan wants us all to lunch at Charleston after the lecture.

Clare [Cherrington] rang up to know where you were as she has bought a picture about which she wants to consult you. She is going to walk here with a lecturer on Sunday afternoon. I have to lunch with Su[3] on Tuesday – so you see how gay I am.

---

1. The £1,000 W. H. Smith Award had been presented on Thursday 4 November in London. TR had gone with LW, then returned to Sussex to garden all day Friday, give lunch to Hamish and Yvonne Hamilton on Saturday, dinner to two local friends, pack, and take the 10.10 p.m. train from Brighton to catch the plane.
2. Quentin Bell was then Professor of Fine Arts at Leeds. On Sunday 28 November he lectured in Brighton.
3. Clare Cherrington was a student at the University of Sussex who became friends with LW. Ling Su-Hua (Mrs Chen) was a Chinese friend of Julian Bell who came to England in the winter of 1946–7. A collection of her stories, *Ancient Melodies*, was published by the Hogarth Press in 1953.

It is 11.30 a.m. and so dark that I can hardly see what I have written. I hope Djerba is nice and that I shall soon hear from you.

Love from your
L

346:  [Sunday] 14 November 1965                    [*Monk's House*]

Dearest, I was very glad to get your letter, but of course you had not been very long on the island. I hope everything has gone well. There is not much to tell you since last I wrote. I dined yesterday with Evelyn [Pember], Odette, and Evelyn's grandchildren. You know what dinner there is like. Evelyn seems quite recovered.

Yesterday I had a curious pair a Spaniard and a Miss Epton from Seaford to take photographs in connection, I think, with a book or article on Virginia in Spanish. Then I had a visit from Lilla [Healing] and Monk.[1] He was ecstatic, but his mother did not like him at all. I think he knew the place, me, and her. Unfortunately I had to say that I would dine at Kingston Lodge. I wish you would return and save me from that.

It has turned brilliant sunny weather again, but cold with 10 degrees of frost last night.

With love from your
Leonard

347:  [Monday] 15 November 1965                           *Djerba*

Dearest L

I was so glad to have your letter to-day, & I was phsycic [sic] because I knew there would be one. I'm very sorry the weather has been so beastly with you & that Fred has pains in his tum. We had a great thunderstorm last Tuesday night which raged all night & produced a wet but not cold morning. We went off on a bus tour round the island in streaming rain. However by the time we were back at midday it was clearing & in the afternoon we had a very good walk. Since then the weather has been full sun, but yesterday there was a very strong wind. Temperature round about 62 all through the days & dropping at night,

1. The Spaniard was José Suarez from *La Prensa* in Argentina. Monk had been staying with Lilla Healing.

but not as much as I had expected. We plunge into that pool in the guide
book every morning before breakfast & most days we go to the beach 7
miles off to bathe. Twice we have walked there. This morning we went
for a sail with a delightful fisherman. Sailing is not for the new comer
here, as there are only narrow channels which are continually dredged
out through which one can sail – otherwise there's no depth of water. It
was quite heavenly this morning with a brilliant clear sky & only the
right amount of wind. We are tremendously glad we are here & not in
either of the beach hotels. These are quite stuffed with Germans. One
has a heated swimming pool which we have named the Hippopotamus
pool. There is a care free old German who floats around in it & he looks
like this.

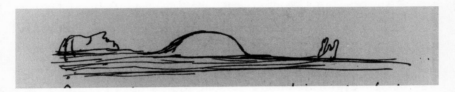

Our company come & go continually but are much more agreeable &
not so many. There is a nice little garden with Olive trees & two peacocks
– beyond is a rough farmish bit in which there is a large solemn Ewe who
has *three* little lambs. All the dogs are kept in the yards & never allowed
to run about the streets. At night they all bark all night. We are going to
spend the last two nights in Tunis. This may or may not be a good idea as
to get there we have to get up at 3.30 in the morning. We are being very
healthy & open air & walking a great deal.[1] Yesterday we must have done
nearly twelve miles. My catarrh is considerably better. I think the bathing
& sea air are good for it. We would very much like to come to Quentin's
lecture but we shall have, I think, Gillian [Tulip] for that week-end.
Would that be all right?

I hope Bessie is behaving herself & not being a nuisance. I'm sorry she
isn't going to share the £1,000 with Co-Co, after all Anneliese said you
could see her tail wagging & that ought to bring her 'some little thing' as
old Robinson used to say. It will be simply lovely to see you & to hear

1. Djerba was a complete rest for especially Ian, whose health TR had been increasingly worried
about since February, when he had had a heart attack. 'Ian looks better,' she wrote in her diary,
'but still has a tired face & not in good spirits. The heart affair has obviously psychological effects
as well as physical ones. I have lost the knack of writing an interesting diary, I feel this is all very
dull' (19.11.65). From now on their holidays would be 'very healthy' ones.

your voice. I think we will arrive latish Sunday afternoon as this way we travel by day & not by night. Fondest love your T.

348:    Monday [18 July 1966]        *S.S. Dab Chick, Grand Union Canal*
                                      *going towards Autherly Junction*

Dearest

It is quite different from how I imagined it would be.[1] Not the Dab Chick that I had imagined right. Small neat, doubled up, I mean one is doubled up, but quite adequate. What is different is England – there aren't *any* motor cars in England, not one. No aeroplanes no noise of any sort except birds & an occasional sheep or cow. It is incredibly beautiful & apparently there are miles & miles & miles with no house road or even barn – yet it is all cultivated country not barren moors. This morning, we have just had breakfast and it is seven o'clock, is beyond everything lovely. Peerless sun, no wind, that's the other thing that has gone with the motor cars etc there's no wind either. Here moored in to a tall grassy bank the grasses don't stir. Yesterday I admit we had violent rain storms which weren't so nice but even then it *looked* lovely. If it stays sunny I doubt if we'll ever come back. One gets used in a moment to the small confined arrangements & there are lots of good things about this also.

We are about to moor at somewhere called Wheaten Aston where we hope there's a shop. There are no pubs to telephone you from – in fact there is nothing but fields & trees.

I must post this now—

Fondest love, I don't wish you were here, because you don't mind about beauty & it *is* rather cold.

> your
> T

1. The canal trip was taken just after TR and LW returned from the United States and Canada where they visited Boston, Washington, South Carolina, the Humphreys in the Hudson Valley and the Grahams in Ontario. While they were away Harold Wilson had submitted LW's name for membership in the Order of the Companions of Honour. This he declined, as Virginia Woolf had when offered the same by Ramsay MacDonald. He wrote to Wilson, 'I have always been (heretically) against the giving and accepting of honours and I have often in the past said so. Much as I appreciate your kindness, I cannot, therefore, accept it, but I hope that you will not think the worst of me' (LW to HW, 11.5.66).

349:    Saturday mid-day [23 July 1966]          *Market Drayton*

Dearest

We have handed over our Dab Chick at 10 this morning. All correct &
no accidents. It was really very enjoyable & the last 2½ days have been
glorious. It's warm to-day but not quite so sunny.

The Shropshire Union Canal was superbly beautiful all the way. The
Worcs Staffs Canal which we went into for one day & night – near
Wolverhampton was not nearly so nice. Locks are hard work but we
managed them. We are sending off this & a P.C. or two before setting off
for Merioneth. We saw Kingfishers yellowhammers greenfinches herons
warblers stacks of wrens. Meadow sweet & fresh cut hay scented the air
all the way.

One got into the somewhat strange rhythm of life pretty quickly. It
reminded me of camping with Fuzzells in the very early Scot's holidays,
before the Glen. We don't think we'll be home before mid-day *Friday* as
we think we'll spend 2 nights on the way instead of one.

We are now off to the Hughes, pretty grubby we are though we have
preserved the essential decencies!

I miss you & *much* look forward to seeing you to-day week.

Fondest love
T

350:    Friday [10] February 1967          *Enton [Hall, Godalming, Surrey]*

Dearest

All is going well here, & I do really think it was a sensible thing to do.
It is all excellently arranged, very clean & professional: You arrive & are
shown your room & told to take your clothes off & come down to the
Consulting Room. There a nice young osteopathic man writes down all
your facts on a card & says you will be on a fruit diet. (Only lemon &
water for Parsons). So you put your clothes on again & we then went for
a very pleasant walk. Back at 4 o'clock when you're given a cup of tea. An
orange & piece of pineapple for me at 7.30. Lemon water for Parsons. We
stayed in our room reading or listening to the news etc until bed time.
We've stuck to this, the 'public rooms' are large warm & comfortable but
of course inhabited by other inmates who don't look very enticing.
Yesterday we both had an osteopathic treatment & then a blanket bath.
This means they wrap you up in an enormous amount of coverings, just

like a mummie [sic] & then hot you up with an electric blanket. You are supposed to sweat but I hardly did. Then you are given a shower & let go. We repeated the pattern of the day before, having another very nice walk. At 7.30 A.M. they bring you a glass of hot water & an orange. You stay in bed till about ten when one of the osteopaths comes round & tells you what they are going to do to you. To-day it was a very thorough & very pleasant massage. The masseur said to me 'are you a painter' this he divined by the fact that I had stiff muscles on the right hand side of my neck & shoulder! I find the total rest of both inside & all the other parts of me very beneficial. You won't know me when I get back. I was 10 stone 4½ when I came in & am now 10 – 1. Parsons has lost 4½ lbs. He's to be allowed an orange for lunch![1]

It will be nice to be back again, one has a curious feeling here as if one had been translated to another life.

I think about you a great deal.

    Much love

      T


351:   [Friday] 10 February 1967          *Monk's House*

Dearest,

It is very pleasant to hear your voice even for 3 minutes – for I miss you greatly. I hope I gain all the lbs which you and Ian lose. It is the most wonderful morning here with sun and warmth that I am typing this for the first time in my work room.

Yesterday Lilla [Healing] appeared after lunch but stayed only half an hour; she thought I might like to be taken for a drive – but there was a cold wind and I thought it better to stay in. Then Deirdre [Bland][2] came to tea with a description of the ceremony at Buckingham Palace. Lilla is bringing me the chicken and other stores this afternoon.

Louie is brimming over with local gossip this morning. Conrad [Mayer] has given notice to Henry Robinson and is furious with him.

1. As part of IMP's regime they had gone to a health spa so he could lose weight. TR was hardly overweight; she was 5 ft 8 in.
2. Her brother, Rupert Hart-Davis, had been knighted in January. In the seventies Deirdre Bland and her husband Anthony opened the Southover Gallery in Lewes. TR exhibited there six times: 10–28 February [?]; 23 March–13 April 1974 (the exhibit sold out quickly and IMP replenished it with pictures he took from the walls at Juggs until TR realised what he was doing); 9–27 May 1978; 13–31 October 1981; 15 October–2 November 1985; 17 November–December 1987.

Agricultural workers' wages went up this week by 6/-, but Conrad was told that he could not get the rise because he is earning more than £14 a week. All right, said Conrad, then I leave you next week.[1]

Then Sergei [Nolbandov] and the Parish Council arranged for a litter basket to be put near the shop. This was done this morning, the basket being on a cement stand. But it was put on what Janson claims to be his land. So when Louie went to the shop, Janson's lorry and men appeared and dug up the litter basket. What is going to happen now I dont know.

Dearest, how I wish you were here and I long for Thursday.

> Your
> Leonard

352:   [Sunday] 12 February 1967                          *Monk's House*

Dearest,

It was very nice to get your letter and hear of your strange life. I put this piece of notepaper in my type writer meaning to write you a proper letter, but, before I had typed a word, [Dr] Rutherford appeared and stayed until 1.15. He found me quite sound in heart, blood pressure, and lungs, and thought I was progressing all right. It is now rather late afternoon and I must catch the post with this.

Yesterday Gilbert Smith rang me up from Brighton where they were staying two nights and they came to tea. They sent you all love. They were very much upset because a few days ago their most beloved cat – was it called Sim? – was killed by a car. It really was awful.

Our dealing with Lilla [Healing] was highly successful as she brought me stores on Friday afternoon and had to leave at once for an appointment with a hairdresser. I had a short visit from Tony [Bland].

I keep on thinking of Thursday when you will be here.

> Love from your
> Leonard

353:   [Saturday] 22 April 1967                               *Dublin*

Dearest

A fine persistent rain is falling over Dublin's fair city, producing an

---

1. Conrad Mayer married Louie Everest in 1963. He worked on Henry Robinson's farm at Iford.

utterly grey light. I have been out to the Nat Gal & come back with two bunches of yellow tulips to cheer me up. In the great goodness of my heart I have put one bunch in Mrs S[mallwood]'s room. She & Ian are at the conference & return with six or eight others for lunch. There was a large shouting reception at the Nat Gal last night, most of the old familiar faces were there. Poor little Rachel Ward[1] looking somehow even smaller & wizened. She had brought the second baby of her mentally deranged daughter with her. She wants a long quiet talk with me which I think will take place on Monday.

This hotel is near, but not on, the green. It is comfortable has all the necessary appurtenances like one's own loo. A very large window looks out over a higgle of roofs of all sorts. Flat, pointed, new, old – The Nat Gal is not very full of plums. It is very old fashioned in that I was the only person there.

There are excellent Poussins & that's about the best thing they've got. The Lane bequest pictures are in another gallery all together. It was too wet to go & find it so I came back here with my tulips & am writing to you instead.

I very nearly missed the aeroplane. The train from Lewes was forty minutes late – I found Ian in a frightful tiz at Vic Sq. about to set off for Brompton Rd because he thought I must have gone straight there in mistake. However all was well. They were working on the line & sent us back from Cooksbridge to get on to another line, we then missed our place & had to keep on waiting for trains to pass us. The lilac is out here, so Dublin must be warmer than London.

> Fondest love & to all animals
> from Your
> T

354:    Monday 2[4] April 1967                           *Dublin*

Dearest

They have gone off to an all day session & I have packed up & before going out for some air (this hotel is absolutely red hot) I am writing you a line. Yesterday we had a short & lovely time on the hills – most beautiful, but a long dreary drive through endless shabby streets to get to it. We are remorselessly clipped to Mrs S. In a way it might have been

1. The Parsons were at a Booksellers Association conference. Rachel Ward was the wife of Alan Ward, a distinguished bookseller in Sheffield who was then president of the Association, and in charge of the conference.

better to be in the horrid big Hiltonish hotel where the conference is, though everyone who is there says it's Hell – but we wouldn't have had to endure quite so much of the excruciating boredom of her company. As always she alternates between being as sweet & as crochety as possible.

Ireland of course belongs to her & it makes it difficult to look with anything but a sullen eye about one. However those hills & lakes yesterday were simply wonderful. Great shiny lakes, not penned in by mountains, but with medium gentle hills rolling away on all sides – Not like the Pentlands. Being Sunday there were little groups of people walking, or sitting on the low stone walls – all in their bright Sunday best & looking enchanting with the silver lakes behind them. It is extraordinary how the Irish look. They all seem to be 'genuine'. It used to irritate me when I was young & my hair was still dark brown to have people say 'you must be Irish' but in fact enormous numbers have dark brown hair & blue eyes.

I dread our night at the Moynes. We go off from here at five o'clock. I think it is only about twenty minutes drive. I long for to-morrow when we will be off on our own. I have Rachel Ward coming to have lunch with me to-day & then I'm going for a walk with Liz Eccleshare & Virginia Brown[e-Wilkinson].[1] It's a better morning, sun shining which it has not done before until late afternoon. Give my love to darling Peg [Ashcroft]. I greatly look forward to being with you on Sunday night.

> All my love
> T

355:   [Monday] 24 April 1967                                *Monk's House*

Dearest,

I hope your cold is better and that you are enjoying Ireland. It has been pretty chilly here, but is full sun and slightly warmer today after 4 degrees of frost last night. I have been fairly pestered with people. On Saturday I was rung up by a Sussex undergraduate who had written to me last year for information about Lawrence. Could she and two others who were taking exams this year in which Lawrence would occur come and talk about him? They – two female and one male – came to tea yesterday – quite nice and intelligent, but more or less the usual thing, staying 2½

1. Elizabeth Eccleshare, wife of Colin Forster Eccleshare of Cambridge University Press. Virginia Browne-Wilkinson, author and broadcaster, had been a friend of LW's since 1959. After he became ill in 1969 she typed letters for him and stayed with him at weekends so TR could return to Juggs Corner to rest.

hours until told to go. Then I had to go and have tea with Kingsley [Martin] and Dorothy [Woodward] to meet a rather dull doctor.

This morning I was rung up by Deirdre [Bland] who wants to bring Rupert to see the garden tomo[rr]ow. Then I had a letter from Enid Jones saying that she thought I was angry with her because her son had bought the land next the cottages. He will not use it and ca[n] she come and see me. Unwillingly I have invited her for a drink.

I wish you were here. Bessie and all animals well and with me send love
> L

356:    [Tuesday] 4 July 1967                                                *Toulouse*

Dearest

We are sitting facing a stream of traffic between us & the station. We have 2 hrs to wait for a train to Castelnaudary – & then the boat – Now in train & almost at Castelnaudary.

*Wed morn* – We found the Escargot, its a very nice boat indeed – high luxe. Comfortable bunks & all sorts of amenities. Castelnaudary seems a charming old town & we were anchored in a quiet wide canal. We mean to stow all our gear this morning. Last night we were shown how to work the boat by an extremely nice French guardien called M Barthé. Gilbert [Smith] learned all the knots. It has two diesel engines. The last people who were also friends of John's left everything in perfect order & even a vase of charming wild flowers. We were pretty tired when we finally sat down to slices of cold rolled shoulder (Mr Hyde!) & fresh very good tomatoes. We had two hours at Orly changing aeroplanes & then two at Toulouse waiting for our train. We'd a great deal of luggage & of course there are no porters at all. So the heaving out & in of innumerable cases was tiring & very hard work. We also had a girl attached to us from Paris onwards. She was English on her way to a holiday with friends near Toulouse. When she got to Paris she found they had booked her on the aeroplane for the wrong day so there was great anxiety for her – whether she'd be allowed on. She was finally & we travelled the rest of the way together.

I'm sending this now as Ian says I must come & buy milk.

Fondest love from
> your
> T.

357:   Sunday, 9 July 1967                                      *Le Canal du Midi*

Dearest

   We are now in a superb stretch of this canal & there are 30 miles of it
without locks – so all is considerably more restful. It has really been very
good – wonderful sunshine & a brisk refreshing breeze. The boat is
luxurious. Full sized dining saloon & two good cabins with comfortable
bunks. A galley for cooking & a loo & shower. Hot water when the Ascot
works. Daphne [Smith] & I have now managed to slow the men up & we
are no longer going on as fast as possible to get to the sea.[1] We have
abandoned the sea & are content to look at, & walk in, the superb country
side. Lots & lots of white admirals & of course continual cicadas.
Everyone so far has been extraordinarily kind & helpful. We've only had
one meal off the boat. We buy loads of fruit & bread & paté & drink bottles
& bottles of wine at about 3/- a bottle. I pick a daily bunch of wild flowers
to decorate the cabin. Nothing spectacular but very pretty. I found one fine
head of some sort of Alium & there is quite a lot of that smallish white
Clematis which you once had, & here there is lots of Spartium Junceum
[Spanish Broom]. We are between Narbonne & Béziers. We can see the far
line of the Pyrenees away to the South. The landscape has been lovely all
the way but is now truly superb. The canal is fairly wide & there is
practically no traffic on it. We are all very well. At first the managing of the
boat caused tensions. It has very powerful engines. Both Ian & Gilbert
were jumpy & kept Daphne & me somewhat on the hop. It was partly our
fault, I decided on reflection, we were too anxious to do everything they
wanted at the double & so made ourselves into victims & so they bullied a
bit. I reflected on this – told Daphne & now all is sweet as silk!

   Fondest love dearest
     from your
        T.

358:   Friday 13 October 1967                                  *Shipton-on-Stour*

Dearest

   Here we safely are. We visited Blenheim on the way – I'm too middle
class for that sort of magnificence. The truth is that, on that scale, nothing

---

1. They got to the sea on Tuesday the 11th but once into the Mediterranean TR recorded in her
diary that the 'ship was leaping about like a dolphin so with a great deal of emphasis Daphne & I
determined they must return, which we did very quickly'.

really *looks* beautiful. It's grand & impressive but not beautiful. The outside is the best, as is so often the way. We had a lovely walk to-day in brilliant sunshine & with a cloudless sky. It grew colder in the afternoon & is just spotting with rain now at 6.30. We go to Romeo & J to-morrow night. Then nothing until Wednesday when we have two – All's Well & Coriolanus. It was unfortunate that we couldn't get seats for All's Well except that matinée.

I left Juggs with some relief. There were four work men in the house. Mr Parry hard at the sitting room. A man from Pettit's to re-do the kitchen ceiling & two of Mr Clark's chaps finishing off the conservatory. I do hope Conrad [Mayer] didn't mind about the staging. It was all my fault. The little garden here is still full of roses & dahlias & clematis in flower on the front door. I hope Bessie is behaving & not giving you any trouble. Thank you for sending the telephone account. It was a previous one that you paid. I'm writing to ask them to send another of the one Ian has mislaid.

> Fondest love dearest
>> Your
>>> T

I'm writing on my knee & have nothing but three envelopes to rest the paper on, so forgive the bad writing.

<u>Sat morning</u>

Not so gay this morning – Ian has a cold & I have a small stye – the first I've ever had. I keep on telling myself it's nothing & 'think what Dadie [George Rylands][1] went through' but it is very unpleasant all the same. Added to these ills it is blowy & raining. But 'it makes a nice change, so you mustn't complain'.

> Much love
>> T

1. Dr George (Dadie) Humphrey Wolferstan Rylands CH, CBE (1902–1999), Shakespearian director, lecturer in English Literature, Dean, Bursar and Director of Studies at King's College, Cambridge. Rylands became an Apostle in 1922; while writing his thesis he worked at the Hogarth Press. He acted in and produced many plays, directing John Gielgud and Peggy Ashcroft in 1945, and greatly influencing Michael Redgrave and younger directors Peter Hall and Robin Midgley. For the British Council he recorded the whole Shakespearian canon. He was chairman of the Apollo Society (1946–72), chairman of the directors and trustees of the Arts Theatre in Cambridge (1946–82), a governor of the Old Vic (1945–78) and a member of the Council of RADA. He was a close friend of LW and the Parsons and often stayed at Juggs Corner.

359:  [Sunday] 15 October 1967                          *Monk's House*

Dearest,

I only hope you are not having the kind of weather we have been 'enjoying' here. For the moment, immediately after Sunday breakfast, the sun is shining with a marvellous and enormous rainbow over the western downs – which is unusual; we very rarely have morning rainbows. Otherwise it had been roaring winds, dripping mist, and sometimes heavy rain. One downpour at night was so heavy that I got up to see whether the water was cascading in through the front door – it just didn't.

It has been practically impossible to do anything in the garden except pick up apples blown from the trees. Delos shrieks his disapproval; his only consolation that he managed to steal my mackerel which I left for two minutes unattended to on top of the frigidaire and he instantly whipped it off on to his side table. All animals well and Bessie so far has been very good.

Deirdre [Bland] rang up and came to lunch on Friday and I am going to dine with them tonight. She brought with her the agent's brochure about the sale of Iford Manor. It is being sold in nine lots. Under a vow of secrecy Louie told me that Conrad had heard an interesting bit of information about this.

That is all my news except that I miss you, if that is new; love from
    Your
    Leonard


360:  Tuesday [17 October 1967]                          *Shipston*

Dearest

I was so glad to have your letter yesterday. We've had a wild night of gale & rain & the mill stream is tearing by right up to the arabes[que] of the bridge. The little moorhen is careering about, suddenly the owner of a huge river. I thought the river might come in as I listened during the night to the battering rain – but thank goodness it didn't.

We've decided to go & see Coventry Cathedral today. Ian's cold seems to have responded well to rough treatment – walking in wind & rain, & my eye, which Katie [probably Lee] said was a septic cyst & not a stye is almost well. We had bad weather on our visit to them, but a drive to them through lovely country. The cottage is just how I imagined it would be. Very nice, rather dark, with a good garden &, of course, wonderful rich soil. They say they are coming to Monks in two weeks. We, so far, have seen Alls Well. We thought it was going to be Romeo & Juliette [sic] on Saturday, but were mistaken. We have a severe day tomorrow with R & J in the afternoon & Coriolanus at night. I miss you very much

      fondest love T.


361:   [Friday 12 April 1968]       *Esperia Palace Hotel, Athens*

Dearest

   We are here – safely after a quick flight no stops. We left London Air Port at 12.30 & arrived at 5 o'clock (Athens' time) that is about an hour later than our time. Of course we have come in for Good Friday – & having had an excellent dinner in a Restaurant facing the Akropolis we have taken nearly an hour in a taxi to get back to the hotel because of procession. Little boys with censers & fine old priests in Piero della Francesca hats. I am scribbling this on my knee at 10 o'clock while we wait for our travel agent to arrive & tell us about to-morrow. I know we take a bus at 6 o'clock in the morning & Ian says he thinks it takes about 6 hours to our embarkation point.

   I needn't tell you how much I think of our wonderful visit & how much I would like to have it all again.[1] The moment when one sees Greece from the air is something which we in this age have invented, & it is a moment of glorious beauty. It is violently windy, sunny but not too warm. They seem to have had the same sort of weather as we have – hot last week & now a return to windy & cool. I trust it will blow itself out before we get to Skiathos.

   This is a very nice quiet hotel just behind the square where the Grande Bretagne & the George IV are. We have bed room & loo & bath. There is a small restaurant & they say they will give us coffee & rolls in our room to-morrow morning. It doesn't have that balcony view of the Acropolis that the first hotel we stayed in had, but is more comfortable.

   I didn't send a cable to the office, being Saturday to-morrow I thought you'd get this on Monday which would be as good.

   My second telephone call, when I spoke to Louie, was to ask you to

---

1. TR and LW were in Athens on their way to and from Israel in April–May 1957, and again in 1961. 'The trip with L which must have been almost exactly this time of year, was an exception. We had perfect weather the whole time.'

send a card to Kay [Jones] & Julia [Draper] to say as we weren't returning until Sunday we couldn't have a meal that night – Now I think I've made one of my usual mistakes & that the date we fixed was the 28th so if you've done nothing about them don't – but if you have – please explain & forgive me for being unbearably woolly.

I miss you very much, & already feel as if I'd been away for weeks.

I think if you wrote to me at this hotel – to await arrival – I'd get it when we return on Tuesday week.

    All my love
      T


362:   Wednesday [17 April 1968][1]        *Villa Maria, Skiathos*

Dearest,

This is a very beautiful island & now the weather is superb. We had three cool days, on one of which we attended a barbecue on the beach when the English inhabitants roasted two Pascal lambs which we ate with suitable sandy flavouring. Bruce [Todd]'s house is delightful, & we have a superb little secluded beach to ourselves. It is better than sand, it is finely ground marble & the sea makes a specially delicious sound as it sighs back & forwards across it. There are a scattering of similar villas built by English visitors, but Bruce's is off on it's own with a truly glorious view. Heaps of wild flowers but too late for the bulbs. I am hoping to find more orchids, so far have found Laxiflora & a Scriapis [sic] both in Fl[ower]s of the Mediterranean. Cistus everywhere.

I feel as if I'd been away for weeks & can't believe it isn't yet *one* week. No letter yet from you. I am giving this to someone who goes to Athens to-morrow to be posted there. The trip here was very interesting. The bus went later than we thought not 6 o'clock but 8. It took 2½ hours & the boat 3½. It was very rough just before we got here but we both survived. I've met one or two nice cats & one dog, not many animals except Don Quixote donkeys tied up to Olive trees.

I miss you very much all love T.


1. This aerogram is stamped Athens, 26 April 1968, but it was clearly held up because of the censorship (see letter 364 and note).

363:   [Sunday] 21 April 1968                    [*Monk's House*]

Dearest,

   The volume of pleasure which one suffers is enormous and unending.
As you know, what I really suffer from is loneliness. Peggy, Nicky, and
the French youth arrived at 8.35 on Friday evening. At midnight Nicky
and the Frenchman drove off to Lullington.[1] They reappeared yesterday
morning, but sailed for France later. It was a frantic day yesterday with
the horticultural show going on all day backwards and forwards to the
Village Hall. I won six firsts, one second, and one third – much the most
of anyone to Vout [Van der Kieft]'s[2] delight. In the afternoon Deirdre
[Bland] and Lucy appeared and had tea. Tonight Peggy and I dine with
the Blands. Last night Ursula [Mommins] dined. I thought the day would
probably never end, but it did about midnight. In half an hour Barbara
[Warner][3] and her daughter who are staying at Lullington are coming to
lunch.

   It is high summer with a temperature of 73 and no wind.

   I wish we were here alone if only for 24 hours. I long to hear from you
   Love from your
        Leonard


364:   [Saturday] 27 April 1968                  [*Monk's House*]

Dearest,

   Your letter took six days to arrive here from Athens. I expect all letters
are censored which explains why your postcards arrived at the office days
before this was delivered here.[4] The consequence is that it is extremely
improbable that this will reach you before you leave Athens.

   I write on the outside chance that it may. It has been perfect summer
weather here full sun nearly all day and little or no wind. Everything

1. Nicholas Hutchinson, actor and director, was Peggy Ashcroft's son. Ashcroft and Jeremy
Hutchinson had bought a house, Deep Thatch, at Lullington in 1961.
2. LW's last gardener and the person who found him in the upstairs sitting room when he took
suddenly ill in April 1969.
3. Barbara Hutchinson was Jeremy Hutchinson's older sister. She had first married Victor
Rothschild and then writer Rex Warner. Lucy was their daughter.
4. In December 1967 King Constantine had attempted unsuccessfully to overthrow the military
junta which had been in power since April. He had been exiled to Rome and the country was under
the rule of Col. Georgios Papadopoulous. Political arrests were numerous and political torture
alleged. LW was right about the censorship of mail.

rushing out in the garden – the flowering cherries roared out in two days and so have the viburnums. I eat asparagus and seakale. The dogs and cats are well. I let Kay know according to your message, but I dont quite understand what you mean in your letter, so I have done nothing.

Peggy left Monday and I have had a very quiet time since. Barbara and her daughter Lucy came from Lullington to lunch on Monday and it was so hot that we had it in the garden. We dined Sunday night with the Blands. I have just been rung up by Deirdre to ask whether she and all her daughter's family can come and see the garden this afternoon. Mr and Mrs Naderer asked me whether they could come and see the garden last Tuesday and they did so in the most Christian friendliness on all sides. So you see how lonely I am.

But I miss you all the same. Love from
Leonard

365:    Monday [29 April] 1968                    [*Villa Maria*] *Skiathos*

Dearest

How glad I was to have your letter yesterday – it took a week. This is my third to you – I wish you were here at this moment, because though you might not have enjoyed all I know you'd be happy here & now. I am sitting on Bruce's terrace, about 200 feet above the little beach, *our* beach – not another soul has been on it. To get to it you walk down a mule track (but no mules) between olive trees & hundreds of sparkling flowers. Bruce & his friend Arthur went home yesterday & we go into Skiathos for the night & off on the ferry at 7.45 to-morrow morning. This is our last hr & 45 mins before the very efficient Col Osborne & his wife fetch us. We are five miles up a switchback road from Skiathos, hardly made up, & rather alarming. We have seen one car go over, but luckily it was caught by bushes & the young man uninjured. All the air is full of the smell of cistus & mastic. We are at the height of the cistuses, pink & white in masses everywhere. Too late for bulbs. It must be almost the same time as our glorious trip. The Peleponese landscape is more beautiful & more what I think of as Greece. This island has a lot of stone pines on it & is therefore much greener & one does not have that wonderful pink fawn colour everywhere. But the sea is superb & the islands, sometimes near & sometimes lost in a haze. We've bathed twice a day. The water is cold enough to make the initial plunge 'a thought' but once in it is glorious. Sparkling & crystal clear. The beach is a wonderful ground marble. Not ground fine enough to be sticky sand but loose & gentle to feet & to bodies lying in it. Dear Bruce could not have been a kinder host. He always brought a little refrigerator bag down to the beach & gave us iced Retsina after our bathe. His friend, Arthur Taylor, never came down to the beach being a little decrepit, so it was just the three of us – & now that it is just the two of us I have no pants on & only a little loose sleeveless jacket. We hope to see Belinda [Keown] for dinner to-morrow or Wed. We leave for Hungary early Thursday, I'll post this in Athens as posts here are very unreliable, added to which almost every day has been a public hol. I'm glad you won all the prizes in the show. Your week-end sounds to have been one lovely whirl. I hope this last one was more peaceful. Forgive very bad hand writing, I'm writing on my knee in blazing sun. You obviously had it much hotter the week end we left than we had here, when it was grey & windy for three days.

This may be my last letter but I'll try & send a card from Hungary.

fondest love T

X

366:    Wednesday 1 May 1968 [postcard]                         *Athens*

We've come in for as many public holidays as we had in Israel! To-day was one; & we had a delightful picnic with Belinda on Hymettus. It is boiling hot. We go to-morrow at crack of dawn to Hungary. I was so glad to have your letter here & hope you have had mine. I feel as if I'd been away for six months. Went to the Parthenon last evening. So glorious. Standing lightly in the full sun, no shadows, as if the columns were made by the blue sky shapes between. all love T.

367:    Saturday 4 May 1968 [postcard]                         *Budapest*

Though the picture is of Greece I am, as you see, in another land. All is well. Very comfortable & every one friendly & kind. Weather warm, slight rain last night. I think of you & of cats & dogs a great deal & am very much looking forward to being home again on Sunday week. Much fond love

T.

368:     [Saturday] 4 May 1968                              *Monk's House*

Dearest, I was so glad to get your letters and hear that everything is going well – also that at last you had got mine. It is very curious weather here. One day horrible (though not really cold), the next absolutely marvellous. It was beautiful yesterday and again a perfect morning today. It is years since the blossom has been as good as it is. The cherries are absolutely covered in flowers. The two cherries on the croft from which last year the birds took almost all the buds are solid with flowers. I took the meat for the cats to Anneliese on Wednesday and went up and had a look at your garden. Everything seemed very trim and also down at the cottage.

I went to town on Wednesday instead of Tuesday and went to the Cranium dinner which I had not done for ages. A very old man with a bald head, who, I thought, must be ten years older than I am, turned out to be Michael MacCarthy, whom, when I was 35 and he a small boy at Miss Fry's school, we used to take out for treats at Richmond. The rest of the company was Bunny, Richard Garnett, Lionel Penrose, Julian Trevelyan,[1] and an unknown bearded man. Then Quentin rang up and wanted to come and ask questions, so I had him and Olivia [Anne Olivier Bell] to lunch yesterday, and we played bowls in summer weather. On Tuesday I drove to Backsettown for the annual meeting of trustees. Tonight I have Julia and Kay to dine.

Harold Nicolson[2] is dead. I am beginning to feel that I am an only survivor.

I wish it were tomorrow week.

Love from your<br>Leonard

1. Michael MacCarthy (1907–1973), farmer, son of Desmond and Molly MacCarthy. Lionel Sharples Penrose (1898–1972) FRS, MA, MD, FRCVP retired from the Galton professorship of eugenics at University College London in 1965; his publications include *The Biology of Mental Defect* (1949) and *The Objective Study of Crowd Behaviour* (1951). Julian Otto Trevelyan (1910–1988), lithographer and painter; his publications include: *Indigo Days* (1957), *Etching: Modern Methods of Intaglio Printmaking* (1963), *The Artist and His World* (1960), *A Place, a State* (1975). Richard Garnett (b. 1923), typographer and publisher, son of (Ray) Rachel Marshall and David (Bunny) Garnett, and grandson of Constance and Edward Garnett; his books include *The Silver Kingdom, The White Dragon, Jack of Dover* and *Constance Garnett: A Heroic Life*.
2. Sir Harold Nicolson (1886–1968), author and critic, husband of Vita Sackville-West. He was in the diplomatic service in Madrid (1910) and Constantinople (1911) before being transferred to the Foreign Office in 1914. In 1940–1 he was parliamentary secretary to the Minister of Information, and was a governor of the BBC 1941–6. He held several other public positions and wrote many books.

369:    Tuesday 10 September 1968 [postcard]        *Polzeath, Cornwall*

We've had a glorious day here (yesterday) & it looks like being another
to-day. We've bathed & walked & all is delightful. I miss you & look
forward to being back.

    Fondest love
        T.


370:    [Wednesday] 11 September 1968                      *Polzeath*

Dearest L.

    It is all very jolly here & so far we've had steady sun. This is a real
holiday house bought by Dick's father & mother forty years or more ago.
It is quite large & looks out to the sea & the side of a beautiful rough hill
side. The household also is a holiday one. From Dick's mother over
eighty, to Elizabeth's daughter [Rachel], eighteen months.[1]

    This little creature is absolutely charming. She charges about at great
speed with nothing on & never cries. Elizabeth is the best mother I've
ever seen & the child shows in her behaviour just how good she is. E *never*
talks quickly or crossly to her & *never* talks down to her, but always talks
to her reasonably. The child is just beginning to talk. She can say a lot of
words & is on the edge of saying a sentence & she can sing the first line of
Three Blind Mice in tune – more than I can do! The husband may be
going to get an important part in a film & has been sent for to go to Rome
for a test.

    The coast is still wonderfully beautiful though of course the inevitable
houses have crept up some lovely headlands.

    We've bathed each day – very cold but nice all the same – I've found
Autumn squill & Lady's tresses. I've been having a tiresome eye. It had a
nasty sort of boil as I left, in the lower lid. It's almost better but has been
a bit of a bore.

    I'm to go & do some food shopping. Dearest love. I miss you very
much

        T.

---

1. Elizabeth was the youngest child of Nora and Richard David. She was then married to Martin
Potter. On one of her many visits to Polzeath, TR painted five panels of a dresser, each with a
different family of flowers on a deep orange-pink base.

371:   [Monday] 7 October 1968                                    *Shipston*

Dearest,

I'm writing this outside in the clear morning sun with the most superb blue sky stretched over me.

Saturday was a real endurance test. As you know the ribs for some reason became much worse on Friday. They were just as bad on Saturday & I couldn't drive the car at all. Poor Ian had to stick to the wheel all the way. I kept on having these frightful spasms.[1]

We got to Long Crendon in time, & to the Church where we found Mrs S[mith] who had kept two seats for us. Church was packed with the usual assortment of old girls in petal hats & young ones in pink fly away ones. It's awful the marriage service, worse really than the burial one. Anyway, that over we made for maison Smith.[2] There must have been four hundred of us. A marquee, very well done, had been put up in the garden enclosing a willow tree – all very pretty but *too many people*. Then followed hours of trying to eat with a fork off a plate held in one hand while you also tried to drink champagne with the other. We didn't get away until 5.15 & *then* we left before the bridal pair. Gay looked very sweet, truly happy, she was bursting with it – which is I suppose another way of saying – 'The Bride looked radiant'. My spasms had eased off a bit. They seemed to prefer me to stand. The evening here with Peg, Dadie was very nice except that I *did* feel pretty awful. Mercifully the spasms stopped & I had none yesterday. It still feels stiff & achy, which is quite bearable. We had lunch with Peg & Dadie at Peg's friend's house, which is enface de maison Priestl[e]y & *that* is really Marble Halls – enormous white wedding cake outside & there *are* marble floors within![3] To-day it is most gloriously fine & this sweet country is looking absolutely it's best. I wish very much you were here. Very much love as always,

     T


372:   [Thursday] 10 October 1968                                 *Shipston*

Dearest, Fortitude – that's what you need when you break ribs. Next time

---

1. TR had broken some ribs.
2. Gabrielle (Gay) Smith, daughter of Gilbert and Daphne Smith, married David Edwards on Saturday 5 October at 12.30. The luncheon was at Baker's Close, Long Crendon.
3. Kissing Tree House, Alveston, Warwickshire, was J. B. Priestley's last home. A long stretch of marble-floored corridor ran from the front door through the large house to a window at its end.

I do so I shall snatch my dagger out of my belt & giving it to you I'll yell 'Dispatch dispatch', like so many of the young Stratford actors who have no speaking part & wait all evening for that dying groan. Anyhow, by dint of Codeine & fortitude I am surprisingly enough very much enjoying this week. It is *such* lovely deep farming country with such splendid great elm trees all about in it.

Have to go – so this must be closed up bringing you as always

Tons of love,

T

On Tuesday morning, 15 April 1969, Leonard was found sitting in a chair upstairs at Monk's House unable to speak intelligibly. The next day he could, but although he knew everyone he was unable to put a name to a face. When Trekkie asked hers he smiled and quoted Swinburne:

And the best and the worst of this is
    That neither is most to blame
If you have forgotten my kisses
    And I have forgotten your name.

In the following months she rarely left his side. Leonard recovered enough to answer mail, check the proofs of the last volume of his autobiography, go into the garden and to Lewes; but he continued to weaken. He died on 14 August and was cremated the next day when Juliette Alvin could come to play Bach and Peggy Ashcroft to read 'Lycidas'. Trekkie buried his ashes under the surviving elm on the lawn of Monk's House. On 11 October in Tunisia with Ian and Granville Coghlan, she wrote in her diary: 'I am half in Sussex all the time, wanting and dreading the return.'

Ian died of a heart attack at Juggs Corner on 29 October 1980. Trekkie stayed in the house and continued to paint, welcome old friends, and enrich the lives of younger and newer ones. When her eyesight and arthritis became too troublesome, she moved into a sheltered flat in Lewes where she died a couple of months later, on 29 July 1995.

# Index